Deregulation and Efficiency of Indian Banks

India Studies in Business and Economics

The Indian economy is considered to be one of the fastest growing economies of the world with India amongst the most important G-20 economies. Ever since the Indian economy made its presence felt on the global platform, the research community is now even more interested in studying and analyzing what India has to offer. This series aims to bring forth the latest studies and research about India from the areas of economics, business, and management science. The titles featured in this series will present rigorous empirical research, often accompanied by policy recommendations, evoke and evaluate various aspects of the economy and the business and management landscape in India, with a special focus on India's relationship with the world in terms of business and trade.

For further volumes:
http://www.springer.com/series/11234

Sunil Kumar • Rachita Gulati

Deregulation and Efficiency of Indian Banks

Springer

Sunil Kumar
Faculty of Economics
South Asian University
New Delhi, India

Rachita Gulati
Department of Humanities and Social Sciences
Indian Institute of Technology Roorkee
Roorkee, Uttaranchal, India

ISBN 978-81-322-1544-8 ISBN 978-81-322-1545-5 (eBook)
DOI 10.1007/978-81-322-1545-5
Springer New Delhi Heidelberg New York Dordrecht London

Printed on acid-free paper

Springer is part of Springer Science+Business Media (www.springer.com)

Preface

From the late 1960s through the early 1990s, the Indian banking system was marked by a high degree of regulation, and all the signs of financial repression were present in the system. The levels of profitability of banks were low by international standards; the volume of bad loans was on the rise; the banks had little loanable resources for commercial lending due to high level of pre-emption; and the banks served as sort of 'quasi-fiscal instruments' for the government. Since 1992, India's policy makers are following a financial deregulation programme and have adopted a gradualist and cautious approach in introducing regulatory changes for creating a competitive, efficient and resilient banking system. Conspicuous banking reforms that have been introduced during the past two decades for augmenting bank efficiency include licensing of new private banks, deregulation of interest rates, reduction in pre-emption of resources, implementation of prudential norms, greater autonomy to public sector banks, allowing banks to raise resources from capital market, and introduction of sound banking regulation and supervisory frameworks.

Given the broad sketch of banking reforms portrayed above, one may ask whether the efficiency and productivity performance of Indian banks since the launching of reforms in 1992 has improved. In this book, we have made an attempt in this direction. In particular, our endeavour here is to evaluate the efficiency performance of Indian banking industry in the post-reforms period by looking at the trends of cost efficiency and total factor productivity growth across different ownership types and size classes. The main research question addressed in this book is: Did financial deregulation spur the efficiency and productivity of Indian banks? Some supplementary questions that have also been addressed in this book are: (i) Does the inclusion of non-traditional activities in the specification of banks' output vector affect the efficiency of banks? (ii) Are foreign banks always better performers? (iii) Does size matter in the banking industry? (iv) Are there any economies or diseconomies of scale in the banking sector? (v) What are most influential bank-specific variables affecting the efficiency and productivity growth of banks? We expect that the empirical findings of this research work may provide some important insights to both policy makers and bank managers and would be helpful for the design of better management strategies for Indian banks.

This book is organised into eight chapters. The first chapter offers a general introduction to the context. The second chapter is devoted to the developments in Indian banking sector. The next two chapters are devoted to literature review of empirical studies and methodological frameworks available in the literature on bank efficiency. The rest of the book is focused on assessing the efficacy of India's approach to financial deregulation. In particular, to reach at the appropriate of bank's inputs and outputs, we investigated the relevance of the inclusion of non-traditional activities in the specification of banks' output vector by analysing their effect on the efficiency of Indian banks. We also focused on the issue of to what extent the relative rankings of distinct ownership groups are affected by the omission of a proxy for non-traditional activities in the output vector. To see whether the financial deregulation programme has had a salutary impact on the performance of Indian banks, we looked at the evolution of cost efficiency and total factor productivity growth of Indian banks during the 16-year period under evaluation. We also delved deeper into the issue of bank efficiency and ownership. The book really contributes to the extant literature on bank efficiency in India and bears important policy implications for further reforms in the Indian banking sector. We feel that the empirical applications provided in the book would be useful for students, academicians, practitioners and policy makers alike.

The completion of this book would never have been possible without the support of a number of individuals. Firstly, our deepest appreciation goes to Prof. Subrata Sarkar, Prof. Jayati Sarkar and Prof. Susan Thomas, all from Indira Gandhi Institute of Development Research, Mumbai, for their intellectual and enthusiastic support. We are grateful to Dr. Balwant Singh, Retired Advisor, Reserve Bank of India, Mumbai; Dr. Rajesh Bhattacharya, Assistant Professor, Indian Institute of Management Calcutta, Kolkata; and Dr. Dil Bahadur Rahut, Programme Manager, International Maize and Wheat Improvement Center, Addis Ababa, Ethiopia, for their help, encouragement and incisive comments at various stages of our project. This work has also benefited from the comments of Prof. Fadzlan Sufian, University of Putra, Malaysia. The first author would also like to extend a special thanks to two leading exponents of university administration in India Dr. Ajaib Singh Brar, Vice Chancellor, Guru Nanak Dev University, Amritsar, and Dr. G.K. Chadha, President, South Asian University, New Delhi, for their patronage and moral support. The author would like to extend special thanks to his wife, Dr. Neetu Bala, and daughters who have cheerfully given up many precious evenings and weekends that rightfully belonged to them in order to make it possible for him to complete this book. The second author wishes to express her gratitude and sincere regards to Prof. Gautam Sinha, Director, Indian Institute of Management Kashipur, Uttarakhand, for all his unending support and encouragement during the process of this research and for giving her the chance to undertake this challenge. She wishes to express her gratitude to her mother, Ridhi Gulati, siblings and guardians who always remained very cooperative and helpful during the time-consuming task of preparing this book. Finally, the authors would like to thank the publisher for the constructive cooperation and patience, understanding and encouragement during the time it took to complete the book.

Sunil Kumar
Rachita Gulati

Contents

Abbreviations

AE	Allocative Efficiency
ALCO	Asset Liability Management Committee
AR	Assurance Region
ARC	Asset Reconstruction Company
ATM	Automated Teller Machine
BCC	Banker, Charnes and Cooper
BFS	Board of Financial Supervision
BIS	Bank for International Settlements
BLP	Branch Licensing Policy
BPLR	Benchmark Prime Lending Rate
CACLS	Capital Adequacy, Asset Quality, Liquidity Compliance, and Systems
CAMELS	Capital Adequacy, Asset Quality, Management, Earnings, Liquidity, and Systems
CBS	Core Banking Solutions
CCR	Charnes, Cooper and Rhodes
CD	Certificates of Deposit
CDR	Corporate Debt Restructuring
CE	Cost Efficiency
COLS	Corrected Ordinary Least Squares
CP	Commercial Paper
CR	Concentration Ratio
CRAR	Capital to Risk-Weighted Assets Ratio
CRM	Customer Relationship Management
CRR	Cash Reserve Ratio
CRS	Constant Returns-to-Scale
DEA	Data Envelopment Analysis
DFHI	Discount and Finance House of India
DFIs	Development Financial Institutions
DMU	Decision Making Unit
DRI	Differential Rate of Interest

DRS	Decreasing Returns-to-Scale
DRT	Debt Recovery Tribunal
EFFCH	Efficiency Change
EFT	Electronic Funds Transfer
FB	Foreign Bank
FDH	Free Disposal Hull
FDI	Foreign Direct Investment
FE	Fixed-Effects
GDP	Gross Domestic Product
GDR	Global Depository Receipt
GLS	Generalised Least Squares
GOI	Government of India
HHI	Herfindahl-Hirschman index
ICT	Information and Communication Technology
IDBI	Industrial Development Bank of India
IFR	International Financing Review
INFINET	Indian Financial Network
INR	Indian National Rupee
IRS	Increasing Returns-to-Scale
LAF	Liquidity Adjustment Facility
LBS	Lead Bank Scheme
LIBOR	London Inter-Bank Offered Rate
M&As	Mergers and Acquisitions
MLE	Maximum Likelihood Estimation
MPI	Malmquist Productivity Index
NBs	Nationalised Banks
NDRS	Non-decreasing Returns-to-Scale
NDTL	Net Demand and Time Liability
NIRS	Non-increasing Returns-to-Scale
NPA	Non-performing Asset
NPB	New Private Bank
NPL	Non-performing Loan
NRI	Non-resident Indian
OBS	Off-balance Sheet
OLS	Ordinary Least Squares
OPB	Old Private Bank
PB	Private Bank
PLR	Prime Lending Rate
PSB	Public Sector Bank
PTE	Pure Technical Efficiency
RBI	Reserve Bank of India
RE	Random-Effects
RoA	Return on Assets
RRB	Regional Rural Bank

RTS	Returns-to-scale
SARFAESI	Securitisation and Reconstruction of Financial Assets and Enforcement of Security Interest
SBI	State Bank of India
SBM	Slack-based Measure
SCB	Scheduled Commercial Bank
SE	Scale Efficiency
SFA	Stochastic Frontier Approach
SLR	Statutory Liquidity Ratio
TE	Technical Efficiency
TECH	Technological Change
TFA	Thick Frontier Analysis
TFP	Total Factor Productivity
VRS	Variable Returns-to-Scale
VSAT	Very Small Aperture Terminal

List of Figures

List of Tables

About the Authors

Dr. Sunil Kumar is currently serving as an Associate Professor of Economics at the Faculty of Economics, South Asian University (SAU), New Delhi. He is also associated with Punjab School of Economics, Guru Nanak Dev University, Amritsar. He has more than 20 years of teaching experience in subjects related to Quantitative Methods, Macroeconomics, and Econometrics. His research interests include data envelopment analysis, stochastic frontier analysis, banking efficiency and industrial productivity. He has published more than three dozen research papers in journals of national and international repute including Economic Change and Restructuring, Macroeconomics and Finance in Emerging Market Economies, the American Journal of Accounting and Finance, International Journal of Productivity and Performance Management, International Review of Economics, Benchmarking, Global Business Review, etc. He also wrote a research book entitled, "Productivity and Factor Substitution: Theory and Analysis". His professional memberships include the Indian Society of Regional Science and Indian Economic Association.

Dr. Rachita Gulati is an Assistant Professor in Economics at Department of Humanities and Social Sciences, Indian Institute of Technology (IIT) Roorkee, Uttarakhand. Before joining IIT Roorkee, she was a core faculty of Indian Institute of Management (IIM) Kashipur, Uttarakhand. Her teaching interests include Applied Econometrics, Managerial Economics, and Quantitative Methods for Economists and her research interests include Efficiency and Productivity Analysis using Frontier Approaches and the Indian Banking Sector. Her research work focuses on financial economics in India and bears important policy implications for further reforms in the Indian banking sector. She has published research papers in journals of national and international repute. In 2008, she received the Best Paper Award from the Global Academy of Business and Economics Research (GABER), USA.

Chapter 1
Introduction

1.1 Background

It has been well documented in the literature that the efficiency of the banking system is germane to the performance of the entire economy because only an efficient system guarantees the smooth functioning of nation's payment system and effective implementation of the monetary policy. Rajan and Zingales (1998) asserted that a sound banking system serves as an important channel for achieving economic growth through the mobilisation of financial savings, putting them to productive use, and transforming various risks. The efficiency of the banking system also has direct implications for social welfare. Society benefits when a country's banking system becomes more efficient, offering more services at a lower cost (Valverde et al. 2003). Owing to aforementioned socio-economic implications of banking efficiency, the analyses of relative efficiency of banks gained a lot of popularity in recent years among the policy makers, bank managers, bank investors and academicians. The information obtained from a banking efficiency analysis can be used either (i) to inform government policy by assessing the effects of deregulation, mergers or market structure on efficiency; (ii) to address research issues by describing the efficiency of an industry, ranking its firms or checking how measured efficiency may be related to the different efficiency techniques employed; or (iii) to improve managerial performance by identifying 'best practices' and 'worst practices' associated with high and low measured efficiency, respectively, and encouraging the former practices and while discouraging latter (Berger and Humphrey 1997).

The banking sector has undergone a significant transformation throughout the world since the early 1980s under the impact of deregulation, globalisation, financial innovation and technological progress (Reserve Bank of India 2008b). The Indian banking sector has not remained insulated from the global trends. With the avowed objective to enhance efficiency and productivity of banks through competition, the policy makers embarked on the programme of financial

S. Kumar and R. Gulati, *Deregulation and Efficiency of Indian Banks*, India Studies in Business and Economics, DOI 10.1007/978-81-322-1545-5_1, © Springer India 2014

deregulation in the year 1992. From the late 1960s through the early 1990s, the Indian banking sector was marked by a high degree of regulation, and parameters like business growth and branch network were the major performance criteria. During this period, the Government of India (GOI) extensively used the banking system as an instrument of public finance (Hanson and Kathuria 1999). Substantial and increasing volumes of credit were channelled to the government at below-market rates through high and increasing cash reserve requirements (CRR) and statutory liquidity requirements (SLR) in order to fund a large and increasing government deficit at relatively low cost (Sen and Vaidya 1997). In fact, the heavy hand of government has been omnipresent in the banking sector, especially in the working of public sector banks (PSBs), and there was very limited market-based decision making. Furthermore, the competition in the banking sector was virtually absent. Bank deposit and lending rates were mostly controlled, and high statutory pre-emption and directed lending requirements left banks with little funds for commercial lending (Bhattacharyya and Patel 2003). Reddy (1998) observed that during this period, for every rupee of deposit in banks, only about one-third to one-half was available for lending to the commercial sector.

Further, rates of return were low by international standards; the capital base had eroded; non-performing assets were on the rise; and customer service was below expectation (Sarkar 2004). More important, lack of proper disclosure norms led to many problems being kept under cover. Poor internal controls raised serious doubts about the integrity of the system itself (Reddy 1998). In such an operating environment, many banks became unprofitable, inefficient and unsound owing to their poor lending strategies and lack of internal risk management under government ownership (Joshi and Little 1996; Shirai 2002). Jagirdar (1996) observed that the average return on assets (ROA) in the second half of the 1980s was only about 0.15 % which was abysmally low by all standards. Further, in 1992–1993, non-performing assets (NPAs) of 27 PSBs amounted to 24 % of total credit, only 15 PSBs achieved a net profit, and half of the PSBs faced negative net worth (Shirai 2002). This not only reduced banks' incentives to operate properly but also undermined regulators' incentives to properly supervise banks' performances (Shirai and Rajasekaran 2002). All in all, all the signs of 'financial repression' were found in the system, and the state of the banking sector in India could be described as a classic example of 'financial repression' à la MacKinnon and Shaw (Mohan 2007). The main consequence of this financial repression was an ascent in the volume of bad loans due to ineffective credit evaluation system and poorer risk assessment policies. Further, poor disclosure standards abetted corruption by window-dressing the true picture of banks. The overstaffing, over-branching and undue interference by labour unions resulted in huge operating losses. This led to a gradual decline in the profitability and efficiency of Indian banks, especially under public ownership. In fact, in late 1990s, Indian banking system was on the verge of a crisis and lacking viability even in its basic function of financial intermediation.

For getting rid of this distressed banking system, the policy makers[1] felt a need for reform measures to improve the health of the Indian banking system. Consequently, the first phase of banking reforms was set in motion in the year 1992 based on the recommendations of the Committee on the Financial System (1991).[2] The key objective of the reforms was to transform the operating environment of the industry from a highly regulated system to a more market-oriented one with a view to increase competitiveness and efficiency (Sarkar 2004). Nevertheless, it is significant to note that the main focus of the reforms process was to increase the profitability and efficiency of the then-existing PSBs that controlled about 90 % of all deposits, assets and credit (Shirai 2002). The reforms process heralded the beginning of implementing prudential norms consisting of capital adequacy ratio, asset classification, income recognition and provisioning, and the deregulation of the operating environment (Agarwal 2000). In order to impart more vitality and autonomy to banks in their operations, the policy makers successfully adopted the route of partial privatisation of PSBs, interest rate deregulation, relaxing entry norms for domestic private and foreign banks and removal of 'financial repression' through reduction in statutory pre-emption. This phase of banking reforms produced some favourable outcomes as reflected by the fact that most of the banks had achieved the international standards of capital adequacy norm of 8 % of the risk weighted assets, had earned operating profits and had reduced significantly the proportion of non-performing assets (NPAs) to the total assets (Sarma 1995).

The success of the first phase of banking reforms catalysed the move towards the next phase in the year 1998. The recommendations of the Committee on Banking Sector Reforms (1998)[3] provided the blueprint for second phase of banking reforms. The key focus of this phase has been on strengthening the foundations of the banking system as well as on issues like upgradation of technology and human resource development (Bhaumik and Mukherjee 2001). The basic tenet of reform measures in this phase was to usher in transparency in financial statements, diversification of ownership and strong corporate governance practices to mitigate the prospects of systemic risks in the banking sector. In view of that, prudential norms have been made more stringent and tighter to bring these at par with international standards. On the whole, the thrust of the banking reforms programme since 1992 was on (i) the promotion of efficiency through competition and market orientation and (ii) strengthening the shock absorptive capacity of the system through adoption of prudential norms and tightening of supervision.

Although the broad contours of reform measures in the banking sector have been provided by the aforementioned committees, a large number of committees and

---

[1] In India, the policy makers that have been entrusted with the task of formulating the policies for banking sector comprise the Reserve Bank of India (Central Bank), Ministry of Finance and related government and financial sector regulatory entities.

[2] This committee is popularly known as Narasimham Committee I, named after its chairman M. Narasimham.

[3] This committee is popularly known as Narasimham Committee II, named after its chairman M. Narasimham.

working groups have been constituted for addressing specific issues in the banking sector. During the last 20 years, an extensive programme of banking reforms has been followed for strengthening of market institutions and allowing greater autonomy to the banks. The details on various reform measures and their impact on the structure of Indian banking industry have been documented. In this context, reference may be made to the works of Sen and Vaidya (1997), Hanson and Kathuria (1999), Arun and Turner (2002), Shirai (2002), Bhide et al. (2002), Yoo (2005), Hanson (2005), Reddy (2005b) and Roland (2008). However, a brief discussion of the areas in which reforms have been introduced is presented here. First, the structure of administered interest rates has been almost totally dismantled in a phased manner.[4] The purpose of deregulating interest rates was to stimulate healthy competition among the banks and to encourage their operational efficiency. Second, for making available a greater quantum of resources for commercial purposes, statutory pre-emptions have gradually been lowered.[5] Third, towards strengthening PSBs, GOI recapitalized these banks to avert any financial crisis and to build up their capital base for meeting minimum capital adequacy norms.[6] Further, the policy makers permitted PSBs to expand their capital base with equity participation by private investors up to the limit of 49 %.[7] Fourth, the policy makers introduced improved prudential norms related to capital adequacy,[8] asset classification[9] and income recognition in line with international norms, as well as increased disclosure level.[10] Fifth, the burden of directed sector lending has been gradually reduced by (a) expanding the definition of priority sector lending[11] and (b) liberalising lending

[4] Except non-resident Indian (NRI) deposits, small loans up to INR 0.2 million and export credit, the interest rates are fully deregulated.

[5] The combined pre-emptions under CRR and SLR, amounting to 63.5 % of net demand and time liabilities in 1991 (of which CRR was 25 %), have since been reduced, and presently, the combined ratio stands below 35 % (of which, the SLR is at its statutory minimum at 24 %).

[6] The GOI has injected about 0.1 % of GDP annually into weak public sector banks (Hanson 2005; Rangarajan 2007). During the period 1992–1993 to 2001–2002, GOI contributed some INR 177 billion, about 1.9 % of the 1995–1996 GDP, to nationalised banks (Mohan and Prasad 2005).

[7] In 1993, the State Bank of India (SBI) Act, 1955 was amended to promote partial private shareholding. The SBI became the first PSB to raise equity in the capital markets. The amendment of the Banking Regulation Act in 1994 allowed the PSBs to raise private equity up to 49 % of paid-up capital. Since then 20 PSBs have diversified their ownership, although the government has remained as the largest shareholder.

[8] India adopted the Basel Accord Capital Standards in April 1992. An 8 % capital adequacy ratio was introduced in phases between 1993 and 1996, according to bank ownership and scope of their operations. Following the recommendations of Narasimham Committee II, the regulatory minimum capital adequacy ratio was later raised to 10 % in the phased manner.

[9] The time for classification of assets as nonperforming has been tightened over the years with a view to move towards the international best practice norm of 90 days by end 2004.

[10] From 2000 to 2001, the PSBs are required to attach the balance sheet of their subsidiaries to their balance sheets.

[11] Priority sector has been redefined to comprise small and marginal farmers, tiny sector of industry, small business and transport operators, village and cottage industries, rural artisans and other weaker sections.

rates on advances in excess of INR 0.2 million. Sixth, entry regulations for domestic private and foreign banks have been relaxed to infuse competition in the banking sector.[12] Seventh, impressive institutional reforms have been introduced to strengthen the supervisory authorities.[13] Eighth, PSBs have been allowed to rationalise some branches while branch licensing has been removed.

While India's approach to banking reforms has been in line with global trends, one unique feature of this approach is that instead of launching the banking reforms in a 'big bang' fashion, Indian policy makers pursued a 'cautious' or 'gradualist' approach to strengthen accounting, legal, supervisory and regulatory frameworks pertaining to the banking sector. In sum, the process of reforms was initiated in a gradual and properly sequenced manner so as to have a reinforcing effect (Reddy 2007). The policy makers sought to consistently upgrade the banking sector by adopting the international best practice through a consultative process.

During the post-deregulation years since 1992, Indian banking system has undergone significant changes. A remarkable trend is the shift from traditional banking activities such as lending and deposit-taking to a more universal banking character with financial market activities such as brokerage and portfolio management growing in importance. Thus, the traditional role of banks as mere financial intermediaries has since altered, and risk management has emerged as the defining attribute. While deregulation has opened up new avenues for banks to augment their incomes, it has also entailed greater competition and, consequently, greater risks.

A positive externality of the banking reforms process has been the building up of the institutional architecture in terms of markets, and creation of enabling environment through technological and legal infrastructure and improvement in managerial competence (Bhide et al. 2002). The most notable achievement of banking industry is the significant improvement in capital adequacy and asset quality. This has been achieved despite convergence of the prudential norms with international best practice. The capital adequacy ratio has increased to 14.5 % for scheduled commercial banks at end-March 2010, which is much above the international norm. Commercial banks' net profits are at 1.13 % and 1.05 % of total assets during 2008–2009 and 2009–2010, up from 0.16 % in 1995–1996. The net non-performing assets declined to 0.94 % of net advances during 2008–2009 from 8.91 % in 1995–1996. Further, the intermediation process has also improved during the post-reforms years. In the post-1992 period, a wave of voluntary mergers and acquisitions swept through the industry as banks tried to cut cost and achieve economies of scale.

---

[12] In 1993, the RBI issued guidelines concerning the establishment of new private sector banks. Nine new private banks have entered the market since then. In addition, over twenty foreign banks have started their operations since 1994.

[13] A high-powered Board of Financial Supervision (BFS) has been constituted in 1994. BFS exercised the power of supervision in relation to the banking companies, financial institutions and non-banking companies, creating an arm's-length relationship between regulation and supervision. On-site supervision was introduced in 1995, and annual supervision of CAMELS was introduced in 1997.

With the completion of about 20 years of banking reforms process, it seems pertinent to take stock of the impact of reform measures on the efficiency of commercial banks. A theoretical proposition appears in the banking literature that a deregulatory process increases competitive forces in the financial system so that 'banks not allocating their resources efficiently would perish unless they could become like their efficient competitors by producing more output with existing inputs' (Alam 2001). In the spirit of this proposition, an ascent in input-conserving efficiency of Indian banks during the post-deregulation years would reflect a positive response by the banks to the reform measures and, thus, signals the success of the reforms process in accomplishing its goal of attaining high operating efficiency in Indian banking industry.

1.2 Motivation, Objectives and Significant Research Questions

As noted above, the thrust of the banking reforms programme was not only on the improvement of operating efficiency through inculcating the spirit of competition among Indian banks but also on strengthening the shock absorptive capacity of the banking system through the adoption of internationally accepted prudential regulations. Accordingly, the Reserve Bank of India (RBI) has thus far promoted, among others, the participation of foreign banks, technological upgradation in the banking sector, recapitalisation of public sector banks, liberalisation of the branch authorisation policy, adoption of innovative policy measures for financial inclusion and application of countercyclical prudential measures (Reserve Bank of India 2010).

How the deregulation of banking environment has influenced the way banks transformed their resources into banking services and outputs has remained largely unexplored in Indian context. In this regard, a continuous year-to-year assessment of performance of banks is crucial because the banking industry has undergone financial innovations and shocks throughout the 1990s due to either the changing regulations or unexpected shocks. Therefore, there are strong reasons to expect that efficiency measures of banks may have fluctuated over short periods of time. Hence, we felt a need to examine the efficiency performance of the Indian banking industry over a longer period so that we could evaluate not only the impact of these regulatory changes but also the effects of such shocks, including substantial improvement in banking technology, on the efficiency of banks.

In the Indian context, strengthening of regulatory and accounting frameworks for ensuring financial stability and improvement of allocative and productive efficiency of banking industry is the core agenda of the RBI and GOI. Therefore, any attempt to evaluate trends in efficiency of Indian banks in resource allocation and utilisation process during the post-deregulation years will not only assist government instrumentalities and banking regulators in policy making but will also enable the banks' management to improve the way in which they allocate and use resources in the production process. With this in mind, we outline the objectives of the book.

The broad objective of the research is to examine how deregulatory measures in the Indian banking sector during the post-reforms years (1992–1993 to 2007–2008) affected the growth of cost efficiency and total factor productivity (TFP) in the Indian banking industry. In particular, the major objectives of this study are as follows:

(i) To undertake a comprehensive review of the banking reforms introduced in the Indian banking industry since 1992
(ii) To gauge the impact of inclusion or exclusion of non-traditional activities on cost efficiency estimates for Indian banks
(iii) To examine trends in cost, allocative, technical, pure technical and scale of the Indian banking industry as a whole and across distinct ownership groups and various size classes during the post-deregulation period
(iv) To analyse the nature of returns-to-scale (RTS) in Indian banking industry
(v) To explore the influential factors that affect cost efficiency and its component measures of Indian banks
(vi) To study the impact of the deregulation process on the total factor productivity (TFP) growth of Indian banks

In light of aforementioned objectives of the study, we primarily focused on seeking the answers to the following research questions:

(i) Does the inclusion of non-traditional activities in the specification of banks' output affect the efficiency of Indian banks?
(ii) Do deregulatory measures spur the efficiency and productivity of Indian banks?
(iii) Are foreign banks always better?
(iv) Does size matter in Indian banking industry?
(v) Are there any economies or diseconomies of scale in the Indian banking sector?
(vi) What are most influential bank-specific variables affecting efficiency and TFP growth of Indian banks?

The Indian banking sector is of particular interest for a number of reasons. First, as noted above, one unique feature of India's approach to financial deregulation is that instead of launching the banking reforms in a 'big bang' fashion, Indian policy makers pursued a 'cautious' or 'gradualist' approach. This offers a great scope for examining whether reforms should be carried out in a big bang fashion or sequenced for removing regulatory and operating constraints slowly over the years so as to augment the resource-use efficiency of the distressed banks. Second, deregulation of the banking sector led to the creation of a level playing field in which all banks – private or government controlled, domestic or foreign – have been subjected to the same prudential norms and standard regulations and have been allowed significant liberty to design and price products on both sides of the balance sheet, to choose asset portfolios and to enter into and exit from regional and local markets (Bhaumik and Dimova 2004). Against this backdrop, it is pertinent to know how banks with different ownership types reacted to regulatory changes in terms of efficiency change. Thirdly, Indian banking is a considerable component of Asian financial markets, and it shares quite similar characteristics with the banking system of other Asian countries. Since most Asian countries have embarked on the path of deregulation or are contemplating to do so, an empirical investigation into the effects of deregulation on the dynamics of efficiency and productivity change in the Indian case could provide useful policy suggestions to those countries.

1.3 Contribution of the Book

From the survey of empirical literature on the banking efficiency in India, it has been observed that existing studies concerning the efficiency of Indian banks have not been of a comprehensive nature. The present study is targeted to enrich the extant literature on the efficiency of Indian banks by providing a detailed analysis of some significantly understated and hitherto neglected aspects relating to the efficiency of Indian banks. In particular, the contribution of the present study to the existing literature is in following directions.

First, the study provides a detailed analysis of trends in cost efficiency and TFP growth of the Indian banking industry as a whole and across distinct ownership groups and size classes during the post-deregulation period. Such a detailed and comprehensive analysis is not available in the existing literature. Further, the sample period, investigated by previous Indian bank studies, is generally not long enough to shed much light on the impact of banking reforms programme. In contrast, this study uses a longer sample period (16 years) which covers both the first phase of banking reforms (1992–1993 to 1997–1998) and the second phase of banking reforms (1998–1999 to 2007–2008). In particular, the sample period is marked by drastic and intensive banking reforms involving significant governance changes in all types of scheduled commercial banks.

Second, the present study examines the growth behaviour of five alternative measures of banking efficiency, namely, cost, allocative, technical, pure technical and scale efficiencies, as a way to strengthen the validity of inference drawn on the basis of empirical results. This is really somewhat missing in the existing studies on the efficiency of Indian banks. Previous studies generally computed one or two efficiency measures and drew the inferences based on those efficiency measures.

Third, this research work has been carried out to verify the relevance of including non-traditional activities in the output vector. Recently, the researchers highlighted the expanding involvement of banks in off-balance sheet (OBS) activities and their impact on efficiency performance of banks. It is worth noting here that majority of recent studies on efficiency in Indian banks have accounted for non-traditional activities by including non-interest income in the output vector as a proxy for these activities. However, to the best of our knowledge, none of these studies have investigated the impact of inclusion or exclusion of these activities on the efficiency estimates. Thus, a clear void exists in the extant literature since no study has been conducted to analyse how the entire distribution of efficiency scores differs when these activities are not considered. The present study has made an attempt in this direction and is targeted to enrich the extant literature on the efficiency of Indian banks by providing a detailed analysis of this significantly understated and hitherto neglected aspect related to efficiency of Indian banks.

Fourth, recent research found that risk variables significantly alter X-inefficiency of the banks. Keeping this in view, we have incorporated the risk element in the efficiency appraisal of the Indian banks. This is accomplished by including equity as a quasi-fixed input variable in the input–output specification used for computing different efficiency measures.

Fifth, we employ a non-radial Malmquist productivity index (MPI) approach as suggested by Tone (2001) to decompose total factor productivity (TFP) change to its distinct components, namely, technical efficiency change (capturing the catching-up effect) and technological change (measuring the frontier-shift effect). To the best of our knowledge, this is perhaps the first empirical study to estimate TFP growth of Indian banks by using the slack-based measure (SBM) model to compute input-oriented distance functions. Earlier attempts in measuring TFP change in Indian banks made use of radial MPI approach, which does not deal with input/output slacks directly.

Sixth, the existing literature on the banking efficiency does not provide clear and robust results with respect to the key determinants of efficiency of Indian banks. In this study, we made efforts to explore the potential determinants of banking efficiency, such as profitability, asset quality and size. To this end, we employ the so-called two-stage DEA procedure and applied panel data-based random-effects Tobit model, which is perhaps not utilised earlier in banking efficiency analyses of Indian banks.

Seventh, this study provides a detailed analysis of the nature of returns-to-scale in the Indian banking industry. In particular, we made use of López-Cortés and Snowden's (1998) scale deficiency index and applied Fukushige and Miyara's (2005) procedure for testing the statistical significance of returns-to-scale at the industry level.

1.4 Structure of the Book

This book aims at bridging the research gaps in the extant literature by empirically investigating the different aspects of bank efficiency in India. To present the discussion in a lucid way, we have organised the book into eight chapters, including the present one.

In the current chapter, we have illuminated the background of the study and highlighted the precise objectives and contributions of the book. Chapter 2 provides a history of the Indian banking industry and discusses the process of transformation of banking industry from a state of high degree of regulation to deregulation and liberalisation. The current structure of Indian banking industry is also presented in this chapter. In Chap. 3, various parametric and non-parametric approaches used in the banking efficiency analyses have been discussed. Chapter 4 presents a thematic survey of empirical literature on banking efficiency. The prominent issues in the banking efficiency literature have also been discussed.

Chapters 5, 6 and 7 are empirical in nature. In Chap. 5, an attempt has been made to examine the relevance of including a proxy for non-traditional activities in the output specification of Indian banks. Further, efforts have been made to measure to what extent the relative rankings of individual banks and ownership groups are affected by the inclusion or exclusion of non-interest income as a proxy for non-traditional activities. Chapter 6 explains the evolution of cost efficiency and its component measures in Indian banking industry during the post-deregulation years. In this chapter, we also explored (i) efficiency differences across distinct ownership groups and various size classes, (ii) nature of returns-to-scale in Indian banking industry and (iii) the key factors influencing interbank variations in cost efficiency and its components. Chapter 7 provides empirical evidence on TFP growth of Indian banking industry during the post-deregulation period. Factors explaining variations in TFP growth and its components have also been discussed. Chapter 8 summarises the major findings of this study and recommends policy changes with a view to enhance the efficiency and productivity of banks operating in India. Enunciating the limitations of the study, the chapter ends by providing some directions on possible future research in the area of banking efficiency in India.

Chapter 2
Banking System in India: Developments, Structural Changes and Institutional Framework

2.1 Introduction

The banking sector in India has undergone a sea change since the launching of the banking reforms programme in the year 1992. One of the foremost objectives of this programme was to instill greater competition in the banking system for augmenting profitability, efficiency and productivity of the banks. With the purpose to impart greater efficiency in the resource allocation process in the banking system, the policy makers gradually implemented a series of reform measures like dismantling of administrated interest rate structure, reduction in statutory pre-emptions in the form of reserve requirements and liberal entry of *de novo* private banks. The efforts have also been made to strengthen the shock absorptive capacity of the system through adoption of prudential norms in the line with the international best practices and tightening of supervision. Consequent to the reform measures introduced over the last 20 years, the Indian banking sector has experienced significant institutional and structural changes.

Against this background, this chapter aims to delineate the important historical developments in the Indian banking industry and to review the major banking reforms since the early 1990s. The chapter also discusses the structural changes and transformations that have been taken place in Indian banking industry since the initiation of banking reforms process. In particular, this chapter aimed at providing necessary background for understanding the empirical analysis of banking efficiency in India that presented in the subsequent chapters of this book.

The chapter unfolds as follows. The next section provides an overview of the historical developments in the Indian banking sector. It also reviews the evolution of the banking reforms over the last two decades. The subsequent section outlines major structural changes and transformations that have taken place in the post-reforms years. The current structure of Indian commercial banking industry is summarised in the penultimate section. The final section is concluding in nature.

S. Kumar and R. Gulati, *Deregulation and Efficiency of Indian Banks*, India Studies in Business and Economics, DOI 10.1007/978-81-322-1545-5_2, © Springer India 2014

2.2 Developments in Indian Banking Sector

Modern banking in India began with the establishment of a limited number of banks by British agency houses for financing of trade in the raw materials needed for British industries. The Indian enterprises made a significant entry into banking business by establishing joint-stock banks only during the early 1920s, which got strengthened by the growing nationalist sentiment and the spread of the Swadeshi movement. However, the economic power in the joint-stock banks was concentrated in the hands of a few families, who managed to make the bulk of its finance available to themselves, favoured groups and their concerns. Moreover, the bulk of bank advances was diverted to industry, particularly to large- and medium-scale industries and big and established business houses, while the needs of vital sectors like small-scale industry, agriculture and exports tended to be neglected. It was only due to the impact of the diversification and growth of Indian industry during the Second World War and also the emphasis of 5-year plans on industrial development in the 1950s that Indian banks changed their banking policies and stance to a certain extent.

With the prime objective to channel the credit towards hitherto neglected priority sectors of the economy in accordance with the national planning priorities, the Government of India (GOI) introduced a scheme of *social control* over banks in 1967 and nationalised 14 major commercial banks in 1969 and then 6 banks in 1980. Following nationalisation, there was significant branch expansion, especially in rural areas. Further, the GOI increasingly used the banking system as an instrument of public finance. At the end of the 1980s, all the signs of 'financial repression' such as excessively high-reserve requirements, credit controls, interest rate controls, strict entry barriers, operational restrictions and predominance of state-owned banks were present in the Indian banking system. On recognising the signs of financial repression and their adverse effects on the health of banks, the policy makers embarked upon a comprehensive programme of banking reforms in the year 1992. In the following years, reforms covered the areas of (a) liberalisation, including interest rate deregulation, the reduction of statutory pre-emptions and the easing of directed credit rules; (b) stabilisation of banks; (c) partial privatisation of state-owned banks; (d) changes in the institutional framework; and (e) entry deregulation for both domestic and foreign banks. The subsequent changes led the Indian banking system truly competitive and a well-structured system resilient from financial crisis.

For analytical purposes, we divide the aforementioned developments in the Indian banking system into four distinct phases. The first phase, so-called initial formative phase, covers the evolution of the banking system in India before independence. The second phase, which is called as *foundation phase* in our analysis, is confined to the period from 1947 to the early 1960s. This phase witnessed the foundation for a sound banking system in the country. The third phase which is designated as the *expansion phase* began in mid-1960s but gained momentum after second round of nationalisation of banks and continued until the late 1980s. The fourth phase that is labelled as the *reform phase* covers the period from 1992 to the present and is marked by a period of transition from a highly regulated banking industry to a contestable industry.

2.2.1 Initial Formative Phase: Prior to Independence

In the eighteenth century, English agency houses[1] in Calcutta and Bombay began to conduct banking business, besides their commercial business, based on the principle of unlimited liability. However, modern banking in India began with the establishment of three Presidency banks.[2] Bank of Bengal was first of the Presidency bank which was established in 1806 with a capital of INR 5 million. Bank of Bombay and Bank of Madras were other two Presidency banks, which started their operations in 1840 and 1843 with a capital of INR 5.2 million and INR 3 million, respectively. After the passage of Act VII in 1860, private banks in the form of joint-stock companies with limited liability began to appear. The first Indian-owned private bank was the Allahabad Bank set up in Allahabad in 1865, the second, Punjab National Bank, was established in 1895 in Lahore, and the third, Bank of India, started its operations in 1906 in Mumbai. The Swadeshi movement of 1906 provided a great impetus to joint-stock banks of Indian ownership, and many more Indian commercial banks such as Central Bank of India, Bank of Baroda, Canara Bank, Indian Bank and Bank of Mysore were established between 1906 and 1913. By the end of December 1913, the total number of reporting commercial banks in the country reached to 56.[3] In 1921, the three Presidency banks were merged to form the Imperial Bank of India. Prior to the establishment of Reserve Bank of India in 1935, the Imperial Bank of India was functioning as a central bank and performed three sets of functions, viz. commercial banking, central banking and the banker to the government. In 1930, the banking system, in all, comprised 1,258 banking institutions registered under Indian Companies Act, 1913.

[1] A type of business organisation recognisable as managing agency took form in a period from 1834 to 1847. Managing agency system came into existence when an agency house first promoted and acquired the management of a company. This system with no counterpart in any other country functioned as an Indian substitute for a well-organised capital market and an industrial banking system of western countries.

[2] They were known as Presidency banks as they were set up in the three Presidencies that were the units of administrative jurisdiction in the country for the East India Company. The Presidency banks were governed by Royal Charters. These banks issued currency notes until the enactment of the Paper Currency Act, 1861, when this right to issue currency notes by the Presidency banks was abolished and that function was entrusted to the Government.

[3] It comprises of 3 Presidency banks, 18 class 'A' banks (with capital of greater than INR 0.5 million), 23 class 'B' banks (with capital of INR 0.1 million to 0.5 million) and 12 exchange banks. Exchange banks were foreign-owned banks that engaged mainly in foreign exchange business in terms of foreign bills of exchange and foreign remittances for travel and trade. Classes A and B were joint-stock banks.

To look into the problems of Indian banking system, especially that of bank failures and lack of spread of banking in rural areas, the Indian Central Banking Enquiry Committee was set up in 1929. The committee noted that the commercial banks played a negligible role in financing the requirements of agricultural production and co-operative credit. The main recommendations of the committee were (i) to establish a central bank for the country and (ii) to enact a special Banking Act to monitor the activities of commercial banks. On the basis of these recommendations of the committee, the Reserve Bank of India Act was passed in 1934, and the Reserve Bank of India (RBI) came into existence in 1935 as a central banking authority of the country. Between 1936 and 1945, many small banks failed due to low capital base, insufficient liquid assets and presence of bad debts. Further, the process of failure of banks continued in the post-independence period. This is evident from the fact that by the end of 1948, over 45 large banks (out of more than 600 banks) were closed down.

2.2.2 Foundation Phase: From 1947 to the Early 1960s

The banking crisis and failure of a large number of banks during 1940s underlined the need for regulating and controlling Indian commercial banks. In 1949, two significant steps have taken in this direction. First, the GOI nationalised the RBI through enacting Reserve Bank of India (Transfer to Public Ownership) Act, 1948, to transform it into a state-owned entity. Second, the Banking Companies Act, 1949 (later rechristened as Banking Regulation Act), was enacted with a view to empower the RBI to regulate, supervise and develop the activities of commercial banks in India. The act bestowed unlimited powers upon the RBI to inspect any banking company with the objective of satisfying itself regarding the eligibility for a licence, opening of branches, amalgamation and compliance with the derivatives issued by the central bank. It has since become the 'regulatory backbone' of contemporary banking regulation (Pasricha 2007). After independence, central banking in the country was not only confined to the regulation and supervision but also aligned its activities to attain the planned development objectives of the government. The commercial banks were considered unique among financial institutions and were assigned a role of conduit in channelizing the resources to most productive uses in the economic planning process. However, banks failed to penetrate into rural and semiurban areas, and credit requirements of agriculture and small-scale enterprises were really neglected.

To bring about wider diffusion of banking facilities and to change an uneven distributive pattern of bank lending, the RBI commissioned the All India Rural Credit Survey Committee in 1951. The committee submitted its report in 1954 and recommended the creation of a strong, integrated state-partnered commercial banking institution entrusted with the task of opening branches in the rural and semiurban areas. Accepting the recommendation of the committee, the GOI nationalised the Imperial Bank of India in 1955 and converted it into State Bank of India (SBI) with the enactment of State Bank of India Act, 1955. This was the starting point for the nationalisation of commercial banks in India (Roland 2008). In 1959, the State Bank of India (Subsidiary Banks) Act was passed to enable SBI to take over eight princely state-associated banks (now five) as its subsidiaries.[4] The SBI and its associates were entrusted with the task of serving the banking needs of neglected areas (Kumbhakar and Sarkar 2003). There were also many bank failures in the early 1960s, affecting the flow of credit to agriculture and small industry (Mohan and Prasad 2005).

2.2.3 Expansion Phase: From the Mid-1960s to the Late 1980s

In order to correct the perceived imbalance in the lending practices of banks, the GOI decided to introduce the scheme of *social control* in December 1967. The main objective of social control was to achieve a wider spread of bank credit, prevent its misuse, direct a larger volume of credit flow to priority sectors and make it more effective instrument of economic development. Nevertheless, the policy did not work as well as the government had anticipated. In order to achieve the desired policy objectives, the GOI nationalised 14 major commercial banks with deposits of over INR 0.5 billion in 1969 by promulgating the Banking Companies (Acquisition and Transfer of Undertakings) Ordinance, 1969, and six more banks with deposits exceeding INR 2 billion in 1980 by propagating the Banking Companies (Acquisition and Transfer of Undertakings) Ordinance, 1980.[5] With that, over 90 % of the banking business was brought under the control of GOI. The major objectives of bank nationalisation were to (i) prevent few corporations from controlling all the banking businesses, (ii) limit the concentration of wealth and economic power by using the resources mobilised by banks to achieve egalitarian growth, (iii) mobilise the savings of general public (including in remote areas) and (iv) pay more attention to priority sectors (agriculture and small industry). While doing so, the GOI made it adequately clear that the role of banking in an economy such as India's must be "inspired by a larger social purpose" and must "subserve national priorities and objectives such as rapid growth in agriculture, small industry, and exports" (Pasricha 2007).

---

[4] State Bank of Bikaner, State Bank of Hyderabad, State Bank of Indore, State Bank of Jaipur, State Bank of Mysore, State Bank of Patiala, State Bank of Saurashtra and State Bank of Travancore are the eight associate banks of SBI. It is worth mentioning here that the State Bank of Bikaner and State Bank of Jaipur have been merged into one bank, namely, State Bank of Bikaner and Jaipur. Recently, in 2008 and 2010, State Bank of Saurashtra and State Bank of Indore have merged with State Bank of India.

[5] The fourteen commercial banks that nationalised in 1969 were Central Bank of India, Bank of Maharashtra, Dena Bank, Punjab National Bank, Syndicate Bank, Canara Bank, Indian Overseas Bank, Indian Bank, Bank of Baroda, Union Bank, Allahabad Bank, United Bank of India, UCO Bank and Bank of India, and six that nationalised in 1980 were Andhra Bank, Corporation Bank, New Bank of India, Oriental Bank of Commerce, Punjab & Sind Bank and Vijaya Bank.

Following nationalisation, there was significant branch expansion to mobilise the savings and a visible increase in the flow of bank credit to priority sectors. The number of bank branches significantly increased from 5,026 in 1960 to about 8,187 in 1969, with the share of rural (urban) branches rose from 16.5 (33.5)% to 17.6 (41.6)% (Reserve Bank of India 2008a). It is significant to note here that on the eve of nationalisation, the banks still had a definite urban orientation. To tackle the problem of urban orientation, the RBI has taken two significant steps: (i) initiated specific schemes like Lead Bank Scheme (LBS) and Differential Rate of Interest (DRI) Scheme and (ii) designed the branch licensing policy (BLP). The Lead Bank Scheme, a district-level system of credit planning, monitoring and oversight, was introduced in 1969 to ensure meeting of the targets of priority sector lending. In addition, the Differential Rate of Interest Scheme was introduced in 1972 to extend credit to low-income people in rural areas at concessional rates of interest. Further, the branch licensing policies[6] have been implemented since 1977 up until 1990 to ensure that the banking infrastructure was sufficient to narrow regional disparities in the availability of banks (Kochar 2005).

Subsequently, in 1977, RBI imposed 1:4 licence rule, which aimed that for every branch opened in an already banked (urban) location, a commercial bank must open four branches in unbanked (rural) locations. This led to the expansion of the rural branches at a higher speed. Consequent of this branch expansion policy, the number of total branches increased to about 60,220 in 1990, indicating a total increase of over 51,000 branches relative to the number that has been observed in 1969. The share of rural branches in total branches rose to about 58 % in 1990 from 17.6 % in 1969. The population per bank office declined rapidly from 65,000 in 1969 to 13,756 in 1990. Alongside the share of bank credit and savings which accounted for by the rural branches rose from 1.5 % to 3 %, respectively, to 15 % each. The credit–deposit ratio in rural areas increased from 37.6 % in 1969 to 60.6 % in 1990. Further, increased financial intermediation in the rural areas aided output and employment diversification out of agriculture. Consequently, the share of credit to the rural sector in total bank credit increased from 3.3 % in 1969 to 14.2 % in 1990. After nationalisation, the focus on directed lending helped largely in availability of credit to the borrowers at lower end.

Ketkar and Ketkar (1992) and Ketkar (1993) observed that bank nationalisation had been a mixed blessing. Aggressive bank branch expansion, especially in the rural areas, has increased financial savings and investment, but the credit controls in the form of directed lending had an adverse effect on the deposit mobilisation, efficiency and profitability of the banks, especially of public sector banks (PSBs). On the whole, the post-nationalisation scenario was dominated by a uniform conglomerate of banks in the public sector with an increased branch network and

[6] The Government of India implemented three branch licensing policies (BLPs) between 1979 and 1990. The first covered the period January 1979 to December 1981, while the second BLP ran from April 1982 through March 1985. The third branch licensing policy guided branch expansion between April 1985 and March 1990.

little differentiation in terms of products and services offered. Besides this, Indian commercial banks, especially PSBs, have made remarkable progress in achieving social goals and bringing financial deepening along with catering the needs of planned development in a mixed economy framework.

From the beginning of 1970s to mid-1980s, the GOI increasingly used the banking system as an instrument of public finance (Hanson and Kathuria 1999). Substantial and increasing volumes of credit were channelled to the government at below-market rates through high and increasing cash reserve requirements (CRR) and statutory liquidity requirements (SLR) in order to fund a large and increasing government deficit at relatively low cost (Sen and Vaidya 1997). The commercial banks, especially PSBs, were obliged to allocate a substantial part of their total loan portfolio to the priority sectors at a subsidised rate that was below the market rate of interest. Furthermore, the deposits and lending rates were being strictly determined by the government. The CRR and SLR were raised to highest levels. There was virtually no autonomy to the banks even in taking decision to open new bank branches. The government also tightly regulated the licensing of market entry of new domestic and foreign banks. Also, the competition in the banking sector was virtually absent. In fact, the heavy hand of government has been omnipresent in the banking sector, especially in the working of PSBs; and there was very limited market-based decision making.

Further, rates of return were low by international standards; the capital base had eroded; non-performing assets were on the rise; and customer service was below expectation (Sarkar 2004). More important, the lack of proper disclosure norms led to many problems being kept under cover. Poor internal controls raised serious doubts about the integrity of the system itself (Reddy 1998). As a result, many banks became unprofitable, inefficient and unsound owing to their poor lending strategies and lack of internal risk management under government ownership (Joshi and Little 1996; Shirai 2002). Jagirdar (1996) observed that the average return on assets (ROA) in the second half of the 1980s was only about 0.15 % which was abysmally low by all the standards. Further, in 1992–1993, non-performing assets (NPAs) of 27 PSBs amounted to 24 % of total credit; only 15 PSBs achieved a net profit, and half of the PSBs faced negative net worth (Shirai 2002). This not only reduced banks' incentives to operate properly and hence their performance but also undermined regulators' incentives to properly supervise banks' performances (Shirai and Rajasekaran 2002). In sum, all the signs of financial repression such as excessively high-reserve requirements, credit controls, interest rate controls, strict entry barriers, operational restrictions and predominance of state-owned banks were present in the Indian banking system.

Recognising the growing deficiencies in the banking system, the GOI decided in mid-1980s to overhaul the regulatory environment of Indian banking industry. The initial impetus in this direction was the recommendations of the Committee to Review the Working of the Monetary System (Chairman: S. Chakravarty 1985). This committee which is popularly known as Chakravarty Committee undertook the comprehensive review of the working of monetary system and suggested the ways to improve the effectiveness of monetary policy as an instrument for planned economic development. The major recommendations of the committee include, *inter alia*, (i) shifting to 'monetary targeting' as a basic framework of monetary policy, (ii) emphasis on the objectives of price policy and economic growth, (iii) coordination between monetary and fiscal policy and (iv) suggestion of a scheme of interest rates in accordance with valid economic criteria.

The recommendations of the Chakravarty Committee guided far-reaching transformation in the conduct of monetary policy in India. There was a shift to a new policy framework for the conduct of monetary policy by introducing monetary targeting. In addition, the recommendations of the Report of the Working Group on the Money Markets (Chairman: N. Vaghul 1987) led to the development of the money market in the country. The significant steps that have been taken for developing the money market include the introduction of new financial instruments (such as 182-day Treasury Bills, Certificates of Deposits (CDs), Commercial Paper (CP) and Participation Certificates) and the development of Discount and Finance House of India (DFHI) in 1988. These changes enabled the creation of new institutional arrangements to support the process of monetary targeting. But these reform measures have failed to address the causes of financial repression in the banking sector since these measures were primarily aimed at the efficient functioning of monetary policy (see Panel A of Table A.1 for detailed recommendations of various committees introduced during this phase).[7]

On the whole, from the early 1970s through the late 1980s, the role of market forces in the Indian banking system was almost missing, and excess regulation in terms of high liquidity requirements and state interventions in allocating credit and determining the prices of financial products have resulted in serious financial repression. The main consequence of this financial repression was an ascent in the volume of bad loans due to ineffective credit evaluation system and poorer risk assessment policies. Further, poor disclosure standards abetted corruption by window-dressing the true picture of banks. The overstaffing, over-branching and undue interference by labour unions resulted in huge operating losses. This led to a gradual decline in the profitability and efficiency of Indian banks, especially of PSBs. In fact, in the late 1980s, Indian banking system was on the verge of a crisis and lacking viability even in its basic function of financial intermediation.

2.2.4 *Reform Phase: Early 1990s Onwards*

The most significant phase in the history of Indian banking industry began in the year 1992 when on realising the presence of financial repression and to seek an escape from any potential crisis in the banking sector, the GOI embarked upon a comprehensive banking reforms plan with the objective of creating a more diversified, profitable, efficient and resilient banking system. The country's approach to introduce

---

[7] Note that Table A.1 is given in the Appendix.

reforms in banking and financial sector was guided by 'Pancha Sutra' or five principles: (i) cautious or sequencing of reform measures, (ii) introduction of norms that were mainly reinforcing, (iii) introduction of complementary reforms across sectors (monetary, fiscal, external and financial sectors), (iv) development of financial institutions and (v) development and integration of financial markets (Reserve Bank of India 2008a, p. 110). It is worth noting here that instead of launching the banking reforms in a 'big bang' fashion, Indian policy makers pursued the 'cautious' or 'gradualist' approach to strengthen accounting, legal, supervisory and regulatory frameworks pertaining to the Indian banking sector.

The evolution of the banking sector in this phase can be divided into two subphases. The first phase of reforms introduced consequent to the release of the Report of the Committee on the Financial System (Chairperson: M. Narasimham 1992a). The focus of this phase of the reforms was economic deregulation targeting at relaxing credit and interest rates controls and removing restrictions on the market entry and diversification (see Panel B of Table A.1 for detailed recommendations of this committee). The second phase of reforms, introduced subsequent to the recommendations of the Committee on the Banking Sector Reforms (Chairperson: M. Narasimham 1998). This phase focused on strengthening the prudential regulations and improving the standards of disclosure and levels of transparency to minimise the risks that banks assume and to ensure the safety and soundness of both individual banks and the Indian banking system as a whole. The major emphasis of this phase was on increasing the minimum capital adequacy ratio; recognition of market risks; tightened assets classification, income recognition and provisioning norms; introduction of Asset-Liability Management System, etc. (see Panel B of Table A.1 for detailed recommendations of this committee). On the whole, the key objective of the reforms process was to transform the operating environment of the banking industry from a highly regulated system to a more market-oriented one, with a view to increase competitiveness and efficiency (Sarkar 2004).

Although the broad contours of reform measures in the financial sector have been provided by the aforementioned committees, a large number of committees/working groups have been constituted since 1992 for addressing the specific issues in the banking sector. For example, Janakiraman Committee (1992b) investigated irregularities in fund management in commercial banks and financial institutions. Padmanabhan Committee (1996b) focused on the on-site supervision of banks and recommended the implementation of CAMELS rating methodology for on-site supervision of the banks. Khan Committee (1997b) suggested measures for bringing about harmonisation in the lending and working capital finance by banks and Development Financial Institutions (DFIs). Verma Committee (1999c) concentrated on restructuring of weak PSBs. The committee identified 3 weak banks, viz. Indian Bank, United Commercial Bank and United Bank of India, and made the suggestion to introduce Voluntary Retirement Fund for enabling banks to reduce excess manpower. Vasudevan Committee (1999a) recommended the strategy of upgradation of the existing technology in the banking sector. Mittal Committee (2001b) made recommendations on the regulatory and supervisory frameworks of internet banking in India. Mohan Committee (2009b) which is popularly known as Committee on

Financial Sector Assessment has suggested significant measures to improve the stability and resilience of the Indian financial system (see Table A.1 for detailed recommendations of these committees/working groups).

In the post-reforms years, a large number of major policy developments have taken place in the Indian banking system for enhancing the operational efficiency and profitability of banks (see Table 2.1 for year-wise details on these developments). Nevertheless, the key banking reforms to uproot the banking system from financial repression and distress have been taken in the following directions. First, for making available a greater quantum of resources for commercial purposes, the statutory pre-emptions have gradually been lowered. Second, the structure of administered interest rates has been almost totally dismantled in a phased manner. Third, the burden of directed sector lending has been gradually reduced by (a) expanding the definition of priority sector lending and (b) liberalising lending rates on advances in excess of INR 0.2 million. Fourth, entry regulations for domestic and foreign banks have been relaxed to infuse competition in the banking sector. Fifth, the policy makers introduced improved prudential norms related to capital adequacy, asset classification and income recognition in line with international norms, as well as increased disclosure level. Sixth, towards strengthening PSBs, GOI recapitalized public sector banks to avert any financial crisis and to build up their capital base for meeting minimum capital adequacy ratio as per Basel norms.

To sum up, during the last 20 years, the policy makers adopted a cautious approach in introducing the reform measures, which were basically targeted to improve the performance of banks in their operations and to inculcate a competitive spirit in them. Apart from achieving greater efficiency by introducing competition through new private banks and increased operational autonomy to PSBs, the banking reforms were also aimed at enhancing financial inclusion, funding economic growth and better customer service to the public. It is worth noting that the banking reforms since 1992 have brought significant structural changes and transformations in the Indian banking system. A detailed record of these changes is presented in the next section.

2.3 Structural Changes and Transformations in the Indian Banking Sector

As noted above, the banking reforms undertaken in India from 1992 onwards were aimed at not only ensuring the safety and soundness of banks but at the same time making them efficient, functionally diverse and competitive. The reforms transformed the landscape of Indian banking industry from a highly regulated market place to a dynamic and market-oriented one. Reforms also provided required functional autonomy to the banks in decision making in accordance with market signals. In fact, reforms brought about significant structural changes and

Table 2.1 List of major policy changes in Indian commercial banking sector since 1992–1993

Year	Major policy developments
1992–1993	• Report of the Narasimham Committee on the Financial System submitted its recommendations
1993–1994	• Cut in statutory liquidity ratio (SLR) and cash reserve ratio (CRR) in the phased manner to reduce statutory pre-emptions of loanable funds • Introduction of risk-weighted capital adequacy norm and prudential norms for asset classifications, income recognition and provisioning of banks • Reduction in the number of prescribed lending rates from six to three • Announcement of norms for floating new private sector banks • Valuation of investments in government securities on the basis of market prices • Constitution of Debt Recovery Tribunals to adjudicate on bad loans made by banks
1994–1995	• Deregulation of interest rates on loans over INR 0.2 million • Freedom to banks to decide their Prime Lending Rates (PLR) and to link loan rates to PLR • Permission to nationalised banks to raise capital up to 49 % of equity from capital market • Amendment to the State Bank of India Act, 1955, to allow the bank to access equity market • Prescription of prudential norms for Non-Performing Assets (NPAs) • Budget provision of INR 57 billion to recapitalized banks to meet new provisioning norms
1995–1996	• Introduction of Banking Ombudsman Scheme[a] • Streamlining of the cash credit system • Abolishment of Minimum Lending Rate on loans above INR 0.2 million
1996–1997	• The State Bank of India issued Global Depository Receipt (GDR) and became the first Indian bank to be listed on stock exchange overseas • Introduction of the concept of Local Area Banks
1997–1998	• Operationalisation of first shared payment ATM network system • Granting of conditional autonomy to the public sector banks • CRR was cut from 13 % to 10 %
1998–1999	• Report of the Narasimham Committee on the Banking Sector Reforms submitted its recommendations • Revision of capital adequacy norms • Deregulation of the rates of interest on foreign currency deposits with the restriction that these rates are not more than LIBOR rates • Deregulation of interest rates on term deposits
1999–2000	• Working Group on Restructuring Weak Public Sector Banks under the chairmanship of M.S. Verma submitted its report • Issuance of guidelines on asset–liability management • Tightening of the provisioning norms for government securities and state government guaranteed loans and assigning risk weights to this category of investment • Permission to banks to operate different PLRs for different maturities of loans
2000–2001	• Given freedom to the banks to price loans of INR 0.2 million • CRR reduced to 7.5 % from 8 % and again reduced to 5.5 % • Advised banks to formulate policies for recovery/write off/compromise and negotiated settlements

(continued)

Table 2.1 (continued)

Year	Major policy developments
2001–2002	• Guidelines issued for raising subordinated debt for inclusion in Tier II capital by foreign banks operating in India • Guidelines issued on foreign direct investment (FDI) in the banking sector • Issued guidelines on market risk management
2002–2003	• Bank rate reduced by 25 basis points to 6.25 % with effect from February 29th, 2002 • CRR reduced by 25 basis points to 4.75 % with effect from November 16th, 2002 • Public sector banks introduced one-time settlement schemes giving opportunity to the borrowers for settlement of their outstanding dues/NPA accounts below a prescribed value ceiling
2003–2004	• RBI gave freedom to commercial banks to determine interest rates on loans and advances • Banks were given freedom to decide all aspects relating to renewal of overdue deposits • Prudential guidelines on banks' investment in non-SLR securities were issued to contain risks • Banks were allowed to raise long-term bonds with a minimum maturity of 5 years
2004–2005	• Banks were advised to ensure strict compliance with the three accounting standards relating to discounting operations, intangible assets and impairment of assets • Banks were advised to inform their accountholders, at least 1 month in advance of any change in the prescribed minimum balance and the changes that may be levied if the minimum balance is not maintained
2005–2006	• Banks which have maintained capital of at least 9 % risk-weighted assets for both credit risks and market risks as on March 31st, 2006, would be permitted to treat the entire balance in the International Financing Review (IFR) as Tier I capital • Reverse repo rate and repo rate have increased by 25 basis points each from October 26th, 2005 to 5.25 % and 6.25 %, respectively • Banks were advised to have a well documented policy and a fair practices code for credit card operations • Banks were advised to develop appropriate delivery channels of electronic payment services • Guidelines for securitization of standard assets issued to all banks
2006–2007	• To improve the credit delivery mechanism, the revised guidelines on lending to the priority sector were issued • The final guidelines on the revised capital adequacy framework (Basel II) were issued to banks in India on April 27th, 2007
2007–2008	• RBI brought policy changes in statutory pre-emptions to insulate the Indian economy from global financial market turmoil • Provisioning requirement for all types of standard assets was reduced to a uniform level of 0.4 %
2008–2009	• Report of the Committee on Financial Sector Assessment submitted its recommendations • CRR was reduced by 250 basis points to 6.5 % of net demand and time liabilities (NDTLs) with effect from October 11th, 2008. Further, CRR was reduced by 50 point basis to 6 % and 5.5 % of NDTL with effect from October 25th, 2008 and November 8th, 2008, respectively

(continued)

Table 2.1 (continued)

Year	Major policy developments
	• SLR was reduced by 100 basis points to 24 % of NDTLs with effect from November 8th, 2008 • The repo rate was reduced by 50 basis points to 7.5 % on November 3rd, 2008 and 100 basis points to 6.5 % on December 8th, 2008. The reverse repo rate was also reduced by 100 basis points to 5 % on December 8th, 2008 • Report of the High Level Committee constituted to review the Lead Bank Scheme and improve its effectiveness to be submitted by December 2008 • The interest rate ceilings on deposits were increased by 75 basis points on November 15th, 2008

Source: Compiled by the authors from the various issues of (i) Report on Trend and Progress of Banking in India, RBI, Mumbai, and (ii) Indian Banking Year Book, Indian Bank's Association, Mumbai

[a]The Banking Ombudsman Scheme was introduced in June 1995 under the provisions of the Banking Regulation Act, 1949. The scheme has been authorised to look into customer complaints against deficiency in banking services and covers all scheduled commercial banks having business in India, except RRBs and scheduled primary co-operative banks

transformations in the Indian banking sector by recapitalizing the ailing banks, allowing profit making banks to access the capital market and infusing the competitive element in the market through the entry of new private banks. The major structural changes and transformations that have taken place in the Indian banking sector in the post-reforms years are discussed below.

2.3.1 Increased Availability of Lendable Resources

With the objective to enhance the quantum of lendable resources at the disposal of banks, RBI made concrete steps to reduce statutory pre-emptions in the form of cash reserve ratio (CRR) and statutory liquidity ratio (SLR) during the post-reform years.[8] This is also done to ensure the appropriate modulation of liquidity in response to the evolving situation (Reserve Bank of India 2007). The RBI through this reform measure made an effort to move commercial banks away from direct instruments of monetary control to indirect instruments. Accordingly, a phased reduction in the SLR and the CRR was undertaken beginning January 9th, 1993 and April 17th, 1993, respectively.

With a view to augment the lendable resources of banks to enable them to meet the genuine productive requirements of credit, the CRR of scheduled commercial banks which was 15 % of net demand and time liabilities (NDTLs) between July 1st, 1989, and October 8th, 1992, was brought down in phases to 9.5 % by November 22nd, 1997. During this period, the CRR on NDTLs was abridged by

[8] SLR indicates the minimum proportion of net demand and time liabilities (NDTLs) that the bank has to maintain in the form of gold, cash or other approved securities, while CRR refers to a portion of NDTLs (deposits) which commercial banks have to keep/maintain with RBI.

as much as 5 % points. The level of CRR on NDTLs was further reduced to 4.5 % by September 18th, 2004, before the onset of withdrawal of monetary accommodation in September 2004 (see Table 2.2). Later, by August 20th, 2008, the CRR for scheduled commercial banks was hiked to 9 % of NDTLs. This boost in CRR is made in different phases: (i) during 2006–2007, the CRR has been increased to 5.5 % of NDTLs by a cumulative of 100 basis points (four equal phases of 25 basis points each); (ii) during 2007–2008, the CRR has been raised further by 150 basis points (two hikes of 25 basis points and two of 50 basis points) to 7.5 % of banks' NDTLs; and (iii) beginning 2008–2009, the CRR has been increased by 150 basis (six phases of 25 basis points each) to the level of 9 % of NDTLs. This hike in the CRR, over the years, has been done to drain excess liquidity, pre-empt the stoking of demand pressures and contain inflation expectations.

The CRR was then sharply reduced by 250 basis points to 6.5 % of NDTLs with effect from the October 11, 2008. It was further reduced by 100 basis points from 6.5 % to 5.5 % of NDTLs in two stages, i.e. by 50 basis points with retrospective effect from the October 25th, 2008, and by further 50 basis points with effect from the November 8th, 2008. Later, the CRR has been brought down by 50 basis points to 5 % of NDTLs. In all, the RBI is judiciously using the CRR to manage swings in liquidity conditions, consistent with the objectives of price and financial stability.

The base SLR was progressively brought down from peak rate of 38.5 % of NDTLs on February 29th, 1992 to a minimum stipulated level of 25 % by October 25th, 1997. Moreover, the SLR on NDTLs was reduced in a phased manner from 38.5 % to 33.74 % on September 17th, 1994 to 27 % in March 1997 and 25 % on October 25th, 1997 (see Table 2.3). The SLR on NDTLs has further been reduced to 24 % in November 2008. In November 2009, the RBI again revised the SLR to be maintained in the form of NDTLs and increased the proportion of SLR investment in NDTLs to 25 %. The increase in SLR is due to banks preference to park their funds in low risk and low return instruments against the backdrop of prevailing uncertainties.

2.3.2 *Movements Towards Market-Driven Interest Rate System*

Deregulation and rationalisation of the interest rate structure have been a key component of the banking sector reforms process. This has not only helped in improving the competitiveness and resource allocation process in the banking system but has also facilitated the monetary transmission mechanism. Moreover, it has also enabled banks to price their products keeping in view the risk and return perceptions and to introduce innovative deposit products. With progressive deregulation of interest rates, banks can have considerable flexibility to decide their deposit and lending rate structures and manage their assets and liabilities with greater efficiency. On the lending side, banks are free to prescribe their own lending rates, including the Prime Lending Rate (PLR). On the deposit side, banks have been given the freedom to offer a fixed rate or a floating rate subject to the approval of their boards.

Table 2.2 Changes in cash reserve ratio (CRR)

Effective date	Rate (%)	Effective date	Rate (%)	Effective date	Rate (%)
January 1st, 1992	15	January 17th, 1998	10.5	September 18th, 2004	4.75
April 21st, 1992	15	March 28th, 1998	10.25	October 2nd, 2004	5
October 8th, 1992	15	April 11th, 1998	10	December 23rd, 2006	5.25
April 17th, 1993	14.5	August 29th, 1998	11	January 6th, 2007	5.5
May 15th, 1993	14	March 13th, 1999	10.5	February 17th, 2007	5.75
June 11th, 1994	14.5	May 5th, 1999	10	March 3rd, 2007	6
July 9th, 1994	14.75	November 6th, 1999	9.5	April 14th, 2007	6.25
August 6th, 1994	15	November 20th, 1999	9	April 28th, 2007	6.5
November 11th, 1995	14.5	April 8th, 2000	8.5	August 4th, 2007	7
December 9th, 1995	14	April 22nd, 2000	8	November 10th, 2007	7.5
April 27th, 1996	13.5	July 29th, 2000	8.25	April 4th, 2008	7.75
May 5th, 1996	13	August 12th, 2000	8.5	May 10th, 2008	8
July 6th, 1996	12	February 24th, 2001	8.25	May 24th, 2008	8.25
October 26th, 1996	11.5	March 10th, 2001	8	July 5th, 2008	8.5
November 9th, 1996	11	May 19th, 2001	7.5	July 19th, 2008	8.75
January 4th, 1997	10.5	November 3rd, 2001	5.75	August 20th, 2008	9
January 18th, 1997	10	December 29th, 2001	5.5	October 11th, 2008	6.50
October 25th, 1997	9.75	June 1st, 2002	5	October 25th, 2008	6
November 22nd, 1997	9.5	November 16th, 2002	4.75	November 8th, 2008	5.50
December 6th, 1997	10	June 14th, 2003	4.5	January 1st, 2009	5

Source: Handbook of Statistics on Indian Economy (various issues), RBI, Mumbai

Table 2.3 Changes in statutory liquidity ratio (SLR)

Effective date	Rate (%)
February 29th, 1992	38.5
January 9th, 1993	38.25
February 6th, 1993	38
March 6th, 1993	37.75
August 21st, 1993	37.5
September 18th, 1993	37.25
October 16th, 1993	34.75
August 20th, 1994	34.25
September 17th, 1994	33.75
October 29th, 1994	31.5
October 25th, 1997	25
November 8th, 2008	24
November 7th, 2009	25

Source: Handbook of Statistics on Indian Economy (various issues), RBI, Mumbai

Table 2.4 The process of interest rates deregulation in Indian banking industry

Deposit rate deregulation
April 1992: Interest rates freed between 46 days and 3 years and over but ceiling prescribed
October 1995: Deposits of maturity over 2 years exempted from stipulation of ceilings
July 1996: Ceiling on the deposits over 1 year has been relaxed
October 1997: Interest rates on term deposits were fully deregulated
November 2004: Minimum maturity period of 15 days reduced to 7 days for all deposits
October 2011: Deregulation of the savings bank deposit interest rate
Lending rate deregulation
1992–1993: Six categories of lending rates
5 slabs for below INR 0.2 million
Minimum lending rate above INR 0.2 million
October 1994: Lending rate freed for loans above INR 0.2 million and minimum rate abolished
October 1996: Banks to specify maximum spread over Prime Lending Rate (PLR)
1997–1998: Separate PLRs permitted for cash credit/demand loans and term loans above 3 years. Floating Rate permitted
1998–1999: PLR made ceiling for loans up to INR 0.2 million
1999–2000: Tenor linked PLR introduced
2001–2002: PLR made benchmark rate; sub PLR permitted for loans above INR 0.2 million
2002–2003: Bank-wise PLRs made transparent on RBI website
2003–2004: Computation of Benchmark PLR rationalised tenor linked PLRs abolished

Source: Report on Currency and Finance 2003–2008, RBI, Mumbai

The structure of interest rates, which had become extremely complex in the pre-reforms period, was first rationalised and then deregulated, barring a few rates both on the deposits and lending sides. Prior to October 25th, 2011, except saving deposit account, non-resident Indian (NRI) deposits, small loans up to INR 0.2 million and export credit, all the interest rates were fully deregulated. Recently, RBI also deregulated the savings bank deposit interest rate. Deregulation of the savings deposit rate is set to reduce the historical advantage that public sector banks enjoyed in current and savings account (CASA) as hungry private banks raise interest rates to attract deposits.

Table 2.4 presents the process of interest rate deregulation in Indian banking industry. The deregulation of deposit rates began when banks were allowed to set interest rates for maturities between 15 days and up to 1 year subject to a ceiling of 8 % effective April 1985. However, this freedom was withdrawn by the end-May 1985. The process of deregulation was resumed in April 1992 by replacing the existing maturity-wise prescriptions by a single ceiling rate of 13 % for all deposits above 46 days. The ceiling rate was brought down to 10 % in November 1994 but was raised to 12 % in April 1995. Banks were allowed to fix the interest rates on deposits with maturity of over 2 years in October 1995, which was further relaxed to maturity over 1 year in July 1996. In October 1997, the deposit rates were fully deregulated by removing its linkage to bank rate. Consequently, RBI gave freedom to commercial banks to fix their own interest rates on term deposits of various maturities with the prior approval of their respective Boards of Directors/Asset-Liability Management Committee (ALCO).

Table 2.5 Movements of interest rates in Indian banking industry

Year	Deposit rates (%) 1–3 years	Over 3 years and up to 5 years	Above 5 years	Minimum lending rates (%)
1991–1992	11	13	13	19
1992–1993	11	11	11	17
1993–1994	10	10	10	14
1994–1995	11	11	11	15
1995–1996	12	13	13	16.5
1996–1997	11.00–12.00	12.00–13.00	12.50–13.00	14.50–15.00
1997–1998	10.50–11.00	11.50–12.00	11.50–12.00	14
1998–1999	9.00–11.00	10.50–11.50	10.50–11.50	12.00–13.00
1999–2000	8.50–9.50	10.00–10.50	10.00–10.50	12.00–12.50
2000–2001	8.50–9.50	9.50–10.00	9.50–10.00	11.00–12.00
2001–2002	7.50–8.50	8.00–8.50	8.00–8.50	11.00–12.00
2002–2003	4.25–6.00	5.50–6.25	5.50–6.25	10.75–11.50
2003–2004	4.00–5.25	5.25–5.50	5.25–5.50	10.25–11.00
2004–2005	5.25–5.50	5.75–6.25	5.75–6.25	10.25–10.75
2005–2006	6.00–6.50	6.25–7.00	6.25–7.00	10.25–10.75
2006–2007	7.50–9.00	7.75–9.00	7.75–9.00	12.25–12.50
2007–2008	8.25–8.75	7.50–9.00	7.50–9.00	12.25–12.75
2008–2009	8.00–8.75	7.75–8.50	7.75–8.50	11.50–12.50

Source: Handbook of Statistics on Indian Economy 2008–2009, RBI, Mumbai

The movement in interest rates since 1992–1993 is shown in Table 2.5. The term deposit rates of scheduled commercial banks for all maturities over 1–3 years moved down significantly to 4.00–5.25 % in 2003–2004 from 11 % in 1992–1993. Similarly, the interest rates on deposits of 3–5 years and above have also softened to 5.25–5.50 % in 2003–2004 from a considerably high level of 13 % during the period 1991–1992. This reduction in the deposit rates across all maturities has been found to have a favourable impact over the cost of funds to the banking sector. During 2004–2005, interest rates offered on deposits by banks for all the maturities were hardened, with an objective to reduce liquidity and contain inflationary pressures. This is indicated by the fact that the interest rates offered by commercial banks on deposit with 1–3 years and above 3 years maturity moved up from 5.25–5.50 % and 5.75–6.25 % in 2004–2005 to 8.00–8.75 % and 7.75–8.50 % in 2008–2009, respectively.

The lending rates of commercial banks have deregulated and rationalised initially from six to four categories in 1992–1993 and further to three categories in 1993–1994. The process of rationalising the interest rate structure received a major impetus with the abolition of the minimum lending rate for credit limits of over INR 0.2 million with effect from October 18th, 1994. The only lending rates that continued to be regulated were those pertaining to exports, small loans of up to INR 0.2 million and the Differential Rate of Interest (DRI) scheme. Since February 1997, commercial banks were required to announce a Prime Lending Rate (PLR) for advances for over INR 0.2 million uniformly applicable to all the branches taking into account the cost of funds and transaction cost with the approval of their boards.

Lending interest rates of scheduled commercial banks have declined from the extremely high level of 19 % in 1991–1992 to 12.00–13.00 % in 1998–1999 (see Table 2.5). Thereafter, the decline in PLRs has somewhat muted given the structural rigidities such as high non-interest operating expenses and cost of servicing non-performing loans. Furthermore, banks have mobilised a large proportion of their deposits at relatively high fixed rates, which also limited the downward shift in the PLRs. The concept of Benchmark Prime Lending Rates (BPLRs) was introduced by the RBI on April 29th, 2003 to address the need for transparency in banks' lending rates and also to reduce the pricing of loans. Banks are now free to prescribe respective BPLRs and are also permitted to offer floating-rate loan products linked to market benchmark in a transparent manner.

In all, there has been a considerable flattening of the term structure of deposit rates during the last several years, with the degree of moderation being higher for longer-term deposits. Interest rates were deregulated to a significant degree not only to aid movement of monetary policy, but also because administered interest rate regime proved to be inefficient and costly. Thus, with the initiation of reforms, Indian banks have gradually moved to an almost entirely market-driven interest rate system from a completely government-determined interest rate structure (Chakrabarti 2005).

2.3.3 *Heightened Competition*

One of the most significant structural changes that has occurred in the Indian banking industry is the increase in the level of competition in the market. The deregulation process has infused the competition in the banking sector by allowing the liberal entry of new private sector and foreign banks and introduction of new financial products and technology. The reforms process has shifted the focus of public sector dominated banking system from social banking to a more efficient and profit-oriented industry. While the reforms process has resulted in the private sector replacing the government as the source of resources for PSBs, the infusion of private-equity capital has led to shareholder's challenges to bureaucratic decision making. PSBs also face increasing competition not only from private and foreign banks but also from growing non-banking financial intermediaries like mutual funds and other capital market entities.

The heightened competition is evident from the fact that the top 3- and 5-bank concentration ratios (CR_3 and CR_5) for Indian banking industry have followed a declining trend during the post-reforms years. In particular, we note that the advance-based CR_3 and CR_5 ratios have dropped from 42.16 % and 52.4 % in 1991–1992 to 30.51 % and 40.07 % in 2008–2009, respectively (see Table 2.6). The asset-based CR_3 and CR_5 ratios have declined from 40.89 % and 51.35 % in 1991–1992 to 30.35 % and 38.99 % in 2008–2009. Further, the fall in the deposit-based CR_3 and CR_5 ratios occurred to the level of 28.8 % and 38.2 % in 2008–2009 from 37.09 % and 48.56 % in 1991–1992, respectively. The evidence of growing competitive pressures in Indian banking industry is also well supported by

Table 2.6 Market concentration in Indian banking industry during the post-reforms years

	Total assets			Deposits			Advances		
Year	CR_3	CR_5	HHI	CR_3	CR_5	HHI	CR_3	CR_5	HHI
1991–1992	40.89	51.35	1010	37.09	48.56	790	42.16	52.40	1030
1992–1993	38.30	49.08	910	35.33	46.81	750	40.93	51.28	1000
1993–1994	37.67	48.75	890	34.77	46.58	740	38.66	49.44	860
1994–1995	35.59	46.29	790	33.52	45.08	690	36.19	47.02	780
1995–1996	35.39	45.84	790	33.28	44.94	690	36.33	46.57	780
1996–1997	34.49	45.00	750	32.51	44.09	660	35.44	45.84	730
1997–1998	34.17	44.59	720	32.53	43.90	650	35.97	46.16	740
1998–1999	34.58	44.51	750	33.48	44.22	700	34.76	45.25	720
1999–2000	33.88	43.65	740	32.89	43.47	690	33.45	43.89	700
2000–2001	34.74	44.32	790	34.09	44.16	740	33.41	44.05	690
2001–2002	34.21	43.53	720	33.15	43.26	710	31.97	42.52	600
2002–2003	33.53	42.88	700	32.75	42.40	690	31.63	42.55	600
2003–2004	32.17	41.52	640	31.29	40.43	620	30.99	41.76	580
2004–2005	32.00	40.72	610	31.02	40.72	620	31.02	40.72	620
2005–2006	31.94	40.77	570	30.71	40.45	560	30.71	40.45	560
2006–2007	31.10	39.92	540	29.97	39.79	530	29.97	39.79	570
2007–2008	30.52	38.84	536	28.56	37.78	510	30.76	39.67	546
2008–2009	30.35	38.99	574	28.80	38.20	567	30.51	40.07	578

Source: Authors' calculations
Note: CR_3 and CR_5 are top 3- and 5-bank concentration ratios, and *HHI* represents Herfindahl-Hirschman index

the declining trend of Herfindahl-Hirschman (HHI) index.[9] Table 2.6 and Fig. 2.1 show the evolution of three types of HHI indices (based on total assets, deposits and advances). The HHI index for total assets has declined from 1,010 in 1991–1992 to 574 in 2008–2009. The similar trend was discernible from the market structure indicators based on size of bank deposits and advances. The deposit-based and advance-based HHI indices have also dropped to 510 and 546 in 2007–2008 from 790 and 1,030 in 1991–1992, respectively.

2.3.4 *More Exposure to Off-Balance Sheet (OBS) Activities*

Another significant transformation that has occurred in Indian banking industry during the post-reforms years is the decline in traditional banking activities and consequent increase in fee-producing non-traditional activities. Traditionally, the core business of the Indian banks has been deposits taking and lending with the

[9] The Herfindahl-Hirschman index is defined as the sum of squares of market shares and varies between 0 and 10,000. In practice, markets in which HHI is below 1,000 are considered as 'loosely concentrated', between 1,000 and 1,800 as 'moderately concentrated' and above 1,800 as 'highly concentrated'.

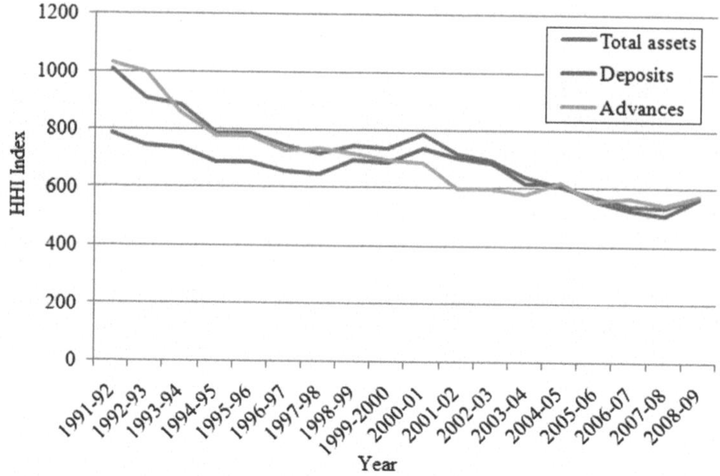

Fig. 2.1 Trends of HHI index during the post-reforms years

purpose to generate interest incomes. But with the financial deregulation during the 1990s, coupled with revolutionary advances in the ICT-based technology, the very nature of the activities of Indian banks has changed. Indian banks are now deriving an ever-increasing percentage of income from sources other than traditional ones such as trading in securities, commission, exchange and brokerage, portfolio management services, underwriting and providing backup liquidity. Thus, banks in India witnessed a significant shift from traditional banking activities to a more universal banking character with financial market activities like brokerage and portfolio management growing in importance.

In recent years, an exposure of Indian banks to off-balance sheet operations which include forward exchange contracts, guarantees, acceptances, endorsements, etc., increased manifold. Banks have responded to OBS activities imaginatively and vigorously in an effort both to retain their traditional customer base and to boost fee income from sources, which are largely or wholly free from capital requirements. These activities act as the vehicles of information and risk sharing services, and contribute to an overall diversification of a bank's output and lead to an increase in its productivity levels.

Table 2.7 provides the trend in OBS activities in Indian commercial banking industry during the period spanning from 1996–1997 to 2008–2009. It is clear from the table that OBS activities showed a significant growth over the period of reforms, reflecting the impact of deregulation, risk management operations, diversification of income and new business opportunities thrown up by advances in information technology. Total off-balance sheet exposure of banks has increased from INR 3,183.9 billion in 1996–1997 to INR 144.98 trillion in 2007–2008. This increase in OBS activities is primarily propelled by the rise in forward exchange contracts. Further, leveraged positions in derivatives as a means of diversifying income, improvements in technology (trading and information services) and increasing use of derivatives as tools for risk mitigation appear to have contributed to the

Table 2.7 Off-balance sheet activities of Indian commercial banks since 1996–1997

Year	1996–1997	1997–1998	1998–1999	1999–2000	2000–2001	2001–2002	2002–2003	2003–2004	2004–2005	2005–2006	2006–2007	2007–2008	2008–2009
Panel A: All banks													
Forward exchange contracts	2,092.8 (31.1)	3,511.51 (44.14)	3,347.59 (35.21)	4,243.15 (38.38)	5,535.96 (42.75)	6,350.95 (41.36)	7924.79 (46.64)	11,828.65 (59.92)	21,969.48 (93.27)	32,801.78 (117.66)	55,852.56 (161.25)	1,08,762.28 (251.4)	79,152.11 (151)
Guarantees given	523.52 (7.78)	587.74 (7.39)	628.14 (6.61)	670.23 (6.06)	714.49 (5.52)	842.54 (5.49)	903.41 (5.32)	1,018.48 (5.16)	1,234.76 (5.24)	1,614.51 (5.79)	2,196.17 (6.34)	2,955.06 (6.8)	4,170.64 (8)
Acceptances endorsements	567.65 (8.43)	571.19 (7.18)	605.18 (6.37)	929.50 (8.41)	1,279.30 (9.88)	1,660 (10.81)	2,827.57 (16.64)	5,085.74 (25.76)	5,120.82 (21.74)	8,079.11 (28.98)	16,268.40 (46.97)	33,268.53 (76.9)	23,396.86 (44.6)
Total contingent liabilities	3,183.98 (47.31)	4,670.45 (58.71)	4,580.92 (48.18)	5,842.88 (52.85)	7,529.75 (58.15)	8,853.50 (57.66)	11,655.78 (68.6)	17,932.88 (90.84)	28,325.08 (120.25)	42,495.41 (152.43)	74,317.14 (214.58)	1,44,985.87 (335.1)	1,06,719.61 (203.6)
Panel B: Public sector banks													
Forward exchange contracts	686.32 (12.34)	1,090.69 (16.80)	1,071.80 (13.92)	1,421.95 (15.97)	1,995.65 (19.38)	2,092.40 (18.00)	2,641.86 (20.55)	3,131.84 (21.29)	4,164.27 (23.47)	5,053.15 (25.08)	6,129.35 (25.12)	9,941.09 (33.9)	10,401.39 (27.6)
Guarantees given	370.39 (6.66)	405.40 (6.24)	419.91 (5.45)	428.37 (4.81)	439.93 (4.27)	481.50 (4.17)	535.55 (4.17)	628.45 (4.27)	794.97 (4.48)	1,038.38 (5.15)	1,377.15 (5.64)	1,750.78 (5.8)	2,559.18 (6.8)
Acceptances endorsements	401.84 (7.22)	391.45 (6.03)	402.75 (5.23)	490.62 (5.51)	551.76 (5.36)	718.86 (6.22)	888.48 (6.91)	1,103.66 (7.5)	1,879.72 (10.6)	2,330.52 (11.57)	3,006.26 (12.32)	6,976.37 (23.1)	6,133.66 (16.3)
Total contingent liabilities	1,458.56 (26.22)	1,887.56 (29.08)	1,894.47 (24.6)	2,340.95 (26.29)	2,987.35 (29.01)	3,292.78 (28.49)	4,065.9 (31.63)	4,863.96 (33.06)	6,838.96 (38.55)	8,422.06 (41.8)	10,512.77 (43.09)	18,668.24 (61.8)	19,094.22 (50.7)
Panel C: New private sector banks													
Forward exchange contracts	84.09 (52.04)	155.94 (60.31)	236.63 (61.41)	343.77 (58.34)	408.88 (51.91)	476.97 (27.34)	726.62 (37.81)	1,532.66 (62.16)	2,781.24 (94.46)	4,284.20 (101.6)	7,003.01 (119.74)	12,173.67 (163.3)	9,196.98 (115.60)
Guarantees given	19.06 (11.8)	31.48 (12.18)	41.16 (10.68)	57.41 (9.74)	70.87 (9.00)	145.03 (8.31)	156.38 (8.14)	173.97 (7.06)	201.39 (6.84)	270.83 (6.42)	420.09 (7.18)	655.71 (8.8)	934.2 (11.70)
Acceptances endorsements	34.04 (21.07)	36.44 (14.09)	42.23 (10.96)	66.06 (11.21)	98.06 (12.45)	239.79 (13.75)	776.58 (40.41)	1,829.7 (74.2)	1,997.43 (67.84)	3,346.38 (79.36)	5,158.28 (88.2)	10,269.43 (137.7)	6,119.2 (76.9)
Total contingent liabilities	137.20 (84.9)	223.87 (86.59)	320.02 (83.06)	467.25 (79.29)	577.81 (73.35)	861.80 (49.4)	1,659.59 (86.36)	3,536.34 (143.42)	4,980.07 (169.15)	7,901.42 (187.39)	12,581.39 (215.12)	23,098.81 (309.8)	16,250.37 (204.3)

(continued)

Table 2.7 (continued)

Year	1996–1997	1997–1998	1998–1999	1999–2000	2000–2001	2001–2002	2002–2003	2003–2004	2004–2005	2005–2006	2006–2007	2007–2008	2008–2009
Panel D: Old private sector banks													
Forward exchange contracts	62.71 (14.11)	138.90 (25.16)	112.70 (17.21)	148.07 (20.25)	184.51 (21.81)	173.90 (18.65)	216.56 (20.63)	238.85 (19.79)	418.07 (31.32)	415.34 (27.74)	504.91 (31.45)	854.54 (43.9)	966.61 (41.7)
Guarantees given	18.64 (4.19)	20.35 (3.69)	25.40 (3.88)	25.66 (3.51)	29.54 (3.49)	33.02 (3.54)	37.98 (3.62)	40.31 (3.34)	46.45 (3.82)	57.15 (3.82)	66.13 (4.12)	92.72 (4.8)	104.86 (4.5)
Acceptances endorsements	14.26 (3.21)	15.55 (2.82)	20.62 (3.15)	27.41 (3.75)	32.46 (3.84)	32.95 (3.54)	46.05 (4.39)	82.57 (6.84)	135.14 (10.13)	157.76 (10.54)	148.48 (9.25)	164.11 (8.4)	96.86 (4.2)
Total contingent liabilities	95.62 (21.51)	174.81 (31.67)	158.73 (24.24)	201.15 (27.51)	246.52 (29.14)	239.89 (25.73)	300.60 (28.64)	361.74 (29.96)	599.67 (44.93)	630.27 (42.09)	719.53 (44.81)	1,111.37 (57.1)	1,168.34 (50.4)
Panel E: Foreign banks													
Forward exchange contracts	1,259.68 (224.69)	2,125.97 (325.63)	1,926.45 (251.6)	2,329.34 (281.29)	2,946.9 (289.41)	3607.66 (321.84)	4,339.73 (372)	6,925.29 (510.56)	14,605.89 (950.68)	23,049.08 (1143.39)	42,215.27 (1518.45)	85,792.97 (2356.3)	58,587.13 (1310.2)
Guarantees given	115.41 (20.59)	130.49 (19.99)	141.66 (18.5)	158.77 (19.17)	174.14 (17.1)	182.98 (16.32)	173.47 (14.87)	175.74 (12.96)	191.95 (12.49)	248.12 (12.31)	332.79 (11.97)	455.84 (12.5)	572.41 (12.8)
Acceptances endorsements	117.49 (20.96)	127.73 (19.57)	139.56 (18.23)	345.39 (41.71)	597.01 (58.63)	668.37 (59.63)	1,116.45 (95.7)	2,069.79 (152.59)	1,108.51 (72.15)	2,244.43 (111.34)	7,955.37 (286.15)	15,858.63 (435.6)	11,047.14 (247.1)
Total contingent liabilities	1,492.59 (266.24)	2,384.19 (365.18)	2,207.68 (288.33)	2,833.52 (342.17)	3,718.06 (365.15)	4,459.02 (397.78)	5,629.67 (482.57)	9,170.82 (676.11)	15,906.36 (1035.33)	25,541.64 (1267.04)	50,503.43 (1816.56)	1,02,107.44 (2804.4)	70,206.67 (1570.1)

Source: Report on Trend and Progress of Banking in India (various issues), RBI, Mumbai
Note: Amount in billions, figures in parentheses are annual variation in percent

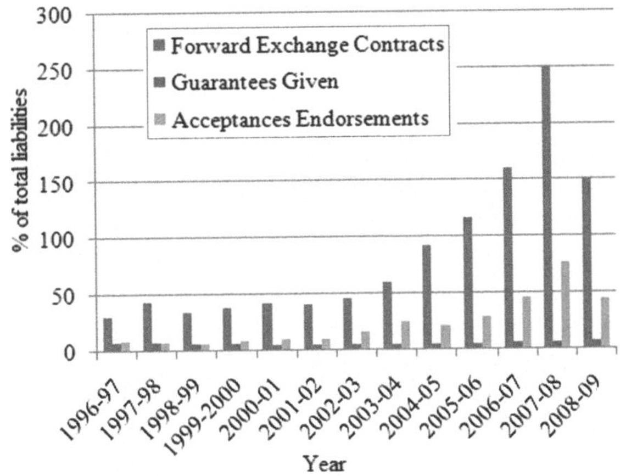

Fig. 2.2 Components of off-balance sheet items for scheduled commercial banks

growth in OBS exposures. The sharp growth in off-balance sheet exposure reflected the banks' attempt to diversify their sources of income (also see Fig. 2.2).

Among bank groups, foreign banks constituted the largest share in OBS activities since 1996–1997, followed by new private banks, old private sector banks and public sector banks, respectively. The level of OBS activities in the foreign banks has risen from INR 1,492.59 billion in 1996–1997 to INR 102.11 trillion in 2007–2008. Apart from foreign banks, new private banks have shown uplift in their OBS exposure. The income of these banks from OBS activities has increased to INR 23,098.81 billion in 2007–2008 as compared to INR 137.2 billion in 1996–1997. However, the same has increased from INR 95.62 billion in 1996–1997 to INR 1,111.37 billion in 2007–2008 for old private sector banks, and INR 1,458.56 billion in 1996–1997 to INR 18,668.24 billion in 2007–2008 for public sector banks. These figures reveal that PSBs and old private banks are still generating more of their income from traditional activities rather than relying more on OBS activities.

It is worth noting here that the financial year 2008–2009 marked an exception to the rising trend of OBS exposure in the Indian banking industry. We noted a fall in OBS exposures in 2008–2009 which is evident from the fact that revenue generated by these activities declined to INR 106.719 trillion in 2008–2009 in comparison of INR 144.98 trillion in 2007–2008. This decline occurred partly due to strengthening of prudential regulations, which adversely affected the exposures of banks to OBS activities. Further, the decline in OBS was especially evident in the case of foreign banks. Apart from the foreign banks, the new private sector banks, old private banks and public sector banks have also witnessed a decline in their income from OBS activities in the financial year 2008–2009.

2.3.5 *Improvement in Asset Quality*

One of the widely used parameters to judge the financial health of the banking sector is the quality of asset portfolio of the banks. The level of non-performing assets (NPAs) is the most important indicator to reflect the asset quality, credit risk and efficiency in the allocation of resources to productive sectors. The high level of NPAs in banks has been a matter of grave concern for the policy makers since it creates bottlenecks in the smooth flow of credit in the economy. In fact, NPAs constitute a real economic loss to the nation since the money locked up in NPAs is not available for productive purposes. In the post-reforms period, all the segments of Indian banking industry experienced a decline in the incidence of problem loans. It is well conceived that an improvement in asset quality is reflected by a declining trend of gross and net NPAs ratios. It has been observed that in the Indian banking industry as a whole, the gross and net NPAs as a percentage of advances (total assets) have declined from 15.7 % (7 %) and 8.1 % (3.3 %) in 1996–1997 to 2.3 % (1.3 %) and 1.1 % (0.6 %) in 2008–2009, respectively (see Table 2.8 and Fig. 2.3). Among the bank groups, the ratios consistently declined for the public and old private sector banks, while it showed wide fluctuations in case of new private and foreign banks. Improvement in credit appraisal process, new legal initiatives aimed at faster NPA resolution, and greater provisions and write-offs enabled by greater profitability contributed to this decline. It is noteworthy here that the level of NPAs among new private and foreign banks has shown an increase during the financial year 2008–2009. This is because of the active role of new private and foreign banks in the real estate and housing loans segments.

Over the decade, the RBI has taken several measures to expedite the recovery of NPAs by strengthening the various channels of recovery such as Debt Recovery Tribunals (DRTs), Lok Adalats, Corporate Debt Restructuring (CDR) mechanism, Asset Reconstruction Companies (ARCs), one-time settlement schemes and the SARFAESI Act.[10] These measures have prompted the banks to concentrate more on recovery of chronic NPAs, then on preventing slippage of new accounts. Further, attempts have been made to restructure the banks through technology upgradation, better management control system, performance targets, emphasis on corporate governing and accountability starting yielding positive results. Better internal control and increased efficiency at all levels have contributed for reduction in non-performing assets. This has comfortably placed the banks with regard to their asset quality.

Among the various channels of recovery available to banks for dealing with NPAs, the DRTs and SARFAESI Act have been the most effective in terms of the amount recovered. In 2008–2009, the amount of NPAs recovered was highest under the DRTs, followed by SARFAESI Act. This is evident from the fact that the level of the NPAs recovered by DRTs and SARFAESI Act are 81.1 % and 33 %, respectively (see Table 2.9). Moreover, the SARFAESI Act has recovered maximum amount of NPAs, followed by DRTs during the financial year 2007–2008.

[10] The GOI enacted the Securitisation and Reconstruction of Financial Assets and Enforcement of Security Interest (SARFAESI) Act, 2002, which provided for enforcement of security interest for realisation of dues without the intervention of courts or tribunals. The act also provided for sale of financial assets by banks/FIs to securitization companies (SCs)/reconstruction companies (RCs).

Table 2.8 Gross and net NPAs of Indian banking industry during the post-reforms years

Year	Public sector banks	Old private sector banks	New private sector banks	Foreign banks	All banks	Public sector banks	Old private sector banks	New private sector banks	Foreign banks	All banks
	Gross NPAs/gross advances (%)					*Net NPAs/net advances (%)*				
1992–1993	23.2	–	–	–	–	–	–	–	–	–
1993–1994	24.8	–	–	–	–	–	–	–	–	–
1994–1995	19.5	–	–	–	–	10.7	–	–	–	–
1995–1996	18.0	–	–	–	–	8.9	–	–	–	–
1996–1997	17.8	10.7	2.6	4.3	15.7	9.2	6.6	2.0	1.9	8.1
1997–1998	16.0	10.9	3.5	6.4	14.4	8.2	6.5	2.6	2.2	7.3
1998–1999	15.9	13.0	5.7	7.0	14.6	8.1	8.4	4.1	2.0	7.5
1999–2000	14.0	10.8	4.1	7.0	12.7	7.4	7.1	2.9	2.4	6.8
2000–2001	12.4	11.1	5.1	6.8	11.4	6.7	7.3	3.1	1.9	6.2
2001–2002	11.1	11.0	8.9	5.4	10.4	5.8	7.1	4.9	1.9	5.5
2002–2003	9.4	8.9	7.6	5.3	8.8	4.5	5.5	4.6	1.8	4.4
2003–2004	7.8	7.6	5.0	4.6	7.2	3.0	3.9	2.4	1.5	2.9
2004–2005	5.5	6.0	3.6	2.9	5.2	2.1	2.7	1.9	0.9	2.0
2005–2006	3.6	4.4	1.7	2.0	3.3	1.3	1.7	0.8	0.8	1.2
2006–2007	2.7	3.0	1.9	1.8	2.5	1.1	0.9	1.0	1.0	1.0
2007–2008	2.2	2.3	2.4	1.8	2.3	0.8	0.7	1.1	0.9	1.0
2008–2009	2.0	2.3	2.9	4.0	2.3	0.7	0.9	1.3	1.7	1.1
	Gross NPAs/total assets (%)					*Net NPAs/total assets (%)*				
1992–1993	11.8	–	–	–	–	–	–	–	–	–
1993–1994	10.8	–	–	–	–	–	–	–	–	–
1994–1995	8.7	–	–	–	–	4.0	–	–	–	–
1995–1996	8.2	–	–	–	–	3.6	–	–	–	–
1996–1997	7.8	5.2	1.3	2.1	7.0	3.6	3.1	1.0	0.9	3.3
1997–1998	7.0	5.1	1.5	3.0	6.4	3.3	2.9	1.1	1.0	3.0
1998–1999	6.7	5.8	2.3	2.9	6.2	3.1	3.6	1.6	0.8	2.9
1999–2000	6.0	5.2	1.6	3.2	5.5	2.9	3.3	1.1	1.0	2.7

(continued)

Table 2.8 (continued)

Year	Public sector banks	Old private sector banks	New private sector banks	Foreign banks	All banks	Public sector banks	Old private sector banks	New private sector banks	Foreign banks	All banks
2000–2001	5.3	5.2	2.1	3.0	4.9	2.7	3.3	1.2	0.8	2.5
2001–2002	4.9	5.2	3.9	2.4	4.6	2.4	3.2	2.1	0.8	2.3
2002–2003	4.2	4.3	3.8	2.4	4.0	1.9	2.6	2.2	0.8	1.9
2003–2004	3.5	3.6	2.4	2.1	3.3	1.3	1.8	1.1	0.7	1.2
2004–2005	2.7	3.2	1.6	1.4	2.5	1.0	1.4	0.8	0.4	0.9
2005–2006	2.1	2.5	1.0	1.0	1.8	0.7	0.9	0.4	0.4	0.7
2006–2007	1.6	1.8	1.1	0.8	1.5	0.6	0.6	0.5	0.3	0.6
2007–2008	1.3	1.3	1.4	0.8	1.3	0.6	0.4	0.7	0.3	0.6
2008–2009	1.2	1.3	1.8	1.5	1.3	0.6	0.5	0.8	0.7	0.6

Source: Report on Trend and Progress of Banking in India (various issues), RBI, Mumbai

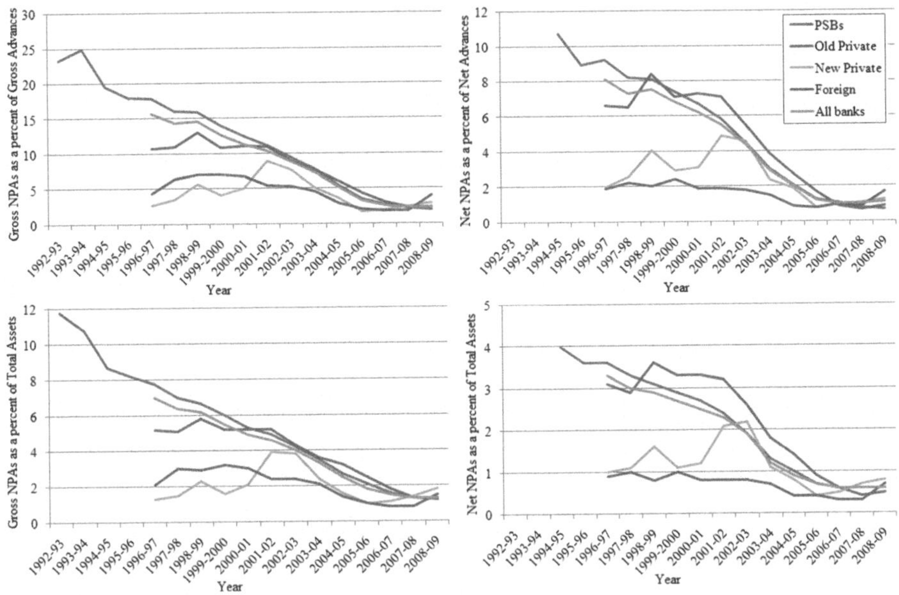

Fig. 2.3 Trends in gross and net NPAs of Indian commercial banks (*Source*: Authors' elaboration)

2.3.6 *Penetration of Information Technology*

In the post-reforms years, information technology and the communication networking systems have revolutionised the functioning of Indian banks. By using state-of-the-art technology, Indian banks, irrespective of the ownership pattern, have developed necessary management information systems which aid in taking scientific decisions. Further, Indian banks are now using advanced banking technologies to provide better service quality to their customer in a cost-effective manner. The first step that most of Indian banks have taken in the use of technology is the computerisation of branches. Since the major part of the transactions arises at the branches, data processing and transmission has become comparatively easier after computerisation. Thus, the process of computerisation marked the starting point of all the technological initiatives taken by Indian banks.

Since the early 1990s, there has been a phenomenal growth in the number of banks who have computerised most of the businesses of their branches. While new private sector banks, foreign banks and old private sector banks have already put in place to 'core banking solutions', PSBs are still adopting similar systems.[11] Nevertheless, all the PSBs have already crossed the 90 % level of computerisation of their

[11] The core banking solutions provides a host of benefits such as anywhere banking, anywhere access and quick funds movement at optimal costs and in an efficient manner.

Table 2.9 Recovery of NPAs by scheduled commercial banks through various channels (Amount in billions)

Year		Recovery channels: One-time settlement-compromise schemes	Lok Adalats	DRTs	SARFAESI Act	ARCs
2003–2004	Number of cases referred	1,39,562	1,86,100	7,544	2,661#	–
	Amount of NPAs involved	15.10	10.63	123.05	78.47	–
	Amount of NPAs recovered	6.17	1.49	21.17	11.56	–
	% of NPAs recovered	40.9	14.0	17.2	14.7	–
2004–2005	Number of cases referred	1,32,781	1,85,395	4,744	39,288#	368
	Amount of NPAs involved	13.32	8.01	143.17	132.24	–
	Amount of NPAs recovered	8.80	1.13	26.88	23.91	145.06
	% of NPAs recovered	66.1	14.1	18.8	18.1	–
2005–2006	Number of cases referred	10,262	1,81,547	3,524	38,969#	–
	Amount of NPAs involved	7.72	11.01	61.23	98.31	–
	Amount of NPAs recovered	6.08	2.23	47.10	34.23	–
	% of NPAs recovered	78.8	20.3	76.9	34.8	–
2006–2007	Number of cases referred	–	1,60,368	4,028	60,178#	–
	Amount of NPAs involved	–	7.58	91.56	90.58	–
	Amount of NPAs recovered	–	1.06	34.63	37.49	–
	% of NPAs recovered	–	14.0	37.8	41.4	–
2007–2008	Number of cases referred	–	1,86,535	3,728	83,942#	–
	Amount of NPAs involved	–	21.42	58.19	72.63	–
	Amount of NPAs recovered	–	1.76	30.20	44.29	–
	% of NPAs recovered	–	8.2	51.9	61.0	–
2008–2009	Number of cases referred	–	5,48,308	2,004	61,760#	–
	Amount of NPAs involved	–	40.23	41.30	120.67	–

(continued)

Table 2.9 (continued)

Year		Recovery channels				
		One-time settlement-compromise schemes	Lok Adalats	DRTs	SARFAESI Act	ARCs
	Amount of NPAs recovered	–	0.96	33.48	39.82	–
	% of NPAs recovered	–	5.4	81.1	33.0	–

Source: Report on Trend and Progress of Banking in India (various issues), RBI, Mumbai
Notes: (i) DRTs and ARCs stand for Debt Recovery Tribunals and Asset Reconstruction Companies, and (ii) # indicates number of notices issued

Table 2.10 Computerisation of banks in India during the most recent years

Year	Fully computerised branches			
	Public sector banks	Old private sector banks	New private sector banks	Foreign banks
2004–2005	71.0	100.0	100.0	100.0
2005–2006	77.5	100.0	100.0	100.0
2006–2007	85.6	100.0	100.0	100.0
2007–2008	93.7	100.0	100.0	100.0
2008–2009	95.0	100.0	100.0	100.0

Source: Report on Trend and Progress of Banking in India (various issues), RBI, Mumbai

businesses. The directive by the central vigilance commission to achieve 100 % computerisation has resulted in renewed vigour in these banks towards fulfilment of this requirement, which could go a long way to improve customer services. Table 2.10 provides the information regarding the extent of computerisation in Indian commercial banks, especially PSBs during the most recent years. The proportion of the branches of PSBs which achieved full computerisation increased from 71 % in 2004–2005 to 95 % in 2008–2009, indicating that the extent of computerisation in Indian banking industry is pacing up. Thus, continuous progress is being made by the banks to achieve a higher target, as more than 90 % PSBs have already been computerised. On the whole, the process of computerisation of the Indian banking sector is almost in the stage of completion.

Besides making expenditure to computerise their branches, Indian banks, especially PSBs, are also making heavy investment in new delivery channels such as anywhere banking, telebanking, mobile banking, net banking, automated teller machine (ATMs), credit cards, debit cards, smart cards, call centre, customer relationship management (CRM) and data warehousing. The main objectives of such efforts are (i) to offer the service quality that is being provided by foreign and new private domestic banks, (ii) to provide their customers greater flexibility and convenience as well as to reduce servicing costs, (iii) to reduce the time lag in funds

Table 2.11 Number and proportion of ATMs in scheduled commercial banks

Year		Public sector banks	Old private sector banks	New private sector banks	Foreign banks	All banks
2004–2005	On-site ATMs	4,753	800	1,883	218	7,654
	Off-site ATMs	5,239	441	3,729	579	9,988
	Total ATMs	9,992	1,241	5,612	797	17,642
	Total ATMs as percent of total branches	*21.1*	*27.5*	*333.1*	*329.4*	*32.8*
2005–2006	On-site ATMs	6,587	1,054	2,255	232	10,128
	Off-site ATMs	6,021	493	3,857	648	11,019
	Total ATMs	12,608	1,547	6,112	880	21,147
	Total ATMs as percent of total branches	*26.3*	*33.9*	*313.44*	*339.8*	*38.6*
2006–2007	On-site ATMs	10,289	1,104	3,154	249	14,796
	Off-site ATMs	6,040	503	5,038	711	12,292
	Total ATMs	16,329	1,607	8,192	960	27,088
	Total ATMs as percent of total branches	*32.9*	*34.9*	*328.1*	*351.6*	*47.5*
2007–2008	On-site ATMs	12,902	1,436	3,879	269	18,486
	Off-site ATMs	8,886	664	5,988	765	16,303
	Total ATMs	21,788	2,100	9,867	1,034	34,789
	Total ATMs as percent of total branches	*41.2*	*47.2*	*279.9*	*377.4*	*56.9*
2008–2009	On-site ATMs	17,379	1,830	5,166	270	24,645
	Off-site ATMs	9,898	844	7,480	784	19,006
	Total ATMs	27,277	2,674	12,646	1,054	43,651
	Total ATMs as percent of total branches	*49.2*	*57.2*	*300.8*	*359.7*	*67.6*

Source: Report on Trend and Progress of Banking in India (various issues), RBI, Mumbai

transfer and (iv) to eliminate error-prone paper work. Thus, the banks have been positioning themselves as a one-stop shop financial service provider with fairly exhaustive range of products. Apart these, banks have also been entering into the business of selling third-party products such as mutual funds and insurance to the retail customers. Consequently, the commercial banks as well as other financial institutions in India have switched over to ICT-based modern automated banking systems from their out-dated manual-based banking systems.

Table 2.11 exemplifies the spread of new delivery channels like self-service terminals, popularly known as ATMs, in Indian banking industry. ATMs are cash dispensers, which enable the customers to withdraw cash even if the bank is closed. The number of ATMs installed in the country has increased from 17,642 in 2004–2005 to 43,651 in 2008–2009. Alternatively, the proportion of total ATMs as a percentage of total branches grew by 34.8 % (67.6 % in 2008–2009 vs. 32.8 % in 2004–2005). Further, new private sector banks constituted the largest share of ATMs in 2004–2005, followed closely by foreign banks, old private banks and public sector banks. However, of all the ATMs installed in the country during 2008–2009, foreign banks had the largest share followed by new private sector banks. On comparing the number of off-site and on-site ATMs installed, it has been noted that new private sector banks had the largest number of off-site ATMs in 2008–2009, while public sector banks have the largest number of on-site ATMs. Further, foreign banks had more off-site ATMs than on-site ATMs in all the financial years.

2.3.7 Consolidation Through Mergers

To achieve a higher level of efficiency and profits, mergers and acquisitions (M&As) in the banking sector have become the most potent activity in the majority of the countries in the world. One of the principal objectives behind the mergers and acquisitions in the banking sector is to reap the benefits of economies of scale. With the intensification of competition in the Indian banking industry through deregulation, partial privatisation and entry of new private and foreign banks, the process of consolidation in the recent years through mergers has become more market-driven rather than forced one. The RBI has been encouraging the consolidation process, wherever possible, given the inability of small banks to compete with large banks that enjoy enormous economies of scale and scope. A drive towards the consolidation of the banking sector through the process of M&As of weak and small banks with stronger ones has been set in motion to protect the interests of depositors, avoid possible financial contagion that could result from individual bank failures and also to reap the benefits of synergy (Reserve Bank of India 2008b). In fact, the policy makers consider the bank mergers as a possible avenue for improving the structure and efficiency of the Indian banking industry.

Table 2.12 lists out the banks' M&As that took place in the Indian banking industry over the last two decades. It has been observed that of 24 M&As that took place during the post-reforms period, as many as 18 mergers took after 1999. It is worth mentioning here that though the mergers in India were primarily triggered by weak financials of the bank being merged, but in the most recent years, there has also been the mergers between healthy and well-functioning banks, which were driven by business and commercial considerations (Leeladhar 2008). Leaving aside the distress and forced merger of Ganesh Bank of Kurundwad and the Federal Bank, all the remaining mergers between the private sector banks in the post-1999 period are voluntary and market-driven mergers between healthy and financially sound banks, and are primarily guided by the profitability considerations. For example, the merger of HDFC Bank and Centurion Bank of Punjab is a voluntary merger of two strong banks, which is purely based on the profitability motives. In sum, the recent phase of consolidation in Indian banking industry presents a healthy trend which is somewhat on the lines suggested by the Narasimham Committee I.

Table 2.12 Bank mergers in India during the post-reforms years

S. No.	Name of transferor bank-institution	Name of transferee bank-institution	Date of amalgamation
1	New Bank of India	Punjab National Bank	September 4th, 1993
2	Kashi Nath Seth Bank Ltd.	State Bank of India	January 1st, 1996
3	Bari Doab Bank Ltd.	Oriental Bank of Commerce	April 8th, 1997
4	Punjab Co-operative Bank Ltd.	Oriental Bank of Commerce	April 8th, 1997
5	Bareilly Corporation Bank Ltd.	Bank of Baroda	June 3rd, 1999
6	Sikkim Bank Ltd.	Union Bank of India	December 22nd, 1999
7	Times Bank Ltd.	HDFC Bank Ltd.	February 26th, 2000
8	Bank of Madura Ltd.	ICICI Bank Ltd.	March 10th, 2001
9	ICICI Ltd.	ICICI Bank Ltd.	May 3rd, 2002
10	Benares State Bank Ltd.	Bank of Baroda	June 20th, 2002
11	Nedungadi Bank Ltd.	Punjab National Bank	February 1st, 2003
12	South Gujarat Local Area Bank Ltd.	Bank of Baroda	June 25th, 2004
13	Global Trust Bank Ltd.	Oriental Bank of Commerce	August 14th, 2004
14	IDBI Bank Ltd.	IDBI Ltd.	April 2nd, 2005
15	Bank of Punjab Ltd.	Centurion Bank Ltd.	October 1st, 2005
16	Ganesh Bank of Kurundwad Ltd.	Federal Bank Ltd.	September 2nd, 2006
17	United Western Bank Ltd.	IDBI Ltd.	October 3rd, 2006
18	Bharat Overseas Bank Ltd.	Indian Overseas Bank	March 31st, 2007
19	Sangli Bank Ltd.	ICICI Bank Ltd.	April 19th, 2007
20	Lord Krishna Bank Ltd.	Centurion Bank of Punjab Ltd.	August 29th, 2007
21	Centurion Bank of Punjab Ltd.	HDFC Bank Ltd.	May 23rd, 2008
22	State Bank of Saurashtra	State Bank of India	August 13th, 2008
23	Bank of Rajasthan	ICICI Bank Ltd.	August 13th, 2010
24	State Bank of Indore	State Bank of India	August 26th, 2010

Source: Report on Currency and Finance (various issues), RBI, Mumbai

2.4 Current Structure of Indian Banking Sector

The Reserve Bank of India (RBI) is the central bank of the country that regulates the operations of other banks, manages money supply and discharges other myriad responsibilities that are usually associated with a central bank. The banking system in India comprises commercial and co-operative banks, of which the former accounts for more than 90 % of the total assets of the banking system. Commercial banks operating in India are governed by different statutory provisions depending upon their status as a corporate body established by an Act of Parliament or a banking company registered under the Banking Companies Act, 1956, after obtaining a banking licence from RBI. Based on the submission of filing statutory returns to RBI, all the commercial banks are bifurcated into (i) scheduled commercial banks and (ii) nonscheduled commercial banks. The scheduled commercial banks are those banks which are listed in Schedule II of the Reserve Bank of India Act, 1934, and have paid-up capital and reserves of more than INR 0.5 million.

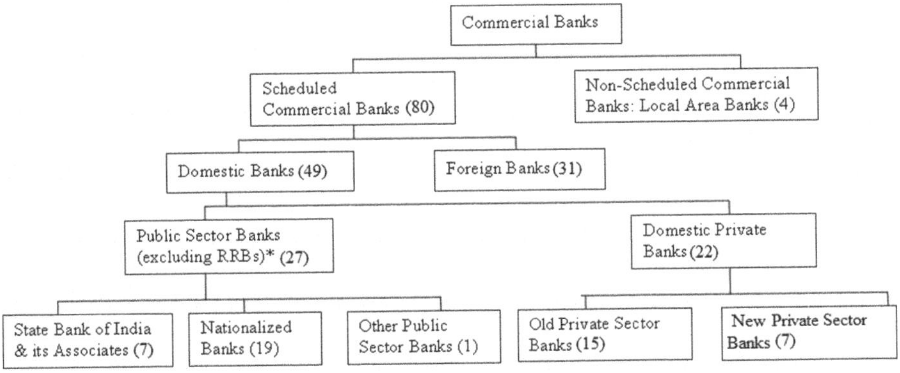

Fig. 2.4 Structure of Indian commercial banking industry (as on end-March 2009) (Notes: Figures in parenthesis indicate number of banks in each group, and '*' stand for Regional Rural Banks)

They have to fulfil certain provisions in line with RBI Act and have an advantage of accessing the credit from the RBI at an hour of need. For the purpose of assessment of performance of banks, the RBI classifies scheduled commercial banks (in terms of their ownership and function) into two categories: (i) domestic banks and (ii) foreign banks. Figure 2.4 provides the structure of Indian commercial banking industry in the financial year 2008–2009.

Of the 80 scheduled commercial banks operating in India during the financial year 2008–2009, 49 banks are domestic, and the remaining 31 are foreign banks. The domestic banks can be further categorised as *public sector banks* (PSBs) and *private sector banks*. Public sector banks include (a) State Bank of India (SBI) and its associate banks, (b) nationalised banks and (c) other public sector banks. Of the total 27 PSBs, 7 banks belong to State Bank of India (SBI) group, 19 are nationalised banks (NBs) and the IDBI Bank is included in the category of other PSBs. The banks belonging to SBI and NB groups operate under the same regulatory environment and may exhibit variations in efficiency due to differences in their managerial skills and practices, nature of business and government patronage. Some key differences in institutional characteristics of these groups in terms of ownership, functions and organisational structure are listed out as follows.

First, the SBI was established under the State Bank of India Act, 1955, and its seven subsidiary banks[12] which were established under the State Bank of India Act, 1959, while the 19 nationalised banks were established under the two acts, i.e. Banking Companies (Acquisition and Transfer of Undertakings) Act, 1970, and Banking Companies (Acquisition and Transfer of Undertakings) Act, 1980. Thus, the banks in SBI and NB groups are governed by the different statutes. Second, the RBI

[12] In 2008, the number of associate banks has reduced to six from seven because of the merger of State Bank of Saurashtra with the State Bank of India. Further, the number has reduced to five with the merger of State Bank of Indore with State Bank of India itself in 2010.

owns the majority share of SBI, while the shares of subsidiary banks are owned by the SBI. On the other hand, nationalised banks are wholly owned by the Government of India. Third, SBI besides carrying out its normal banking functions also acts as an agent of the Reserve Bank of India. SBI undertakes most of the government business transactions (including major borrowing programmes), thereby earning more non-interest income than nationalised banks (Shanmugam and Das 2004). However, this privilege has not been bestowed upon the nationalised banks. Fourth, the SBI has a well-defined system of decentralisation of authority; while in case of nationalised banks, the organisational structure differs across banks.

Private sector banks consist of domestic private banks which can further be classified as old private banks that are in business prior to 1996 and new private banks that are established after 1996. As on end-March 2009, private sector banking segment comprised of 15 old private sector banks and 7 new private sector banks. According to the guidelines issued by the RBI in January 2001 for entry of new private banks, the initial minimum paid-up capital should be INR 2 billion which shall be increased to INR 3 billion in subsequent 3 years after the commencement of business. The new private banks are less labour-intensive, have limited number of branches, have adopted modern technology and are more profitable. The private sector banks, particularly new ones, have brought in state-of-the-art technology and tapped new markets such as retailing, capital markets and bancassurance. Also, these banks accessed low-cost NRI funds and managed the associated forex risk for them. At present, these banks are giving competition to the public sector banks since their inception. Though both public and private sector banks are integral part of Indian banking system and operate under the guidelines of RBI; nevertheless, their ownership and functioning differ vastly.

To date, there are 31 foreign banks operating in India with 295 branches. For a foreign bank to operate in India, the minimum capital requirement of USD 25 million, spread over three branches, i.e. USD 10 million for the first branch, additional USD 10 million for the second branch and further USD 5 million for third branch has been stipulated. Foreign banks tend to follow 'exclusive banking' by offering services to a small number of clients, particularly to high-income groups, TNCs and big corporate groups. Therefore, their operations are confined only to metropolitan cities and Tier I cities.[13] As far as their strength is concerned, it lies in their technology, vast capital resources, considerable international exposure and well established networking. They garner more of their income from fee-based activities. According to the guidelines issued by Committee on Financial Sector Assessment in 2009, the GOI and RBI could consider the following issues while reviewing the roadmap of foreign banks:

(i) Foreign banks can operate in the country either through branches or the subsidiary route.

---

[13] Cities in India are categorised as Tier 1, Tier 2 and Tier 3 cities on the basis of the population of the city. Tier 1 cities are those cities where population is more than five million, Tier 2 are those cities where population is between one million and five million, and Tier 3 are those cities where population is less than one million.

(ii) The branch licensing policy of these entities could broadly be structured on the lines of that followed in case of new private banks, but consistent with country's WTO commitments.
(iii) In the case of foreign banks adopting the subsidiary route, the foreign shareholding should not exceed 74 %.
(iv) These banks should be listed on the stock exchanges as this would enhance market discipline.
(v) There could be a need to have independent board members for subsidiaries of foreign banks to protect the interest of all stakeholders.
(vi) The expansion of foreign banks should not affect the credit flow to agriculture and small and medium enterprises.

Table 2.13 provides summary details of different types of commercial banks (excluding regional rural banks) as on the end-March 2009. It has been observed that among the domestic banks, PSBs have a countrywide network of branches and account for over 70 % of the total banking business. However, since the inception of banking reforms, their share has come down significantly from a peak of 90 % in 1991.[14] The State Bank of India holds the dominant market position among all the scheduled commercial banks. It is the world's largest commercial bank in terms of branch network with a staggering 16,323 branches as on end-March 2009. Further, the nationalised banks have expanded their network to 39,786 branches and cater to the socio-economic needs of a large mass of the population, especially the weaker section and in the rural areas. This indicates that PSBs have strong presence at rural and semiurban areas and employ a large number of staff. About 85 % of branches of the commercial banks in India belong to PSBs. Further, their share in total employment provided by the commercial banking industry is about 78 %. In brief, PSBs command a lion's share of Indian banking industry. The share of domestic banks (both public and private sector banks) is more than 90 % in all the business parameters of the Indian banking industry. However, foreign banks have a minuscule share (less than 9 %) in the all business parameters and operate exclusively in urban and metropolitan areas.

Since the initiation of the process of banking reforms in 1992, the share of PSBs in the business parameters of banking industry has declined due to intensive price and non-price competition that has emerged in the wake of relaxed entry norms during the post-reforms years. For maintaining their share and achieving sustainable growth in the highly competitive environment, PSBs are offering a number of innovative products and services and constantly improving delivery channels to attract new customers and retain the existing ones. Further, to offer the service quality, PSBs are making heavy investment in information technology regularly to switch over to ICT-based modern automated banking systems from their out-dated manual-based banking systems.

---

[14] This is evident from the fact that the share of public sector banks in deposits, advances and total assets of Indian banking industry has declined from 87.9 %, 89.3 % and 87.2 % during the financial year 1992–1993 to 76.6 %, 75.3 % and 71.9 % during the financial year 2008–2009, respectively.

Table 2.13 Structure of commercial banking in India* (as at end-March 2009)

Bank group	No. of banks	Branches	Staff	Investments	Advances	Deposits	Total assets
		Number		Amount in billions			
I. *Public sector banks (a + b)*	27	56,109	7,34,661	10,126.66	22,601.56	31,127.48	37,667.16
Market share (%)		85.8	78.0	69.9	75.3	76.6	71.9
a. State Bank of India Group	7	16,323	2,68,598	3,576.24	7,396.06	10,070.42	12,802.12
Market share (%)		29.1	36.6	35.3	32.7	32.4	34.0
b. Nationalised banks and IDBI Ltd.	20	39,786	4,66,063	6,550.42	15,205.49	21,057.06	24,865.05
Market share (%)		70.9	63.4	64.7	67.3	67.6	66.0
II. *Indian private sector banks*	22	9,011	1,76,410	3,064.55	5,753.36	7,363.79	10,274.65
Market share (%)		13.7	18.7	21.1	19.2	18.1	19.6
III. *Foreign banks in India*	31	292	30,304	1,303.54	1,654.15	2,140.77	4,471.49
Market share (%)		0.4	3.2	9.0	5.5	5.3	8.5
IV. *Total Indian domestic (public and private banks (I + II))*	49	65,120	9,11,071	13,191.21	28,354.92	38,491.27	47,941.81
Market share (%)		99.5	96.8	91.0	94.5	94.7	91.5
V. *Total commercial banks (I + IV)*	80	65,412	9,41,375	14,494.75	30,009.06	40,632.04	52,413.31
Market Share (%)		100	100.0	100.0	100.0	100.0	100.0

Source: Authors' calculations from Statistical Tables Relating to Banks in India (2008–2009)
Note: (i) '*'indicates the exclusion of Regional Rural Banks

2.5 Conclusions

The main purpose of this chapter is to trace out the evolution of Indian banking industry and to examine the policy changes since the early 1990s that transformed the Indian banking system to a market-driven and sound banking system from a highly regulated and financially repressed system. It has been observed that from the early 1970s through the late 1980s, the role of market forces in the Indian banking system was almost missing, and excess regulation in terms of high liquidity requirements and state interventions in allocating credit and determining the prices of financial products resulted in serious financial repression. Realising the presence of the signs of financial repression and to seek an escape from any potential crisis in the banking sector, the Government of India embarked upon a comprehensive banking reforms plan in 1992 with the objective of creating a more diversified, profitable, efficient and resilient banking system. The main agenda of reforms process was to focus on key areas: (i) restructuring of PSBs by imparting more autonomy in decision making, and by infusing fresh capital through recapitalisation and partial privatisation; (ii) creating contestable markets by removing entry barriers for *de novo* domestic private and foreign banks; (iii) improving the regulatory and supervisory frameworks; and (iv) strengthening the banking system through consolidation. To meet this agenda, the policy makers heralded an episode of interest rates deregulation, standardised minimum capital requirements as per Basel norms, prudential norms relating to income recognition, assets classification and provisioning for bad loans, and changes in the legal and supervisory environment.

Subsequent to the implementation of the extensive financial liberalisation programme implemented in 1992, the banking system of India witnessed visible structural changes and transformations during the past 20 years. Use of the state-of-the-art banking technology, increased availability of lendable resources, heightened competition, a trend towards the market-driven interest rate system, improvement in asset quality, imposition of capital market discipline, drive towards consolidation through mergers, greater exposures of non-traditional activities, etc., are the key structural changes and transformations that have occurred in the post-deregulation period, which transformed the Indian banking system from a weak and crisis prone system to a sound and efficient system which is resilient to external shocks, and able to play its vital role in the development of the economy.

Chapter 3
Measurement of Bank Efficiency: Analytical Methods

3.1 Introduction

This chapter reviews various frontier approaches that have been utilised extensively in the applied research on bank efficiency. Earlier, the regulators, managers, investors and analysts generally relied on financial accounting ratios to assess the relative efficiency of banks. The main reasons for using ratios as a tool for performance evaluation are to allow comparison among similar-sized banks and to control for sector-specific characteristics permitting the comparison of individual bank's ratios with some benchmark for the sector (Halkos and Salamouris 2004). An inspection of literature provides that many different ratios have been employed to examine various aspects of a bank's performance. For instance, intermediation cost, interest spread, operating expenditure, cost to income ratio, return on assets, return on equity, business per employee, income per employee and business per branch, among others, are some commonly used accounting ratios for assessing the financial performance of the banking units (Reserve Bank of India 2008c).

Though financial accounting ratios are simple to use and relatively easy to understand, but their use to measure bank performance is subject to many criticisms. The financial ratios do not take account the differences in the business undertaken by different banks, which will in turn be reflected in different combinations of inputs and outputs (Tripe 2004). DeYoung (1998) suggests that blind pursuit of accounting-based benchmarks might reduce a bank's cost efficiency by cutting back on those expenditures necessary to run the bank properly. Further, Berger et al. (1993a) note that financial ratios may be misleading because they do not control for product mix or input prices. Owing to aforementioned intricacies of the financial accounting ratios, the frontier efficiency analysis gained tremendous popularity in measuring the efficiency of banking industry. Bauer et al. (1998) suggested that frontier efficiency analysis is superior to the financial ratios' analysis, since it is based on the recognition that some banks will not be as successful as others in meeting their objectives. The frontier techniques measure the performance of each bank in an industry relative to the *efficient frontier* consisting

S. Kumar and R. Gulati, *Deregulation and Efficiency of Indian Banks*, India Studies in Business and Economics, DOI 10.1007/978-81-322-1545-5_3, © Springer India 2014

of dominant banks in the industry. A bank is classified as fully efficient if it lies on the frontier and inefficient if its outputs can be produced more efficiently by another set of banks. It is significant to note here that each frontier technique involves various models for deriving a measure of best practice for the sample of banks and then determine how closely individual banks lie relative to this standard. The best practice is usually in the form of an *efficient frontier* that is estimated using econometric or mathematical programming techniques. The frontier techniques summarise bank performance in a single statistic that controls for the differences among banks in a sophisticated multidimensional framework that has its roots in economic theory. Further, frontier efficiency measures dominate the traditional ratio analysis in terms of developing meaningful and reliable measures of bank performance. Owing to these features of frontier methodology, the conventional ratio analysis is becoming obsolete.

The available frontier efficiency approaches can be grouped into two major estimation techniques: (i) parametric and (ii) non-parametric approaches. In parametric approaches, a specific functional form of the production function like Cobb–Douglas and transcendental logarithmic (translog) is required to specify a priori. The efficiency is then assessed in relation to this function with constant parameters and will be different depending on the chosen functional form. On the other hand, non-parametric approaches do not specify a functional form, but nevertheless require certain assumptions about the structure of production technology (e.g. free disposability,[1] convexity[2]). In the non-parametric approaches, a separate mathematical programming problem is needed to solve for obtaining the efficiency scores for individual banks included in the sample. Further, non-parametric approaches are deterministic in nature since these approaches postulate that all the distances from the *efficient frontier* are assumed to be caused by inefficiency.

To present the analytical framework for computing the efficiency scores using each frontier approach, the rest of the chapter is organised as follows. Section 3.2 discusses the Data Envelopment Analysis (DEA) approach for measuring efficiency in a cross-sectional data setting. Section 3.3 introduces the underlying framework of widely used DEA models in panel data setting. The strengths, limitations, basic requirements and outcomes from a DEA methodology are discussed in Sect. 3.4. Section 3.5 presents the Free Disposal Hull (FDH) approach for measuring the efficiency of banks. Section 3.6 discusses the parametric efficiency measurement approach of Stochastic Frontier Analysis (SFA). Further, the details on the other parametric approaches are given in the Sect. 3.7. In Sect. 3.8, a comparative analysis of DEA and SFA techniques is presented. In particular, this section focuses on why both the approaches produce different estimates of bank's efficiency. The final section concludes the discussion.

---

[1] Free disposability means that the destruction of goods is not expensive.

[2] Convexity implies that the efficient frontier includes all linear combinations of dominant units.

3.2 Data Envelopment Analysis (DEA)

DEA is a linear (mathematical) programming-based non-parametric approach first originated in the literature by Charnes et al. (1978) as a reformulation of the Farrell's (1957) single-output, single-input radial measure of technical efficiency to the multiple-output, multiple-input case. The subsequent developments in DEA are very extensive. Interested parties are directed to those provided by Seiford and Thrall (1990), Ali and Seiford (1993), Charnes et al. (1994), Seiford (1996), Zhu (2003), Ray (2004) and Copper et al. (2007). What follows is a general discussion of DEA with primary attention directed to describe a few widely used DEA models. DEA calibrates the level of technical efficiency (TE) on the basis of an estimated discrete piecewise frontier (or so-called efficient frontier or best practice frontier or envelopment surface) made up by a set of *Pareto-efficient* decision making units (DMUs).[3] In all instances, these *Pareto-efficient* banks located on the *efficient frontier*, compared to the others, use minimum productive resources given the outputs (input-conserving orientation), or maximise the output given the inputs size (output-augmenting orientation), and are called the *best practice performers* or *reference units* or *peer units* within the sample of banks. These *Pareto-efficient* banks have a benchmark efficiency score of unity that no individual bank's score can surpass. In addition, it is not possible for the *Pareto-efficient* unit to improve any input or output without worsening some other input or output. It is significant to note that the *efficient frontier* provides a yardstick against which to measure the relative efficiency of all other banks that do not lie on the frontier. The banks which do not lie on the *efficient frontier* are deemed relatively inefficient (i.e. Pareto nonoptimal banks) and receive a TE score between 0 and 1. The efficiency score of each bank can be interpreted as the radial distance to the *efficient frontier*. In short, the DEA forms a non-parametric surface frontier (more formally a piecewise linear convex isoquant) over the data points to determine the efficiency of each bank relative to this frontier.

Using actual data for the banks under consideration, DEA employs linear programming technique to construct *efficient* or *best practice frontier*. In fact, a large number of linear programming DEA models have been proposed in the literature to compute efficiency of individual banks corresponding to different technical or behavioural goals. Essentially, each of these various models seeks to establish which of *n* banks determine the *efficient frontier*. The geometry of this surface is prescribed by the specific DEA model employed. Nevertheless, for the analytical purpose, we can classify DEA models used in banking efficiency models in two broad categories: (i) non-allocation DEA models and (ii) allocation DEA models.

[3] DMUs are usually defined as entities responsible for turning input(s) into output(s), such as firms and production units. In this book, DMUs refer to the individual banks. A DMU must have at least some degree of freedom in setting behavioural goals and choosing how to achieve them.

3.2.1 Non-allocation DEA Models

The non-allocation DEA models compute relative TE scores for individual banks without using any information on prices of inputs and outputs. Before discussing the methods for efficiency measurement, it is necessary to look at the different perspectives of technical efficiency. *Technical efficiency* (TE) refers to the conversion of physical inputs, such as labour and capital, into outputs relative to best practice. TE, thus, relates to the productivity of inputs (Sathye 2001). It is a comparative measure of how well it actually processes inputs to achieve its outputs, as compared to its maximum potential for doing so, as represented by its production possibility frontier (Barros and Mascarenhas 2005). Accordingly, TE of the bank is its ability to transform multiple resources into multiple financial services (Bhattacharyya et al. 1997b). A bank is said to be technically inefficient if it operates below the frontier. A measure of TE helps to determine inefficiency due to the input/output configuration as well as the size of operations.

Charnes et al. (1994) described three possible orientations in DEA models for computing TE scores: (i) *input-oriented models* are the models where banks are deemed to produce a given amount of outputs with the minimum possible amount of inputs (inputs are controllable). In this orientation, the inefficient banks are projected onto the *efficient frontier* by decreasing their consumption of inputs. Input minimisation allows us to determine the extent to which a bank can reduce inputs while maintaining the current level of outputs; (ii) *output-oriented models* are models where banks are deemed to produce with given amounts of inputs the maximum possible amount of outputs (outputs are controllable). In this orientation, inefficient banks are projected onto the *efficient frontier* by increasing their production of outputs. Output maximisation might be used when the inputs are constrained, and emphasis is on increasing the outputs; and (iii) *base-oriented models* (or *additive* or *non-oriented* models) are models where banks are deemed to produce the optimal mix of inputs and outputs (both inputs and outputs are controllable). Here, the inefficient banks are projected onto the *efficient frontier* by simultaneously reducing their inputs and increasing their outputs to reach an optimum level.

Figure 3.1 describes the different orientations used in DEA framework using the simple case of a single-input and single-output production system. QQ′ represents *efficient frontier*, and Bank D is an inefficient unit. Point I constitutes the benchmark for inefficient Bank D in the input-oriented model. The relative efficiency of Bank D is given by the ratio of distances $D_I I/D_I D$. Point O is the projection of D in the output-oriented model. The relative efficiency of Bank D is then $DD_o/D_o O$. Finally, point B is the base-projection of Bank D in the base-oriented model.

In the empirical studies, the researchers have widely utilised the input-oriented and output-oriented models. An illustration of the TE measurement from input-oriented perspective is provided in Fig. 3.2. The figure illustrates a two-dimension *efficient frontier* in input space (i.e. an isoquant $L(y)$) in which all four banks (A, B, C and D) produce the same amount of output y but with varying amounts of inputs x_1 and x_2. The *efficient frontier* in input space is defined by banks A, B, C and D that require minimum inputs to produce the same level of output. These units are

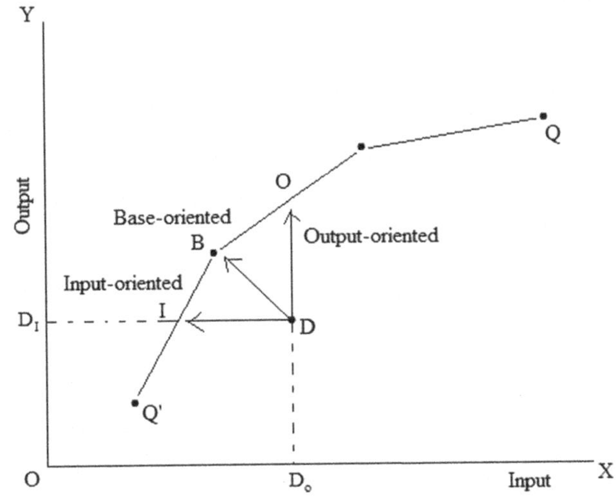

Fig. 3.1 Orientations in DEA (*Source*: Charnes et al. 1994)

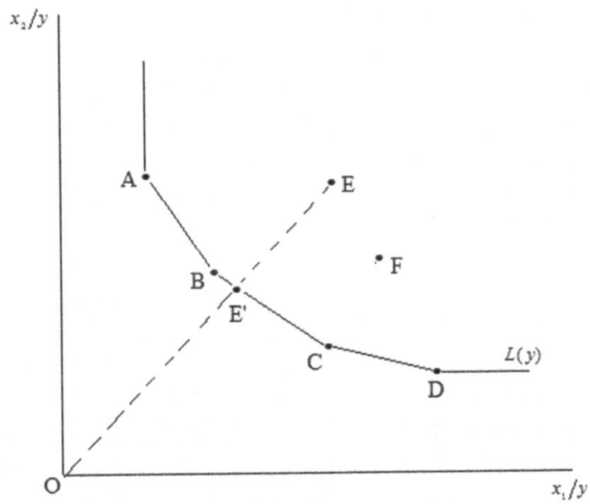

Fig. 3.2 Input-oriented technical efficiency (*Source*: Authors' elaboration)

labelled as efficient banks and have TE score equal to 1. On the other hand, banks E and F are inefficient because both require more of each input to produce the same amount of output. In input-oriented context, a measure of TE for an inefficient bank can be defined as

$$\theta_{\text{input}} = \frac{\text{Minimum input}}{\text{Actual input}}$$

The measure of TE for Bank E is defined as $\theta^{E}_{\text{input}} = \text{OE}'/\text{OE}$. It is significant to note that θ^{E} is less than 1. Further, the inefficient Bank E can move on to the *efficient frontier* (and in a way get the status of efficient bank in Farrell's sense) by a radial (or proportional) reduction in inputs by amount EE′.

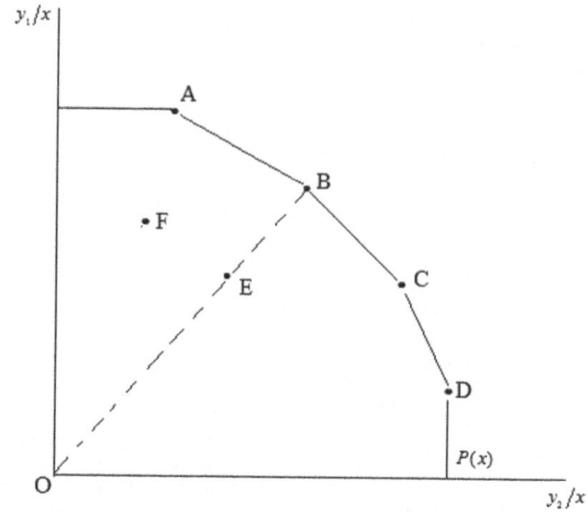

Fig. 3.3 Output-oriented technical efficiency (*Source*: Authors' elaboration)

Figure 3.3 depicts the output-oriented measure of technical efficiency. In this case, the banks A, B, C, D, E and F produce any combination of the two outputs y_1 and y_2 that fall within the production set $P(x)$ using a given amount of inputs. The piecewise linear boundary ABCD is the locus of efficient production and, therefore, banks A, B, C and D are rated as efficient. Banks E and F lies within the production possibility set and are, therefore, rated inefficient. In output-oriented context, TE is defined as the proportion to which outputs can be expanded radially without changing the input level. A measure of TE for an inefficient bank can be defined as

$$\theta_{\text{output}} = \frac{\text{Actual output}}{\text{Maximum output}}$$

To derive the efficiency of Bank E, we simply calculate how far E can be moved towards the frontier along the dotted line through the origin. The measures of TE for Bank E is defined as $\theta^{\text{E}}_{\text{output}} = \text{OE/OB}$. Further, the inefficient Bank E can move on to the *efficient frontier* (and in a way get the status of efficient bank in Farrell's sense) by a radial (or proportional) augmentation in outputs by amount EB.

The widely used non-allocation DEA models to compute technical efficiency scores are the *CCR* model, the *BCC* model, the *additive* model, the *multiplicative* model and the *slack-based* measures (SBM) model. Besides this, the researchers used extensions of CCR and BCC models for specific purposes like ranking of banks and incorporating value judgments, including non-discretionary inputs and outputs. The following subsections discuss various non-allocation DEA models.

3.2.1.1 The CCR Model

In their seminal paper entitled, "Measuring the efficiency of decision making units", which is published in *European Journal of Operational Research*, Charnes et al. (1978) developed a DEA model which got tremendous popularity with the name CCR DEA model. The CCR model is based on the assumptions of constant returns-to-scale (CRS), strong disposability of inputs and outputs and convexity of the production possibility set. The application of CCR model not only provides technical efficiency scores for individual banks but also provides vital information on input and output slacks and reference set for inefficient banks. There are two distinct variants of the CCR model: input-oriented CCR model (CCR-I) and output-oriented CCR model (CCR-O).

CCR-I

To illustrate input-oriented CCR DEA model, consider a set of n banks ($j = 1, \ldots, n$), utilising quantities of inputs $x \in R^m_+$ to produce quantities of outputs $y \in R^s_+$. We can denote x_{ij} the amount of the ith input used by the bank j ($i = 1, \ldots, m$) and y_{rj} the amount of the rth output produced by the bank j ($r = 1, \ldots, s$). In the CCR model, the multiple-inputs and multiple-outputs of each bank are aggregated into a single virtual input and virtual output, respectively. The input-oriented TE score for target bank 'o' can be obtained by solving the following fractional programming model:

$$\max_{u,\nu}\ h_o(u,\nu) = \frac{\text{Virtual Output}_o}{\text{Virtual Input}_o} = \frac{\sum_{r=1}^{s} u_r y_{ro}}{\sum_{i=1}^{m} \nu_i x_{io}}$$

$$\begin{aligned} &\text{subject to} \\ &\frac{\sum_{r=1}^{s} u_r y_{rj}}{\sum_{i=1}^{m} \nu_i x_{ij}} \le 1 && j = 1, \ldots, n \\ &u_r \ge \varepsilon && r = 1, \ldots, s \\ &\nu_i \ge \varepsilon && i = 1, \ldots, m. \end{aligned} \tag{3.1}$$

where y_{ro} = the amount of the rth output produced by the bank 'o', x_{io} = the amount of the ith input used by the bank 'o', u_r = the weight given to output r, ν_i = the weight given to input i, ε = a non-Archimedean (infinitesimal) constant.

The objective of this model is to determine positive and unknown input and output weights that maximise the ratio of a virtual output to a virtual input for bank 'o'. The constraints restrict that the ratio of virtual output to the virtual input for each bank to be less than or equal to 1. This implies that the maximal efficiency, h_o^*, is at the most equal to 1. The justification for ε is twofold: first, to ensure that the denominator is never zero and second, to ensure that each input and output is considered. It is important to note that the optimal output and input weights (i.e. u_r^* and v_i^*) are obtained through optimisation (i.e. linear programming solution). Such optimisation is performed separately for each bank in order to compute the weights and efficiency scores.

Charnes and Cooper (1962) developed a transformation from a fractional programming problem to an equivalent linear programming problem. By using the transformation of the variables,

$$\mu_r = tu_r$$
$$\nu_i = tv_i$$
$$t = \frac{1}{\sum_{i=1}^{m} \nu_i x_{io}}.$$

The fractional CCR model (3.1) can be transformed into the following linear programming model, which is popularly known as 'multiplier form' of CCR model:

$$\begin{aligned}
&\max_{\mu,\nu} \; f_o(\mu) = \sum_{r=1}^{s} \mu_r y_{ro} \\
&\text{subject to} \\
&\sum_{i=1}^{m} \nu_i x_{io} = 1 \\
&\sum_{r=1}^{s} \mu_r y_{rj} - \sum_{i=1}^{m} \nu_i x_{ij} \le 0, \qquad j = 1, \ldots, n \\
&\mu_r \ge \varepsilon, \qquad r = 1, \ldots, s \\
&\nu_i \ge \varepsilon, \qquad i = 1, \ldots, m.
\end{aligned} \tag{3.2}$$

The dual programme of the model (3.2), which is popularly known as 'envelopment form' of CCR model, is given as

$$\begin{aligned}
&\min_{\theta^{CCR}, \lambda, s^+, s^-} \; g_o(\theta^{CCR}, s^+, s^-) = \theta_o^{CCR} - \varepsilon \left(\sum_{r=1}^{s} s_r^+ + \sum_{i=1}^{m} s_i^- \right) \\
&\text{subject to} \\
&\sum_{j=1}^{n} \lambda_j x_{ij} + s_i^- = \theta_o^{CCR} x_{io}, \qquad i = 1, \ldots, m \\
&\sum_{j=1}^{n} \lambda_j y_{rj} - s_r^+ = y_{ro}, \qquad r = 1, \ldots, s \\
&\lambda_j \ge 0, \qquad j = 1, \ldots, n \\
&s_r^+, s_i^- \ge 0 \\
&0 < \varepsilon \le 1.
\end{aligned} \tag{3.3}$$

Note that the primal model has $n + s + m + 1$ constraints while the dual has $m + s$ constraints. The number of banks (n) should usually be considered larger than the number of inputs and outputs ($m + s$) in order to provide a fair degree of discrimination of results. In view of this, it is clear that dual model (3.3) will be simpler to solve as it has $n + 1$ fewer constraints than the primal model (3.2). It should be noted that both the primal (multiplier form) and dual (envelopment form) problems have the same solutions.

The scalar θ_o^{CCR}, corresponding to bank o's TE score, represents the largest possible radial contraction that is proportionally applied to the bank o's inputs in order to project it to a point on the *efficient frontier* that corresponds to the minimal consumption of inputs $\left(\sum_{j=1}^{n} \lambda_j x_{ij} + s_i^-\right)$ required to produce bank o's current output levels $\left(\sum_{j=1}^{n} \lambda_j y_{rj} - s_r^+\right)$. For inefficient banks, the value of $\theta_o^{CCR} < 1$ represents the proportion of inputs that the bank should be using to produce its current levels of outputs, such that $1 - \theta_o^{CCR}$ corresponds to bank o's level of technical inefficiency. The value of θ_o^{CCR} is limited to be $0 < \theta_o^{CCR} \leq 1$. Any non-zero values of λ_j indicate that an efficient bank is in the reference set of bank 'o'. The s_i^- input slack term equals the input excess that remains in input i of bank 'o' after the radial contraction was applied to bank o's inputs, and the s_r^+ output slack term equals the shortfall in the production of output r. The ε term in the objective function represents a small positive number (10^{-6}) whose purpose is to maximise the sum of the slacks should more than one optimal solution exists. Doing so, however, can lead to some theoretical difficulties that can be avoided by solving the CCR model in two stages. In Stage 1, the model is solved for the optimal value of θ_o^{CCR} (i.e. θ_o^{*CCR}), while in Stage 2, the value of θ_o^{CCR} is fixed to θ_o^{*CCR} and the model is solved such that it maximises the values of the slacks. These stages are outlined below.

Stage 1 focuses on obtaining the TE scores in Farrell-Debreu's sense by ignoring the presence of non-zero slacks. For getting TE score for bank 'o', the model (3.4) is to be solved:

$$
\begin{aligned}
&\theta_o^{*CCR} = \min_{\lambda,\, \theta^{ccr}} \theta_o^{CCR} \\
&\text{subject to} \\
&\sum_{j=1}^{n} \lambda_j x_{ij} \leq \theta_o^{CCR} x_{io} && i = 1, \ldots, m \\
&\sum_{j=1}^{n} \lambda_j y_{rj} \geq y_{ro} && r = 1, \ldots, s \\
&\lambda_j \geq 0, && j = 1, \ldots, n.
\end{aligned}
\tag{3.4}
$$

θ_o^{*CCR} represent the input-oriented TE score of bank 'o'. After calculating model (3.4), we obtain input and output slack values as

$$s_i^- = \theta_o^{*CCR} x_{io} - \sum_{j=1}^{n} \lambda_j x_{ij} \qquad i = 1, \ldots, m$$

$$s_r^+ = \sum_{j=1}^{n} \lambda_j y_{rj} - y_{ro} \qquad r = 1, \ldots, s$$

where s_i^- and s_r^+ represent input and output slacks, respectively.

In Stage 2, we optimise the slacks by fixing $\theta^{*\,CCR}$ in the following linear programming problem:

$$\begin{aligned}
&\max_{\lambda, s^+, s^-} \left(\sum_{r=1}^{s} s_r^+ + \sum_{i=1}^{m} s_i^- \right) \\
&\text{subject to} \\
&\sum_{j=1}^{n} \lambda_j x_{ij} + s_i^- = \theta_o^{*CCR} x_{io}, \qquad i = 1, \ldots, m \\
&\sum_{j=1}^{n} \lambda_j y_{rj} - s_r^+ = y_{ro}, \qquad r = 1, \ldots, s \\
&\lambda_j \geq 0, \qquad j = 1, \ldots, n.
\end{aligned} \tag{3.5}$$

The solution of the model (3.5) yields optimal values of input and output slacks s_i^{-*} and s_r^{+*}.

The interpretation of the results of envelopment model (3.3) can be summarised as follows: (i) the bank '*o*' is *Pareto-efficient* if and only if $\theta_o^{*CCR} = 1$ and $s_i^{-*} = s_r^{+*} = 0$ for all i and r. Otherwise, if $\theta_o^{*CCR} < 1$ then the bank '*o*' is inefficient, i.e. the bank '*o*' can either increase its output levels or decrease its input levels, and (ii) the left-hand side of the envelopment model is usually called the 'reference set', and the right-hand side represents a specific bank under evaluation. The non-zero optimal λ_j^* represents the benchmarks for a specific bank under evaluation. The reference set provides coefficients (λ_j^*) to define the hypothetical efficient bank. The reference set or the efficient target shows how inputs can be decreased and outputs increased to make the bank under evaluation efficient.

CCR-O

The output-oriented CCR model focuses on maximal movement via proportional augmentation of output for a given level of inputs. To drive CCR-O model, we minimise the inefficiency of bank '*o*' given by the ratio of virtual input to virtual output under the constraints that so defined inefficiency cannot be lower than one for itself or for any of the other banks. The required optimisation problem is

$$\min_{u,v} \; z_o(u,v) = \frac{\text{Virtual Input}_o}{\text{Virtual Output}_o} = \frac{\sum_{i=1}^{m} v_i x_{io}}{\sum_{r=1}^{s} u_r y_{ro}}$$

$$\begin{aligned} &\text{subject to} \\ &\frac{\sum_{i=1}^{m} v_i x_{ij}}{\sum_{r=1}^{s} u_r y_{rj}} \geq 1 && j = 1, \ldots, n \\ &u_r \geq \varepsilon && r = 1, \ldots, s \\ &v_i \geq \varepsilon && i = 1, \ldots, m. \end{aligned} \tag{3.6}$$

Again the Charnes and Cooper (1962) transformation for fractional programming yields the linear programming model, popularly known as output-oriented multiplier (primal) and envelopment (dual) models, as follows:

Model orientation	Multiplier model (primal)	Envelopment model (dual)
Output-oriented CCR model	$\min_{\mu,\nu} \; w_o(\nu) = \sum_{i=1}^{m} \nu_i x_{io}$ subject to $\sum_{r=1}^{s} \mu_r y_{ro} = 1$ $\sum_{i=1}^{m} \nu_i x_{ij} - \sum_{r=1}^{s} \mu_r y_{rj} \geq 0$ $\mu_r, \nu_i \geq \varepsilon$	$\max_{\phi^{CCR}, \lambda, s^+, s^-} \; h_o(\phi^{CCR}, s^+, s^-) = \phi_o^{CCR} + \varepsilon\left(\sum_{r=1}^{s} s_r^+ + \sum_{i=1}^{m} s_i^-\right)$ subject to $\sum_{j=1}^{n} \lambda_j x_{ij} + s_i^- = x_{io}$ $\sum_{j=1}^{n} \lambda_j y_{rj} - s_r^+ = \phi_o^{CCR} y_{ro}$ $\lambda_j, s_i^-, s_r^+ \geq 0$

Like model (3.3), the output-oriented envelopment CCR model is also solved in a two-stage process. First, we calculate ϕ_o^{*CCR} by ignoring the slacks. Then we optimise the slacks by fixing ϕ_o^{*CCR} in the following linear programming problem:

$$\begin{aligned} &\max_{\lambda, s^+, s^-} \left(\sum_{r=1}^{s} s_r^+ + \sum_{i=1}^{m} s_i^-\right) \\ &\text{subject to} \\ &\sum_{j=1}^{n} \lambda_j x_{ij} + s_i^- = x_{io} && i = 1, \ldots, m \\ &\sum_{j=1}^{n} \lambda_j y_{rj} - s_r^+ = \phi_o^{*CCR} y_{ro} && r = 1, \ldots, s \\ &\lambda_j \geq 0, && j = 1, \ldots, n. \end{aligned} \tag{3.7}$$

3.2.1.2 The BCC Model

The BCC model has been developed by Banker et al. (1984) as an extension of the CCR model to allow for returns-to-scale to be variable. Thus, BCC model computes efficiency scores corresponding to the assumption of variable returns-to-scale (VRS). It is more flexible than the CCR model since it allows for constant, increasing and decreasing returns-to-scale. Banker et al. (1984) showed that solutions to CCR and BCC models allow a decomposition of technical efficiency (TE) into pure technical efficiency (PTE) and scale efficiency (SE) components. Like the CCR model, BCC model also has two variants: input-oriented BCC model (BCC-I) and output-oriented BCC model (BCC-O).

BCC-I

BCC-I model measures the pure technical efficiency of the bank 'o' by solving the following pair of primal (multiplier form) and dual (envelopment) linear programming models:

Model orientation	Multiplier model (primal)	Envelopment model (dual)
Input-oriented BCC model	$\max_{\mu,\nu} f_o(\mu,\mu_o) = \sum_{r=1}^{s} \mu_r y_{ro} - \mu_o$ subject to $\sum_{i=1}^{m} \nu_i x_{io} = 1$ $\sum_{r=1}^{s} \mu_r y_{rj} - \sum_{i=1}^{m} \nu_i x_{ij} - \mu_o \leq 0$ $\mu_r, \nu_i \geq \varepsilon$ μ_o free in sign	$\min_{\theta^{BCC},\lambda,s^+,s^-} g_o(\theta^{BCC}, s^+, s^-) = \theta_o^{BCC} - \varepsilon\left(\sum_{i=1}^{m} s_i^- + \sum_{r=1}^{s} s_r^+\right)$ subject to $\sum_{j=1}^{n} \lambda_j x_{ij} + s_i^- = \theta_o^{BCC} x_{io}$ $\sum_{j=1}^{n} \lambda_j y_{rj} - s_r^+ = y_{ro}$ $\sum_{j=1}^{n} \lambda_j = 1$ $\lambda_j, s_i^-, s_r^+ \geq 0$

Above models differ from their CCR counterparts in the free variable, μ_o, in the primal model and the constraint, $\sum_{j=1}^{n} \lambda_j = 1$, in the dual model. It is worth noting that the convexity constraint, $\sum_{j=1}^{n} \lambda_j = 1$, essentially ensures that an inefficient bank is only 'benchmarked' against banks of a similar size. The free variable, μ_o, relaxes the constant returns-to-scale condition by not restricting the envelopment surface to go through the origin. The BCC model can be solved using a two-phased approach similar to that for the CCR model. The first phase provides θ_o^{*BCC} and then θ_o^{*BCC} is used in the second phase to solve for the input excesses, s_i^{-*}, and output shortfalls, s_r^{+*}.

Because the BCC model imposes an additional constraint, $\sum_{j=1}^{n} \lambda_j = 1$, the feasible region of the BCC model is a subset of that of the CCR model. The relationship between the optimal objective values of the CCR and BCC models is that $\theta_o^{*BCC} \geq \theta_o^{*CCR}$. Therefore, a bank found to be efficient with the CCR model will also be found to be efficient with the corresponding BCC model. A measure of SE for bank 'o' can be obtained as a ratio of efficiency measure from CCR-I model to efficiency measure from BCC-I model, i.e. $\theta_o^{*CCR}/\theta_o^{*BCC}$.

BCC-O

The output-oriented BCC model measures the efficiency of the bank 'o' by solving the following pair of primal (multiplier form) and dual (envelopment) linear programming models:

Model orientation	Multiplier model (primal)	Envelopment model (dual)
Output-oriented BCC model	$\min_{\mu,\nu} \ w_o(\nu,\nu_o) = \sum_{i=1}^{m} \nu_i x_{io} + \nu_o$ subject to $\sum_{r=1}^{s} \mu_r y_{ro} = 1$ $\sum_{i=1}^{m} \nu_i x_{ij} - \sum_{r=1}^{s} \mu_r y_{rj} + \nu_o \geq 0$ $\mu_r, \nu_i \geq \varepsilon$ ν_o free in sign	$\max_{\phi^{BCC},\lambda,s^+,s^-} \ h_o(\phi^{BCC}, s^+, s^-) = \phi_o^{BCC} + \varepsilon\left(\sum_{r=1}^{s} s_r^+ + \sum_{i=1}^{m} s_i^-\right)$ subject to $\sum_{j=1}^{n} \lambda_j x_{ij} + s_i^- = x_{io}$ $\sum_{j=1}^{n} \lambda_j y_{rj} - s_r^+ = \phi_o^{BCC} y_{ro}$ $\sum_{j=1}^{n} \lambda_j = 1$ $\lambda_j, s_i^-, s_r^+ \geq 0$

Again, BCC-O models differ from their CCR counterparts in terms of the free variable, ν_o, in the primal model, and the constraint, $\sum_{j=1}^{n} \lambda_j = 1$, in the dual model. The free variable, ν_o, relaxes the assumption of constant returns-to-scale by not restricting the envelopment surface to go through the origin. The BCC-O model can also be solved using a two-phased approach similar to that for the CCR-O model. The first phase provides ϕ_o^{*BCC} and then ϕ_o^{*BCC} is used in the second phase to solve for the input excesses, s_i^{-*}, and output shortfalls, s_r^{+*}. A measure of SE for bank 'o' can be obtained as a ratio of efficiency measure from CCR-O model to efficiency measure from BCC-O model, i.e. $\phi_o^{*CCR}/\phi_o^{*BCC}$.

3.2.1.3 Additive Model

In the preceding models (CCR and BCC), the projection of inefficient banks to the envelopment surface is based on the model orientation. CCR-I (or BCC-I) model focuses on radial movement towards the frontier through the proportional reduction of inputs, while CCR-O (or BCC-O) model does this through proportional augmentation of outputs. Charnes et al. (1985) introduced the *additive* or *Pareto–Koopmans* (PK) model which provides a non-oriented measure that simultaneously reduces the inputs and augments the outputs by taking the slacks into account when measuring efficiency. The envelopment surface in the additive model is similar to BCC model in that it allows for scale effects creating the same VRS efficiency frontier. This is due to presence of the convexity constraint $\sum_{j=1}^{n} \lambda_j = 1$ in the dual (envelopment form) and, equivalently, μ_o in the primal (multiplier form) problem.

There are several types of additive models, from which we select the following:

$$\max_{\lambda, s^-, s^+} \; g_o(\lambda, s_i^-, s_r^+) = \sum_{r=1}^{s} s_r^+ + \sum_{i=1}^{m} s_i^-$$

subject to

$$\sum_{j=1}^{n} \lambda_j y_{rj} - s_r^+ = y_{ro}$$

$$\sum_{j=1}^{n} \lambda_j x_{ij} + s_i^- = x_{io}$$

$$\sum_{j=1}^{n} \lambda_j = 1$$

$$\lambda_j, s_i^-, s_r^+ \geq 0.$$

The bank '*o*' is ADD-efficient if the optimal value of the above model is equal to zero. If any component of the slack variables is positive then it is inefficient, and the values of non-zero components identify the sources and amounts of inefficiency in the corresponding inputs and outputs. The solution to envelopment model gives the optimal values s_i^{-*} and s_r^{+*}, which can be used to define target values for inputs ($\hat{x}_{io}$) and outputs($\hat{y}_{ro}$).

$$\hat{y}_{ro} = y_{ro} + s_r^{+*} \geq y_{ro}$$
$$\hat{x}_{io} = x_{io} - s_i^{-*} \leq x_{io}$$

The dual problem to the above additive model can be expressed as follows:

$$\min_{\nu, \mu, \mu_o} \; w_o(\nu, \mu, \mu_o) = \sum_{i=1}^{m} \nu_i x_{io} - \sum_{r=1}^{s} \mu_r y_{ro} + \mu_o$$

subject to

$$\sum_{i=1}^{m} \nu_i x_{ij} - \sum_{r=1}^{s} \mu_r y_{rj} + \mu_o \leq 0$$

$$\mu_r \geq 1$$

$$\nu_i \geq 1$$

μ_o free in sign

3.2.1.4 Multiplicative Model

In the preceding DEA models, efficiency is viewed as the sum of outputs divided by the sum of inputs. This means that adding one more output results in added input without any effect on the other outputs. However, in some processes, output levels (or input levels) may be interdependent (Sherman 1988). Charnes et al. (1982) introduced an alternative formulation of DEA known as '*multiplicative model*' which provides a measure of efficiency based on the ratio of the weighted multiplicative product of outputs divided by the weighted multiplicative product of inputs in order to account for interdependencies between input or output levels. The input (v_i) and output (μ_r) weights are applied as powers to the input and output variables as can be seen in the multiplicative formulation below:

$$\begin{aligned}
&\max_{\mu,\nu} \prod_{r=1}^{s} y_{ro}^{\mu_r} / \prod_{i=1}^{m} x_{io}^{v_i} \\
&\text{subject to} \\
&\prod_{r=1}^{s} y_{rj}^{\mu_r} / \prod_{i=1}^{m} x_{ij}^{v_i} \leq 1, \qquad j = 1, \ldots, n \\
&\mu_r \geq 1, \qquad r = 1, \ldots, s \\
&v_i \geq 1, \qquad i = 1, \ldots, m.
\end{aligned} \tag{3.8}$$

Taking logarithms, this may be written as the linear programming problem

$$\begin{aligned}
&\max_{\mu,\nu} \sum_{r=1}^{s} \mu_r \ln(y_{ro}) - \sum_{i=1}^{m} v_i \ln(x_{io}) \\
&\text{subject to} \\
&\sum_{r=1}^{s} \mu_r \ln\left(y_{rj}\right) - \sum_{i=1}^{m} v_i \ln(x_{ij}) \leq 0 \\
&\mu_r \geq 1 \\
&v_i \geq 1
\end{aligned}$$

with dual

$$\begin{aligned}
&\min_{\lambda, s^+, s^-} -\sum_{r=1}^{s} s_r^+ - \sum_{i=1}^{m} s_i^- \\
&\text{subject to} \\
&\sum_{j=1}^{n} \ln(x_{ij})\lambda_j + s_i^- = \ln(x_{io}), \\
&\sum_{j=1}^{n} \ln\left(y_{rj}\right)\lambda_j - s_r^+ = \ln(y_{ro}), \\
&\lambda_j, s_i^-, s_r^+ \geq 0.
\end{aligned}$$

The bank o is efficient in an optimal solution of dual model iff all slacks are zero.

It is worth noting that the envelopment surface in the multiplicative model is piecewise log-linear instead of piecewise linear, which is the envelopment surface for the other DEA models. As with the additive model, a bank 'o' is only considered to be efficient if all its slacks are zero (Cooper et al. 2007). The above model is also called Variant Multiplicative model, which has a constant returns-to-scale envelopment surface. The Invariant Multiplicative model has the same formulation for the primal and the dual except that the convexity constraint in the dual and the variable μ_o in the primal are added to the model. As a result, the envelopment surface will be variable returns-to-scale.

3.2.1.5 Slack-Based Measures (SBM) Model

The standard CCR and BCC DEA models, so defined, are based on the proportional reduction (augmentation) of input (output) vectors and do not take account of slacks. While the additive DEA model can capture slacks, it is neither unit invariant nor able to generate a scalar measure of efficiency. Tone (2001) introduced the slack-based measure (SBM) model to deal with inputs/outputs individually, contrary to the radial approaches that assume proportional changes in inputs/outputs. This scalar measure deals directly with the input excesses and the output shortfalls of the concerned banks. It is invariant to the units of measurement and is monotone increasing in each input and output slack. Furthermore, it is reference set dependent, i.e. the measure is determined only by its reference set and is not affected by statistics over the whole data set.

As far as the orientations in SBM model are concerned, we have input-oriented, output-oriented and non-oriented models. The linear programming problems of the SBM models corresponding to three model orientations are given below:

Input-oriented	Output-oriented	Non-oriented
$\rho_I^* = \min\limits_{\lambda, s^-} 1 - \frac{1}{m}\sum_{i=1}^{m} s_i^- / x_{io}$ subject to $\sum_{j=1}^{n} \lambda_j x_{ij} + s_i^- = x_{io}$ $\sum_{j=1}^{n} \lambda_j y_{rj} \geq y_{ro}$ $\lambda_j, s_i^- \geq 0$	$\rho_o^* = \min\limits_{\lambda, s^+} \frac{1}{1 + \frac{1}{s}\sum_{r=1}^{s} s_r^+ / y_{ro}}$ subject to $\sum_{j=1}^{n} \lambda_j x_{ij} \leq x_{io}$ $\sum_{j=1}^{n} \lambda_j y_{rj} - s_r^+ = y_{ro}$ $\lambda_j, s_r^+ \geq 0$	$\rho^* = \min\limits_{\lambda, s^-, s^+} \frac{1 - \frac{1}{m}\sum_{i=1}^{m} s_i^- / x_{io}}{1 + \frac{1}{s}\sum_{r=1}^{s} s_r^+ / y_{ro}}$ subject to $\sum_{j=1}^{n} \lambda_j x_{ij} + s_i^- = x_{io}$ $\sum_{j=1}^{n} \lambda_j y_{rj} - s_r^+ = y_{ro}$ $\lambda_j, s_i^-, s_r^+ \geq 0$

Note that both the traditional radial and non-radial SBM DEA models yield the same frontier but may yield different efficient targets even when the envelopment models do not have non-zero slacks. The objective function in the SBM model satisfies unit invariant because the numerator and denominator are measured in the

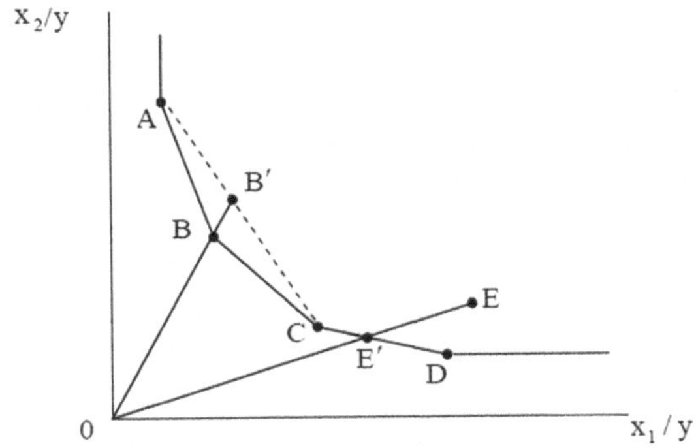

Fig. 3.4 Super-efficiency model (*Source*: Andersen and Petersen 1993)

same units for each bank in the above equation. Furthermore, the non-radial efficiency score also lie between 0 and 1.

3.2.2 *Extensions of Basic Non-allocation DEA Models*

3.2.2.1 Super-Efficiency Models

When a DMU under evaluation is not included in the reference set of the envelopment models, the resulting DEA models are called super-efficiency DEA models (Zhu 2003). The first super-efficiency model has been developed by Andersen and Petersen (1993) to provide strict ranking to all DMUs in the sample. Their idea is explained in Fig. 3.4. Figure illustrates that A, B, C and D are efficient banks which make up the *best practice* frontier. The inefficient Bank E is compared to a reference point which is the linear combination of the nearest peers on the *efficient frontier*. In case of Bank E, the reference (or virtual) point, E′, is the linear combination of C and D. The efficiency score of E is OE′/OE which is less than one. The efficiency score of an inefficient bank remains the same under super-efficiency and standard DEA approach. The difference exists only when it comes to an efficient bank.

Now consider an efficient bank, say Bank B. The efficiency score of Bank B under the standard DEA approach is OB/OB = 1, while the efficiency score under the super-efficiency model is determined by excluding B from the original reference set (line ABCD) and then compare B to the new reference set (line ACD) formed by the remaining efficient banks. Thus, the efficiency score of Bank B under the super-efficiency model will be OB′/OB, which is greater than 1. This implies that even proportional increase in input, B can still remain as an efficient bank. Thus, in the super-efficiency model, all the relative efficient banks would have an efficiency score equal to or greater than 1. This procedure makes the ranking of efficient banks possible (i.e. higher super-efficiency score implies higher rank). However, the inefficient units which are not on the *efficient frontier*, and with an initial DEA score of less than 1, would find their relative efficiency score unaffected by their exclusion from the reference set of banks.

Later, Thrall (1996), Dulá and Hickman (1997), Seiford and Zhu (1999), Xue and Harker (2002), Tone (2002a), Lovell and Rouse (2003) and Bogetoft and Hougaard (2004) show the infeasibility problems in the Andersen and Petersen (A-P) super-efficiency model. To deal with infeasible problems, Tone (2002a) provides a super-efficiency model using the slack-based measure of efficiency, which is non-radial and deals with input/output slacks directly.

The linear programming problems for the super-efficiency models as developed by Andersen and Petersen (1993) and Tone (2002a) corresponding to different model orientations are illustrated as follows:

	Model orientation		
Models↓	Input-oriented	Output-oriented	Non-oriented
Super-efficiency radial (Andersen and Petersen 1993)	$\theta^{*\text{super}} = \min_{\lambda,\theta^{\text{super}}} \theta^{\text{super}}$ subject to $\sum_{j=1, j\neq o}^{n} \lambda_j x_{ij} \le \theta^{\text{super}} x_{io}$ $\sum_{j=1, j\neq o}^{n} \lambda_j y_{rj} \ge y_{ro}$ $\lambda_j \ge 0$	$\phi^{*\text{super}} = \max_{\lambda,\phi^{\text{super}}} \phi^{\text{super}}$ subject to $\sum_{j=1, j\neq o}^{n} \lambda_j x_{ij} \le x_{io}$ $\sum_{j=1, j\neq o}^{n} \lambda_j y_{rj} \ge \phi^{\text{super}} y_{ro}$ $\lambda_j \ge 0$	
Super-efficiency non-radial (Tone 2002a)	$\rho_I^{*\text{super}} = \min_{\lambda,s^-} 1 - \frac{1}{m}\sum_{i=1}^{m} s_i^-/x_{io}$ subject to $\sum_{j=1, j\neq o}^{n} \lambda_j x_{ij} + s_i^- = x_{io}$ $\sum_{j=1, j\neq o}^{n} \lambda_j y_{rj} \ge y_{ro}$ $\lambda_j, s_i^- \ge 0$	$\rho_O^{*\text{super}} = \min_{\lambda,s^+} \frac{1}{1+\frac{1}{s}\sum_{r=1}^{s} s_r^+/y_{ro}}$ subject to $\sum_{j=1, j\neq o}^{n} \lambda_j x_{ij} \le x_{io}$ $\sum_{j=1, j\neq o}^{n} \lambda_j y_{rj} - s_r^+ = y_{ro}$ $\lambda_j, s_r^+ \ge 0$	$\rho^{*\text{super}} = \min_{\lambda,s^-,s^+} \frac{1 - \frac{1}{m}\sum_{i=1}^{m} s_i^-/x_{io}}{1+\frac{1}{s}\sum_{r=1}^{s} s_r^+/y_{ro}}$ subject to $\sum_{j=1, j\neq o}^{n} \lambda_j x_{ij} + s_i^- = x_{io}$ $\sum_{j=1, j\neq o}^{n} \lambda_j y_{rj} - s_r^+ = y_{ro}$ $\lambda_j, s_i^-, s_r^+ \ge 0$

3.2.2.2 Cross-Efficiency Models

The cross-efficiency model was introduced by Sexton et al. (1986) and extended by Oral et al. (1991), Doyle and Green (1994) and Thanassoulis et al. (1995). This method was developed as a DEA extension tool that can be utilised to identify best-performing banks and to rank banks using cross-efficiency scores that are linked to all banks. The basic idea of cross-efficiency models is to use DEA in a peer-appraisal instead of a self-appraisal. A peer-appraisal refers to the efficiency score of a bank that is achieved when evaluated with the optimal weights (input and output weights obtained by means of the output-oriented CRS model) of other banks. There are two principal advantages of cross-efficiency: (i) it provides a unique ordering of the banks, and (ii) it eliminates unrealistic weight schemes without requiring the elicitation of weight restrictions from application area experts (Liang et al. 2008).

To compute cross-efficiency score, consider n banks that are to be evaluated in terms of m inputs and s outputs. Let x_{ij} $(i = 1, \ldots, m)$ and y_{rj} $(r = 1, \ldots, s)$ be the input and output values of bank j $(j = 1, \ldots, n)$. In the first stage, for a specific bank, say bank k, $k \in \{1, \ldots, n\}$, we solve the following input-oriented DEA model proposed by Charnes et al. (1978) to obtain (i) the optimal weights of inputs $(\nu_{1k}^*, \nu_{2k}^*, \ldots, \nu_{mk}^*)$ and (ii) the optimal weight of outputs $(\mu_{1k}^*, \mu_{2k}^*, \ldots, \mu_{sk}^*)$ and efficiency score(θ_{kk}^*).

$$\begin{aligned} &\theta_{kk}^* = \max_{\mu, \nu} \sum_{r=1}^{s} \mu_{rk} y_{rk} \\ &\text{subject to} \\ &\sum_{r=1}^{s} \mu_{rk} y_{rj} - \sum_{i=1}^{m} \nu_{ik} x_{ij} \leq 0 \\ &\sum_{i=1}^{m} \nu_{ik} x_{ik} = 1 \\ &u_{rk}, \nu_{ik} \geq 0. \end{aligned} \tag{3.9}$$

Then $\theta_{kk}^* = \sum_{r=1}^{s} u_{rk}^* y_{rk}$ is referred to as the CCR-efficiency or simple efficiency of bank k. Note here that we need to run the above model for each bank individually. As a result, there are n sets of input and output weights for the n banks. Given the results of the first stage, the weights used by the bank can be utilised for calculating the peer-rated efficiency for each of the other banks. The peer-evaluation (cross-efficiency) score, θ_{kj}^*, indicating the efficiency score for bank j using the weighting scheme of bank k, can be obtained as

$$\theta_{kj}^* = \frac{\sum_{r=1}^{s} \mu_{rk}^* y_{rj}}{\sum_{i=1}^{m} \nu_{ik}^* x_{ij}}.$$

Note here that for each bank has $(n-1)$ cross-efficiencies plus one CCR-efficiency.

Since CCR model may have multiple optimal solutions, this non-uniqueness could potentially hamper the use of cross-efficiency (Baker and Talluri 1997). To resolve this problem, Sexton et al. (1986) introduced a secondary goal to avoid the arbitrariness of cross-efficiency. One of the most commonly used secondary goals is the so-called aggressive formulation for cross-efficiency evaluation suggested by Doyle and Green (1994). In this approach, an attempt is made to minimise the efficiencies of other DMUs while preserving the efficiency of the bank under evaluation. The aggressive formulation suggested by Doyle and Green (1994), which aimed at minimising the secondary goal C_k, is given below:

$$\begin{aligned} & C_k = \min \sum_{r=1}^{s} \left(\mu_{rk} \sum_{j=1, j \neq k}^{n} y_{rj} \right) \\ & \text{subject to} \\ & \sum_{i=1}^{m} \left(\nu_{ik} \sum_{j=1, j \neq k}^{n} x_{ij} \right) = 1 \\ & \sum_{r=1}^{s} \mu_{rk} y_{rk} - \theta_{kk}^{*} \sum_{i=1}^{m} \nu_{ik} x_{ik} = 0 \\ & \sum_{r=1}^{s} \mu_{rk} y_{rj} - \sum_{i=1}^{m} \nu_{ik} x_{ij} \leq 0, \qquad j = 1, \ldots, n; j \neq k \\ & \mu_{rk}, \nu_{ik} \geq 0. \end{aligned} \tag{3.10}$$

The benevolent formulation can be obtained by maximising the secondary goal C_k.

Once the weighting scheme and the cross-efficiencies have been found, we construct a matrix called the 'cross-efficiencies matrix'. Such a matrix for six banks is shown as

DEA cross-efficiencies matrix

	Bank receiving weights						
Bank	1	2	3	4	5	6	Average appraisal of peers
1	θ_{11}^*	θ_{12}^*	θ_{13}^*	θ_{14}^*	θ_{15}^*	θ_{16}^*	A_1
2	θ_{21}^*	θ_{22}^*	θ_{23}^*	θ_{24}^*	θ_{25}^*	θ_{26}^*	A_2
3	θ_{31}^*	θ_{32}^*	θ_{33}^*	θ_{34}^*	θ_{35}^*	θ_{36}^*	A_3
4	θ_{41}^*	θ_{42}^*	θ_{43}^*	θ_{44}^*	θ_{45}^*	θ_{46}^*	A_4
5	θ_{51}^*	θ_{52}^*	θ_{53}^*	θ_{54}^*	θ_{55}^*	θ_{56}^*	A_5
6	θ_{61}^*	θ_{62}^*	θ_{63}^*	θ_{64}^*	θ_{65}^*	θ_{66}^*	A_6
	e_1	e_2	e_3	e_4	e_5	e_6	
	Average appraisal by peers						

In the cross-efficiency matrix, all banks are bounded by $0 \leq \theta_{kj}^* \leq 1$, and the banks in the diagonal θ_{kk}^* depict the CCR-efficiency score as $\theta_{kk}^* = 1$ for efficient banks and $\theta_{kk}^* < 1$ for inefficient banks. Further, e_k is the mean cross-efficiency of the bank k and is calculated in the following way:

$$e_k = \frac{1}{(n-1)} \sum_{j \neq k} \theta_{kj}^*$$

We can use e_k for ranking of banks in the sample. In order to rank the banks, we can simply assign the bank with the highest score a rank of one and the bank with the lowest score a rank of n. A bank is categorised as being overall efficient when it has high average cross-efficiencies; conversely, when it has lower values, it is known as 'false standard' efficient bank.

Furthermore, Doyle and Green (1994) developed the concept of a 'maverick index', which is defined as below:

$$M_k = \left(\theta^*_{kk} - e_k\right)/e_k.$$

The higher the value of M_k, the more the bank can be considered a maverick. Mavericks are those banks that enjoy the greatest relative increment when shifting from peer-appraisal to self-appraisal. If a bank is classified as a maverick, what we are implying is that this bank operates 'far' from the rest of the banks. A maverick bank has high simple efficiency score and low peer efficiency score. Generally, a maverick bank is CCR-efficient but fails to appear in the reference sets of inefficient banks. Alternatively, maverick bank has a very low peer count.

3.2.2.3 Non-discretionary Input and Output Variables Models

Banker and Morey (1986) introduced the DEA models that can be used to model non-discretionary (or uncontrollable) input and output variables. These variables are exogenously fixed variables and not under the control of bank but have significant effect on their performance (Zhu 2003). The models incorporating non-discretionary variables are unique in the sense that (i) the radial contraction (θ) in the inputs, or radial expansion (ϕ) in the outputs, cannot be applied to the non-discretionary variables, and (ii) it eliminates the slacks for non-discretionary inputs and outputs from the objective function since the management has no control over these variables so not interested in their slacks.

To compute the relative efficiency of a bank, let us suppose that the input and output variables may each be partitioned into subsets of discretionary (D) and non-discretionary (ND) variables. Thus,

$$i = \{1, \ldots, m\} = i_D \cup i_{ND} \text{ with } i_D \cap i_{ND} = \varnothing$$
$$\text{and } r = \{1, \ldots, s\} = r_D \cup r_{ND} \text{ with } r_D \cap r_{ND} = \varnothing$$

where i_D, r_D and i_{ND}, r_{ND} refer to discretionary (D) and non-discretionary (ND) input and output variables, respectively, and $\varnothing$ is empty set. The linear programming problems of primal (multiplier) and dual (envelopment) form of the models incorporating non-discretionary input and output variables are defined as follows:

Frontier type↓	Non-discretionary inputs	Non-discretionary outputs
Multiplier form	$\max_{\mu,\nu} \sum_{r=1}^{s}\mu_r y_{ro} - \sum_{i=1, i\in ND}^{m} \nu_i x_{io}$ subject to $\sum_{r=1}^{s}\mu_r y_{rj} - \sum_{i\in ND}\nu_i x_{ij} - \sum_{i\in D}\nu_i x_{ij} \leq 0$ $\sum_{i\in D}\nu_i x_{io} = 1$ $\nu_i \geq \varepsilon,\ i\in D$ $\nu_i \geq 0,\ i\in ND$ $\mu_r \geq \varepsilon$	$\min_{\mu,\nu} \sum_{i=1}^{m}\nu_i x_{io} - \sum_{r=1, r\in ND}^{s} \mu_r y_{ro}$ subject to $\sum_{i=1}^{m}\nu_i x_{ij} - \sum_{r\in ND}\mu_r y_{rj} - \sum_{r\in D}\mu_r y_{rj} \geq 0$ $\sum_{r\in D}\mu_r y_{ro} = 1$ $\nu_i \geq \varepsilon$ $\mu_r \geq \varepsilon,\ i\in D$ $\mu_r \geq 0,\ i\in ND$
Envelopment form	$\min_{\lambda,s^-,s^+} \theta_o - \varepsilon\left(\sum_{i=1, i\in D}^{m} s_i^- + \sum_{r=1}^{s} s_r^+\right)$ subject to $\sum_{j=1}^{n}\lambda_j x_{ij} + s_i^- = \theta_o x_{io},\ i\in D$ $\sum_{j=1}^{n}\lambda_j x_{ij} + s_i^- = x_{io},\ i\in ND$ $\sum_{j=1}^{n}\lambda_j y_{rj} - s_r^+ = y_{ro}$ $\lambda_j, s_i^-, s_r^+ \geq 0$	$\max_{\lambda,s^-,s^+} \phi_o + \varepsilon\left(\sum_{i=1}^{m} s_i^- + \sum_{r=1, r\in D}^{s} s_r^+\right)$ subject to $\sum_{j=1}^{n}\lambda_j x_{ij} + s_i^- = x_{io}$ $\sum_{j=1}^{n}\lambda_j y_{rj} - s_r^+ = \phi_o y_{ro},\ r\in D$ $\sum_{j=1}^{n}\lambda_j y_{rj} - s_r^+ = y_{ro},\ r\in ND$ $\lambda_j, s_i^-, s_r^+ \geq 0$

Note here that Banker and Morey formulation can also be expressed as a VRS model by adding the constraint $\sum_{j=1}^{n} \lambda_j = 1$.

3.2.2.4 Assurance Region Models

The most significant extension of DEA is the concept of assurance region (AR) models or restricted multiplier models as developed by Thompson et al. (1990), which imposes restrictions (constraints) on weights to control how much a bank can freely use the weights to become efficient. As noted, the only restriction on the multiplier DEA models is the positivity of the multipliers imposed by ε, i.e. $\varepsilon > 0$. This flexibility is often advantageous in application of DEA methodology. However, in some situations, it can assign unreasonably low or excessively high values to the multipliers in an attempt to drive the efficiency rating for a particular bank as high as possible (Cooper et al. 2004). In the restricted multiplier models, lower and upper bounds can be established on a weight ratio of a given pair of inputs or outputs to assure that no bank can freely choose to become efficient through using excessive outputs or insufficient inputs (Ozcan 2008). Thus, the banks will reassess their input usage and output production within given limits that are equivalent to policy or managerial restrictions. In order to impose the restrictions on input weights, the additional inequality constraints of the following form need to be incorporated into the multiplier DEA models:

$$\alpha_i \leq \frac{\nu_i}{\nu_{io}} \leq \beta_i \qquad i = 1, \ldots, m. \tag{3.11}$$

The restrictions to outputs weights can be imposed using the following formula:

$$\delta_r \leq \frac{\mu_r}{\mu_{ro}} \leq \gamma_r \qquad r = 1, \ldots, s. \tag{3.12}$$

Here, ν_{io} and μ_{ro} represent multipliers which serve as 'numeraires' in establishing the upper and lower bounds represented here by α_i, β_i and by δ_r, γ_r for the multipliers associated with inputs and outputs where $\alpha_{io} = \beta_{io} = \delta_{ro} = \gamma_{ro} = 1$.

The constraints (3.11) and (3.12) are called assurance regions of Type-I constraints as developed by Thompson et al. (1986). Each of these restrictions link either only input or only output weights. However, Thompson et al. (1990) defined a more precise form of AR models called AR Type-II. AR Type-II models are typically used where some relationship between the output and input concerned is to be reflected (Thanassoulis et al. 1995). Such a model imposes the restriction of a type $\gamma_i \nu_i \geq u_r$. The multiplier form of DEA model is, therefore, modified to include AR constraints and resulting linear programming problem is as follows:

	Model orientation	
Frontier type↓	Input-oriented	Output-oriented
Multiplier form	$\max_{\mu,\nu} \sum_{r=1}^{s} \mu_r y_{ro} + \mu$ subject to $\sum_{r=1}^{s} \mu_r y_{rj} - \sum_{i=1}^{m} \nu_i x_{ij} + \mu \leq 0$ $\sum_{i=1}^{m} \nu_i x_{io} = 1$ $\alpha_i \leq \frac{v_i}{v_{io}} \leq \beta_i$ $\delta_r \leq \frac{\mu_r}{\mu_{ro}} \leq \gamma_r$ $\gamma_i \nu_i \geq u_r$ $\mu_r, \nu_i \geq 0(\varepsilon)$	$\min_{\mu,\nu} \sum_{i=1}^{m} \nu_i x_{io} + \nu$ subject to $\sum_{i=1}^{m} \nu_i x_{ij} - \sum_{r=1}^{s} \mu_r y_{rj} + \nu \leq 0$ $\sum_{r=1}^{s} \mu_r y_{ro} = 1$ $\alpha_i \leq \frac{v_i}{v_{io}} \leq \beta_i$ $\delta_r \leq \frac{\mu_r}{\mu_{ro}} \leq \gamma_r$ $\gamma_i \nu_i \geq u_r$ $\mu_r, \nu_i \geq 0(\varepsilon)$

The generality of these AR constraints provides flexibility in use. Prices, utils and other measures may be accommodated and so can mixtures of such concepts. Moreover, one can first examine provisional solutions that appear to be reasonably satisfactory to decision makers who cannot state the values for their preferences in an a priori manner.

3.2.3 Allocation DEA Models

Allocation DEA models are used to estimate the cost, revenue and profit frontiers to obtain the respective efficiency scores corresponding to three behavioural goal to be pursued by the banks, i.e. cost minimisation, revenue maximisation and profit maximisation. It determines the efficiency scores for individual banks when information on prices of either inputs or outputs or both is given. In particular, allocation models are classified as *cost efficiency* DEA models, *revenue efficiency* DEA models and *profit efficiency* DEA models.

3.2.3.1 Cost Efficiency DEA Models

Cost efficiency DEA models compute the cost efficiency measure for individual banks when information for prices of inputs is given. Let us explain the concept of cost efficiency as used in the frontier efficiency methodological framework. *Cost efficiency* (CE) measure provides how close a bank's cost is to what a best practice bank's cost would be for producing the same bundle of outputs (Weill 2004). Measurement of cost efficiency requires the specification of an objective function and information on market prices of inputs. If the objective of the production unit is that of cost minimisation, then a measure of cost efficiency is provided by the ratio of minimum cost to observed cost (Lovell 1993). A methodological framework to measure cost efficiency of a bank dates back to the seminal work of Farrell (1957). In Farrell's framework, input-oriented technical efficiency is just one component of cost efficiency, and in order to be cost efficient, a bank must first be technically efficient. However, another component of cost efficiency is input-oriented allocative efficiency (AE), which reflects the ability of the bank to choose the inputs in optimal proportions, given their respective prices. AE describes whether the bank is using the right mix of inputs in light of the relative price of each input. It should be noted that allocative efficiency is interpreted as a residual component of the cost efficiency of the bank and obtained from the ratio of cost and technical efficiency scores. It is significant to note that a measure of cost efficiency corresponds to the behavioural goal of the bank and a measure of technical efficiency ignores such goal.

An illustration of these efficiency measures as well as the way they are computed is given in Fig. 3.5.

In Fig. 3.5, it is assumed that the bank uses two inputs, x_1 and x_2, to produce output y. The bank's production frontier $y = f(x_1, x_2)$ is characterised by constant returns-to-scale, so that $1 = f(x_1/y, x_2/y)$, and the frontier is depicted by the efficient unit isoquant Y_oY_o. A bank is said to be technically efficient if it is operating on Y_oY_o. However, technical inefficiency relates to an individual bank's failure to produce on Y_oY_o. Hence, Bank P in the figure is technically inefficient. Thus, for Bank P, the technical inefficiency can be represented by the distance QP. As already noted, a measure of TE is the ratio of the minimum possible inputs of the bank to the bank's observed inputs. Accordingly, the level of TE for Bank P is defined by the ratio OQ/OP. It measures the proportion of inputs actually necessary to produce output. Allocative inefficiencies result from choosing the wrong input combinations given input prices. Now suppose that CC′ represents the ratio of input prices so that cost minimisation point is Q′. Since the cost at point R is same as the cost at Q′, we measure the AE of the bank as OR/OQ, where the distance RQ is the reduction

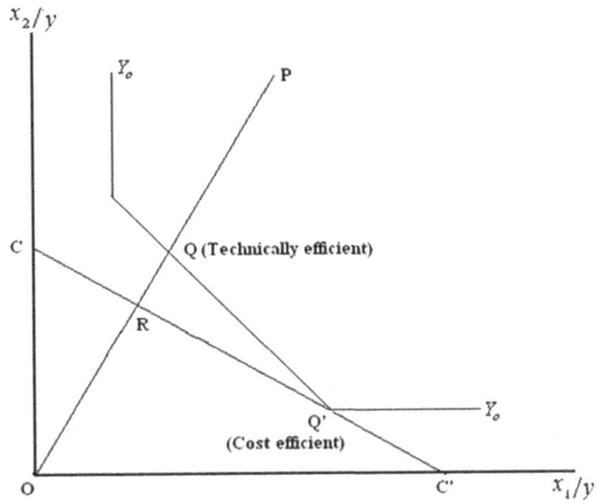

Fig. 3.5 Measurement of cost efficiency (*Source*: Authors' elaboration)

in production costs which could occur if production occurs at Q′. Finally, the cost efficiency of the bank is defined as OR/OP, which can be considered a composite measure efficiency that includes both technical and allocative efficiencies. In fact, the relationship between CE, TE and AE is expressed as

$$\begin{array}{ccccc} \text{CE} & = & \text{TE} & \times & \text{AE} \\ (\text{OR}/\text{OP}) & = & (\text{OQ}/\text{OP}) & \times & (\text{OR}/\text{OQ}). \end{array}$$

The frontier-based measures of cost efficiency always range between 0 and 1.

The banking efficiency literature spells two DEA models for estimating cost efficiency: (i) traditional cost efficiency (CE Type-I) model as proposed by Färe et al. (1985) and (ii) new cost efficiency (CE Type-II) model as suggested by Tone (2002b). It has been pointed out by Tone (2002b) that the traditional cost efficiency model does not take account of the fact that costs can obviously be reduced by reducing the input factor prices. Therefore, the difference between traditional and new cost efficiency measures is that the former use the original input values in the constraints while the latter use the cost values of inputs in the constraints. The linear programming problems for the envelopment form of CE Type-I and Type-II models are given as below:

In the above models, p_i^o is the unit price of ith input for bank 'o', $\widetilde{x}_{io}$ is the (unknown) quantity of ith input for bank 'o' that minimises the cost, $\widetilde{x}^*_{io}$ is the optimal value of $\widetilde{x}_{io}$, x_{ij} is the actual value of the ith input for jth bank, $\overline{\widetilde{x}}_{io}$ is the (unknown) cost of input i for bank'o', $\overline{\widetilde{x}}^*_{io}$ is optimal value of $\overline{\widetilde{x}}_{io}$ and $\overline{x}_{ij} = p_{ij}$ x_{ij} is the actual cost of input i for jth bank. In the CE Type-I model, the unit cost for the bank 'o' to be fixed at p^o and the cost-minimising input-bundle $\widetilde{x}^* = \left(x^*_{1o}, x^*_{2o}, \ldots, x^*_{mo}\right)$ that produces the output y_{ro} is to be found. However, in CE Type-II model, we explicitly find the optimal cost of input i for bank 'o' (i.e. $\overline{\widetilde{x}}^*_{io}$) that produces output y_{ro} independently of the bank's current unit price p^o.

Cost efficiency DEA models

Objective	CE Type-I	CE Type-II
Cost minimisation	$\min_{\lambda,\widetilde{x}} \sum_{i=1}^{m} p_i^o \widetilde{x}_{io}$ subject to $\sum_{j=1}^{n} \lambda_j x_{ij} \le \widetilde{x}_{io}, \quad i = 1, \ldots, m$; $\sum_{j=1}^{n} \lambda_j y_{rj} \ge y_{ro}, \quad r = 1, \ldots, s$; $\lambda_j, \widetilde{x}_{io} \ge 0, \quad j = 1, \ldots, n$. Add $\sum_{j=1}^{n} \lambda_j = 1$ for VRS	$\min_{\lambda,\overline{x}} \sum_{i=1}^{m} \widetilde{\overline{x}}_{io}$ subject to $\sum_{j=1}^{n} \lambda_j \overline{x}_{ij} \le \widetilde{\overline{x}}_{io} \quad i = 1, \ldots, m$; $\sum_{j=1}^{n} \lambda_j y_{rj} \ge y_{ro} \quad r = 1, \ldots, s$; $\lambda_j, \widetilde{\overline{x}}_{io} \ge 0, \quad j = 1, \ldots, n$. Add $\sum_{j=1}^{n} \lambda_j = 1$ for VRS
Cost efficiency	$CE_o = \frac{\text{Minimum cost}}{\text{Actual cost}} = \frac{\sum_{i=1}^{m} p_i^o \widetilde{x}^*_{io}}{\sum_{i=1}^{m} p_i^o x_{io}}$	$CE_o = \frac{\text{Minimum cost}}{\text{Actual cost}} = \frac{\sum_{i=1}^{m} \widetilde{\overline{x}}^*_{io}}{\sum_{i=1}^{m} \overline{x}_{io}}$

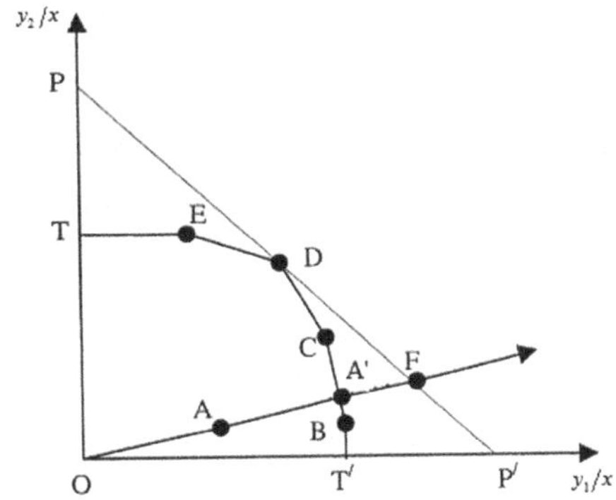

Fig. 3.6 Measurement of revenue efficiency (*Source*: Authors' elaboration)

3.2.3.2 Revenue Efficiency DEA Models

Revenue efficiency measures the change in a bank's revenue adjusted for a random error, relative to the estimated revenue obtained from producing an output bundle as efficiently as the *best practice* bank (Berger and Mester 1997). If the objective of the bank is that of revenue maximisation, then a measure of revenue efficiency is provided by the ratio of actual revenue to maximum or potential revenue. Any difference between the actual and potential revenue is attributable to either because of output-oriented technical inefficiency (producing too few outputs of one or more outputs given the input quantities) or output-oriented allocative inefficiency (producing nonoptimal combination of outputs given their prices).

The measurement of revenue efficiency in the frontier methodological framework is depicted graphically in Fig. 3.6. It is assumed that the bank produces two outputs, y_1 and y_2, using the input x. The production possibility curve is represented by TT′. From the output-oriented framework, a bank is said to technically efficient if it is operating on TT′. Therefore, banks B, C, D and E are output-oriented technically efficient, while Bank A lies below the frontier and is inefficient. In other words, the bank located at point A has a potential to increase the production levels of both outputs to point A′ on the production possibility frontier. Thus, for Bank A, the output-oriented technical inefficiency can be represented by the distance AA′. A measure of output-oriented TE is the ratio of the actual output to maximum outputs of the bank. Accordingly, the level of output-oriented TE for Bank A is defined by the ratio OA/OA′. Now suppose that PP′ represents the iso-revenue line, Bank D is deemed to be revenue efficient. Since the revenue at point F is the same as the cost at D, we measure the output-oriented AE of the bank as OA′/OF, where the distance A′F is the increase in revenue which could occur if production occurs at A′. Finally, the revenue efficiency of the bank is defined as OA/OF, which can be considered a composite measure efficiency that includes both output-oriented technical and allocative efficiencies. Further, the distance AF represents revenue inefficiency for Bank A. In fact, the relationship between RE, TE and AE is expressed as

$$\begin{aligned} \text{RE} \quad &= \quad \text{TE} \quad \times \quad \text{AE} \\ (\text{OA}/\text{OF}) &= \left(\text{OA}/\text{OA}'\right) \times \left(\text{OA}'/\text{OF}\right). \end{aligned}$$

Like cost efficiency models, we have two revenue efficiency models: (i) traditional revenue efficiency (RE Type-I) model (ii) and new revenue efficiency (RE Type-II) model. The difference between these revenue efficiency models is that Type-I model uses the original outputs values in constraints, while Type-II model uses total revenue values of outputs in the constraints. The linear programming problems for traditional and new revenue efficiency models are given as follows:

In the above models, q_r^o is the unit price of rth output for bank 'o', $\tilde{y}_{ro}$ is the (unknown) quantity of rth output for bank 'o' that maximises the revenue, $\tilde{y}^*_{ro}$ is the optimal value of $\tilde{y}_{ro}$, y_{rj} is the actual value of the rth output for jth bank, $\tilde{\overline{y}}_{ro}$ is the (unknown) revenue earned by bank 'o' from output r , $\tilde{\overline{y}}^*_{ro}$ is optimal value of $\tilde{\overline{y}}_{ro}$ and $\overline{y}_{rj} = q_{rj}y_{rj}$ is the actual revenue from output r for jth bank. In the RE Type-I model, the unit price for the bank 'o' to be fixed at q^o and the revenue-maximising output-bundle is to be found. However, in RE Type-II model, we explicitly find the optimal revenue from output r for bank 'o' (i.e. $\tilde{\overline{y}}^*_{ro}$) independently of the bank's current unit price q^o.

3.2.3.3 Profit Efficiency DEA Models

Profit efficiency is the more inclusive concept – taking account of both cost and revenue performance – given that managers have some control over both revenues and costs. In empirical analyses, researchers favour profit efficiency ex ante than cost efficiency because the latter neglects operating revenues and loan losses. In the frontier efficiency measurement framework, a measure of profit efficiency assesses how close a bank comes to generating the maximum possible profit given the levels of input and output prices (quantities) and other exogenous conditions. In other words, profit efficiency improvements occur when a bank moves closer to the profit of a best practice bank under the given conditions. It is provided by the ratio of actual profit to maximum profit. The idea of measuring profit efficiency is conceptualised in Fig. 3.7.

In the figure, the curve OQ shows the production frontier. The actual input–output combination of the Bank A is (x_A,y_A) shown by the point A. Therefore, the profit earned by Bank A is $\pi = q_Ay_A - p_Ax_A$. The set of all (x,y) through A which yield normalised profit π is shown by the line CD. The objective of the Bank A is to reach highest isoprofit line parallel to CD that can be attained at any point on or below the curve OQ. The highest such point on isoprofit line is reached at the point B representing the tangency of the isoprofit line EF with the production frontier. Let the optimal input–output bundle for Bank B is (x^*,y^*). The intercept of this line OE equals the maximum normalised profit π^*. Bank A achieves maximum profit when it is projected on the isoprofit curve EF (say at A*), where maximum profits equals that of Bank B, i.e. $\pi^* = q_Ay_A^* - p_Ax_A^* = q_By_B - p_Bx_B$. Thus, profit efficiency for Bank A would be given by the ratio of actual to maximum profits, i.e. $PE_A = \pi/\pi^*$. Regarding the decomposition of profit efficiency, Kumbhakar and Lovell (2000) states:

Revenue efficiency DEA models

Objective	Revenue type-I	Revenue type-II
Revenue maximisation	$\max_{\lambda,\tilde{y}} \sum_{r=1}^{s} q_r^o \tilde{y}_{ro}$ subject to $\sum_{j=1}^{n} \lambda_j x_{ij} \leq x_{io}, \quad i = 1, \ldots, m$ $\sum_{j=1}^{n} \lambda_j y_{rj} \geq \tilde{y}_{ro}, \quad r = 1, \ldots, s$ $\lambda_j, \tilde{y}_{ro} \geq 0, \quad j = 1, \ldots, n$ Add $\sum_{j=1}^{n} \lambda_j = 1$ for VRS	$\max_{\lambda,\tilde{\bar{y}}} \sum_{r=1}^{s} \tilde{\bar{y}}_{ro}$ subject to $\sum_{j=1}^{n} \lambda_j x_{ij} \leq x_{io} \quad i = 1, \ldots, m$ $\sum_{j=1}^{n} \lambda_j \bar{y}_{rj} \geq \tilde{\bar{y}}_{ro} \quad r = 1, \ldots, s$ $\lambda_j, \tilde{\bar{y}}_{ro} \geq 0, \quad j = 1, \ldots, n$ Add $\sum_{j=1}^{n} \lambda_j = 1$ for VRS
Revenue efficiency	$RE_o = \frac{\text{Actual revenue}}{\text{Maximum revenue}} = \frac{\sum_{r=1}^{s} q_r y_{ro}}{\sum_{r=1}^{s} q_r^o \tilde{y}_{ro}^*}$	$RE_o = \frac{\text{Actual revenue}}{\text{Maximum revenue}} = \frac{\sum_{r=1}^{s} \bar{y}_{ro}}{\sum_{r=1}^{s} \tilde{\bar{y}}_{ro}^*}$

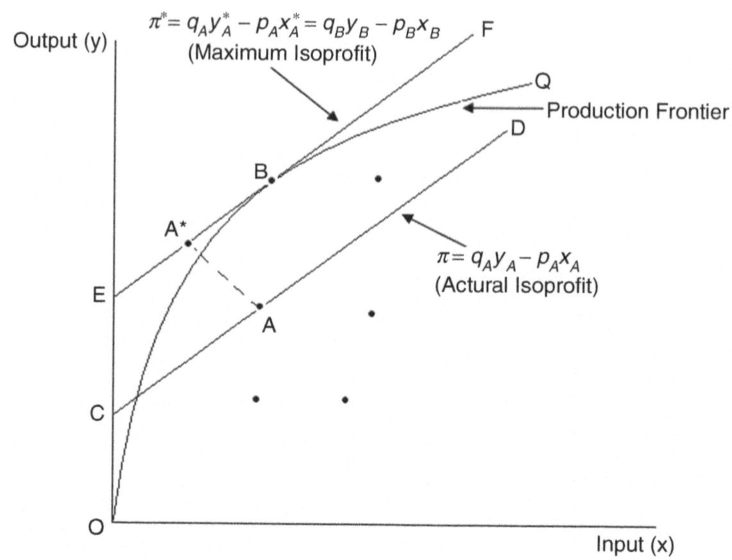

Fig. 3.7 Measurement of profit efficiency (*Source*: Authors' elaboration)

A decomposition of profit efficiency into its constituent parts is somewhat arbitrary, depending on whether an input-oriented or an output-oriented measure of technical efficiency is used.

In the contemporary literature on banking efficiency, two measures of profit efficiency, namely, standard profit efficiency and alternative profit efficiency, have been used by the researchers (see Berger et al. 1993b, Berger and Mester 1997, Cooper et al. 2007, Maudos and Pastor 2003). However, a consensus on the most adequate one was difficult to be achieved. These two measures differ whether or not we consider the existence of market power in the setting of output prices. The estimation of standard profit efficiency (SPE) is based on the assumptions that (i) banks maximise the profits in perfectly competitive input and output markets, and (ii) the prices of outputs and inputs are determined exogenously. Thus, the standard profit function is specified in terms of input and output prices, i.e. $\pi = f(p,q)$. In fact, SPE measures how close a bank is to producing the maximum possible profit given a particular level of input and output prices.

In contrast, the alternative profit efficiency (APE) developed by Humphrey and Pulley (1997) assumes the existence of imperfect competition or banks exercise a form of market power in choosing output prices. However, this market power is limited to output markets and banks remain competitive purchasers of inputs. Thus, alternative profit function is defined in terms of input prices and output quantities, i.e. $\pi = f(p,y)$. In fact, APE measures how close a bank comes to earning maximum profits, given its output levels rather than its market prices. DeYoung and Hassan (1998) listed two advantages of specifying profits as a function of output quantities rather than output prices: (i) it avoids having to measure output prices, which are not available for transactions services and fee-based outputs and can only be imperfectly constructed for loan outputs, and (ii) output quantities tend to vary across banks to a greater degree than do output prices, and as a result explain a larger portion of the variation in profits in regression analysis.

Berger and Mester (1997) noted that alternative profit frontier is preferred over the standard profit frontier when one or more of the following conditions hold: (i) there are substantial unmeasured differences in the quality of banking services; (ii) outputs are not completely variable, so that a bank cannot achieve every output scale and product mix; (iii) output markets are not perfectly competitive, so that banks have some market power over the prices they charge; and (iv) output prices are not accurately measured, so they do not provide accurate guides to opportunities to earn revenues and profits in the standard profit function.

The linear programming problems for (i) traditional standard profit efficiency (SPE Type-I) model as proposed by Färe et al. (1997), (ii) new standard profit efficiency (SPE Type-II)[4] model as suggested by Cooper et al. (2007) and (iii) the alternative profit efficiency (APE) model as developed by Maudos and Pastor (2003) are given below:

The profit efficiency scores so obtained are bounded above and have a maximum value of 1. It ranges over $(-\infty, 1)$ and equals 1 for a best practice bank within the observed data. Profit efficiency can be negative since banks can throw away more than 100 % of their potential profits.

3.3 Panel Data DEA Models

The above discussion on DEA models focused on the efficiency measurement in case of cross-section data setting. However, in general, using cross-section data DEA studies provide a snapshot of relative efficiency performance of banks for a particular year of study. Using longitudinal data or panel data, one can detect efficiency trends of banks over time and track the performance of each bank through a sequence of time periods. Two most common approaches in the DEA literature to capture the variations in efficiency over time in the panel data setting are (i) window analysis and (ii) Malmquist productivity index. This section outlines the distinctive features of these approaches.

3.3.1 Window Analysis

Charnes et al. (1985) developed a method, firstly suggested by Klopp (1985), known as window analysis, which could be used for a panel data comprising the

---

[4] As with cost and revenue efficiency, the difference between SPE Type-I and Type-II is that Type-I model is traditional and commonly uses the original inputs/outputs values in constraints, while Type-II models use cost/revenue values of inputs/outputs in constraints.

Profit efficiency DEA models

Objective	SPE type-I	SPE type-II	APE
Profit maximisation	$\max\limits_{\lambda,\tilde{x},\tilde{y}} \sum_{r=1}^{s} q_r^o \tilde{y}_{ro} - \sum_{i=1}^{m} p_i^o \tilde{x}_{io}$ subject to $\sum_{j=1}^{n} \lambda_j x_{ij} \leq \tilde{x}_{io}, \quad i = 1, \ldots, m$ $\sum_{j=1}^{n} \lambda_j y_{rj} \geq \tilde{y}_{ro}, \quad r = 1, \ldots, s$ $x_{io} \geq \tilde{x}_{io}$ $y_{ro} \leq \tilde{y}_{ro}$ $\lambda_j \geq 0, \quad j = 1, \ldots, n$	$\max\limits_{\lambda,\tilde{\bar{x}},\tilde{\bar{y}}} \sum_{r=1}^{s} \tilde{\bar{y}}_{ro} - \sum_{i=1}^{m} \tilde{\bar{x}}_{io}$ subject to $\sum_{j=1}^{n} \lambda_j \bar{x}_{ij} \leq \tilde{\bar{x}}_{io} \quad i = 1, \ldots, m$ $\sum_{j=1}^{n} \lambda_j \bar{y}_{rj} \geq \tilde{\bar{y}}_{ro} \quad r = 1, \ldots, s$ $\bar{x}_{io} \geq \tilde{\bar{x}}_{io}$ $\bar{y}_{ro} \leq \tilde{\bar{y}}_{ro}$ $\lambda_j \geq 0, \quad j = 1, \ldots, n$	$\max\limits_{\lambda,\tilde{x},\tilde{\bar{y}}} \sum_{r=1}^{s} \tilde{\bar{y}}_{ro} - \sum_{i=1}^{m} p_i^o \tilde{x}_{io}$ subject to $\sum_{j=1}^{n} \lambda_j x_{ij} \leq \tilde{x}_{io}, \quad i = 1, \ldots, m$ $\sum_{j=1}^{n} \lambda_j y_{rj} \geq y_{ro}, \quad r = 1, \ldots, s$ $\sum_{j=1}^{n} \lambda_j \bar{y}_{rj} \geq \tilde{\bar{y}}_{ro}$ $x_{io} \geq \tilde{x}_{io}$ $\bar{y}_{ro} \leq \tilde{\bar{y}}_{ro}$ $\lambda_j \geq 0, \quad j = 1, \ldots, n$
Profit efficiency	$SPE_o = \dfrac{\sum_{r=1}^{s} q_r y_{ro} - \sum_{i=1}^{m} p_i x_{io}}{\sum_{r=1}^{s} q_r \tilde{y}^*_{ro} - \sum_{i=1}^{m} p_i \tilde{x}^*_{io}}$	$SPE_o = \dfrac{\sum_{r=1}^{s} \bar{y}_{ro} - \sum_{i=1}^{m} \bar{x}_{io}}{\sum_{r=1}^{s} \tilde{\bar{y}}^*_{ro} - \sum_{i=1}^{m} \tilde{\bar{x}}^*_{io}}$	$APE_o = \dfrac{\sum_{r=1}^{s} q_r y_{ro} - \sum_{i=1}^{m} p_i x_{io}}{\sum_{r=1}^{s} \tilde{\bar{y}}^*_{ro} - \sum_{i=1}^{m} p_i \tilde{x}^*_{io}}$

observations for various banks over a given period of time. In a panel data setting, window analysis performs DEA over time by using a moving average analogue, where a bank in each different period is treated as if it is a 'different' bank. Specifically, a bank's performance in a particular period is contrasted with its performance in other periods in addition to the performance of the other banks.

The intrinsic advantages of window analysis are as follows. First, when the cross-section observations are small, most of them might be used in the construction of the frontier, reducing the discriminatory power of DEA (Coelli et al. 2005). Thus, the application of DEA to small samples can lead to the 'self-identifiers' problem (Gaganis and Pasiouras 2009). The window analysis is often suggested as a solution to this problem. The windows are used with long panel data set in order to have a large number of sequential. One purpose of window analysis is to relieve degrees of freedom pressure when $m + s$ (i.e. sum of inputs and outputs) is large relative to n (i.e. number of banks in a cross-section). As such, it provides a compromise between running DEA once on one large $n \times T$ pooled panel and running DEA T times on T small cross sections (Fried et al. 2008). Second, window analysis tracks dynamic efficiency trends through successive overlapping windows and, thus, allows for monitoring the performance over time. This may help the managers to take appropriate actions to augment the performance of the bank under consideration. Third, window analysis is a commonly used sensitivity analysis in DEA. It allows for an assessment of the stability of relative efficiency scores over time (Avkiran 2006). The sensitivity in question is to that of external factors that may distort figures for a particular year and a varying group of reference units.

Suppose, there are observations for n different banks over T periods, it is treated as if there are $n \times T$ different banks. In window analysis, the data set, with $n \times T$ observations, is divided into a series of overlapping periods or windows, each of width w ($w < T$), and thus having $n \times w$ banks. Hence, the first window has $n \times w$ banks from period $1,2,\ldots,w$, the second one has $n \times w$ banks for period $(2, 3, \ldots, w, w + 1)$, and so on, and the last window consists of $n \times w$ banks for period $T-w+1,\ldots,T$. In all, for a given set of $n \times T$ observations, there will be $T - w + 1$ separate windows with a size of $n \times w$. These windows are analysed separately. Then a moving average for each observation of banks is calculated by taking average of its scores from each window that attends. There would be w efficiency scores for each observation and the average of these scores is used as the efficiency measurements for the corresponding observation (Ozdincer and Ozyildirim 2008).

Consider a hypothetical panel data set of five banks ($n = 5$) over six ($T = 6$) yearly periods. To perform the analysis using a 3-year ($w = 3$) window, we proceed as follows. Each bank is represented as if it is a different bank for each of the three successive years in the first window (Year 1, Year 2 and Year 3), and an analysis of the 15 ($nw = 5 \times 3$) banks is performed by using DEA model to obtain sharper and more realistic efficiency estimates. The window is then shifted one period, and an analysis is performed on the second 3-year set (Year 2, Year 3 and Year 4) of the five banks. The process continues in this manner, shifting the window forward one period each time and concluding with a final (fourth) analysis of five banks for the last 3 years (Year 4, Year 5 and Year 6). Thus, one performs $T - w + 1$ separate

Table 3.1 Format of DEA window analysis

Bank	Period window	Year 1	Year 2	Year 3	Year 4	Year 5	Year 6
Bank 1	Window 1	$\theta^1_{1,1}$	$\theta^1_{1,2}$	$\theta^1_{1,3}$			
	Window 2		$\theta^1_{2,2}$	$\theta^1_{2,3}$	$\theta^1_{2,4}$		
	Window 3			$\theta^1_{3,3}$	$\theta^1_{3,4}$	$\theta^1_{3,5}$	
	Window 4				$\theta^1_{4,4}$	$\theta^1_{4,5}$	$\theta^1_{4,6}$
Bank 2	Window 1	$\theta^2_{1,1}$	$\theta^2_{1,2}$	$\theta^2_{1,3}$			
	Window 2		$\theta^2_{2,2}$	$\theta^2_{2,3}$	$\theta^2_{2,4}$		
	Window 3			$\theta^2_{3,3}$	$\theta^2_{3,4}$	$\theta^2_{3,5}$	
	Window 4				$\theta^2_{4,4}$	$\theta^2_{4,5}$	$\theta^2_{4,6}$
Bank 3	Window 1	$\theta^3_{1,1}$	$\theta^3_{1,2}$	$\theta^3_{1,3}$			
	Window 2		$\theta^3_{2,2}$	$\theta^3_{2,3}$	$\theta^3_{2,4}$		
	Window 3			$\theta^3_{3,3}$	$\theta^3_{3,4}$	$\theta^3_{3,5}$	
	Window 4				$\theta^3_{4,4}$	$\theta^3_{4,5}$	$\theta^3_{4,6}$
Bank 4	Window 1	$\theta^4_{1,1}$	$\theta^4_{1,2}$	$\theta^4_{1,3}$			
	Window 2		$\theta^4_{2,2}$	$\theta^4_{2,3}$	$\theta^4_{2,4}$		
	Window 3			$\theta^4_{3,3}$	$\theta^4_{3,4}$	$\theta^4_{3,5}$	
	Window 4				$\theta^4_{4,4}$	$\theta^4_{4,5}$	$\theta^4_{4,6}$
Bank 5	Window 1	$\theta^5_{1,1}$	$\theta^5_{1,2}$	$\theta^5_{1,3}$			
	Window 2		$\theta^5_{2,2}$	$\theta^5_{2,3}$	$\theta^5_{2,4}$		
	Window 3			$\theta^5_{3,3}$	$\theta^5_{3,4}$	$\theta^5_{3,5}$	
	Window 4				$\theta^5_{4,4}$	$\theta^5_{4,5}$	$\theta^5_{4,6}$

Source: Authors' elaboration
Note: $\theta^o_{w,t}$ represents the relative efficiency of bank '*o*' in window *w* and period *t*

analysis, where each analysis examines $n \times w$ banks. Table 3.1 depicts window analysis for aforementioned case with a three period moving window.

The results of a window analysis as given in Table 3.1 can be used for the identification of trends in efficiency performance, the stability of reference sets and other possible insights. 'Row views' clarify efficiency performance of the banks in sample. Similar 'Column views' allow comparison of banks across different references sets and hence provide information on the stability of these scores as the references sets change. The utility of the table can be further extended by appending columns of summary statistics for each bank to reveal the relative stability of each banks' results.

3.3.2 Malmquist Productivity Index (MPI)

The Malmquist productivity index, first initiated by Caves et al. (1982a, b) and further developed by Färe (1988), Färe et al. (1994a, b) and others (e.g. Färe et al. 1997, Ray and Desli 1997), has been widely used in the literature of productivity analyses. Although most of the desired properties can be inherited from the conventional Törnqvist (1936) index, the popularity of the MPI is

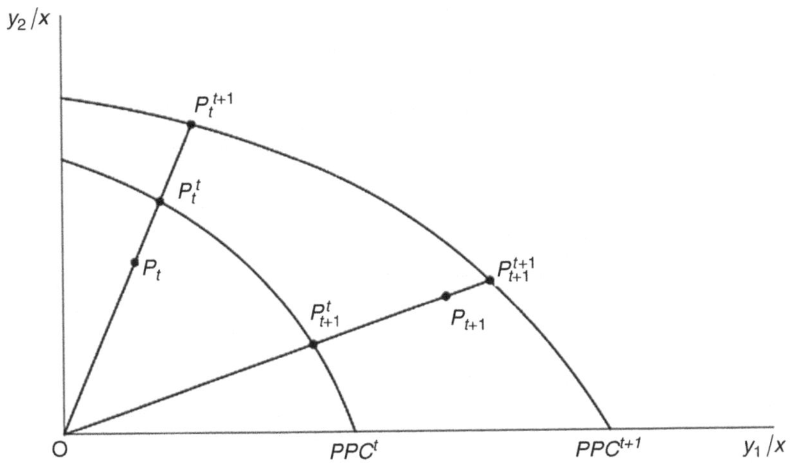

Fig. 3.8 Measuring change in efficiency over time: output-oriented framework (*Source*: Authors' elaboration)

attributed to the fact that TFP can be measured using distance functions without the requirement for information on prices or cost shares of factors.

As noted above, DEA models can be output-oriented or input-oriented. Consequently, the MPI can be defined from output-oriented perspective when the inputs are fixed at their current levels or input-oriented perspective when the outputs are fixed at their current levels. The measurement of MPI from the output-oriented approach is to see how much more output has been produced, using a given level of inputs and the present state of technology, relative to what could be produced under a given reference technology using the same level of inputs. An alternative is to measure MPI from input-oriented approach by examining the reduction in input use, which is feasible given the need to produce a given level of output under a reference technology (Coelli et al. 2005). The idea of computing MPI from output- and input-oriented perspectives is described in detail as follows.

3.3.2.1 A Graphical Conceptualisation

Output-Oriented Framework

Let us consider the Bank P which produces two outputs, y_1 and y_2, from a given level of input x, over two time periods: a base period, t, and an end period, $t + 1$. In Fig. 3.8, PPC^t and PPC^{t+1} refer to the production possibility curves for Bank P in the two time periods, respectively. Clearly, improvements in production technology have occurred (since PPC^{t+1} is outside PPC^t) in a non-neutral way (since the shift in production possibility curves is skewed rather than parallel). Bank P's actual production position has changed from P_t to P_{t+1} over the two periods.

The fact that neither point lies on its associated production possibility curve indicates that the bank is technically inefficient in both time periods.

Now consider the production points of the different time periods separately. The technical efficiency of the bank (using Farrell's output-oriented definition) in time period t (TE_t) and time period $t+1$ (TE_{t+1}) is $TE_t = OP_t/OP_t^t$ and $TE_{t+1} = OP_{t+1}/OP_{t+1}^{t+1}$, respectively. Let us define the output distance function for period t (denoted by $D_o^t(x_t, y_{1t}, y_{2t})$ where the subscript t on the input and output denotes the quantities used in time period t) as the inverse of the maximum amount by which output could be increased (given the level of inputs remains constant) while still remaining within the feasible production possibility set. This is just the value measured by TE_t and so $TE_t = D_o^t(x_t, y_{1t}, y_{2t})^{-1}$. Similarly, it is the case that $TE_{t+1} = D_o^{t+1}(x_{t+1}, y_{1t+1}, y_{2t+1})^{-1}$ where $D_o^{t+1}(x_{t+1}, y_{1t+1}, y_{2t+1})$ denotes the output distance function for period $t+1$ and the subscript $t+1$ on the input and output denotes the quantities used in time period $t+1$.

An examination of the way the productivity of the bank has changed over the two time periods can be approached in two ways, i.e. by using the technology in period t as the reference technology or by using the technology in period $t+1$ as the reference technology. Using the first method, the technical efficiency of the bank at point P_{t+1} is measured by comparing actual output at time $t+1$ relative to the maximum that could be achieved given period t's technology (i.e. OP_{t+1}/OP_{t+1}^t which can be denoted by $D_o^t(x_{t+1}, y_{1t+1}, y_{2t+1})$), and this is compared to the technical efficiency of the bank at point P_t measured by comparing actual output at time t relative to the maximum that could be achieved, also given period t's technology (i.e. OP_t/OP_t^t which can be denoted by $D_o^t(x_t, y_{1t}, y_{2t})$). A measure of the growth in productivity between the two periods using the technology of period t as the reference technology is known as the Malmquist (Malmquist 1953) output-oriented productivity index defined relative to the initial period's technology (M_o^t) and is given as

$$M_o^t = \frac{D_o^t(x_{t+1}, y_{1t+1}, y_{2t+1})}{D_o^t(x_t, y_{1t}, y_{2t})} = \frac{OP_{t+1}/OP_{t+1}^t}{OP_t/OP_t^t} \tag{3.13}$$

Using the second method, the technical efficiency of the bank at point P_{t+1} is measured by comparing the output at time $t+1$ relative to the maximum that could be achieved given time $t+1$'s technology (i.e. OP_{t+1}/OP_{t+1}^{t+1} which can be denoted by $D_o^{t+1}(x_{t+1}, y_{1t+1}, y_{2t+1})$), and this is compared to the technical efficiency of the bank at point P_t measured by comparing the output at time t relative to the maximum that could be achieved also given period $t+1$'s technology (i.e. OP_t/OP_t^{t+1} which can be denoted by $D_o^{t+1}(x_t, y_{1t}, y_{2t})$). The measure of the growth in productivity between the two periods using the technology of period $t+1$ as the reference technology is known as the Malmquist output-oriented productivity index defined relative to the final period's technology (M_o^{t+1}) and is given by

$$M_o^{t+1} = \frac{D_o^{t+1}(x_{t+1}, y_{1t+1}, y_{2t+1})}{D_o^{t+1}(x_t, y_{1t}, y_{2t})} = \frac{OP_{t+1}/OP_{t+1}^{t+1}}{OP_t/OP_t^{t+1}} \tag{3.14}$$

We, therefore, have two measures of the change in productivity over the two periods (n measures in the n period case) and it is unclear which measure is the appropriate one to use, since the choice of base technology would be arbitrary. This problem is overcome by using the Malmquist output-oriented productivity change index (M_o) which is defined as the geometric mean of M_o^t and M_o^{t+1} (Färe et al. 1994a):

$$\begin{aligned} M_o = \sqrt{M_o^t . M_o^{t+1}} &= \sqrt{\frac{D_o^t(x_{t+1}, y_{1t+1}, y_{2t+1})}{D_o^t(x_t, y_{1t}, y_{2t})} \frac{D_o^{t+1}(x_{t+1}, y_{1t+1}, y_{2t+1})}{D_o^{t+1}(x_t, y_{1t}, y_{2t})}} \\ &= \sqrt{\frac{OP_{t+1}/OP_{t+1}^t}{OP_t/OP_t^t} \frac{OP_{t+1}/OP_{t+1}^{t+1}}{OP_t/OP_t^{t+1}}} \end{aligned} \tag{3.15}$$

The index (3.15) can be rewritten as

$$\begin{aligned} M_o &= \frac{D_o^{t+1}(x_{t+1}, y_{1t+1}, y_{2t+1})}{D_o^t(x_t, y_{1t}, y_{2t})} \sqrt{\frac{D_o^t(x_{t+1}, y_{1t+1}, y_{2t+1})}{D_o^{t+1}(x_{t+1}, y_{1t+1}, y_{2t+1})} \frac{D_o^t(x_t, y_{1t}, y_{2t})}{D_o^{t+1}(x_t, y_{1t}, y_{2t})}} \\ &= \frac{OP_{t+1}/OP_{t+1}^{t+1}}{OP_t/OP_t^t} \sqrt{\frac{OP_{t+1}/OP_{t+1}^t}{OP_{t+1}/OP_{t+1}^{t+1}} \frac{OP_t/OP_t^t}{OP_t/OP_t^{t+1}}}. \end{aligned} \tag{3.16}$$

The first component of (3.16) is the ratio of technical efficiency in time period $t + 1$ (the final period) to technical efficiency in time period t (the initial period) and, therefore, measures the change in technical efficiency between the two periods. The ratio equals 1 if there is no change in technical efficiency over the two periods and is greater than 1 (less than 1) if technical efficiency has improved (declined) over the two periods.

The second component measures the change in production technology (i.e. shifts in the frontier) between the two periods t and $t + 1$. It is the geometric mean of the change in technology between the two periods evaluated at x_t and x_{t+1}, respectively. This component has the value 1 when there is no change in production technology, and is greater than 1 (less than 1) if change in production technology has had a positive (negative) effect.

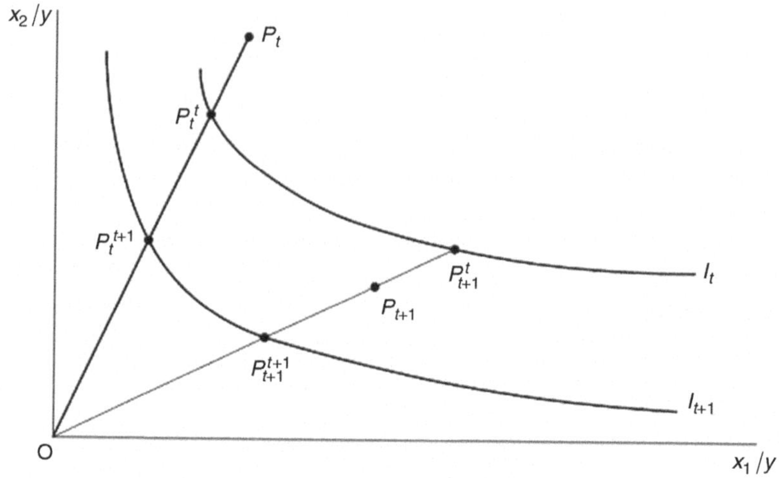

Fig. 3.9 Measuring change in efficiency over time: input-oriented framework (*Source*: Authors' elaboration)

Input-Oriented Framework

The Malmquist productivity index can also be defined in an input-oriented framework. First, we must define the input distance function which is the maximum amount by which all inputs could be reduced (given the level of outputs remains constant) while still remaining in the feasible input set. In Fig. 3.9, the bank now uses two inputs x_1 and x_2 to produce output y, and I_t and I_{t+1} refer to the isoquants in the period t and $t + 1$, respectively. Improvements in production technology have occurred, since I_{t+1} is inside I_t. The observed production points for the bank in time periods t and $t + 1$ are P_t and P_{t+1}, respectively, neither of which is technically efficient since each lies beyond its own isoquant. The value of the input distance function for the bank in time period t is $D_i^t(x_{1t}, x_{2t}, y_t) = OP_t/OP_t^t$. This is the reciprocal of the Farrell input-oriented measure of technical efficiency for Bank P at time t. Similarly, the distance function for Bank P in time period $t + 1$ is $D_i^{t+1}(x_{1t+1}, x_{2t+1}, y_{t+1}) = OP_{t+1}/OP_{t+1}^{t+1}$.

As with the output-oriented approach, the measurement of how productivity, in input-oriented context, has changed over two time periods can be approached in two ways, i.e. by using period t technology or by using period $t + 1$ technology. Using the first method, the technical inefficiency of the bank at point P_{t+1} is measured by comparing the actual input at time $t + 1$ relative to the minimum required given period t's technology (i.e. OP_{t+1}/OP_{t+1}^t which can be denoted by $D_i^t(x_{1t+1}, x_{2t+1}, y_{t+1})$). This is compared to the technical inefficiency of the bank at point P_t measured by comparing the actual input at time t relative to the minimum required, also given period t's technology (i.e. $OP_t/OP_t^t = D_i^t(x_{1t}, x_{2t}, y_t)$). A measure of the change in productivity between the two periods given the technology of period t as the reference technology is known as the Malmquist input-oriented productivity index defined relative to the initial period's technology (M_i^t) and is given as

$$M_i^t = \frac{D_i^t(x_{1t+1}, x_{2t+1}, y_{t+1})}{D_i^t(x_{1t}, x_{2t}, y_t)} = \frac{OP_{t+1}/OP_{t+1}^t}{OP_t/OP_t^t} \tag{3.17}$$

Using the second method, the technical inefficiency of the bank at point P_{t+1} is measured by comparing the actual input at time t relative to the minimum input required given the technology of period $t + 1$ (i.e. $OP_{t+1}/OP_{t+1}^{t+1} = D_i^{t+1}(x_{1t+1}, x_{2t+1}, y_{t+1})$). This is compared with the technical inefficiency of the bank at point P_t measured by comparing the actual input at time t relative to the minimum input required given period $t + 1$'s technology (i.e. OP_t/OP_t^{t+1} which can be denoted by $D_i^{t+1}(x_{1t}, x_{2t}, y_t)$). The Malmquist input-oriented productivity index defined relative to the final period's technology (M_i^{t+1}) is given as

$$M_i^{t+1} = \frac{D_i^{t+1}(x_{1t+1}, x_{2t+1}, y_{t+1})}{D_i^{t+1}(x_{1t}, x_{2t}, y_t)} = \frac{OP_{t+1}/OP_{t+1}^{t+1}}{OP_t/OP_t^{t+1}} \tag{3.18}$$

The problem of the arbitrary choice of which technology to use as the base technology when comparing productivity change over two periods is again overcome by defining the Malmquist input-oriented productivity change index (denoted by M_i) as the geometric mean of M_i^t and M_i^{t+1}:

$$\begin{aligned} M_i = \sqrt{M_i^t . M_i^{t+1}} &= \sqrt{\frac{D_i^t(x_{1t+1}, x_{2t+1}, y_{t+1})}{D_i^t(x_{1t}, x_{2t}, y_t)} \frac{D_i^{t+1}(x_{1t+1}, x_{2t+1}, y_{t+1})}{D_i^{t+1}(x_{1t}, x_{2t}, y_t)}} \\ &= \sqrt{\frac{OP_{t+1}/OP_{t+1}^t}{OP_t/OP_t^t} \frac{OP_{t+1}/OP_{t+1}^{t+1}}{OP_t/OP_t^{t+1}}}. \end{aligned} \tag{3.19}$$

This can rewritten as

$$\begin{aligned} M_i &= \frac{D_i^{t+1}(x_{1t+1}, x_{2t+1}, y_{t+1})}{D_i^t(x_{1t}, x_{2t}, y_t)} \sqrt{\frac{D_i^t(x_{1t+1}, x_{2t+1}, y_{t+1})}{D_i^{t+1}(x_{1t+1}, x_{2t+1}, y_{t+1})} \frac{D_i^t(x_{1t}, x_{2t}, y_t)}{D_i^{t+1}(x_{1t}, x_{2t}, y_t)}} \\ &= \frac{OP_{t+1}/OP_{t+1}^{t+1}}{OP_t/OP_t^t} \sqrt{\frac{OP_{t+1}/OP_{t+1}^t}{OP_{t+1}/OP_{t+1}^{t+1}} \frac{OP_t/OP_t^t}{OP_t/OP_t^{t+1}}}. \end{aligned} \tag{3.20}$$

The components of this index can be interpreted in the opposite way from components of the output-oriented productivity index of (3.16). Specifically, $D_i^{t+1}(x_{1t+1}, x_{2t+1}, y_{t+1})/D_i^t(x_{1t}, x_{2t}, y_t)$ represents the change in technical efficiency between periods $t + 1$ and t and equals 1 if there has been no change and is less than 1 (greater than 1) if there has been a decline (improvement) in technical efficiency. The second component measures the change in production technology between periods $t + 1$ and t and equals 1 if there has been no technical change and is less than 1 (greater than 1) if the effects of production technology have been negative (positive).

3.3.2.2 DEA-Based Estimation of Malmquist Productivity Index

As noted above, the MPI productivity index can be calculated either by using input-oriented or output-oriented distance functions. Distance functions can represent a multi-input-multi-output technology without any behavioural assumptions such as cost minimisation or profit maximisation.

Let $x^t = (x_1^t, \ldots, x_m^t)$ denote a vector of m inputs at time t and $y^t = (y_1^t, \ldots, y_s^t)$ be a vector of s outputs at time t. The production technology at time t, T^t is defined by

$$T^t = \{(x^t, , y^t) : x^t \text{ can produce } y^t\}$$

and it consists of all input–output vectors that are technically feasible at time t. The Shephard's (1970) input distance function is defined on the technology T as

$$D_i^t(y^t, , x^t) = \sup\left\{\theta : \left(\frac{x^t}{\theta}, y^t\right) \in T^t\right\},$$

i.e. as the 'maximal' feasible contraction of x^t.

The output distance function due to Shephard (1970) is defined by

$$D_o^t(x^t, , y^t) = \inf\left\{\phi : \left(x^t, \frac{y^t}{\phi}\right) \in T^t\right\},$$

i.e. the 'minimal' feasible expansion of y^t (Fung et al. 2008).

Assume two time periods t and $t + 1$, respectively, and define in each one of them technology and production as above. Taking time period t as the reference period, the input- and output-oriented MPI are given as

$$MPI_i^{t,t+1}(y^{t+1}, x^{t+1}, y^t, x^t) = \underbrace{\frac{D_i^{t+1}(y^{t+1}, x^{t+1}|CRS)}{D_i^t(y^t, x^t|CRS)}}_{EFFCH_i^{t,t+1}} \times \underbrace{\sqrt{\frac{D_i^t(y^{t+1}, x^{t+1}|CRS)}{D_i^{t+1}(y^{t+1}, x^{t+1}|CRS)} \frac{D_i^t(y^t, x^t|CRS)}{D_i^{t+1}(y^t, x^t|CRS)}}}_{TECH_i^{t,t+1}} \quad \text{and} \tag{3.21}$$

$$MPI_o^{t,t+1}(x^{t+1}, y^{t+1}, x^t, y^t) = \underbrace{\frac{D_o^{t+1}(x^{t+1}, y^{t+1}|CRS)}{D_o^t(x^t, y^t|CRS)}}_{EFFCH_o^{t,t+1}} \times \underbrace{\sqrt{\frac{D_o^t(x^{t+1}, y^{t+1}|CRS)}{D_o^{t+1}(x^{t+1}, y^{t+1}|CRS)} \frac{D_o^t(x^t, y^t|CRS)}{D_o^{t+1}(x^t, y^t|CRS)}}}_{TECH_o^{t,t+1}}. \tag{3.22}$$

The 'CRS' stands for constant returns-to-scale, and it is explicitly recognise that the distance functions are defined relative to CRS technology. From Eqs. 3.21 and 3.22, we note that the MPI is thus defined as the product of *efficiency change* (EFFCH), which is how much closer a bank gets to the *efficient frontier* (*catching-up effect* or *falling behind*), and *technical change* (TECH), which is how much the benchmark production frontier shifts at each bank's observed input mix (*technical progress* or *regress*). MPI can attain a value greater than, equal to or less than unity depending on whether the bank experiences productivity growth, stagnation or productivity decline, respectively, between periods t and $t + 1$. Similarly, EFFCH index takes a value greater than 1 for an efficiency increase, 0 for no efficiency change or less than 1 for an efficiency decrease. Likewise, TECH attains a value greater than 1 for technical progress, 0 for technical stagnation or less than 1 for technical regress.

In order to calculate the productivity of bank '*o*' between t and $t + 1$, we need to solve four different distance functions that make up MPI using either radial or non-radial DEA models. It is worth noting here that both radial and non-radial models compute a distance function as a reciprocal of Farrell's (1957) measure of technical efficiency. For radial MPI, we should consider the linear programming problems outlined below:

Linear programming problems for radial input- and output-oriented distance functions

Input-oriented	Output-oriented
Panel A: Distance function at time t using the reference technology for the period t	
$\left[\hat{D}_i^t(y_o^t, x_o^t)\right]^{-1} = \min\limits_{\theta,\lambda} \theta_o$	$\left[\hat{D}_o^t(x_o^t, y_o^t)\right]^{-1} = \max\limits_{\phi,\lambda} \phi_o$
subject to	subject to
$\sum_{j=1}^{n} \lambda_j x_{ij}^t \leq \theta_o x_{io}^t$	$\sum_{j=1}^{n} \lambda_j x_{ij}^t \leq x_{io}^t$
$\sum_{j=1}^{n} \lambda_j y_{rj}^t \geq y_{ro}^t$	$\sum_{j=1}^{n} \lambda_j y_{rj}^t \geq \phi_o y_{ro}^t$
$\lambda_j \geq 0$	$\lambda_j \geq 0$
Panel B: Distance function at time t + 1 using the reference technology for the period t + 1	
$\left[\hat{D}_i^{t+1}(y_o^{t+1}, x_o^{t+1})\right]^{-1} = \min\limits_{\theta,\lambda} \theta_o$	$\left[\hat{D}_o^{t+1}(x_o^{t+1}, y_o^{t+1})\right]^{-1} = \max\limits_{\phi,\lambda} \phi_o$
subject to	subject to
$\sum_{j=1}^{n} \lambda_j x_{ij}^{t+1} \leq \theta_o x_{io}^{t+1}$	$\sum_{j=1}^{n} \lambda_j x_{ij}^{t+1} \leq x_{io}^{t+1}$
$\sum_{j=1}^{n} \lambda_j y_{rj}^{t+1} \geq y_{ro}^{t+1}$	$\sum_{j=1}^{n} \lambda_j y_{rj}^{t+1} \geq \phi_o y_{ro}^{t+1}$
$\lambda_j \geq 0$	$\lambda_j \geq 0$
Panel C: Distance function at time t using the reference technology for the period t + 1	
$\left[\hat{D}_i^{t+1}(y_o^t, x_o^t)\right]^{-1} = \min\limits_{\theta,\lambda} \theta_o$	$\left[\hat{D}_o^{t+1}(x_o^t, y_o^t)\right]^{-1} = \max\limits_{\phi,\lambda} \phi_o$
subject to	subject to
$\sum_{j=1}^{n} \lambda_j x_{ij}^{t+1} \leq \theta_o x_{io}^t$	$\sum_{j=1}^{n} \lambda_j x_{ij}^{t+1} \leq x_{io}^t$
$\sum_{j=1}^{n} \lambda_j y_{rj}^{t+1} \geq y_{ro}^t$	$\sum_{j=1}^{n} \lambda_j y_{rj}^{t+1} \geq \phi_o y_{ro}^t$
$\lambda_j \geq 0$	$\lambda_j \geq 0$

Panel D: Distance function at time t + 1 using the reference technology for the period t

$$\left[\hat{D}_i^{\,t}\left(y_o^{t+1},x_o^{t+1}\right)\right]^{-1}=\min_{\theta,\lambda}\theta_o$$

subject to

$$\sum_{j=1}^{n}\lambda_j x_{ij}^{t}\le\theta_o x_{io}^{t+1}$$

$$\sum_{j=1}^{n}\lambda_j y_{rj}^{t}\ge y_{ro}^{t+1}$$

$$\lambda_j\ge 0$$

$$\left[\hat{D}_o^{\,t}\left(x_o^{t+1},y_o^{t+1}\right)\right]^{-1}=\max_{\phi,\lambda}\phi_o$$

subject to

$$\sum_{j=1}^{n}\lambda_j x_{ij}^{t}\le x_{io}^{t+1}$$

$$\sum_{j=1}^{n}\lambda_j y_{rj}^{t}\ge\phi_o y_{ro}^{t+1}$$

$$\lambda_j\ge 0$$

It is worth noting here that the estimation of distance functions in the radial MPI is based on DEA model developed by Charnes et al. (1978) which takes no account of slacks. However, non-zero input and output slacks are very likely to present even after the radial efficiency improvement, and often, these non-zero slack values represent a substantial amount of inefficiency. Therefore, in order to fully measure the inefficiency in bank's performance, it is very important to also consider the inefficiency represented by the non-zero slacks in the DEA-based MPI. Tone (2001) proposed three different variants of a non-radial MPI based on slack-based measure (SBM) model that assesses the performance of banks by simultaneously dealing with input excesses and output shortfalls of the banks concerned. The linear programming problems for estimating distance functions using SBM models are outlined as

Linear programming problems for non-radial (SBM) input- and output-oriented distance functions

Input-oriented	Output-oriented

Panel A: Distance function at time t using the reference technology for the period t

Input-oriented:

$$\left[\hat{D}_i^{\,t}\left(y_o^{t},x_o^{t}\right)\right]^{-1}=\min_{\theta,s^-}1-\frac{1}{m}\sum_{i=1}^{m}s_i^-/x_{io}^{t}$$

subject to

$$\sum_{j=1}^{n}\lambda_j x_{ij}^{t}+s_i^-=x_{io}^{t}$$

$$\sum_{j=1}^{n}\lambda_j y_{rj}^{t}\ge y_{ro}^{t}$$

$$\lambda_j,s_i^-\ge 0$$

Output-oriented:

$$\left[\hat{D}_o^{\,t}\left(x_o^{t},y_o^{t}\right)\right]^{-1}=\min_{\phi,s^+}\frac{1}{1+\frac{1}{s}\sum_{r=1}^{s}\frac{s_r^+}{y_{ro}^{t}}}$$

subject to

$$\sum_{j=1}^{n}\lambda_j x_{ij}^{t}\le x_{io}^{t}$$

$$\sum_{j=1}^{n}\lambda_j y_{rj}^{t}-s_r^+=y_{ro}^{t}$$

$$\lambda_j,s_r^+\ge 0$$

Panel B: Distance function at time t + 1 using the reference technology for the period t + 1

Input-oriented:

$$\left[\hat{D}_i^{\,t+1}\left(y_o^{t+1},x_o^{t+1}\right)\right]^{-1}=\min_{\theta,s^-}1-\frac{1}{m}\sum_{i=1}^{m}s_i^-/x_{io}^{t+1}$$

subject to

$$\sum_{j=1}^{n}\lambda_j x_{ij}^{t+1}+s_i^-=x_{io}^{t+1}$$

$$\sum_{j=1}^{n}\lambda_j y_{rj}^{t+1}\ge y_{ro}^{t+1}$$

$$\lambda_j,s_i^-\ge 0$$

Output-oriented:

$$\left[\hat{D}_o^{\,t+1}\left(x_o^{t+1},y_o^{t+1}\right)\right]^{-1}=\min_{\phi,s^+}\frac{1}{1+\frac{1}{s}\sum_{r=1}^{s}\frac{s_r^+}{y_{ro}^{t+1}}}$$

subject to

$$\sum_{j=1}^{n}\lambda_j x_{ij}^{t+1}\le x_{io}^{t+1}$$

$$\sum_{j=1}^{n}\lambda_j y_{rj}^{t+1}-s_r^+=y_{ro}^{t+1}$$

$$\lambda_j,s_r^+\ge 0$$

Panel C: Distance function at time t using the reference technology for the period t + 1

$$\left[\hat{D}_i^{t+1}(y_o^t, x_o^t)\right]^{-1} = \min_{\theta, s^-} 1 - \frac{1}{m}\sum_{i=1}^{m} s_i^- / x_{io}^t$$

subject to

$$\sum_{j=1}^{n} \lambda_j x_{ij}^{t+1} + s_i^- = x_{io}^t$$

$$\sum_{j=1}^{n} \lambda_j y_{rj}^{t+1} \geq y_{ro}^t$$

$$\lambda_j, s_i^- \geq 0$$

$$\left[\hat{D}_o^{t+1}(x_o^t, y_o^t)\right]^{-1} = \min_{\phi, s^+} \frac{1}{1 + \frac{1}{s}\sum_{r=1}^{s} \frac{s_r^+}{y_{ro}^t}}$$

subject to

$$\sum_{j=1}^{n} \lambda_j x_{ij}^{t+1} \leq x_{io}^t$$

$$\sum_{j=1}^{n} \lambda_j y_{rj}^{t+1} - s_r^+ = y_{ro}^t$$

$$\lambda_j, s_r^+ \geq 0$$

Panel D: Distance function at time t + 1 using the reference technology for the period t

$$\left[\hat{D}_i^t(y_o^{t+1}, x_o^{t+1})\right]^{-1} = \min_{\theta, s^-} 1 - \frac{1}{m}\sum_{i=1}^{m} s_i^- / x_{io}^{t+1}$$

subject to

$$\sum_{j=1}^{n} \lambda_j x_{ij}^t + s_i^- = x_{io}^{t+1}$$

$$\sum_{j=1}^{n} \lambda_j y_{rj}^t \geq y_{ro}^{t+1}$$

$$\lambda_j, s_i^- \geq 0$$

$$\left[\hat{D}_o^t(x_o^{t+1}, y_o^{t+1})\right]^{-1} = \min_{\phi, s^+} \frac{1}{1 + \frac{1}{s}\sum_{r=1}^{s} \frac{s_r^+}{y_{ro}^{t+1}}}$$

subject to

$$\sum_{j=1}^{n} \lambda_j x_{ij}^t \leq x_{io}^{t+1}$$

$$\sum_{j=1}^{n} \lambda_j y_{rj}^t - s_r^+ = y_{ro}^{t+1}$$

$$\lambda_j, s_r^+ \geq 0$$

Färe et al. (1994b) enhanced the aforementioned decomposition of MPI by taking EFFCH component and decomposing it into pure technical efficiency change (PECH) and scale efficiency change (SECH) components with respect to variable returns-to-scale (VRS) technology. The input-oriented MPI with enhanced decomposition as developed by Färe et al. is given as

$$MPI_i^{t,t+1}(y^{t+1}, x^{t+1}, y^t, x^t) = \underbrace{\frac{D_i^{t+1}(y^{t+1}, x^{t+1}|VRS)}{D_i^t(y^t, x^t|VRS)}}_{PECH_i^{t,t+1}}$$

$$\times \underbrace{\frac{D_i^{t+1}(y^{t+1}, x^{t+1}|VRS)/D_i^{t+1}(y^{t+1}, x^{t+1}|CRS)}{D_i^t(y^t, x^t|VRS)/D_i^t(y^t, x^t|CRS)}}_{SECH_i^{t,t+1}}$$

$$\times \underbrace{\sqrt{\frac{D_i^t(y^{t+1}, x^{t+1}|CRS)}{D_i^{t+1}(y^{t+1}, x^{t+1}|CRS)} \frac{D_i^t(y^t, x^t|CRS)}{D_i^{t+1}(y^t, x^t|CRS)}}}_{TECH_i^{t,t+1}}. \quad (3.23)$$

The corresponding output-oriented MPI decomposition can be defined in an analogous manner.

The extended decomposition of MPI by Färe et al. (1994b) has been criticised by Ray and Desli (1997) who are having the opinion that 'their use of CRS and VRS within the same decomposition of the MPI raises a problem of internal inconsistency'. The MPI approach gives the correct estimation of TFP change in the presence of CRS technology, while may not accurately measure productivity changes when VRS is assumed for the technology (Grifell-Tatjé and Lovell 1995). The fundamental problem is that the imposition of a VRS technology creates a systematic bias on the productivity measurement derived unless the VRS technology is identical to CRS technology (Odeck 2008). However, various alternatives have been proposed, but none of them has gained widespread acceptance. The debate continues on how a proper Malmquist index can be derived assuming VRS, and complete redo is yet to emerge (see Grifell-Tatjé and Lovell 1999; Balk 2001 for discussion on this issue).

3.4 Strengths, Limitations, Basic Requirements and Outcomes of DEA

3.4.1 Strengths and Limitations

Since the publication of the seminal paper of Charnes et al. in 1978, there have been thousands of theoretical contributions and practical applications in various fields using DEA (Klimberg and Ratick 2008). The bibliographies compiled by Tavares (2002) and Emrouznejad et al. (2008) highlight that over the years, DEA has been applied in many diverse areas such as health care, banking, education, software production, telecommunication, transport, military operations, criminal courts, electric utilities, library services, mining operations and manufacturing. Some notable advantages of DEA which motivated the researchers, including us, to use it over other frontier efficiency measurement techniques are as follows.

First, DEA is able to manage complex production environments with multiple-input and multiple-output technologies (Jacobs 2000). Second, DEA optimises for each individual observation, in place of the overall aggregation, and single optimisation thereafter, performed in statistical regressions. Instead of trying to fit a regression plane through the centre of the data, DEA floats a piecewise linear surface to rest on top of observations (Majumdar and Chang 1996). Third, DEA approach has good asymptotic statistical properties. For instance, DEA is equivalent to maximum likelihood estimation, with the specification of the production frontier in DEA as a non-parametric monotone and concave function instead of a parametric form linear in parameters (Banker 1993). Fourth, DEA produces a scalar measure of efficiency for each unit, which makes the comparison easy (Sowlati and Paradi 2004). Fifth, in DEA, the computations are value-free and do not require specification or knowledge of a priori weights of prices for inputs or outputs (Charnes et al. 1994). DEA does not require any pre-specified functional form between inputs and outputs, i.e. production function (Mirmirani et al. 2008). Therefore, the probability of a misspecification of the production technology is zero

(Jemric and Vujcic 2002). Thus, DEA estimates are unbiased if we assume that there is no underlying model or reference technology (Kittelsen 1999). Sixth, it does not require the establishment of arbitrary cut-off points for classifying efficient and inefficient banks (Rutledge et al. 1995).

On the other hand, the main disadvantages of DEA as summarised by Coelli et al. (2005) are as follows. First, DEA does not account for random error. The deviations from the frontier are assumed to be due to inefficiency. Errors in measurement and random noise can misrepresent real relative efficiency. Second, there is a strong influence of estimated frontier by outliers. If the outlier is a high performance unit with the same characteristics as other units, then it provides a good benchmark for inefficient units. However, if the outlier is operating in a different cultural environment or has some other unique aspect, and therefore has an unfair or unattainable advantage, then other units will receive artificially low scores. Third, DEA is intended for estimating the relative efficiency of a bank, but does not specifically address absolute efficiency. In other words, it measures how well the bank is performing compared to its peers (set of efficient units), but not compared to a theoretical maximum. The main problem arising from this is the impossibility of ranking efficient units; indeed all the efficient units have an efficiency score of 100 %. Fourth, the technique requires a minimum number of units in order to guarantee the necessary degrees of freedom in the model. In principle, all inputs and outputs relevant to the function of the units should be included. However, the larger the number of inputs and outputs in relation to the number of units being assessed, the less discriminating the method appears to be (Thanassoulis 2001). Further, the analyses containing less than the minimum number of units will yield higher efficiency scores and more units on the efficient frontier and hence give a more unfavourable picture.

3.4.2 *Basic Requirements*

The implementation of DEA for assessing the performance of banks requires the fulfilment of certain conditions concerning (number of DMUs, the weights, the environment in which bank is operating, etc.). Ho (2004) described the following basic requirements for implementing DEA so as to get robust efficiency estimates:

(i) The banks must operate in the same cultural environment.[5]
(ii) The model must contain suitable inputs and outputs. For example, a bank measuring productivity should employ a model with variables such as number of employees, number of branches, physical assets, etc. as opposed to square footage, etc., although these can be incorporated into the model if that is required.

[5] Culture is the distinctive management and operational competencies that reflect the firm's technology and processes.

Table 3.2 DEA outcomes and their implications

S. No.	DEA outcomes	Implications
1.	Overall efficiency score (0–100 %)	(a) Quantitative ranking of the banks in an objective, fair, strict and unambiguous manner (b) Gauging the extent of inefficiency
2.	Peer analysis	Identify best-performer(s) in the sample whose practices can be emulated by inefficient bank(s) in the sample
3.	Slacks	(a) Helps to identify waste of critical inputs (b) Helps to identify overproduction of output (c) Helps in designing and implementation of an efficiency improvement programme
4.	Targets	Potential reduction in inputs and potential augmentation of outputs for projecting inefficient banks on to the *efficient frontier*. The targets also help in designing and implementation of an efficiency improvement programme

Source: Authors' elaboration

(iii) Each bank must have a complete set of accurate data for all variables in the model.

(iv) There must be a minimum number of units to study in order to maintain sufficient degrees of freedom. Cooper et al. (2007) provides two such rules to determine the minimum number of banks. They expressed these rules as: $n \geq \max\{m \times s; 3(m + s)\}$, where $n =$ number of banks, $m =$ number of inputs, and $s =$ number of outputs. The first rule of thumb states that sample size should be greater than equal to product of inputs and outputs, while the second rule states that number of observation in the data set should be at least three times the sum of number of input and output variables. For example, if a model includes five inputs and two output variables, there should be at least $\max\{5 \times 2; 3(5 + 2)\} = \max\{10,21\} = 21$ banks.

3.4.3 Outcomes

An implementation of DEA gives the outcomes that not only limited to the efficiency scores alone but also related to the peers to be emulated, presence of slacks in inputs and outputs and potential improvements in the production process. Table 3.2 highlights the implications of various outcomes of DEA for a decision making unit. The most immediate outcome of a DEA analysis is a list of relatively efficient and inefficient banks. Using DEA, the comparatively inefficient banks can be ranked in order of their relative inefficiency to indicate which banks are more inefficient in relation to others. An additional outcome of DEA can be found by calculating the number of times an efficient bank appears within various peer comparison sets for relatively inefficient units.

3.5 Free Disposal Hull (FDH) Analysis

The Free Disposal Hull approach (FDH) was proposed by Deprins et al. (1984) and extended by Tulkens (1993). It is a more general version of the DEA variable returns-to-scale model as it relies only on the strong free disposability assumption[6] for production set and hence does not restrict itself to convex technologies. If the true production set is convex then the DEA and FDH are both consistent estimators. However, FDH shows a lower rate of convergence (due to the less assumption it require) with respect to DEA. On the contrary, if the true production set is not convex, then DEA is not a consistent estimator of the production set, while FDH is consistent.

As deterministic non-parametric methods, DEA and FDH assume no particular functional form for the boundary and ignore measurement error. Instead, the best practice technology is the boundary of a reconstructed production possibility subset based upon directly enveloping a set of observations. However, in FDH, the production possibilities set is composed only of the DEA vertices and the Free Disposal Hull points interior to these vertices (Berger and Humphrey 1997). Since the DEA presumes that linear substitution is possible between observed input combinations on an isoquant which is generated from the observations in piecewise linear form, FDH presumes that no substitution is possible so the isoquant looks like a step function formed by the intersection of lines drawn from observed (local) Leontief-type input combinations. Thus, the FDH frontier has a staircase shape and envelops the data more tightly than the DEA frontier does. Moreover, the FDH frontier is either congruent with or interior to the DEA frontier, and thus, FDH will typically generate larger estimates of average efficiency than DEA (Tulkens 1993).

Figure 3.10 compares DEA and FDH frontiers. The production frontier of FDH as represented by a staircase line ABCDEF is contained in DEA-BCC frontier ABCEF, which in turn is contained in DEA-CCR frontier OCG. The DEA-CCR assumes constant returns-to-scale so that all observed production combinations can be scaled up or down proportionally, and DEA-BCC assumes variable returns-to-scale and is represented by a piecewise linear convex frontier. Thus, FDH, DEA-CCR and DEA-BCC models define different production possibility sets and efficiency scores. As an example, the input-oriented efficiency of Bank T is given by *OI*/*OT*, *OH*/*OT* and *OG*/*OT* as determined by the FDH, DEA-CCR and DEA-BCC models, respectively.

For computing efficiency measures, the FDH model is formulated by adding the additional constraint $\lambda_j \in \{0,1\}$ i.e. λ_j to be binary in the DEA-BCC model so as to relax an assumption of convexity.

---

[6] Aside from the usual regularity axioms (i.e. 'no free lunch', the possibility of inactivity, boundedness and closedness), FDH imposes only strong free disposability in inputs and in outputs and so-called free disposal (Wagenvoort and Schure 1999). The former refers to the fact that any given level of output(s) remains feasible if any of the input is increased, whereas the latter means that with given input(s) it is always possible to reduce output(s).

Fig. 3.10 Free Disposal Hull (*Source*: Tulkens 1993)

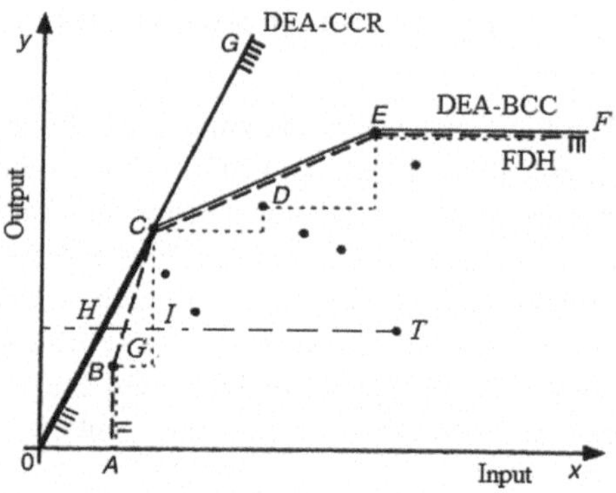

$$
\begin{aligned}
&\min \theta^{FDH} \\
&\text{subject to} \\
&\quad \sum_{j=1}^{n} \lambda_j x_{ij} \le \theta^{FDH} x_{io} && i = 1, \ldots, m \\
&\quad \sum_{j=1}^{n} \lambda_j y_{rj} \ge y_{ro} && r = 1, \ldots, s \qquad (3.24) \\
&\quad \sum_{j=1}^{n} \lambda_j = 1 && j = 1, \ldots, n \\
&\quad \lambda_j \in \{0, 1\} \text{ i.e., binary}
\end{aligned}
$$

3.6 Stochastic Frontier Analysis (SFA)

Another widely used frontier efficiency methodological framework used in applied banking efficiency analyses is stochastic frontier analysis (SFA) which was independently proposed by Aigner et al. (1977) and Meeusen and van den Broeck (1977). Kumbhakar and Lovell (2000) in their excellent book provided an extensive survey of literature on SFA, and therefore, we restrict ourselves on the broad contours of this frontier efficiency measurement approach. Coelli et al. (2003) listed out the main advantages of SFA methodology as follows: (i) environment variables are easier to deal with, (ii) it allows us to conduct statistical tests of hypotheses concerning any parameter restrictions associated with economic theory and (iii) it allows an easier identification of outliers. On the other hand, the main disadvantages of SFA are that estimation results are sensitive to distributional assumptions on the error terms, and it requires large samples for robustness, so it is very demanding regarding data requirements.

The stochastic frontier involves two random components, one associated with the presence of technical inefficiency and the other being a traditional random error.

An appropriate formulation of a stochastic frontier model in terms of a general production function for the ith bank is

$$y_i = f(x_i; \beta)\, e^{v_i} e^{u_i} \tag{3.25}$$

where y_i indicates the observed level of output, x_i is the vector of inputs used in the production process, β is the vector of unknown technological parameters to be estimated, $f(x_i;\beta)$ is the deterministic part of the production function, v_i is the two-sided 'white noise' component representing random disturbance and u_i is a non-negative one-sided disturbance term which accounts for technical inefficiency. In logarithmic terms, this can be written as

$$\ln y_i = \ln f(x_i; \beta) + v_i - u_i = \ln f(x_i; \beta) + \varepsilon_i \tag{3.26}$$

The stochastic production frontier model (3.26) is often referred to as a 'composed error' model since the error term has two components. The important features of the stochastic frontier model can be illustrated graphically. Let us suppose the bank produces the output y_i using only one input x_i. In this case, a Cobb–Douglas stochastic frontier model takes the form

$$\begin{aligned} &\ln y_i = \beta_o + \beta_1 \ln x_i + \nu_i - u_i \\ \text{or} \quad & y_i = \exp(\beta_o + \beta_1 \ln x_i + \nu_i - u_i) \\ \text{or} \quad & y_i = \underbrace{\exp(\beta_o + \beta_1 \ln x_i)}_{\substack{\text{deterministic}\\ \text{component}}} \times \underbrace{\exp(\nu_i)}_{\text{noise}} \times \underbrace{\exp(-u_i)}_{\text{inefficiency}}. \end{aligned} \tag{3.27}$$

Such a frontier is depicted in Fig. 3.11 where we plot inputs and outputs of two banks, A and B, and where the deterministic component of the frontier model has been drawn to reflect the existence of diminishing returns-to-scale. Values of the input are measured along the horizontal axis and outputs are measured on the vertical axis. Bank A uses the input level x_A to produce the output y_A, while Bank B uses the input level x_B to produce the output y_B (these observed values are indicated by the points marked with $\times$). If there were no inefficiency effects (i.e. if $u_A = 0$ and $u_B = 0$), then so-called frontier outputs would be $y_A^* \equiv \exp(\beta_o + \beta_1 \ln x_A + \nu_A)$ and $y_B^* \equiv \exp(\beta_o + \beta_1 \ln x_B + \nu_B)$ for banks A and B, respectively. These frontier values are indicated by the points marked with $\otimes$ in Fig. 3.11. It is clear that the frontier output for Bank A lies above the deterministic part of the production frontier only because the noise effect is positive ($\nu_A > 0$), while the frontier output for Bank B lies below the deterministic part of the frontier because the noise effect of negative ($\nu_B < 0$). It can also be seen that the observed output of Bank A lies below the deterministic part of the frontier because the sum of the noise and inefficiency effects is negative (i.e. $\nu_A - u_A < 0$).

The stochastic production frontier as specified in (3.26) has limited applicability in the banking efficiency analyses since it accommodates only single output and, thus, not consistent with multiple-outputs and multiple-inputs characteristics of the

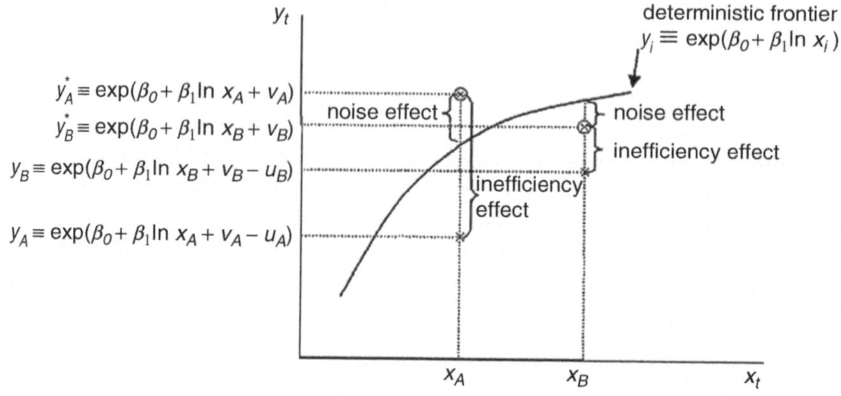

Fig. 3.11 Measuring technical efficiency using stochastic frontier analysis (*Source*: Coelli et al. 2005)

production process of banking firms. Researchers, therefore, generally use the stochastic cost frontier for obtaining the cost efficiency scores for individual banks. The stochastic cost frontier model can be written as

$$\begin{aligned} \ln C_i = c_i &= C(y_i, w_i; \beta) + v_i + u_i \\ &= C(y_i, w_i; \beta) + \varepsilon_i \end{aligned} \tag{3.28}$$

where ln C_i is the logarithm of observed cost of production for the ith bank, C (.) is the functional form of the core of the cost frontier, i.e. the deterministic part, y_i is the logarithm of the output quantity, w_i is a vector of logarithm of input prices, β is a vector of unknown parameters to be estimated, u_i is the non-negative cost inefficiency effect and v_i is the random error which represents noise in the data and is usually specified as white noise. Additionally, u_i and v_i are considered as being independently distributed from each other. The minimum cost of a bank corresponds to the stochastic quantity $\exp(C(y_i,w_i;\beta) + v_i)$, and the measure of cost inefficiency is given by the ratio of minimal to actual cost, i.e.

$$CE_i = \frac{\exp(C(y_i, w_i; \beta) + v_i)}{\exp(C(y_i, w_i; \beta) + v_i + u_i)} = \exp(-u_i). \tag{3.29}$$

Since the random variable u is non-negative, the value of the cost efficiency lies between 0 and 1, with the value of 1 representing totally cost efficient production.

In the stochastic frontier analysis, the estimation of cost efficiency relies on the choice of functional form and estimates of parameter β. To estimate β vector, one can make use of maximum likelihood (ML) method or, in some circumstances, corrected ordinary least squares (COLS) method. However, ML estimators have many desirable large sample (i.e. asymptotic) properties, and therefore, they are often preferred to other estimators as COLS (Coelli et al. 2005). The ML method aims to provide estimates of the production technology parameters (i.e. β) and bank-specific (in)efficiency.

In the ML estimation, introduced by Aigner et al. (1977) and Meeusen and van den Broeck (1977), one proceeds by specifying the likelihood function for the model (3.28) according to the assumption formulated about the distribution of the one-side disturbance u_i. Indeed, while the noise component v_i is essentially always assumed to follow $N(0,\sigma_v^2)$, there are several possibilities as regards the specification of the inefficiency term, which is usually assumed to follow a *truncated-normal*, *half-normal*, *exponential* or *gamma* distribution, anyhow holding the strong assumption that it is independent of the random deviation term and the other regressors. Meeusen and van den Broeck (1977) assume an exponential distribution for u_i, and Aigner et al. (1977) discussed two distributions, the *half-normal* and the *exponential*, as possible candidates for the one-sided error term representing cost inefficiency. Stevenson (1980) first suggested the truncated normal, and Greene (1980, 1990, 1993) has advocated the two-parameter gamma distribution. Lee (1983) suggests the four-parameter Pearson family of distributions. However, there is no a priori basis for choosing one distribution over another, and the worse thing is that different specifications have been found to give different estimates of cost inefficiency (Forsund et al. 1980; Schmidt 1976). In practice, this choice is usually made for reasons of convenience and the most popular choice in the literature has been the half-normal distribution. In all these cases, it is possible to derive the distribution of the composed error term $\varepsilon_i(=v_i + u_i)$ and go back from this up to the likelihood function of the log-linear model (3.28). The score functions allow then to derive the appropriate expressions for the numerical computation of β estimator and the variance of composed error term, σ_ε^2.

Once the parameters are estimated, the centre of interest is the estimation of cost inefficiency, u_i. The u_i must be observed indirectly since direct estimates of only ε_i are available. The procedure for decomposing ε_i into its two components v_i and u_i relies on considering the expected value of u_i conditional upon $\varepsilon_i(=v_i + u_i)$. Jondrow et al. (1982) were the first to specify a half-normal distribution for the one-sided inefficiency component and to derive the conditional distribution $(u_i| v_i + u_i)$. Under this formulation of the half-normal distribution, the expected mean value of inefficiency, conditional upon the composite residual, is defined as

$$E[u_i|\varepsilon_i] = \frac{\sigma\lambda}{1+\lambda^2}\left[\frac{\phi(\varepsilon_i\lambda/\sigma)}{\Phi(-\varepsilon_i\lambda/\sigma)} - \frac{\varepsilon_i\lambda}{\sigma}\right] \tag{3.30}$$

where $\sigma^2 = \sigma_u^2 + \sigma_v^2$ captures inefficiency, for $\lambda = 0$ every observation would lie on the frontier (Greene 1993). $\phi(.)$ and $\Phi(.)$ are, respectively, the probability density function and cumulative distribution function of the standard normal distribution.

The truncated-normal model is a more general form of the half-normal, where u_i is distributed with a modal value of μ (Stevenson 1980). The explicit form for the conditional expectation is obtained by replacing the $\varepsilon_i\lambda/\sigma$ in the half-normal model with: $u_i^* = \varepsilon_i\lambda/\sigma + \mu/\sigma\lambda$. If μ is not significantly different from zero, the model collapses to the half-normal.

If an exponential distribution is imposed, with a density function of the general form $f(u_i) = \theta\exp^{-\theta u_i}$, the conditional expectation is expressed as (Greene 1993):

$$E[u_i|\varepsilon_i] = (\varepsilon_i - \theta\sigma_v^2) + \frac{\sigma_v\phi[(\varepsilon_i - \theta\sigma_v^2)/\sigma_v]}{\Phi[(\varepsilon_i - \theta\sigma_v^2)/\sigma_v]} \quad (3.31)$$

in which θ is the distribution parameter to be estimated.

The more general gamma distribution is formed by adding an additional parameter P to the exponential formulation, such that $f(u_i) = \frac{\theta^P}{\Gamma(P)} u^{P-1} \exp^{-\theta u_i}$ with $u_i \sim G[\theta, P]$ (Greene 1990).

3.6.1 *Panel Data Framework*

Until the work of Pitt and Lee (1981), all efficiency measurement studies were cross-sectional. As pointed out by Schmidt and Sickles (1984), these models have three problems. First, the cost inefficiency of a particular bank can be estimated but not consistently. Second, the estimation of the model and the separation of inefficiency effect from statistical noise require specific assumptions about the distribution of inefficiency effect and statistical noise. Third, it may be incorrect to assume that inefficiency is independent of the regressors. They recommended that a rich panel data can overcome some of these difficulties and listed out the following three principal benefits accruing to panel data in the context of production frontiers:

(i) No strong distributional specification is necessary for the inefficiency disturbance term.
(ii) When inefficiency is measured with panel data, it is estimated consistently as time $T \to \infty$.
(iii) Inefficiency can be measured without assuming that it is uncorrelated with the regressors.

The literature on SFA provides two types of panel data models, namely, time-invariant and time-varying efficiency models.

3.6.1.1 Time-Invariant Efficiency Models

The stochastic cost frontier with time-invariant efficiency can be written as

$$c_{it} = \alpha + x'_{it}\beta + v_{it} + u_i \quad (3.32)$$

where c_{it} represents the logarithm of costs of the ith bank at time t ($i = 1, \ldots, N$; $t = 1, \ldots, T$), x_{it} are the regressors, α and β are the coefficients to be estimated and v_{it} is the error term capturing noise. As the parameters of the model can be estimated in a number of ways, therefore, cost efficiency can be estimated in different ways.

Fixed-Effects Model

The stochastic cost frontier with time-invariant efficiency as described above in (3.32) can be written as

$$c_{it} = \alpha_i + x'_{it}\beta + v_{it}. \tag{3.33}$$

In (3.33), $\alpha_i = \alpha + u_i$ is the common bank effects of the fixed-effects model. The estimate of inefficiency $\hat{u}_i$ is then defined as the distance from the bank-specific intercept $\hat{\alpha}_i$ to the minimal intercept in the sample:

$$\hat{u}_i = \hat{\alpha}_i - \min_i (\hat{\alpha}_i) \geq 0 \tag{3.34}$$

Consequently, $\hat{\alpha} = \min_i (\hat{\alpha}_i)$. The frontier is, thus, shifted to the bank with the smallest estimated intercept and any deviation from this intercept is interpreted as inefficiency. This model is estimated either by adding dummy variables for each of the banks and using OLS or by performing the 'within transformation' and applying OLS to the transformed model. There are some advantages in using the 'Within estimator' model. No assumptions need to be made about a specific distribution of the inefficiency term, as is the case with cross-sectional models. One need not assume that the inefficiency term is not correlated with the regressors. Further, the fixed-effects model has nice consistency properties.

However, the fixed-effects model has a potential serious drawback. Horrace and Schmidt (1996) found wide confidence intervals for the efficiency estimates based on the fixed-effects model. The estimation error and the uncertainty in the identification of the most efficient observation are among the explanations adopted to justify this result. A problem related to the 'Within estimation' is that if important time-invariant regressors are included in the frontier model, these will show up as inefficiency in (3.33) (Cornwell and Schmidt 1996). In other words, the fixed-effects (α_i) capture both variations across banks in time-invariant cost efficiency and all phenomena that vary across banks but are time-invariant for each bank. Unfortunately, this occurs whether or not the other effects are included as regressors in the model. This problem can be solved by estimating model (3.32) in a random-effects context.

Random-Effects Model

In the random-effects model, the inefficiency terms u_i are treated as one-sided *i.i.d.* random variables which are uncorrelated with the regressors x_{it} and the statistical noise v_{it} for all t. The random-effects model can be estimated using either least squares or maximum likelihood techniques. The least squares approach as proposed by Schmidt and Sickles (1984) involves writing the model in the form of the standard error-components model, then applying generalised least squares (GLS).

The ML approach involves making stronger distributional assumptions concerning the u_i's. For example, Pitt and Lee (1981) assumed a half-normal distribution, while Battese and Coelli (1988) considered the more general truncated-normal distribution. In the followings, we briefly discuss these approaches.

Schmidt and Sickles (1984) proposed a random-effects model to compute time-invariant efficiency. In the case of a cost function model, it is defined as

$$\begin{aligned} c_{it} &= \alpha + x'_{it}\beta + v_{it} + u_i \\ &= (\alpha + \mu) + x'_{it}\beta + v_{it} + u_i^* \end{aligned} \tag{3.35}$$

where $\mu = E(u_i) > 0$. In doing this transformation, $u_i^* = u_i - \mu$ has a zero mean by definition and usual GLS panel data techniques apply. Hence, the model can be rewritten as

$$c_{it} = \alpha_i + x'_{it}\beta + v_{it} \tag{3.36}$$

where $\alpha_i = \alpha + u_i$. The estimate of inefficiency $\hat{u}_i$ is then defined (as in the fixed-effects model) as the distance from the bank-specific intercept to the minimal intercept in the sample:

$$\hat{u}_i = \hat{\alpha}_i - \min_i (\hat{\alpha}_i) \geq 0. \tag{3.37}$$

The frontier is thus shifted to the bank with the smallest estimated intercept. The estimate $\hat{\alpha}_i$ is calculated by $\hat{\alpha}_i = 1/T \sum_t \hat{\varepsilon}_{it}$ for each $i = 1, \ldots, N$, where $\hat{\varepsilon}_{it} = c_{it} - x'_{it}\hat{\beta}$ is the composed residual from regression.

Schmidt and Sickles (1984) point out that the random-effects model is more suitable for short panels in which correlation is empirically rejected. Hausman and Taylor (1981) developed a test, based on Hausman (1978), for the hypothesis that the error terms are uncorrelated with the regressors. If the null hypothesis of non-correlation is accepted, a random-effects model is chosen, otherwise a fixed-effects model is appropriate. The Hausman specification test is a test of the orthogonality assumption that characterises the random-effects estimator, which is defined as the weighted average of the Between and Within estimator. The test statistic is

$$H = \left(\hat{\beta}_{FE} - \hat{\beta}_{RE}\right)' \left[\mathrm{var}\left(\hat{\beta}_{FE}\right) - \mathrm{var}\left(\hat{\beta}_{RE}\right)\right]^{-1} \left(\hat{\beta}_{FE} - \hat{\beta}_{RE}\right) \tag{3.38}$$

where $\hat{\beta}_{RE}$ and $\hat{\beta}_{FE}$ are the estimated parameter vectors from the random and fixed-effects models. Under the null hypothesis that the random-effects estimator is appropriate, the test statistic is distributed asymptotically as χ^2 with degrees of freedom equal to the number of the regressors. Henceforth, large values of the H test statistic have to be interpreted as supporting the fixed-effects model. Hausman and Taylor (1981) developed a similar test of the hypothesis that the inefficiency terms are not correlated with the regressors.

The above panel data techniques avoid the necessity of distribution assumptions in both the specification and the estimation of stochastic frontier functions. However, if the latter are known, similar maximum likelihood techniques to the ones applied to the cross-sectional data can be applied to a stochastic production frontier panel data model in order to get more efficient estimates of the parameter vector and of the cost inefficiency scores for each productive unit. In this respect, Pitt and Lee (1981) derived the half-normal counterpart of Aigner et al. (1977) model for panel data, while Kumbhakar (1987) and Battese and Coelli (1988) extend Pitt and Lee's analysis to the normal-truncated stochastic frontier panel data model. The inefficiency can be estimated by the conditional mean $\hat{u}_i = E(u_i|\overline{\varepsilon}_i)$, where $\varepsilon_{it} = u_i + v_{it}$ and $\overline{\varepsilon}_{it} = \frac{1}{T}\sum_{t=1}^{T} \hat{\varepsilon}_{it}$, proposed by Jondrow et al. (1982). Alternatively, Battese and Coelli's (1988) estimator $E(\exp\{-u_{it}\}|\overline{\varepsilon}_i)$ can be used to obtain point estimator bank-specific time-invariant cost inefficiency.

3.6.1.2 Time-Variant Efficiency Models

The assumption of time-invariant efficiency seems to be very unreasonable with large panels, particularly if the operating environment is competitive. In such a situation, it is hard to accept the notion that inefficiency remains constant through many time periods (Kumbhakar and Lovell 2000). Cornwell et al. (1990) and Kumbhakar (1990) were the first to propose a model with efficiency varying with time. The first study suggested the use of several estimation strategies, including fixed-effects and random-effects approaches, while the second study applied a maximum likelihood technique with the assumption that efficiency varies in the same way for all individuals.

If the assumption of a time-invariant inefficiency term is relaxed, the model to be examined is the following:

$$\begin{aligned} c_{it} &= \alpha_{0t} + x'_{it}\beta + v_{it} + u_{it} \\ &= \alpha_{\text{it}} + x'_{it}\beta + v_{it} \end{aligned} \tag{3.39}$$

where α_{0t} is the cost frontier intercept common to all banks in period t and $\alpha_{it} = \alpha_{0t} + u_{it}$ is the intercept for the ith bank in period t. Given that it is possible to estimate α_{it}, the following estimates of the cost efficiency of each bank can be obtained:

$$\hat{u}_{it} = \alpha_{it} - \alpha_{0t} \tag{3.40}$$

where $\alpha_{0t} = \min_i (\hat{\alpha}_{it})$. Since it is not possible to estimate all α_{it} because this would mean having to estimate additional $N \times T$ coefficients in addition to the parameter vector β, Cornwell et al. (1990) proposed the following functional form:

$$\alpha_{it} = \theta_{i1} + \theta_{i2}t + \theta_{i3}t^2 \tag{3.41}$$

which reduces the problem to estimating $N \times 3$ parameters in addition to the ones contained in β. Substituting (3.41) in (3.39), we get the general model:

$$\begin{aligned} c_{it} &= \theta_{i1} + \theta_{i2}t + \theta_{i3}t^2 + x'_{it}\beta + v_{it} \\ &= w'_{it}\delta_i + x'_{it}\beta + v_{it} \end{aligned} \tag{3.42}$$

where $w'_{it} = [1, t, t^2]$, and $\delta_i = \begin{bmatrix} \theta_{i1} \\ \theta_{i2} \\ \theta_{i3} \end{bmatrix}$

When using a fixed-effects model, the estimation procedure starts by finding the 'Within estimator', $\hat{\beta}_w$, then continues by applying OLS to a regression of the residuals $(y_{it} - x'_{it}\hat{\beta}_w)$ to find estimates of the elements of δ_i and then computing $\hat{\alpha}_{it}$ as $w'_{it}\hat{\delta}_i$. Finally, estimates of inefficiency as in (3.40) will be obtained. Cornwell et al. (1990) consider the fixed-effects and random-effects approach. Since time-invariant regressors cannot be included in the fixed-effects model, they develop a GLS random-effects estimator for time-varying cost efficiency model. However, the GLS estimator is inconsistent when the cost inefficiencies are correlated with the regressors; therefore, the authors compute an efficient instrumental variables (EIV) estimator that is consistent in the case of correlation of the efficiency terms with the regressors and that also allows for the inclusion of time-invariant regressors.

Lee and Schmidt (1993) propose an alternative formulation, in which the cost inefficiency effects for each productive unit at a different time period are defined by the product of individual cost inefficiency and time-effects:

$$u_{it} = \delta_t u_i$$

where δ_t's are the time-effects represented by time dummies and the u_i can be either fixed or random bank-specific effects.

On the other hand, if independence and distributional assumptions are available, Maximum Likelihood Estimation technique can also be applied to the estimation of stochastic frontier panel data models where cost inefficiency depends on time. Kumbhakar (1990) suggests a model in which the cost inefficiency effects assumed to have a half-normal distribution vary systematically with time according to the following expression:

$$u_{it} = \delta(t)u_i \text{ and } \delta(t) = \left[1 + \exp\left(bt + ct^2\right)\right]^{-1},$$

where b and c are unknown parameters to be estimated. In this model, the hypothesis of time-invariant cost efficiency can be verified by testing the hypothesis $b = c = 0$.

Another time-varying efficiency model was proposed by Battese and Coelli (1992) who assume cost inefficiency to be an exponential function of time and where only one additional parameter (b) has to be estimated:

$$u_{it} = \delta(t)u_i = \exp[-b(t - T)]u_i \tag{3.43}$$

where u_i's are assumed to be *i.i.d.* following a truncated-normal distribution. The drawback to these two models is that the inefficiency component follows a prescribed functional form, which might or might not be true. Especially in the case of the Battese and Coelli (1992) model, the evolution of the inefficiency component over time is monotonic, i.e. the inefficiency increases or decreases constantly over time, which need not hold in general. Cuesta (2000) specified a model of the form $u_{it} = \delta(t)$ $u_i = \exp[-b_i(t - T)]u_i$. This model generalises the Battese and Coelli (1992) model and allows the temporal pattern of inefficiency effects to vary across banks.

Kumbhakar and Hjalmarsson (1995) model the inefficiency term as

$$u_{it} = a_i + \xi_{it} \tag{3.44}$$

where a_i is a bank-specific component which captures bank heterogeneity also due to omitted time-invariant variables and ξ_{it} is a bank time-specific component which has a half-normal distribution. The estimation of this model is in two steps. In the first step, either a fixed-effects model or a random-effects model is used to estimate all the parameters of the model $c_{it} = \alpha + x'_{it}\beta + v_{it} + u_{it}$, except those in (3.44). In the second step, distribution assumptions are imposed on ξ_{it} and v_{it}. The fixed-effects $(\alpha + a_i)$ and the parameters ξ_{it} and v_{it} are estimated by maximum likelihood, conditioned on the first step parameter estimates.

Battese and Coelli (1995) propose a model for stochastic cost inefficiency effects for panel data which includes explanatory variables. They modelled the inefficiency component as

$$u_{it} = \delta' z_{it} + w_{it} \tag{3.45}$$

where u_{it} are cost inefficiency effects in the stochastic frontier model that are assumed to be independently but not identically distributed, z_{it} is vector of variables which influence efficiencies, and δ is the vector of coefficients to be estimated. w_{it} is a random variable distributed as a truncated-normal distribution with zero mean and variance σ_u^2. The requirement that $u_{it} \geq 0$ is ensured by truncating w_{it} from below such that $w_{it} \geq -\delta' z_{it}$. Battese and Coelli (1995) underline that the assumptions on the error component w_{it} are consistent with the assumption of the inefficiency terms being distributed as truncated-normal distribution $N^+(\delta' z_{it}, \sigma_u^2)$.

3.6.2 Stochastic Distance Functions

Traditional stochastic production frontier models are incapable to provide the technical efficiency scores when there is multiple-outputs since those models accommodate only single output. For computing technical efficiency of the banks in a multiple-outputs and multiple-inputs setting, the researchers are now widely using the stochastic distance functions (see, e.g. Jiang et al. 2009; Cuesta and Orea 2002; Rezitis 2008; Koutsomanoli-Filippaki et al. 2009b). Stochastic distance function approach allows one to deal which multiple-inputs multiple-outputs (Coelli and Perelman 1999) in the form of parametric distance functions, originally proposed by Shephard (1970). The basic idea is that in the case of a given production possibility frontier, for every bank, the distance from the production frontier is a function of the vector of inputs used, x, and the level of outputs produced, y. For the output-oriented model, the distance function is defined as

$$D_o(x, y) = \min\{\theta : y/\theta \in P(x)\} \tag{3.46}$$

where $D_o(x,y)$ is the distance function from the bank's output set $P(x)$ to the production frontier. $D_o(x,y)$ is nondecreasing, positively linearly homogeneous and convex in y and decreasing in x (Coelli and Perelman 1999). θ is the scalar distance by which the output vector can be deflated (see Coelli 2000) and can be interpreted as the level of efficiency. The output distance function aims at identifying the largest proportional increase in the observed output vector y provided that the expanded vector y/θ is still an element of the original output set. If y is located on the outer boundary of the production possibility set then $D_o(x,y) = \theta = 1$ and the utility is 100 % efficient. On the other hand, values of $D_o(x,y) = \theta \leq 1$ indicate inefficient banks lying within the *efficient frontier*.

The input-orientated approach is defined on the input set $L(y)$ and considers, by holding the output vector fixed, how much the input vector may be proportionally contracted. The input distance function is expressed by

$$D_i(x, y) = \max\{\rho : x/\rho \in L(y)\}. \tag{3.47}$$

$D_i(x,y)$ is nondecreasing, positively linearly homogeneous and concave in x and increasing in y (Coelli and Perelman 1999). ρ is the scalar distance by which the input vector can be deflated. If $D_i(x,y) = \rho = 1$, then x is located on the inner boundary of the input set and the bank is 100 % efficient.

In stochastic distance functions approach, the first step is to determine the parametric relationship between inputs and outputs. The most commonly used functional form is the translog function. The translog input distance function D_i in its parametric form with M ($m = 1, \ldots, M$) outputs and K ($k = 1, \ldots, K$) inputs is specified as (Coelli 2000)

$$\begin{aligned} \ln D_i = \alpha_o + \sum_{m=1}^{M} \gamma_m \ln y_m + \sum_{k=1}^{K} \beta_k \ln x_k + \frac{1}{2} \sum_{m=1}^{M} \sum_{n=1}^{M} \gamma_{mn} \ln y_m \ln y_n \\ + \frac{1}{2} \sum_{k=1}^{K} \sum_{l=1}^{K} \beta_{kl} \ln x_k \ln x_l + \sum_{k=1}^{K} \sum_{m=1}^{M} \delta_{km} \ln x_k \ln y_m. \end{aligned} \tag{3.48}$$

In order to maintain the homogeneity and symmetry, a number of restrictions need to be imposed. For homogeneity, the following restrictions have to be considered:

$$\sum_{k=1}^{K}\beta_k = 1,\ \sum_{l=1}^{K}\beta_{kl} = 0 \text{ and} \sum_{k=1}^{K}\delta_{km} = 0$$

For symmetry, two other restrictions have to be fulfilled:

$$\gamma_{mn} = \gamma_{nm} \quad \text{and} \quad \beta_{kl} = \beta_{lk}$$

Imposing homogeneity restrictions by normalising (3.48) by dividing the inputs by one of the inputs x_K delivers the estimating form of the input distance:

$$-\ln x_k = \alpha_o + \sum_{m=1}^{M}\gamma_m \ln y_m + \sum_{k=1}^{K-1}\beta_k \ln\left(\frac{x_k}{x_K}\right) + \frac{1}{2}\sum_{m=1}^{M}\sum_{n=1}^{M}\gamma_{mn}\ln y_m \ln y_n$$
$$+ \frac{1}{2}\sum_{k=1}^{K-1}\sum_{l=1}^{K-1}\beta_{kl}\ln\left(\frac{x_k}{x_K}\right)\ln\left(\frac{x_l}{x_K}\right) + \sum_{k=1}^{K-1}\sum_{m=1}^{M}\delta_{km}\ln\left(\frac{x_k}{x_K}\right)\ln y_m - \ln D_i. \tag{3.49}$$

Here, $\ln D_i$ can be interpreted as error term which reflects the difference between the observed data realisations and the predicted points of the estimated function. Replacing $\ln D_i$ by a composed error term (the stochastic error ν_i and the technical inefficiency u_i) yields the common SFA form. It can be estimated by a stochastic frontier production function defined as $y_i = f(x_i) + \nu_i - u_i$. For $I(i = 1, \ldots, I)$ banks, the econometric specification with $\ln D_i = \nu_i - u_i$, in its normalised form, is expressed by

$$-\ln x_{Ki} = \alpha_o + \sum_{m=1}^{M}\gamma_m \ln y_{mi} + \sum_{k=1}^{K-1}\beta_k \ln\left(\frac{x_{ki}}{x_{Ki}}\right) + \frac{1}{2}\sum_{m=1}^{M}\sum_{n=1}^{M}\gamma_{mn}\ln y_{mi}\ln y_{ni}$$
$$+ \frac{1}{2}\sum_{k=1}^{K-1}\sum_{l=1}^{K-1}\beta_{kl}\ln\left(\frac{x_{ki}}{x_{Ki}}\right)\ln\left(\frac{x_{li}}{x_{Ki}}\right) + \sum_{k=1}^{K-1}\sum_{m=1}^{M}\delta_{km}\ln\left(\frac{x_{ki}}{x_{Ki}}\right)\ln y_{mi} + \nu_i - u_i. \tag{3.50}$$

A distribution for u_i has to be assumed in order to separate stochastic noise and inefficiency effects. One may assume that u_i follows either the half-normal distribution ($u_i \sim N^+[0,\sigma_u^2]$) or the truncated-normal distribution ($u_i \sim N^+[0,\sigma_u^2]$).

3.6.3 *Marrying DEA with SFA*

In recent years, attempts have been made by the researchers to marry DEA with SFA with the objective to reap the benefits of both the approaches in estimating banking efficiency. The first attempt in this direction has been made by Fried et al. (2002). The authors suggested a three-stage approach which begins with

DEA for purging performance evaluation of environmental factors and statistical noise. In the second stage, SFA is applied to trace components of performance attributable to the operating environment of the unit, statistical noise and managerial efficiency. In the third stage, data entered into DEA in Stage 1 are adjusted for the effect of the environment and statistical noise before repeating DEA. Thus, the evaluation emerging from the final stage DEA is said to represent managerial efficiency only.

In Stage 1, Fried et al. (2002) suggested the use of input-oriented variable returns-to-scale DEA with the conventional BCC model. The linear programming problem for envelopment form of BCC-I is given as

$$\begin{aligned}
&\min_{\theta, s_i^-, s_r^+} \quad \theta - \varepsilon\left(\sum_{i=1}^{m} s_i^- + \sum_{r=1}^{s} s_r^+\right) \\
&\text{subject to} \\
&\quad \sum_{j=1}^{n} \lambda_j x_{ij} + s_i^- = \theta x_{io} \\
&\quad \sum_{j=1}^{n} \lambda_j y_{rj} - s_r^+ = y_{ro} \\
&\quad \sum_{j=1}^{n} \lambda_j = 1 \\
&\quad \lambda_j, s_i^-, s_r^+ \geq 0
\end{aligned} \tag{3.51}$$

where x_{ij} is the amount of the ith input used by the bank j, y_{rj} is the amount of the rth output produced by the bank j and s_i^- and s_r^+ represent input and output slacks, respectively. The optimal solution that emerges from the model (3.51) is the preliminary performance evaluation scores that are likely to be confounded by environmental effects and statistical noise.

In Stage 2, Fried et al. (2002) focus on radial slacks (i.e. input contraction) emerging from Stage 1 DEA rather than non-radial slacks (i.e. underproduced output). Using SFA, input slacks are regressed on observable environmental variables and a composed error term that captures statistical noise due to measurement errors and managerial inefficiency. The main justification for SFA is an asymmetric error term that allows for identification of the one-sided error component (i.e. managerial inefficiency) and the symmetric error term component (i.e. statistical noise). The general function of the SFA regressions is represented in (3.52) for the case of input slacks:

$$s_{i,j}^- = f^i\left(z_j; \beta^i\right) + \nu_{i,j} + u_{i,j} \tag{3.52}$$

where $s_{i,j}^-$ is the Stage 1 slack in the ith input for the bank j, z_j is the environmental variables, β^i is the parameter vectors for the feasible slack frontier and $\nu_{i,j} + u_{i,j}$ is composed error structure where $\nu_{i,j} \sim N\left(0, \sigma_{\nu_i}^2\right)$ represents statistical noise, and

$u_{i,j} \geq 0$ represents managerial inefficiency. Similarly, SFA regression for the case of output slacks can be given as follows:

$$s^{+}_{r,j} = f^{r}\left(z_j; \beta^{r}\right) + \nu_{r,j} + u_{r,j} \tag{3.53}$$

The SFA regression model does not require specification of the direction of impact of environmental variables; this can be read from the signs of the parameters. Following each regression, parameters $\beta^{i}, \mu^{i}, \sigma^{2}_{\nu_i}, \sigma^{2}_{u_i}$ are estimated and permitted to vary across N input slack regressions.

In Stage 3, the authors repeat the DEA of Stage 1 by replacing observed input data with input data that have been adjusted for the influence of environmental factors and statistical noise. Thus, the DEA analysis to emerge from Stage 3 represents performance due to managerial efficiency only.

The above three-stage analysis put forward by Fried et al. (2002) begins with traditional DEA using the BCC model. However, the BCC model, while producing unit-invariant (i.e. dimension-free) radial inefficiency estimates, does not generate unit-invariant estimates of non-radial inefficiency (or slacks). For consistent interpretation of DEA and SFA estimates, there is a need to choose a fully unit invariant DEA model. Such a solution exists within the slack-based measure (SBM) of efficiency as suggested by Tone (2001) where it is possible to argue for either output maximisation or input minimisation. However, Fried et al. (2002) arbitrarily select input minimisation and, thus, focus only on input slacks in Stage 2. Thus, Avkiran and Rowlands (2008) modified the research design put forward by the Fried et al. (2002) and proposed a more comprehensive analysis where total input and output slacks are measured simultaneously against the same reference set, facilitated by a non-oriented SBM model that is fully unit-invariant. The linear programming programme for the non-oriented constant returns-to-scale SBM is shown below:

$$\begin{aligned}
&\min\ \rho = \frac{1 - \dfrac{1}{m}\displaystyle\sum_{i=1}^{m} s_i^{-}/x_{io}}{1 + \dfrac{1}{s}\displaystyle\sum_{r=1}^{s} s_r^{+}/y_{ro}} \\
&\text{subject to} \\
&\sum_{j=1}^{n} \lambda_j x_{ij} + s_i^{-} = x_{io} \\
&\sum_{j=1}^{n} \lambda_j y_{rj} - s_r^{+} = y_{ro} \\
&\lambda_j, s_i^{-}, s_r^{+} \geq 0
\end{aligned} \tag{3.54}$$

where s_i^{-} and s_r^{+} represent input and output slacks, respectively. Alternatively, the model can be transformed into

$$\rho = \left(\frac{1}{m}\sum_{i=1}^{m}\frac{x_{io} - s_i^-}{x_{io}}\right)\left(\frac{1}{s}\sum_{r=1}^{s}\frac{y_{ro} + s_r^+}{y_{ro}}\right) \tag{3.55}$$

where the first term represents the mean contraction rate of inputs and the second term represents the mean expansion rate of outputs. In the model (3.54), the bank is deemed to be efficient if the optimal value for the objective function is unity. In other words, for a bank to be efficient, all optimal input slack (input excess) and output slack (output shortfall) must equal zero. In the alternative formulation represented by (3.55), SBM is the product of input and output inefficiencies. In this way, environmental variables are omitted in Stage 1 analysis.

In Stage 2, Fried et al. ignore output slacks and regressed only input slacks on the environmental variables because of their model's input orientation. However, they do acknowledge that a case can be made where both input and output slacks are explained through SFA. As a modification, Avkiran and Rowlands (2008) focus on both input slacks and output slacks and thus provide a more refined measure of organisational efficiency which can be incorporated into managerial decision making with more confidence. Thus, Stage 2 analysis leads to an estimate of $m + s$ (i.e. inputs plus outputs) SFA regressions where slacks measured by SBM for each input (output) are regressed on environmental variables. Parameter estimates obtained from SFA regressions are used to predict input slacks attributable to the operating environment and to statistical noise. Thus, observed inputs can be adjusted for the impact of the environment and statistical noise by

$$x_{i,j}^A = x_{i,j} + \left[\max_j\left\{z_j\hat{\beta}^i\right\} - z_j\hat{\beta}^i\right] + \left[\max_j\left\{\hat{\nu}_{i,j}\right\} - \hat{\nu}_{i,j}\right] \tag{3.56}$$

where $x_{i,j}^A$ is the adjusted quantity of ith input in j^{th} bank, $x_{i,j}$ the observed quantity of ith input in j^{th} bank, $z_j\hat{\beta}^i$ the ith input slack in j^{th} bank attributable to environmental factors and $\hat{\nu}_{i,j}$ the ith input slack in j^{th} bank attributable to statistical noise.

Alternatively,

$$x_{i,j}^A = \left(1 + \text{AdjFactorEnvironment}_{x_{i,j}} + \text{AdjFactorNoise}_{x_{i,j}}\right)x_{i,j} \tag{3.57}$$

where

$$\text{AdjFactorEnvironment}_{x_{i,j}} = \left(\frac{\max_j\left\{z_j\hat{\beta}^i\right\}}{x_{i,j}}\right)\left(\frac{1 - z_j\hat{\beta}^i}{\max_j\left\{z_j\hat{\beta}^i\right\}}\right), \text{ and}$$

$$\text{AdjFactorNoise}_{x_{i,j}} = \left(\frac{\max_j\left\{\hat{\nu}_{i,j}\right\}}{x_{i,j}}\right)\left(\frac{1 - \hat{\nu}_{i,j}}{\max_j\left\{\hat{\nu}_{i,j}\right\}}\right).$$

The first adjustment in the (3.56), $\left[\max_j\left\{z_j\hat{\beta}^i\right\} - z_j\hat{\beta}^i\right]$, levels the playing field regarding the operating environment by placing all units into the least favourable environment observed in the sample. The second adjustment $\left[\max_j \left\{\hat{\nu}_{i,j}\right\} - \hat{\nu}_{i,j}\right]$ places all units in the least fortunate situation (i.e. regarding measurement errors) found in the sample. Hence, banks enjoying relatively favourable operating environments and statistical noise would find their inputs adjusted upwards. Equation 3.57 is the transformation of Fried et al.'s approach to adjusting inputs, where the researcher is better able to see the degree of adjustments attributable to the operating environment and statistical noise. This is achieved by taking ratios instead of differences and arriving at an adjustment factor which multiplies the observed input. The variable 'AdjFactorEnvironment' represents the percent upward adjustment of the observed input for the impact of the environment, and the another variable, 'AdjFactorNoise', captures the percent upward adjustment attributed to statistical noise.

Similarly, observed outputs can be adjusted for the impact of the environment and statistical noise by

$$y^A_{r,j} = y_{r,j} + \left[z_j\hat{\beta}^r - \min_j\left\{z_j\hat{\beta}^r\right\}\right] + \left[\hat{\nu}_{r,j} - \min_j\left\{\hat{\nu}_{r,j}\right\}\right] \tag{3.58}$$

where $y^A_{r,j}$ is the adjusted quantity of rth output in j^{th} bank, $y_{r,j}$ the observed quantity of rth output in j^{th} bank, $z_j\hat{\beta}^r$ the rth output slack in j^{th} bank attributable to environmental factors and $\hat{\nu}_{r,j}$ the rth output slack in j^{th} bank attributable to statistical noise.

Alternatively,

$$y^A_{r,j} = \left(1 + \text{AdjFactorEnvironment}_{y_{r,j}} + \text{AdjFactorNoise}_{y_{r,j}}\right)y_{r,j} \tag{3.59}$$

where

$$\text{AdjFactorEnvironment}_{y_{r,j}} = \left(\frac{z_j\hat{\beta}^r}{y_{r,j}}\right)\left(1 - \frac{\min_j\left\{z_j\hat{\beta}^r\right\}}{z_j\hat{\beta}^r}\right),$$

$$\text{AdjFactorNoise}_{y_{r,j}} = \left(\frac{\hat{\nu}_{r,j}}{y_{r,j}}\right)\left(1 - \frac{\min_j\left\{\hat{\nu}_{r,j}\right\}}{\hat{\nu}_{r,j}}\right)$$

However, to use Eqs. 3.56 or 3.58, it is necessary to distinguish input-sourced statistical noise ($\nu_{i,j}$) from managerial inefficiency ($u_{i,j}$) in the composed error term of the SFA regressions. Once $\nu_{i,j}$ has been estimated for each unit, Eqs. 3.56 or 3.58 can be implemented and observed input usage adjusted. The statistical noise attached to an input usage and in output generation is estimated residually by Eqs. 3.60 and 3.61, respectively, as

$$\hat{E}\left[\nu_{i,j}\middle|\nu_{i,j} + u_{i,j}\right] = s^-_{i,j} - z_j\hat{\beta}^i - \hat{E}\left[u_{i,j}\middle|\nu_{i,j} + u_{i,j}\right] \tag{3.60}$$

and

$$\hat{E}\left[\nu_{r,j}\middle|\nu_{r,j}+u_{r,j}\right]=s_{r,j}^{+}-z_j\hat{\beta}^{r}-\hat{E}\left[u_{r,j}\middle|\nu_{r,j}+u_{r,j}\right]. \tag{3.61}$$

In Stage 3, SBM DEA analysis of managerial efficiency purged of the influence of operating environment and statistical noise. That is, in this final stage of the three-stage efficiency analysis, all units are re-evaluated after inputs and outputs have been adjusted for influences of operating environment and statistical noise.

3.7 Other Parametric Approaches

3.7.1 Distribution Free Approach (DFA)

The distribution free approach (DFA) was originally suggested in Schmidt and Sickles (1984) and introduced by Berger (1993). It assumes that efficiencies are stable over time[7] while random error tends to average out and, thus, requiring little to be assumed about the distributional form of the efficiency measure or random error. In this sense, the methodology is relatively 'distribution free'. DFA specifies a functional form for the efficiency frontier as does SFA, but it uses different way to separate the inefficiencies from the residual. In particular, it is based on a translog system of cost and input cost share equations, and it generates estimates of inefficiency for each bank in each time period. In DFA, the cost function can be estimated either by GLS, as in Schmidt and Sickles (1984), or by using OLS, as in Berger (1993). Since DFA does not require any assumption about the distribution of either inefficiency or the random error, it is easier to implement than SFA. Some significant studies on the use of DFA in the banking industry are Berger (1993), Allen and Rai (1996), DeYoung (1997), Dietsch and Lozano-Vivas (2000), Rime and Stiroh (2003), Matousek and Taci (2004) and Weill (2007).

In order to estimate cost efficiency, let us suppose there is a sample of banks indexed $i = 1,\ldots, I$ in each of T time periods indexed $t = 1,\ldots..,T$. For each bank, we observe expenditure E_{it}, a vector y_{it} of outputs produced, and a vector w_{it} of input prices paid. A translog system consisting of a cost equation and its associated input cost share equations can be written as

$$\begin{aligned} \ln E_{it} &= \ln c(y_{it}, w_{it}; \beta^t) + v_{it} + u_i, \\ \frac{w_{nit}x_{nit}}{E_{it}} &= s_{nit}(y_{it}, w_{it}; \beta^t) + v_{nit}, \qquad (n = 2, \ldots, N) \end{aligned} \tag{3.62}$$

[7] DFA is also known as stability-over-time approach as it assumes that efficiencies are stable over time.

This system is estimated separately for each time period, and so the technology parameter vector has a time superscript. Within each time period the error vector $[v_{it}, v'_{nit}]'$ captures the effects of random statistical noise, and the error component $u_i \geq 0$ measures the cost of bank-specific cost inefficiency. Since $E(v_{nit}) = 0$, allocative efficiency is imposed, and so u_i captures the cost of technical inefficiency only. Zellner's Seemingly Unrelated Regression (SUR) estimator is used to estimate model (3.62). It is assumed that the u_i are random effects distributed independently of the regressors. For each producer, the cost equation residuals $\hat{\varepsilon}_{it} = \hat{v}_{it} + \hat{u}_i$ are averaged over time to obtain the average residual, $\hat{\varepsilon}_i = (1/T) \sum_t \hat{\varepsilon}_{it}$. On the assumption that the random-noise error component v_{it} should tend to average zero over time, $\hat{\varepsilon}_i = (1/T)\sum_t \hat{\varepsilon}_{it} \cong \hat{u}_i$ provide an estimate of the cost inefficiency error component. To ensure that estimated cost inefficiency is non-negative, $\hat{\varepsilon}_{it}$ is normalised on the smallest value, and we obtain

$$\text{In}\, Eff_{it} = \exp\{-[\hat{\varepsilon}_i - \min_i(\hat{\varepsilon}_i)]\}$$

where $\min_i(\hat{\varepsilon}_i)$ is the minimum value of the average error term for all banks in the sample. This estimator is similar to the GLS panel data estimator in which u_i is treated as a random-effects, and this similarity suggests that it is appropriated when I is large relative to T and when the u_i are orthogonal to the regressors. However, it differs from GLS in that the structure of the underlying production technology is allowed to vary through time. Berger (1993) noted that since the elements of v_{it} may not fully cancel out through time for each producer, $\hat{\varepsilon}_i$ may contain elements of luck as well as inefficiency. To alleviate this problem, he recommended truncating the distribution of CE_i at its qth and $(1-q)$th quantiles.

A disadvantage of DFA is the requirement that cost efficiency be time invariant, and this becomes less tenable as T increases. However, DFA also has two distinct virtues. First, being based on a sequence of T separate cross-sectional regressions, it allows the structure of production technology to vary flexibly through time (although excessive variation in $\hat{\beta}^t$ would be difficult to explain). Second, it does not impose a distributional assumption on the u_i, it lets the data reveal the empirical distribution of the $\hat{\varepsilon}_{it} \cong \hat{u}_i$.

3.7.2 Thick Frontier Analysis (TFA)

Berger and Humphrey (1991, 1992) developed another distribution free way of estimating cost frontiers using a single cross section or a panel, the so-called Thick Frontier Analysis (TFA). The TFA specifies a functional form for the frontier cost function. In contrast to SFA which imposes arbitrary assumptions about the normal and half-normal distributions, and orthogonality between X-inefficiencies and regressors, TFA imposes no distributional assumptions on either inefficiency or random error. It assumes that deviations from predicted costs within the highest and lowest cost quartiles of observations (stratified by size class) represent random error, while deviations in predicted costs between the highest and lowest quartiles represent inefficiencies (Berger and Humphrey 1997).

In TFA, instead of estimating a precise frontier bound, a cost function is estimated for the lowest average cost quartile of banks, which may be thought of as a 'thick frontier', where the banks exhibit an efficiency greater than the sample average. Similarly, the cost function for the highest average cost quartile is also estimated where the banks assumed to have less efficiency than the sample average. The difference in the predicted costs between these two 'thick frontiers'[8] or 'cost functions' can be split into two factors. First is explained by market factors related to the available exogenous variables and the second factor cannot be explained, i.e. the 'inefficiency residual'. The predicted cost differences between highest and lowest cost quartiles between market factors and inefficiency residual can de decomposed as

$$\text{Diff} = \left[\hat{AC}^{Q4} - \hat{AC}^{Q1}\right]/\hat{AC}^{Q1}$$

where $\hat{AC}^{Q1}$ and $\hat{AC}^{Q4}$ represent the mean average cost of lowest and highest cost quartiles, respectively. The part of Diff owing to the exogenous market factors is given by:

$$\text{Market} = \left[\hat{AC}^{Q4*} - \hat{AC}^{Q1}\right]/\hat{AC}^{Q1}$$

The remaining differences in average cost that cannot be attributed to the exogenous variables constitute the measured inefficiency residual as given by:

$$\text{Ineff} = \left[\hat{AC}^{Q4} - \hat{AC}^{Q4*}\right]/\hat{AC}^{Q1} = \text{Diff} - \text{Market}$$

The distinct advantages of the Thick Frontier Analysis is that (i) any number of exogenous variables may be added to the cost equation without changing the number of comparison banks or necessarily creating a downward bias in the inefficiency estimate, (ii) even if the errors terms within quartiles represent inefficiencies rather than random errors as maintained, the thick frontier approach remains a valid comparison of the average inefficiencies of high and low cost banks, and (iii) it reduces the effect of extreme points in the data, as can DFA when the extreme average residuals are truncated. However, an important caveat of TFA is that the measured efficiency under TFA is sensitive to the assumptions about which fluctuations are random and which represent efficiency differences (Berger 1993). For example, if random errors follow a thick-tailed distribution and tend to be large in absolute value, while inefficiencies follow a thin-tailed distribution and tend to be small, then TFA may not yield precise estimates of the overall level of inefficiencies.

[8] The frontier is called *thick* in order to indicate that best practice banks are allowed to be positioned close to the frontier but not necessarily at the frontier.

However, Berger and Humphrey (1991) argued that 'precise measurement is not our purpose rather, our goals are to get a basic idea of the likely magnitude of inefficiencies in banking and to identify their sources by decomposing them into several categories'.

3.7.3 Recursive Thick Frontier Analysis (RTFA)

Recursive Thick Frontier Analysis (RTFA) was developed by Wagenvoort and Schure (1999, 2006). It is panel estimation approach which avoids imposing distributional assumptions on the inefficiency component of the error term. Unlike other frontier approaches, RTFA works well even if the number of time periods in the panel data set is small. RTFA is based on the assertion that if deviations from the frontier of X-efficient banks are completely random then one must observe for this group of banks that the probability of being located either above or below the frontier is equal to a half. This hypothesis can be tested for panel data sets but requires sorting of the full sample into a group of X-inefficient and X-efficient banks. The cost frontier is estimated using only the observations of the latter category by applying the 'trimmed least squares' (TLS) estimator (see Koenker and Bassett 1978). Once the frontier is established, the X-efficiency can be computed as

$$XEFF_{ti} = x_{ti}\beta^*_{TLS}/y_{ti}.$$

Here, x_{ti} represents a k-dimensional input bundle and y_{ti} is an output bundle. β^*_{TLS} is TLS estimator of β. RTFA allows X-inefficiency to vary over time and be dependent on the explanatory variables of the frontier model.

Two important points are to be emphasised. First, in RTFA, the efficient banks are selected on the basis of their distance to the regression line instead of their average costs as in TFA. Second, even in the case where the observations of both the inefficient and efficient banks are drawn from a normal distribution, it is unlikely that the computed residuals of the regression equation are exactly normally distributed.

3.8 Comparison of DEA and SFA

In the banking efficiency literature, the most commonly used parametric approach is SFA and non-parametric approach is DEA. As already noted, both SFA and DEA have a range of advantages and disadvantages, which may influence the choice of methods in a particular application. The principal advantage of SFA is that it allows the test of hypothesis concerning the goodness of fit of the model. However, the major disadvantage is that it requires specification of a particular frontier function (like Cobb–Douglas or translog), which may be restrictive in most cases.

Table 3.3 Comparison of DEA and SFA

S. No.	Characteristic	Data Envelopment Analysis	Stochastic frontier analysis
1.	Nature	Non-parametric approach	Parametric approach
2.	Functional specification	DEA does not require any a priori assumption about the selection of particular form of technical, cost or profit function relating to inputs and outputs	SFA requires assumption about the particular form of technical, cost or profit function being estimated and the distribution of efficiency. Thus, the efficiency is then assessed in relation to this function with constant parameters and will be different depending on the chosen functional form
3.	Frontier estimation	DEA constructs a piecewise linear-segmented efficient frontier with minimal assumption about the underlying technology making it less susceptible to specification error but with no scope for random error	SFA constructs a smooth parametric frontier which accounts for stochastic error but requires specific assumptions about the technology and the inefficiency term which may be inappropriate or very restrictive (such as half-normal or constant inefficiency over time)
4.	Handling of inputs and outputs	DEA has the advantage that it is able to manage complex production environments with multiple-input and multiple-output technologies	SFA production frontier cannot manage multiple-outputs. However, cost and profit frontier can accommodate multiple-outputs
5.	Efficiency outcome	DEA efficiency estimates are based on a comparison of the input–output levels of an individual bank with those of a very small subset of efficient units	SFA efficiencies are based on estimated average parameter values in the regression model
6.	Random noise	DEA is a nonstatistical (i.e. non-stochastic) method and makes no assumptions about the stochastic nature of the data. Thus, DEA is deterministic in nature. The non-stochastic nature of DEA implies that either the data are observed without error or the relationship between inputs and outputs is deterministic	SFA is a statistical or econometric method tends to make assumptions about the stochastic nature of the data. Thus, SFA allows for statistical or random 'noise' in data
7.	Sample size	DEA works particularly well with small samples	SFA needs large samples to avoid lack of degrees of freedom

Source: Authors' elaboration

Furthermore, the major advantage of the DEA is that it does not require the specification of a particular functional form for the technology. The main disadvantage is that it is not possible to estimate parameters for the model and hence impossible to test hypothesis concerning the performance of the model.

Table 3.3 provides a comparison of DEA and SFA on various aspects. It is significant to note here that though DEA and SFA are widely used by the researchers in their empirical analyses on the efficiency of banks, but no consensus has been reached in the literature about the appropriate and preferred estimation methodology (Iqbal and Molyneux 2005, Staikouras et al. 2008).

3.9 Conclusions

The main objective of this chapter is to review the various analytical methods which are being used by the researchers to measure bank efficiency. It has been observed that the frontier efficiency measurement methods made the traditional financial accounting ratios' analysis completely obsolete and outdated. From the deep inspection of literature, we note that Data Envelopment Analysis (DEA) and stochastic frontier analysis (SFA) are the predominant frontier approaches that have attracted many empirical studies. Both the approaches have their distinct advantages and disadvantages. DEA has an advantage of computing efficiency scores in multiple-inputs and multiple-outputs production setting without specifying any functional form and distribution of the inefficiency term, but makes no room for noise and lacks hypothesis testing. On the other hand, though the efficiency estimates from SFA accommodate the noise, yet these estimates are very sensitive to the choice of functional form and distribution of the inefficiency term. In sum, no agreement has been reached on the superiority of one method over the others, and choice of a particular method is primarily guided by the data considerations and an individual preference.

Chapter 4
A Survey of Empirical Literature on Bank Efficiency

4.1 Introduction

The purpose of this chapter is to provide a comprehensive but not an exhaustive survey of the empirical literature on bank efficiency. Over the past several years, substantial research efforts have gone into measuring the efficiency of banks using frontier efficiency measurement techniques like Stochastic Frontier Analysis, Data Envelopment Analysis, and Thick Frontier Analysis. However, earlier studies were mainly confined to the banking system of the USA and other well-developed European countries (see, for instance, the survey articles of Berger et al. 1993a; Berger and Humphrey 1997; Berger and Mester 1997). Berger and Humphrey (1997) in their extensive international literature survey documented 130 studies on efficiency of financial institutions covering 21 countries. Of these studies, only eight studies examined the efficiency of banks in the developing and Asian countries (including 2 in Japan). Thus, a lopsided distribution of the studies in favour of industrially advanced countries was confirmed by the existing surveys on the subject matter.

In recent years, we have seen a plethora of empirical studies, which focused on the different strands of research in bank efficiency in developing and transition countries. This motivated us to undertake a fresh survey of literature on the bank efficiency. In particular, we identified four broad nonmutually exclusive research areas in which significant efforts have been made by the researchers in the recent years. The first research area includes those empirical works which examined the impact of deregulation and liberalisation measures on the efficiency of the banking system. The second key area focuses on the issue of bank ownership and efficiency. The studies covered under this area examine whether ownership structure of banking firms plays a significant role in determining efficiency or, in simple words, whether or not private banks are more efficient than state-owned banks. Another significant area covered in this survey concentrates on the cross-country comparisons of bank efficiency. The final research area which has been explored in

S. Kumar and R. Gulati, *Deregulation and Efficiency of Indian Banks*, India Studies in Business and Economics, DOI 10.1007/978-81-322-1545-5_4, © Springer India 2014

the present survey concentrates on the effects of mergers and acquisitions (M&As) on the efficiency and productivity of acquiring banks.

The rest of the chapter is organised as follows. Section 4.2 presents the literature review of bank efficiency studies that assessed the effects of deregulatory policy actions on banks' efficiency performance. The review of the studies on ownership and bank efficiency is provided in Sect. 4.3. Section 4.4 provides a review of the studies on cross-country comparisons of bank efficiency. Section 4.5 lists out the research efforts delineating the effects of M&As on efficiency gains of acquiring banks. The penultimate section provides details on the major issues in bank efficiency analyses. The final section is concluding in nature.

4.2 Deregulation and Bank Efficiency

Until the late 1980s, financial repression policies were responsible for the poor operations of banks in most developing and emerging economies. In many of these economies, the banking industry was heavily controlled by the government. Banks were subjected to a large number of limitations such as restrictions on the expansion of loan portfolios, high pre-emptions of loanable funds and ceilings on interest rates. Due to high degree of regulation and controlled environment, banks in most of these countries lost versatility in their operations and consequently experienced a fall in profitability, efficiency and productivity. To get rid of financial repression, these economies embarked upon the process of financial deregulation and liberalisation of the banking sector. The deregulation policies aimed at eliminating government control and intervention, enhancing competition, improving resource allocation and acquiring more efficient financial institutions, by making them less state directed and by exposing them to increased market competition (Barajas et al. 2000). Consequently, there has been a proliferation of academic studies on examining the impact of deregulation and liberalisation on the efficiency and productivity of the banking system.

In theory, financial liberalisation is expected to improve bank efficiency (Berger and Humphrey 1997). The elimination of government control and intervention aims at restoring and strengthening the price mechanism, as well as improving the conditions for market competition (Hermes and Lensink 2008). This stimulates the efficiency of banks in resource utilisation process. Competitive pressures induce the banks to become more efficient by reducing overhead costs, improving on overall bank management, improving risk management and offering new financial instruments and services (Denizer et al. 2000). Since 1990s, there is a flurry of studies on the effect of deregulation on efficiency and productivity of banks. Nevertheless, the empirical results have been mixed (Berger and Humphrey 1997). Results appear to vary depending on the country, bank ownership and size (Avkiran 2000).

4.2.1 International Experience

Notable studies which reported a positive impact of deregulation on the efficiency and productivity of banks are Berg et al. (1992) for Norway; Zaim (1995), Isik and Hassan (2003a) and Isik (2007) for Turkey; Maghyereh (2004) for Jordan; Leightner and Lovell (1998) and Chantapong and Menkhoff (2005) for Thailand; Chen et al. (2005), Berger et al. (2005) and Fu and Heffernan (2007) for China; Patti and Hardy (2005) and Burki and Niazi (2010) for Pakistan; Mukherjee et al. (2001), Alam (2001) and Berger and Mester (2003) for US; Kumbhakar et al. (2001), Tortosa-Ausina (2002b), Maudos and Pastor (2003) and Kumbhakar and Lozano-Vivas (2005) for Spain; Avkiran (2000), Neal (2004) and Sturm and Williams (2004) for Australia; Rebelo and Mendes (2000) and Canhoto and Dermine (2003) for Portugal; Hasan and Marton (2003) for Hungary; Schmid (1994) and Ali and Gstach (2000) for Austria; López-Cortés (1997) for Mexico; Bertrand et al. (2007) for France; Ariss (2008) for Lebanon; Gilbert and Wilson (1998), Park and Weber (2006) and Banker et al. (2010) for Korea; Gjirja (2004) for Sweden; Girardone et al. (2004) for Italy; Matousek and Taci (2004) for Czech Republic; Hauner and Peiris (2005) for Uganda; Matthews and Ismail (2006) and Njie (2007) for Malaysia; Dacanay III (2007a) for Philippines; Huang et al. (2008) and Hsiao et al. (2010) for Taiwan; Sufian (2007a) for Singapore; Asaftei and Kumbhakar (2008) for Romania; Noulas (2001) and Chortareas et al. (2009) for Greece; and Fethi et al. (2011) for Egypt. Panel A of Table 4.1 provides the major finding(s) of aforementioned studies.

In contrast to aforementioned studies, there are some studies which reported a negative or insignificant effect of deregulatory measures on the efficiency and productivity of banks. Some prominent studies in this context are Humphrey (1991, 1993), Humphrey and Pulley (1997), Grabowski et al. (1994), Elyasiani and Mehdian (1995), Wheelock and Wilson (1999) and Mehdian et al. (2007) for US; Grifell-Tatjé and Lovell (1996) and Lozano-Vivas (1998) for Spain; Kumbhakar and Wang (2007), Ariff and Can (2008) and Fu and Heffernan (2009) for China; Fukuyama and Weber (2002) for Japan; Christopoulos and Tsionas (2001) for Greece; Dogan and Fausten (2003) for Malaysia; Sathye (2002) for Australia; Havrylchyk (2006) for Poland; Denizer et al. (2000, 2007) and Ozkan-Gunay and Tektas (2006) for Turkey; Rizvi (2001) for Pakistan; Hao et al. (2001) and Mahadevan and Kim (2001) for Korea; Cook et al. (2001) for Tunisia; and Kwan (2006) for Hong Kong, among others. Panel B of Table 4.1 presents the major conclusion(s) of above reported studies.

Overall, there is no consensus about the impact of deregulation on the efficiency of banks across different economies. In some countries, the banking sector is benefited from deregulation and liberalisation policies, whereas in others, the efficiency performance of banks seemed not to be affected or deteriorated. Of 72 studies reviewed, 47 studies (i.e. 65 %) conclude that deregulation and liberalisation have had a positive effect on the banks' performance. That is, banks tend to respond positively to more liberal environment, and banks' efficiency and

Table 4.1 Impact of deregulation on the efficiency of banks in different countries

Author (year)	Country	Period of the study	Efficiency, productivity and performance measures	Methodological framework		Major finding(s)
				Efficiency	Productivity	
Panel A: Studies showing a positive effect of deregulation						
Berg et al. (1992)	Norway	1980–1989	TE and TFP growth	DEA	Malmquist productivity index	There is a rapid productivity growth in Norwegian banking as a result of deregulation
Schmid (1994)	Austria	1987–1991	TE	DEA	–	Technical efficiency of Austrian banks improved substantially in the period following 1980s
Zaim (1995)	Turkey	Two points of time, i.e. 1981 and 1990	CE, TE and AE	DEA	–	The post-1980 financial liberalisation policies succeeded in enhancing both technical and allocative efficiency of Turkish banks
López-Cortés (1997)	Mexico	1982–1995	TE, PTE and SE	DEA and Window analysis	–	An inefficiency gap between Mexican banks was reduced during the post-deregulation period
Gilbert and Wilson (1998)	Korea	1980–1994	TE and TFP growth	DEA	Malmquist productivity index	Privatisation and deregulation of the 1980s have led to the significant improvement in the productivity of the Korean banking sector
Leightner and Lovell (1998)	Thailand	1989–1994	TE and TFP growth	DEA	Malmquist productivity index	Financial liberalisation had a significant and positive impact on total factor productivity growth of Thai banks
Ali and Gstach (2000)	Austria	Four points of time, i.e. 1990,1995, 1996, 1997	TE and TFP growth	DEA	Malmquist productivity index	Deregulation spurred the competition which in turn brought a slight improvement in the technical efficiency of Austrian banks
Avkiran (2000)	Australia	1986–1995	TE and TFP growth	DEA	Malmquist productivity index	There is an increase in productivity growth in Australian banks during the period of deregulation

Mukherjee et al. (2001)	USA	1984–1990	TE and TFP growth	DEA	Malmquist productivity index	Deregulation has brought a significant improvement in efficiency and productivity indices of US banks
Rebelo and Mendes (2000)	Portugal	1990–1997	TE, PTE, SE and TFP growth	DEA	Malmquist productivity index	Portuguese banks observed an improvement in the efficiency and productivity during the deregulation period
Alam (2001)	USA	1980–1989	TE and TFP growth	DEA	Malmquist productivity index	US banks have experienced a productivity progress during the 1980s that was mainly due to shift in technology than changes in efficiency
Kumbhakar et al. (2001)	Spain	1986–1995	PE	SFA	–	Deregulation and liberalisation have had a positive impact on the productivity of Spanish saving banks
Noulas (2001)	Greece	1993–1998	TE	DEA	–	Financial deregulation has led to an improvement in the technical efficiency of private and state-controlled Greek banks
Tortosa-Ausina (2002b)	Spain	1985–1995	CE	DEA	–	Deregulation has brought improvement in the cost efficiency of Spanish banks
Berger and Mester (2003)	USA	1991–1997	Cost productivity, profit productivity	SFA		Profit productivity of US banks has improved substantially with the advent of reforms
Canhoto and Dermine (2003)	Portugal	1990–1995	TE, PTE, SE and TFP growth	DEA	Malmquist productivity index	The technical efficiency of Portugal banks has improved during the deregulation period
Isik and Hassan (2003a)	Turkey	1981–1990	TE, PTE, SE and TFP growth	DEA	Malmquist productivity index	The efficiency and productivity of all forms of Turkish banks have improved significantly after the deregulation
Hasan and Marton (2003)	Hungary	1993–1997	CE and PE	SFA	–	The liberal policies of deregulation have brought an improvement in the efficiency of the Hungarian financial institutions

(continued)

Table 4.1 (continued)

Author (year)	Country	Period of the study	Efficiency, productivity and performance measures	Methodological framework		Major finding(s)
				Efficiency	Productivity	
Maudos and Pastor (2003)	Spain	1985–1996	CE, SPE and APE	DEA	–	Cost- and profit efficiency of Spanish banks, both commercial and savings banks, has improved in the period of structural change and increased competition
Girardone et al. (2004)	Italy	1993–1996	CE	SFA	–	Mean X-inefficiency of Italian banks tends to decline over time and for all bank sizes reflecting a positive impact of deregulation
Gjirja (2004)	Sweden	1998–2002	CE, TE, AE, PTE, SE and TFP growth	DEA	Malmquist productivity index	The efficiency and productivity of Swedish banks have improved during the period of financial globalisation and liberalisation
Maghyereh (2004)	Jordan	1984–2001	TE, PTE, SE and TFP growth	DEA	Malmquist productivity index	Financial liberalisation programme of the early 1990s was successful in bringing an observable increase in the efficiency of Jordan banks
Matousek and Taci (2004)	Czech Republic	1993–1998	CE	DFA	–	The efficiency of Czech banking sector increased with an increase in competition through privatisation during the analysed period
Neal (2004)	Australia	1995–1999	CE, TE, AE and TFP growth	DEA	Malmquist productivity index	There is a significant improvement in the cost efficiency and productivity of Australian banking sector over the period of liberalisation and deregulation
Sturm and Williams (2004)	Australia	1988–2001	TE, PTE, SE and TFP growth	DEA and SFA	Malmquist productivity index	The efficiency and productivity of Australian banks seem to have increased in the post-deregulation period

Berger et al. (2005)	China	1994–2001	PE	SFA	–	The Chinese commercial banks experienced higher profit efficiency with the increased foreign bank entry and competition
Chen et al. (2005)	China	1993–2000	CE, TE and AE	DEA	–	The financial deregulation of 1995 has improved cost efficiency levels including both technical and allocative efficiency
Chantapong and Menkhoff (2005)	Thailand	1995–2003	CE	SFA	–	The cost efficiency of banks in Thailand has caught up to best practice standards after the financial deregulation
Hauner and Peiris (2005)	Uganda	1999–2004	TE	DEA	–	The financial sector reforms pursued by Uganda are successful in bringing about improvement in the technical efficiency of banking system
Kumbhakar and Lozano-Vivas (2005)	Spain	1986–2000	TFP growth	SFA	–	Deregulation has contributed positively to the productivity growth of Spanish banks
Patti and Hardy (2005)	Pakistan	1985–2002	CE and APE	DFA	–	The liberalisation and reforms, including the privatisation of major banks, seem to have positive impact on the Pakistani banks' performance
Matthews and Ismail (2006)	Malaysia	1994–2000	TE, PTE, SE and TFP growth	DEA	Malmquist productivity index	Efficiency and productivity of Malaysian banks, both domestic and foreign, have increased during the period of analysis
Park and Weber (2006)	Korea	1992–2002	TFP growth	DEA	Malmquist productivity index	The Korean banking industry experienced productivity growth during the post-deregulation period
Bertrand et al. (2007)	France	1978–1999	ROA, concentration index, AE	Traditional financial ratios	–	French banks have improved their monitoring and screening functions along with their efficiency after the reforms of 1980s

(continued)

Table 4.1 (continued)

Author (year)	Country	Period of the study	Efficiency, productivity and performance measures	Methodological framework		Major finding(s)
				Efficiency	Productivity	
Dacanay III (2007a)	Philippines	1992–2004	CE and PE	SFA	–	Financial liberalisation of 1994 has brought a modest improvement in cost and alternative profit efficiency of Philippine commercial banks
Isik (2007)	Turkey	1981–1990	TFP growth	DEA	Malmquist productivity index	Deregulation had a positive impact on the productivity growth of Turkish banks
Fu and Heffernan (2007)	China	1985–2002	ROA, ROE, concentration ratio, market share, CE, SE	Traditional financial ratios and SFA	–	Financial reforms have brought an improvement in cost X-efficiency of Chinese banks during the reforms period
Njie (2007)	Malaysia	1999–2005	CE, TE, PTE, SE, AE and TFP growth	DEA	Malmquist productivity index	Cost inefficiency among Malaysian banks has declined with the onset of financial liberalisation measures
Sufian (2007a)	Singapore	1993–2003	TE, PTE and SE	DEA	–	An overall efficiency of Singapore's banking industry has shown an upward trend due to deregulation in the latter years of the study period
Asaftei and Kumbhakar (2008)	Romania	1996–2002	CE	SFA and Shadow cost functions	–	Technical efficiency of all types of Romanian banks improved in the post-regulation period
Ariss (2008)	Lebanon	1990–2001	CE	SFA	–	Cost efficiency of Lebanese banks has improved during the period of financial deregulation and liberalisation
Huang et al. (2008)	Taiwan	2001–2004	TFP growth	DEA	Malmquist productivity index	Financial restructuring has brought a substantial improvement in productivity growth of Taiwanese commercial banks

Chortareas et al. (2009)	Greece	1998–2003	CE, PE and TFP growth	DEA	Malmquist productivity index	Greek banks seem to enjoy relatively high cost- and profit efficiency during the period of analysis. Further, the productivity of Greek banks has also recorded a positive trend
Burki and Naizi (2010)	Pakistan	1991–2000	CE, AE, TE, PTE and SE	DEA	–	Deregulation has brought improvement in the cost efficiency and productivity of Pakistani banks since 1996
Hsiao et al. (2010)	Taiwan	2000–2005	TE	DEA	–	Financial restructuring has improved the operating efficiency of Taiwanese banks
Banker et al. (2010)	Korea	1995–2005	CE, AE, TE, PTE and SE	DEA	–	Average technical efficiency of Korean banks has improved during the post-reforms period
Fethi et al. (2011)	Egypt	1984–2002	TE, PTE, SE and TFP growth	DEA	Malmquist productivity index	Liberalisation policies have had a positive impact on the efficiency and productivity of Egyptian banks
Panel B: Studies showing a negative effect of deregulation						
Humphrey (1991, 1993)	USA	1977–1988	TFP growth	EFA	–	Deregulation and liberalisation seem to have a negative effect on US banks' productivity
Grabowski et al. (1994)	USA	Three points of time, i.e. 1979, 1983 and 1987	CE, AE, TE, PTE and SE	DEA	–	Deregulation policies do not seem to have a favourable effect on the efficiency of US banking firms
Elyasaini and Mehdian (1995)	USA	Two points of time, i.e. 1979 and 1988	CE,AE, TE, PTE and SE	DEA	–	Deregulation does not seem to have a favourable effect on the efficiency of US banks
Grifell-Tatjé and Lovell (1996)	Spain	1986–1991	TFP growth	DEA	Malmquist productivity index	Deregulation has brought no productivity gains in Spanish savings banking industry

(continued)

Table 4.1 (continued)

Author (year)	Country	Period of the study	Efficiency, productivity and performance measures	Methodological framework		Major finding(s)
				Efficiency	Productivity	
Humphrey and Pulley (1997)	US	1977–1988	PE	TFA	–	Deregulation of interest rates in the early 1980s has led to the decline in the efficiency of US banks
Lozano-Vivas (1998)	Spain	1985–1991	CE	TFA	–	Deregulation has led to decrease in relative cost efficiency for Spanish commercial banks and no significant improvement for savings banks
Wheelock and Wilson (1999)	USA	1984–1993	TE and TFP growth	DEA	Malmquist productivity index	Average productivity as well as technical efficiency of US banks has declined with the advent of reforms
Christopoulos and Tsionas (2001)	Greece	1993–1998	CE, TE and AE	SFA	–	Deregulation has brought no significant improvement in the cost efficiency of Greek banks
Cook et al. (2001)	Tunisia	1992–1997	TE	DEA	–	Deregulation policies have been less successful in improving the efficiency of Tunisian banks
Hao et al. (2001)	Korea	1985–1995	CE	SFA	–	The financial deregulation of 1991 was found to have had little or no significant effect on the level of bank efficiency in Korea
Mahadevan and Kim (2001)	Korea	1986–1996	TFP growth	DEA	Malmquist productivity index	Financial deregulation did not improve the productivity growth of Korean banks
Rizvi (2001)	Pakistan	1993–1998	TE, PTE, SE and TFP growth	DEA	Malmquist productivity index	Financial liberalisation has a negative impact on the efficiency and productivity of Pakistani banks

Fukuyama and Weber (2002)	Japan	1992–1996	TE	DEA	–	Japanese banks experienced significant decline in TFP growth throughout the analysed period
Sathye (2002)	Australia	1995–1999	TFP growth	DEA	Malmquist productivity index	Deregulation started in early 1980s has brought a decline in total factor productivity of Australian banks. Alternatively, deregulation did not lead to improvement in productivity of Australian banks
Dogan and Fausten (2003)	Malaysia	1989–1998	TE and TFP growth	DEA	Malmquist productivity index	The regulatory reforms and liberalisation are not sufficient conditions for an improvement of efficiency and productivity of Malaysian banks
Havrylchyk (2006)	Poland	1997–2001	CE, AE, TE, PTE and SE	DEA	–	Deregulation has not brought any improvement in the Polish banks' efficiency
Kwan (2006)	Hong Kong	1992–1999	CE	SFA	–	The X-efficiency of Hong Kong banks has been found to decline over the period of study
Ozkan-Gunay and Tektas (2006)	Turkey	1990–2001	TE	DEA	–	The mean technical efficiency of Turkish banks has declined during the period 1990–2001
Denizer et al. (2000, 2007)	Turkey	1970–1994	TE, PTE and SE	DEA	–	Liberalisation programmes of 1980s have brought no significant improvements in the efficiency of Turkish banks
Kumbhakar and Wang (2007)	China	1993–2002	TE and TFP growth	SFA	–	Deregulation has not brought any improvement in the efficiency of Chinese banks
Mehdian et al. (2007)	USA	1990–2003	CE, AE, TE, PTE and SE	DEA	–	Financial deregulation and globalisation has been a cause for decline in the overall efficiency of US commercial banks

(continued)

Table 4.1 (continued)

Author (year)	Country	Period of the study	Efficiency, productivity and performance measures	Methodological framework		Major finding(s)
				Efficiency	Productivity	
Ariff and Can (2008)	China	1995–2004	CE, SPE and APE	DEA	–	No significant improvement in the cost- and alternative profit efficiency levels of Chinese banks during the period of deregulation
Fu and Heffernan (2009)	China	1985–2002	CE	SFA	–	X-efficiency for the Chinese banks declined significantly in the second phase of reforms following 1993–2003

Source: Authors' compilation

Notes: (i) *DEA, SFA, DFA, TFA* and *EFA* are the acronyms for data envelopment analysis, stochastic frontier analysis, distribution free approach, thick frontier analysis and econometric frontier analysis, respectively, and (ii) *CE, TE, AE, RE, PTE, SE, SPE* and *APE* stand for cost, technical, allocative, revenue, pure technical, scale, standard profit and alternative profit efficiencies, respectively

productivity improved significantly during the post-deregulation period. However, the remaining 25 studies (i.e. 35 %) conclude that deregulation has deteriorated the efficiency performance of banks.

In all, the effect of deregulation on the efficiency and productivity of the banking sector seems highly dependent on the specific economic environment of each country. The reported adverse effect in a few studies may be due to the short-term effects of liberalisation such as credit rationing, high spreads and weakening loan quality (Musonda 2008). These problems tend to be exacerbated under an unstable macroeconomic environment which is often associated with the early years of reforms. This suggests that the hypothesis stating that deregulation always improves efficiency and productivity may be rejected.

4.2.2 Indian Experience

The literature on bank efficiency in India shows that a good number of studies have assessed the impact of the transition from regulation to competition on the efficiency and productivity of banks. The studies that broadly confirmed a positive impact of deregulatory policies on the efficiency of banks include Bhattacharyya et al. (1997a, b), Ram Mohan and Ray (2004b), Shanmugam and Das (2004), Das et al. (2005), Ataullah and Le (2006), Chatterjee (2006), Sensarma (2006), Mahesh and Bhide (2008), Rezvanian et al. (2008), Reserve Bank of India (2008c), Das and Ghosh (2009), Kumar and Gulati (2009b, 2010), Ray and Das (2010) and Zhao et al. (2008, 2010). There are also a few studies which reported either an adverse or insignificant effect of deregulatory policy actions on the performance of banks (see, e.g. Kumbhakar and Sarkar 2003; Galagedera and Edirisuriya 2005; Das and Ghosh 2006, and Sensarma 2005, 2008). All in all, the empirical evidence about the impact of deregulation on efficiency of Indian banks has been found to be mixed in the literature, but an overwhelming majority of studies has shown a positive impact of deregulation and liberalisation on the efficiency performance of banks. Table 4.2 reports the main findings of Indian studies.

4.3 Bank Ownership and Efficiency

Another highly explored area in the literature is the relationship between bank ownership and efficiency. The studies in this research area primarily focus on computing efficiency gaps across banks belonging to different ownership types. According to Altunbas et al. (2001), agency issues associated with different types of firms' ownership are the key concern in many banking systems where state-owned banks operate alongside private sector institutions. The empirical studies from this area are primarily aimed at the testing of validity of *property right hypothesis* (Alchian 1965; De Alessi 1980), *principal–agent framework*, and *public choice*

Table 4.2 Impact of deregulation on the efficiency of Indian banks

Author (year)	Period of the study	Efficiency, productivity and performance measures	Methodological framework		Major finding(s)
			Efficiency	Productivity	
Panel A: Studies showing a positive effect of deregulation					
Bhattacharyya et al. (1997a)	1970–1992	TFP growth	SFA	–	Deregulation has a positive impact on the total factor productivity growth of Indian public sector banks
Bhattacharyya et al. (1997b)	1986–1991	TE	DEA	–	Deregulation has led to an improvement in the efficiency of Indian commercial banks
Ram Mohan and Ray (2004b)	1992–2000	RE, TE and AE	DEA	–	There is an improvement in the revenue efficiency of Indian banks. A convergence in performance between public and private sector banks has been noticed in the post-reforms era
Shanmugam and Das (2004)	1992–1999	TE	SFA	–	During the deregulation period, Indian banking industry showed a progress in terms of efficiency of raising non-interest income investments and credits
Das et al. (2005)	1997–2003	TE, CE, RE and PE	DEA	–	The efficiency of Indian banks in general and of the bigger banks in particular has improved during the post-reforms period
Ataullah and Le (2006)	1992–1998	TE	DEA	–	Technical efficiency of Indian banks, especially of the foreign banks, has improved during the post-liberalisation era
Chatterjee (2006)	1995–2002	CE	SFA	–	The average cost inefficiency of Indian domestic banks has declined during the study period
Sensarma (2006)	1986–2000	CE and TFP growth	SFA	–	Deregulation in Indian banking industry especially in its public sector banking segment has achieved the objectives of reduction in intermediation costs and improving TFP

Zhao et al. (2008)	1992–2004	TE and TFP growth	DEA	Malmquist productivity index	After an initial adjustment phase, Indian banking industry has experienced a sustained TFP growth driven mainly by technological progress
Mahesh and Bhide (2008)	1985–2004	CE, PE and advance efficiency	SFA	–	The cost- and profit efficiency of Indian banks has improved after deregulation
Rezvanian et al.(2008)	1998–2003	CE, TE, AE, PTE and SE	DEA	–	An ascent in cost efficiency in all ownership groups and industry as a whole has taken place due to its allocative efficiency component rather than technical efficiency component
Reserve Bank of India (2008c)	1991–2007	CE, TE and AE	DEA	–	Efficiency has improved across all bank groups during the study period, and most of the observed efficiency gains have emanated after few years of reforms, i.e. from 1997 to 1998 onwards
Das and Ghosh (2009)	1992–2004	CE and APE	DEA	–	Liberalisation of the banking sector in India has produced positive results in improving the cost- and profit efficiencies of banks
Kumar and Gulati (2009b)	1993–2006	TE	DEA	–	Deregulation has not only brought a significant improvement in technical efficiency of Indian public sector banks but also narrowed down the efficiency gaps
Ray and Das (2010)	1997–2003	CE and SPE	DEA	–	The cost efficiency levels for Indian banks have improved during the post-reforms period
Kumar and Gulati (2010)	1993–2008	CE, AE and TE	DEA	–	Deregulation has had a positive impact on the cost efficiency levels of Indian public sector banking industry over the period of study
Zhao et al. (2010)	1992–2004	CE	SFA	–	Deregulation has improved the performance of Indian banks and fostered competition in the lending market

(continued)

Table 4.2 (continued)

Author (year)	Period of the study	Efficiency, productivity and performance measures	Methodological framework: Efficiency	Methodological framework: Productivity	Major finding(s)
Panel B: Studies showing a negative effect of deregulation					
Kumbhakar and Sarkar (2003)	1985–1996	CE and TFP growth	Shadow cost function	–	A significant TFP growth has not been observed in Indian banking sector during the deregulatory regime. Further, public sector banks have not responded well to deregulatory measures
Sensarma (2005)	1986–2003	PE	SFA	–	Profit efficiency of Indian banks has shown a declining trend during the period of deregulation
Galagedera and Edirisuriya (2005)	1995–2002	TE and TFP growth	DEA	Malmquist productivity index	Deregulation has brought no significant growth in the productivity of Indian banks
Das and Ghosh (2006)	1992–2002	TE, PTE and SE	DEA	–	The period after liberalisation did not witness any significant increase in number of efficient banks, and some banks have high degree of inefficiency during the period of liberalisation
Sensarma (2008)	1986–2005	APE	SFA	–	The profit efficiency and productivity of Indian banks has declined following deregulation and liberalisation

Source: Authors' compilation

Notes: (i) *DEA, SFA, DFA, TFA* and *EFA* are the acronyms for data envelopment analysis, stochastic frontier analysis, distribution free approach, thick frontier analysis and econometric frontier analysis, respectively, and (ii) *CE, TE, AE, RE, PTE, SE, SPE* and *APE* stand for cost, technical, allocative, revenue, pure technical, scale, standard profit and alternative profit efficiencies, respectively

theory (Niskanen 1975; Levy 1987). According to the property right hypothesis, private enterprises should perform more efficiently and profitably than public enterprises. Principal–agent framework and public choice theory complement the property right hypothesis and highlight the importance of management being constrained by capital market discipline. The theoretical argument is straightforward: a lack of capital market discipline weakens owners' control over management, making management freer to pursue its own agenda and giving it fewer incentives to be efficient. On account of the lack of market discipline, the management in state-owned banks experiences a lower intensity of environmental pressure and therefore may operate less efficiently than privately owned banks. In addition, state-owned banks may have inferior incentives to achieve economic efficiency than privately owned banks and may lack the information on which to make management decisions efficiently (Figueira et al. 2006).

The effect of foreign ownership on bank efficiency has also been the focus of many empirical studies. In particular, these studies aimed at testing the presence of *home field advantage hypothesis* and the *global advantage hypothesis* formulated by Berger et al. (2000) in the banking systems. First, the *home field advantage hypothesis* predicts that domestic-owned banks are generally more efficient than foreign-owned banks due to the absence of structural agency costs that foreign-owned banks are confronted with. According to this hypothesis, distance between the principal (the parent bank in the home country) and the agent (the subsidiary or branch in the host country), creates a structural agency cost or organisational diseconomies for a foreign-owned bank to operate or monitor its subsidiary from a distance. Other factors leading to a comparative advantage for domestic banks are differences in language, culture, currency, regulatory and supervisory structures, other country-specific market features, bias against foreign institutions and other explicit or implicit barriers.

Second, the *global advantage hypothesis* states that foreign-owned banks are more efficient due to some comparative advantages that domestic-owned banks lack. These advantages stem from advanced technologies, more superior managerial skills, more efficient organisations due to stiff competition in the home market, a more active market for corporate control and a better access to an educated labour force with the ability to adapt to new technologies. Berger et al. (2000) considered two forms of the global advantage hypothesis, namely, *the general global advantage* and *the limited global advantage*. In the general form, efficiently managed foreign banks, regardless of the nation in which they are headquartered, are able to overcome any cross-border disadvantages and operate more efficiently than domestic banks in other nations. However, in the limited form of the hypothesis, only the efficient banks headquartered in one or a limited number of nations with specific favourable market, regulatory, or supervisory conditions can operate more efficiently than domestic banks in other nations.

Research on the aforementioned issues broadly suggests that in developed nations, the efficiency disadvantages of foreign-owned banks relative to domestically owned banks tend to outweigh the efficiency advantages on average, with some notable exceptions. In developing nations, the situation may often be reversed with the efficiency advantages of foreign-owned banks outweighing the disadvantages on average (Berger 2007). In other words, foreign banks in developing countries are more efficient than domestic banks, while foreign banks in developed countries are less efficient than domestic banks (Claessens et al. 2001). Our survey of literature presented in Table 4.3 largely lends a support to above inferences. We note that the existing literature is ambivalent on the issue of efficiency behaviour across different ownership type groups. Keeping this in view, we attempt to summarise the results of the studies showing the impact of ownership on the efficiency of banks belonging to distinct ownership types.

4.3.1 International Experience

From the deep scan of the studies reviewed in the Table 4.3, we note that the studies which broadly conclude that foreign banks are more efficient than domestic banks largely belong to developing nations (see, for instance, Jemric and Vujcic (2002), Kraft et al. (2006) for Croatia; Hasan and Marton (2003) for Hungary; Chantapong and Menkhoff (2005) for Thailand; Hauner and Peiris (2005) for Uganda; Havrylchyk (2006) for Poland; Matthews and Ismail (2006) for Malaysia; Burki and Niazi (2010) for Pakistan; Ariff and Can (2008), Berger et al. (2009) for China; Isik (2007, 2008) for Turkey; Asaftei and Kumbhakar (2008) for Romania; Ariss (2008) for Lebanon; Karas et al. (2008) for Russia, among others). However, there exists a few studies from the developing nations which conclude that foreign banks are worse performers than domestic banks (see, for instance, Dacanay III (2007a) for Philippines; Hadad et al. (2008) for Indonesia; Matousek et al. (2008) for Turkey; Fethi et al. (2011) for Egypt; Sufian (2009a) for Malaysia; Staub et al. (2010) for Brazil). The studies which reached to the conclusion that no significant efficiency differences exist between domestic and foreign banks include Nikiel and Opiela (2002) for Poland, Fuentes and Vergara (2007) for Chile, Kyj and Isik (2008) for Ukraine and Delis et al. (2009) for Greece.

The existing literature belonging to developed nations is also ambivalent on the issue of efficiency differences between foreign and domestic banks. Table 4.3 further lists the studies from developed economies which found that foreign-owned banks perform more poorly on average than domestic banks (see, for instance, DeYoung and Nolle (1996), Chang et al. (1998) for US; Altunbas et al. (2001) for Germany, among others). On the other hand, the studies by Matousek and Taci (2004) for Czech Republic and Sturm and Williams (2004) for Australia have documented that foreign banks perform better than domestic banks.

Thus, the extant literature is inconclusive on the issue of efficiency differences between foreign and domestic banks. Of 30 studies reviewed, 17 studies found that foreign banks perform better than domestic banks on all performance measures, nine studies opinioned that domestic banks are better performers than foreign banks, and the remaining four studies found no significant difference (or mixed results) among foreign and domestic banks. These differences in the results may be

Table 4.3 Impact of ownership on the efficiency of banks in different countries

Author (year)	Country	Period of the study	Methodological framework	Efficiency, productivity and performance measures	Major finding(s)
Panel A: Foreign > domestic					
Jemric and Vujcic (2002)	Croatia	1995–2000	DEA	TE and PTE	Foreign banks are significantly more efficient than domestic banks
Hasan and Marton (2003)	Hungary	1993–1997	SFA	CE and PE	Foreign banks and banks with higher foreign bank ownership involvement outperform domestic banks
Matousek and Taci (2004)	Czech Republic	1993–1998	DFA	CE	Cost efficiency of foreign banks is, on average, higher than those of domestic banks, both small and big, in Czech Republic
Sturm and Williams (2004)	Australia	1988–2001	SFA- and DEA-based Malmquist productivity index	TE, PTE, SE and TFP growth	Foreign banks are more efficient than private banks in Australia during the post-deregulation period
Chantapong and Menkhoff (2005)	Thailand	1995–2003	SFA	CE	The foreign banks seem to be more efficient than domestic banks
Hauner and Peiris (2005)	Uganda	1999–2004	DEA	TE	Foreign banks are on average more efficient than domestic banks in Uganda
Havrylchyk (2006)	Poland	1997–2001	DEA	CE, AE, TE, PTE and SE	Foreign banks are more efficient than domestic-owned banks
Kraft et al. (2006)	Croatia	1994–2000	SFA	CE	Foreign banks seem to have strong efficiency advantages over domestic banks
Matthews and Ismail (2006)	Malaysia	1994–2000	DEA-based Malmquist productivity index	TE, PTE, SE and TFP growth	Foreign banks in Malaysia are more efficient and productive than domestic banks over the study period
Isik (2007)	Turkey	1981–1990	DEA-based Malmquist productivity index	TFP growth	Foreign banks experienced greater productivity and technological and efficiency improvements than domestic private and public sector banks in Turkey

(continued)

Table 4.3 (continued)

Author (year)	Country	Period of the study	Methodological framework	Efficiency, productivity and performance measures	Major finding(s)
Asaftei and Kumbhakar (2008)	Romania	1996–2002	SFA	CE	State-owned banks are more cost-inefficient than domestic private, foreign branches and representative offices
Ariss (2008)	Lebanon	1990–2001	SFA	CE	Foreign banks are more efficient than domestic banks in the early 1990s, but in the later period domestic banks catch up on their peers to become as efficient as foreign banks
Ariff and Can (2008)	China	1995–2004	DEA	CE, SPE and APE	Joint-stock commercial banks are on average more cost- and profit efficient than state-owned banks
Isik (2008)	Turkey	1981–1996	DEA-based Malmquist productivity index	TE and TFP growth	Foreign banks are most efficient and productive than domestic banks in Turkey
Karas et al. (2008)	Russia	Two points in time, i.e. 2002 and 2006	SFA	CE	Foreign banks in Russia are more efficient than domestic private banks. Further, domestic public banks are more efficient than domestic private banks
Berger et al. (2009)	China	1994–2003	SFA	CE, PE	Foreign banks have outperformed the domestic banks
Burki and Niazi (2010)	Pakistan	1991–2000	DEA	CE, AE, TE, PTE and SE	Foreign and private banks are more efficient vis-à-vis state-owned banks in terms of cost, technical and allocative efficiencies
Panel B: Domestic > foreign					
DeYoung and Nolle (1996)	USA	1985–1990	DFA	PE	Foreign-owned US banks are less profit efficient US-owned banks
Chang et al. (1998)	USA	1984–1989	SFA	CE	Foreign-owned multinational banks are significantly less cost efficient than domestically-owned banks in the USA
Altunbas et al. (2001)	Germany	1989–1996	SFA and DFA	CE and PE	Public German banks are more cost- and profit efficient than their mutual and private counterparts

Dacanay III (2007a)	Philippines	1992–2004	SFA	CE and SPE	Foreign banks are more cost-inefficient than domestic banks in the Philippines
Hadad et al. (2008)	Indonesia	Cross-sectional data for the year 2007	DEA	TE	State-owned banks outperform the foreign banks in Indonesia
Matousek et al. (2008)	Turkey	2000–2005	SFA	CE	State banks are more cost efficient than the private and the foreign banks in each year of the study period
Sufian (2009a)	Malaysia	2001–2004	DEA-based Malmquist productivity index	TFP growth	Domestic banks' productivity levels are relatively higher compared with the foreign banks in Malaysia
Staub et al. (2010)	Brazil	2000–2007	DEA	CE, TE and AE	State-owned banks are significantly more efficient than foreign and private banks
Fethi et al. (2011)	Egypt	1984–2002	DEA-based Malmquist productivity index	TE and TFP growth	State-owned banks are most efficient than joint-ventured, foreign and private banks
Panel C: No significant differences (or mixed results)					
Nikiel and Opiela (2002)	Poland	1997–2000	SFA	CE and PE	Foreign banks outperform domestic banks in cost efficiency; however, opposite is true for profit efficiency measure
Fuentes and Vergara (2007)	Chile	1990–2004	SFA	CE and SPE	Domestic banks are more profit efficient than foreign banks in Chile, although their cost efficiency remains same
Kyj and Isik (2008)	Ukraine	1998–2003	DEA	TE, PTE and SE	There is no significant difference in technical, pure technical and scale efficiencies between domestic- and foreign-owned Ukrainian banks
Delis et al. (2009)	Greece	1993–2005	DEA and SFA	CE and PE	State-owned banks are more cost efficient than private banks, while at the same time private banks are more profit efficient than state-owned banks

Source: Authors' compilation

Notes: (i) *DEA, SFA, DFA, TFA* and *EFA* are the acronyms for data envelopment analysis, stochastic frontier analysis, distribution free approach, thick frontier analysis and econometric frontier analysis, respectively, and (ii) CE, TE, AE, RE, PTE, SE, SPE and APE stand for cost, technical, allocative, revenue, pure technical, scale, standard profit and alternative profit efficiencies, respectively

due to differences in sample periods, country coverage, varying performance measures and/or techniques used. Further, the results of the majority of reviewed studies clearly agree the aforementioned statement that foreign banks in developing countries are more efficient than domestic banks, while the opposite is true for developed nations.

4.3.2 *Indian Experience*

In the literature on Indian banking industry, we found mixed evidence concerning the issue of bank ownership and efficiency. Table 4.4 presents the major finding (s) of the Indian studies on banking efficiency. We have categorised these studies in the following seven distinct categories (see Panel A–G of the table for details).

(a) Public > Private > Foreign
Bhattacharyya et al. (1997b), Galagedera and Edirisuriya (2005), Das and Ghosh (2006), Sensarma (2006, 2008), Mahesh and Bhide (2008), Das and Ghosh (2009) and Tabak and Tecles (2010) concluded that the public sector banks are more efficient than private banks followed by foreign banks. Thus, of the total studies reviewed, eight studies fall in this category.
(b) Public > Foreign > Private
This category includes the research efforts of Sathye (2003), Ram Mohan and Ray (2004a), Shanmugam and Das (2004), Ataullah and Le (2006) and Ray and Das (2010). They found that public sector banks were higher on efficiency front followed by foreign banks and private banks. In all, five studies have been included in this category.
(c) Private > Public > Foreign
The studies of Mukherjee et al. (2002) and Kumar and Gulati (2009a) inferred that private banks have the highest efficiency, followed by public sector banks and foreign banks. Only two studies fall in this category.
(d) Private > Foreign > Public
Chatterjee and Sinha (2006) and Zhao et al. (2010) noted that public sector banks are least efficient followed by foreign banks and private banks. In other words, private banks are more efficient than foreign banks and public sector banks. Not more than two studies came forward with this conclusion.
(e) Foreign > Public > Private
Ataullah and Le (2006) and Zhao et al. (2008) conclude that foreign banks as a group have been found to be more efficient than public sector banks followed by private banks.
(f) Foreign > Private > Public
This category includes the studies by Sarkar et al. (1998), Chakrabarti and Chawla (2005), Das et al. (2005) and Debasish (2006). Only four studies found that foreign banks are relatively more efficient than private and public sector banks.

Table 4.4 Impact of ownership on the efficiency of Indian banks

Author (year)	Period of the study	Methodological framework	Efficiency, productivity and performance measures	Major finding(s)
Panel A: Public > Private > Foreign (or Public > Private)				
Bhattacharyya et al. (1997b)	1986–1991	DEA	TE	The public sector banks had the highest efficiency followed by private and foreign banks
Galagedera and Edirisuriya (2005)	1995–2002	DEA	TE, PTE, SE and TFP growth	Public sector banks outperform private banks in terms of efficiency and productivity
Das and Ghosh (2006)	1992–2002	DEA	TE, PTE and SE	Banks with public ownership are more efficient than their private counterparts including foreign banks
Sensarma (2006)	1986–2000	SFA	CE and TFP growth	The cost efficiency of public banks has been higher relative to private banks followed by foreign banks in the post-deregulation period
Sensarma (2008)	1986–2005	SFA	APE and TFP growth	Public sector banks were more profit efficient than private banks prior to deregulation, and their difference becomes insignificant after deregulation. Further, both the bank groups outperform foreign banks in terms of profit efficiency
Mahesh and Bhide (2008)	1985–2004	SFA	CE, PE and advance efficiency	Public sector banks are more efficient than private and foreign banks in India
Das and Ghosh (2009)	1992–2004	DEA	CE and SPE	State-owned banks appear to have higher levels of cost- and profit efficiency than private and foreign banks
Tabak and Tecles (2010)	2000–2006	Bayesian SFA	CE and PE	Public banks are the most efficient, followed by private and foreign banks
Panel B: Public > Foreign > Private				
Sathye (2003)	Cross-sectional data for the year 1998	DEA	TE	The efficiency of private banks is paradoxically lower than that of PSBs and foreign banks

(continued)

Table 4.4 (continued)

Author (year)	Period of the study	Methodological framework	Efficiency, productivity and performance measures	Major finding(s)
Ram Mohan and Ray (2004a)	1992–2000	DEA	TE, AE and RE	PSBs perform significantly better than private banks but not differently from foreign banks
Shanmugam and Das (2004)	1992–1999	SFA	TE	The banks belonging to SBI group are more technically efficient than foreign banks followed by nationalised and private domestic banks
Ataullah and Le (2006)	1992–1998	DEA	TE	Public sector banks are relatively more efficient than domestic private and foreign banks in generating loans and advances
Ray and Das (2010)	1997–2003	DEA	CE and SPE	An average cost- and profit efficiency of state-owned banks is much higher than foreign banks, nationalised banks and domestic private banks in that order
Panel C: Private > Public > Foreign (or Private > Public)				
Mukherjee et al. (2002)	1996–1999	DEA	TE	Private banks are more efficient than both public and foreign banks
Kumar and Gulati (2009a)	Cross-sectional data for the year 2006–2007	DEA	TE, PTE and SE	Private banks are more technically efficient than public sector banks
Panel D: Private > Foreign > Public				
Chatterjee and Sinha (2006)	Cross-sectional data for the year 1996–1997, 1998–1999, 2000–2001 and 2002–2003	DEA	CE, TE and AE	Public sector banks lagged behind the private sector banks both in terms of technical and allocative efficiency
Zhao et al. (2010)	1992–2004	SFA	CE	Public sector banks have been found to be more cost efficient than foreign and domestic private banks during the period of deregulation

Panel E: Foreign > Public > Private				
Ataullah and Le (2006)	1992–1998	DEA	TE	Foreign banks lead the public and domestic private banks in generating income from their operations
Zhao et al. (2008)	1992–2004	DEA	TE, PTE, SE and TFP growth	Foreign banks as group took a lead in terms of efficiency followed by public and private bank groups
Panel F: Foreign > Private > Public				
Sarkar et al. (1998)	1994–1995	Traditional financial ratios	ROA	Foreign banks are better performers than private and public banks
Chakrabarti and Chawla (2005)	1990–2002	DEA	TE	The public sector banks have lagged behind their private and foreign counterparts in terms of efficiency performance
Das et al. (2005)	1997–2003	DEA	TE, CE, RE and PE	The efficiency of foreign banks has been found to be much higher than private and public banks
Debasish (2006)	1997–2004	DEA	TE	Foreign-owned banks are, on an average, more efficient than domestic private and public sector banks
Panel G: No significant difference				
Reserve Bank of India (2008c)	1991–2007	DEA	CE, TE and AE	No significant differences in any of the efficiency measures between public and private sector banks

Source: Authors' compilation
Notes: (i) *DEA, SFA, DFA, TFA* and *EFA* are the acronyms for data envelopment analysis, stochastic frontier analysis, distribution free approach, thick frontier analysis and econometric frontier analysis, respectively, and (ii) *CE, TE, AE, RE, PTE, SE, SPE* and *APE* stand for cost, technical, allocative, revenue, pure technical, scale, standard profit and alternative profit efficiencies, respectively

(g) No significant difference
The study by Reserve Bank of India (2008c) concluded that there exist no significant differences in the efficiency levels across different ownership groups.

On the whole, we note that Indian studies on banking efficiency often reach seemingly contradictory findings in terms of relative ranking of the different ownership groups because of differences in specification of inputs and outputs, methods of estimation (DEA, SFA), time period, functional forms, behavioural assumptions (production, cost, profit optimisation), etc. In sum, there exists no clear picture about the dominance of a particular ownership group over others in Indian banking industry. Thus, there exists a clear inconsistency in the ranking of distinct ownership groups on the basis of efficiency measure.

4.4 Cross-Country Efficiency Comparisons

Another significant research area in the bank efficiency literature that received the considerable attention of the researchers is the comparisons of efficiency levels across countries. The main objective of cross-country studies is to get valuable information regarding the competitiveness of banks in sampled countries, a concern of particular importance in an increasingly harmonised financial world. In their excellent survey article, Berger and Humphrey (1997) noted that out of 130 studies reviewed, the focus of only five studies was cross-country efficiency comparisons. The first cross-country study was conducted by Berg et al. (1993) which presented a comparative analysis of bank efficiency in Finland, Norway and Sweden. The results of cross-country comparative efficiency studies are difficult to interpret because the regulatory and economic environments faced by banks are likely to differ importantly across nations and because the level and quality of service associated with deposits and loans in different countries may differ in ways that are difficult to measure (Berger and Humphrey 1997).

In most of the cross-country efficiency studies, a single common efficient frontier is estimated for comparing the efficiency of banking systems across countries. Bos and Schmiedel (2007) revealed a paradox in such cross-border studies, where banks are usually compared to a common efficient frontier, thereby assuming that banks across different countries have access to the same technology. They are of the opinion that when the frontier is applied to each sample country and the performance of each individual banking institution is compared against the best practice bank in that country, efficiency results cannot be compared across borders. On this issue, Dietsch and Lozano-Vivas (2000) commented that the assumption of a common efficient frontier could yield misleading efficiency estimates for banks from different countries as such approaches do not control for cross-country differences in regulatory, demographic and economic conditions that are beyond a bank's control. However, some recent studies made an attempt to avoid the bias inherent in cross-border bank efficiency comparisons by incorporating country-specific environmental conditions (see, for instance, Dietsch and Lozano-Vivas 2000; Chaffai et al. 2001; Lozano-Vivas et al. 2001, 2002; Grigorian and Manole 2006). It has been observed that the efficiency scores tend to be higher when cross-country heterogeneity is considered, indicating that part of the inefficiency can be explained by these heterogeneous factors. Therefore, neglecting these factors may cause underestimated efficiency score. To resolve the issue of incorporating heterogeneity in the efficiency estimation framework to a larger extent, Bos and Schmiedel (2007) developed a meta-frontier methodological framework for estimating 'truly' comparable efficiencies across countries using a meta-frontier which accounts for different underlying technologies in the banking systems of the sample countries.

From the review of extant literature, we find that most of the cross-country efficiency studies focus on the European market. However, more recently, the developments like privatisation, deregulation and consolidation in the developing countries influenced the researchers to conduct cross-country studies to evaluate the impact of these changes on the efficiency of banks across these countries. Table 4.5 lists out the cross-border studies that have been carried out with an objective to study the impact of deregulation and liberalisation on the efficiency of banks in different countries. It will be prudent to keep in mind that the consequences of liberalisation may also differ across countries. It may deteriorate or enhance the efficiency of banks. The studies which examined the positive impact of deregulation on the efficiency of banks include Ataullah et al. (2004), Howcroft and Ataullah (2006), Jaffry et al. (2007), Nguyen and Williams (2005) and Shen et al. (2009) for a sample of Southeast Asian countries; Casu and Molyneux (2003), Casu et al. (2004), Espitia-Escuer and Garcia-Cebrian (2004), Brissimis et al. (2008) and Kondeas et al. (2008) for European Union nations; Chang and Luh (2000) for 19 Asia-Pacific countries; Kwan (2003) for seven Asian countries; Weill (2007), Košak et al. (2009) and Koutsomanoli-Filippaki et al. (2009a) for Central and Eastern European (CEE) countries; Figueira and Nellis (2007) for Portugal and Spain; and Hermes and Nhung (2010) for a sample of ten Latin American and Asian countries, among others. In contrast to aforementioned studies, there are a few cross-country studies that reported either an adverse or insignificant impact of deregulation and liberalisation policies on the efficiency and productivity of banks in different nations, for example, Fries and Taci (2005) for European nations, Ariss et al. (2007) for six GCC countries and Perera et al. (2007) for four South Asian countries.

It is worth noting here that the studies by Ataullah et al. (2004), Howcroft and Ataullah (2006), Jaffry et al. (2007), Perera et al. (2007) and Shen et al. (2009) included India in the sample along with other Southeast Asian economies while examining the impact of deregulatory policies (see Panels A.1 and B.1 of Table 4.5 for details). Shen et al. (2009) found that India was the most efficient among ten Asian countries included in the sample. From our survey, we note that of 19 cross-country studies reviewed, only five studies have included India in cross-country efficiency comparisons. Further, maximum of eight cross-country studies have been carried out for European countries, and remaining are specified for other regions.

Table 4.6 presents the summary results of those cross-country studies which have concentrated on the issue of bank ownership and efficiency. The findings from these studies have also been found to be mixed. The studies of Fries and Taci (2005),

Table 4.5 Impact of deregulation on the efficiency of banks – a cross-country analysis

Author (year)	Country	Period of the study	Efficiency, productivity and performance measures	Methodological framework	Major finding(s)
Panel A: Studies showing a positive effect of deregulation					
Panel A.1: Studies including India					
Ataullah et al. (2004)	India and Pakistan	1988–1998	TE, PTE, SE	DEA	The overall technical efficiency of the banking industry of India and Pakistan has improved following the financial liberalisation
Howcroft and Ataullah (2006)	India and Pakistan	1988–1998	TE and TFP growth	DEA and Malmquist productivity index	The TFP growth in the banking sector of both India and Pakistan has improved slowly during the study period. Also, loan-based model revealed more improvement in TFP growth than income-based model
Jaffry et al. (2007)	India, Pakistan, Bangladesh	1993–2001	TE and TFP growth	DEA and Malmquist productivity index	There is a substantial improvement in the technical efficiency and productivity of the banks across Indian subcontinent
Panel A.2: Studies excluding India					
Chang and Luh (2000)	19 Asian-Pacific countries	1965–1990	TFP growth	Malmquist productivity index	The overall productivity of banks in East Asian economies has improved during the period under study
Casu and Molyneux (2003)	5 European countries (France, Germany, Italy, Spain, UK)	1993–1997	TE and PTE	DEA	The average efficiency scores for almost all the European countries have improved over the period of analysis
Kwan (2003)	7 Asian countries	1992–1999	CE	SFA	Operating efficiency of Asian banks has improved over time

Casu et al. (2004)	5 European countries (France, Germany, Italy, Spain, UK)	1994–2000	CE and TFP growth	DEA, SFA and Malmquist productivity index	There exists a productivity growth in the Italian and Spanish banking sector, whereas the growth has been observed to be modest for French, German and British banks in the study period
Espitia-Escuer and Garcia-Cebrian (2004)	9 European Union countries	1988–1999	TE	SFA	The technical efficiency of all EU banks has improved in the period under analysis
Nguyen and Williams (2005)	5 Southeast Asian countries (Indonesia, Korea, Malaysia, Philippines and Thailand)	1990–2002	APE	SFA	Financial liberalisation has led to improvement in the profit efficiency of the banking sectors of Southeast Asian countries since 1996
Figueira and Nellis (2007)	Portugal and Spain	1992–2003	TE and TFP growth	DEA and Malmquist productivity index	Both Spanish and Portuguese banks have indeed become more efficient and productive with the intensification of reforms measures during the study period
Weill (2007)	6 CEE countries and 11 Western European countries	1996–2000	CE	SFA	The efficiency of banks in CEE and Western European countries has improved, but the increase in efficiency is higher in CEE nations than in Western European countries
Brissimis et al. (2008)	10 European Union countries	1994–2005	TE and TFP growth	DEA and Malmquist productivity index	Banking reforms and competition exerted a positive impact on bank efficiency and productivity of EU nations
Hermes and Nhung (2010)	10 Latin American and Asian countries	1991–2000	TE, PTE and SE	DEA	Financial liberalisation programmes appeared to have a positive impact on the efficiency of banks in the countries belonging to Latin America and Asia

(continued)

Table 4.5 (continued)

Author (year)	Country	Period of the study	Efficiency, productivity and performance measures	Methodological framework	Major finding(s)
Kondeas et al. (2008)	15 European Union nations	1989–1995	CE	SFA	Reduction in regulatory barriers has led to the improvement in the efficiency and productivity of the banks in the countries across European Union
Koutsomanoli-Filippaki et al. (2009a)	4 CEE countries (Hungary, Poland, Czech Republic and Slovakia)	1999–2003	PE	SFA	Financial reforms appeared to assert a significant positive impact on profit efficiency of the banking industry of CEE countries
Košak et al. (2009)	8 new EU member states (5 CEE and 3 Baltic states)	1996–2006	CE	SFA	Cost efficiency of all the new EU member states has increased over time
Panel B: Studies showing a negative effect of deregulation					
Panel B.1: Studies including India					
Perera et al. (2007)	4 South Asian countries (India, Bangladesh, Pakistan and Sri Lanka)	1997–2004	CE	SFA	Cost efficiency of the banks in South Asian countries has shown a decline over the study period
Panel B.2: Studies excluding India					
Fries and Taci (2005)	15 East European transition nations	1994–2001	CE	SFA	With the advancement of reforms, the cost efficiency of transition nations has declined significantly
Ariss et al. (2007)	6 GCC countries (Bahrain, Kuwait, Oman, Qatar, Saudi Arabia, United Arab Emirates)	1999–2004	CE, AE, TE, PTE and SE	DEA	GCC countries experienced a decline in the efficiency of the banks but with different degree in the post-deregulation period

Source: Authors' compilation

Notes: (i) *DEA, SFA, DFA, TFA* and *EFA* are the acronyms for data envelopment analysis, stochastic frontier analysis, distribution free approach, thick frontier analysis and econometric frontier analysis, respectively; and (ii) *CE, TE, AE, RE, PTE, SE, SPE* and *APE* stand for cost, technical, allocative, revenue, pure technical, scale, standard profit and alternative profit efficiencies, respectively

Table 4.6 Impact of ownership on the efficiency of banks – a cross-country analysis

Author (year)	Country	Period of the study	Efficiency, productivity and performance measures	Methodological framework	Major finding(s)
Panel A: Foreign > Domestic					
Weill (2003)	Czech Republic and Poland	Cross-sectional data for the year 1997	CE	SFA	Foreign banks are more cost efficient than domestic banks
Ataullah et al. (2004)	India and Pakistan	1988–1998	ROA, TE, PTE and SE	DEA and traditional financial ratios	Domestic private and foreign banks are more technically efficient than public sector banks in both countries
Fries and Taci (2005)	15 East European transition nations	1994–2001	CE	SFA	Privatised banks with majority foreign ownership are the most efficient than the banks with domestic ownership in East European nations
Nguyen and Williams (2005)	5 Southeast Asian countries	1990–2002	APE	SFA	Foreign-owned banks are, on average, significantly more profit efficient than domestic banks in selected Southeast Asian countries, except the Philippines
Grigorian and Manole (2006)	17 European transition countries	1995–1998	TE	DEA	Foreign-owned banks are significantly more efficient than domestic banks in transition economies
Panel B: Domestic > Foreign					
Kablan (2007)	6 West African Economic Monetary Union (WAEMU) countries	1993–1996	TE, CE and TFP growth	DEA and SFA	Foreign banks are the most efficient ones, followed by state-owned WAEMU banks

(continued)

Table 4.6 (continued)

Author (year)	Country	Period of the study	Efficiency, productivity and performance measures	Methodological framework	Major finding(s)
Perera et al. (2007)	4 South Asian countries (India, Bangladesh and Pakistan)	1997–2004	CE	SFA	State-owned banks in South Asian countries are more cost-inefficient than private-owned banks
Barry et al. (2008)	6 Asian countries (Hong Kong, Indonesia, South Korea, Malaysia, Philippines, and Thailand)	1999–2004	TE, PTE and SE	DEA	Banks owned by minority private shareholders and by foreign investors appeared to be more efficient than state-owned banks during the post-crisis period
Staikouras et al. (2008)	6 Southeast European countries	1998–2003	CE	SFA	Foreign banks and banks with higher foreign ownership are more cost efficient than state-owned banks
Chen (2009)	8 Sub-Saharan African middle-income countries	2000–2007	CE	SFA	Foreign banks are more efficient than public and domestic private banks
Košak et al. (2009)	8 new EU member states (5 CEE and 3 Baltic states)	1996–2006	CE	SFA	Banks with foreign ownership seemed to have higher efficiency scores than domestic banks
Poghosyan and Poghosyan (2010)	11 Central and Eastern European countries	1992–2006	CE	SFA	Foreign Greenfield banks are characterised by superior cost efficiency, compared to domestic and foreign-acquired banks
Miller and Parkhe (2002)	12 EU countries and Switzerland, UK, Argentina, India, Japan, USA, Canada, Chile	1989–1996	PE	SFA	Domestic banks in the selected countries outperformed foreign banks

Zajc (2006)	6 CEE nations (Czech Republic, Estonia, Hungary, Poland, Slovakia and Slovenia)	1995–2000	CE	SFA	Foreign banks are less cost efficient than domestic banks in Central and Eastern European countries
Lensink et al. (2008)	105 countries	1998–2003	CE	SFA	Foreign ownership has a negative effect on the bank efficiency. This indicates that domestic banks are on average more efficient than foreign banks
Thi and Vencappa (2008)	Czech Republic, Hungary and Poland	1994–2004	CE	SFA	Foreign banks are generally more cost efficient than their domestic counterparts
Wezel (2010)	6 Central American countries	2002–2007	TE, AE, SE and CE	DEA and SFA	Domestic and regional banks in Central America are more efficient than foreign banks
Yildirim and Philippatos (2007)	12 CEE nations	1993-2000	CE and APE	SFA and DFA	Foreign banks are found to be more cost efficient, but less profit efficient relative to domestic private and state-owned banks

Source: Authors' compilation

Notes: (i) *DEA, SFA, DFA, TFA* and *EFA* are the acronyms for data envelopment analysis, stochastic frontier analysis, distribution free approach, thick frontier analysis and econometric frontier analysis, respectively, and (ii) *CE, TE, AE, RE, PTE, SE, SPE* and *APE* stand for cost, technical, allocative, revenue, pure technical, scale, standard profit and alternative profit efficiencies, respectively

Grigorian and Manole (2006), Staikouras et al. (2008) and Košak et al. (2009) for a sample of selected European countries found an evidence that foreign banks are more efficient than domestic banks. Similar finding is also qualified by Poghosyan and Poghosyan (2010) for a sample of Central and Eastern European countries. For other regions, the superior performance of foreign banks is corroborated by Nguyen and Williams (2005), Perera et al. (2007) and Barry et al. (2008) for a sample of Asian countries; Chen (2009) for Sub-Saharan African middle-income countries; Weill (2003) for Czech Republic and Poland; Ataullah et al. (2004) for India and Pakistan; and Kablan (2007) for West African Economic Monetary Union countries.

In contrast, Zajc (2006) reported a lower efficiency of foreign banks compared with domestic banks for Central and Eastern European countries, while Wezel (2010) reached at this conclusion for a sample of six Central American countries. Nevertheless, the study by Miller and Parkhe (2002) for a sample of 12 EU nations along with Switzerland, UK, Argentina, India, Japan, USA, Canada and Chile; Lensink et al. (2008) for 105 developed and developing countries; and Thi and Vencappa (2008) for Czech Republic, Hungary and Poland concluded that domestic banks were more efficient than foreign banks. Nonetheless, Yildirim and Philippatos (2007) for 12 CEE nations reported mixed evidence.

4.5 Mergers and Acquisitions (M&As) and Bank Efficiency

The last 20 years have witnessed an unprecedented number of mergers and acquisitions (M&As) in the banking systems of most countries. This prompted the research on the effects of M&As on the bank efficiency. Since the mid- to late 1980s, a large part of the research undertaken to evaluate the effects produced by M&A's transactions has been analysed primarily within US banking (see Berger and Humphrey 1997).[1] Nevertheless, since 1990s, a significant number of studies has been published that aimed to examine the impact of mergers on the efficiency of banks in the economies other than the USA. The common testable hypothesis in these studies is whether mergers are successful in terms of efficiency improvements of the acquiring banks. It was expected that the process of M&As would be more successful when the acquiring bank is more efficient than the bank being acquired because the superior management team would gain control and use its demonstrated ability to improve the less efficient bank.

DeYoung et al. (2009) in their extensive survey of 150 studies on M&As in financial institutions found no consistent evidence regarding whether, on average, the participating financial firms benefit from M&As; whether the customers of these firms benefit; or whether societal risks have increased or decreased as a result of this activity. Our survey findings are also consistent with DeYoung et al. (2009) and report mixed evidences concerning the effects of mergers on bank efficiency. We note that the bulk of empirical research shows evidence of significant efficiency gains from bank mergers, but a few studies also reported that mergers may not have a beneficial effect in terms of X-efficiency of acquiring banks and the banking industry as a whole (see Table 4.7 for the main findings of the studies reviewed). Most of the

Table 4.7 Impact of M&As on the efficiency and productivity

Author (year)	Country	Period of the study	Methodological framework	Main finding(s)
Panel A: Studies showing positive effect of M&As				
Akhavein et al. (1997)	USA	1981–1989	DFA	Merging banks improved their profit efficiency substantially after mergers
Resti (1998)	Italy	1986–1995	DEA	Merged banks seem to have increased their efficiency in the years after the merger
Avkiran (1999)	Australia	1986–1995	DEA	Acquiring banks are more cost efficient than target banks, indicating that there is a gradual rise in efficiency after the merger exercise
Cuesta and Orea (2002)	Spain	1985–1998	Stochastic output distance function approach	Merged banking firms are more efficient than non-merged firms in Spain
Krishnasamy et al. (2003)	Malaysia	2000–2001	DEA	Malaysian banks have experienced total factor productivity improvement in the period following the merger process
Humphrey and Vale (2004)	Norway	1987–1998	SFA	There is an evidence of cost efficiency improvement resulting from mergers of Norwegian banks
Peng and Wang (2004)	Taiwan	1997–1999	SFA	Bank merger enhanced the cost efficiency of Taiwan's banks
Sufian (2004)	Malaysia	1998–2003	DEA	Merger programme was successful, particularly for the small and medium banks, which have benefited the most from the merger and expansion via economies of scale
Mylonidis and Kenikola (2005)	Greece	Pre-merger period: 1994–1997 Post-merger period: 2000–2002	Traditional financial ratios	Merger activity has a positive impact on Greek banks operating performance
Gourlay et al. (2006)	India	1992–2005	DEA	Mergers led to improvement of efficiency of merging banks
De Guevara and Maudas (2007)	Spain	1986–2002	SFA	The cost efficiency of Spanish banks improved during the period of consolidation, largely due to declines in marginal costs
Sufian et al. (2008)	Singapore	1997–2000	Traditional financial ratios and DEA	Mean overall efficiency of acquiring banks has improved after merger resulting from merger with a more efficient bank

(continued)

Table 4.7 (continued)

Author (year)	Country	Period of the study	Methodological framework	Main finding(s)
Singh (2009)	India	2001–2005	DEA	Mergers do not seem to impact the cost efficiency in an adverse manner
Panel B: Studies showing a negative effect of M&As				
Berger and Humphrey (1992)	USA	n.a.	DFA and traditional financial ratios	There were no efficiency gains associated with mergers in which the acquirer bank was more efficient than acquired bank
Peristiani (1997)	USA	1980–1990	SFA	Acquiring banks failed to improve post-mergers X-efficiency, and the mergers led to no sign of improvements in efficiency
Garden and Ralston (1999)	Australia	1992–1997	DEA	Mergers do not result in an increase in X-efficiency or allocative efficiency in the post-merger period
Rezitis (2008)	Greece	19993–2004	Stochastic output distance function approach	The effects of mergers and acquisition on technical efficiency and total factor productivity growth of Greek banks was negative
Wu (2008)	Australia	1983–2001	DEA	Mergers have resulted in poorer efficiency performance of merged bank
Panel C: Studies showing inconclusive evidences about M&As				
Liu and Tripe (2002)	New Zealand	1989–1998	DEA	The possible effects of mergers on efficiency gains remain inconclusive. Some banks were more efficient post-merger while others remained inefficient post-merger
Berger and Mester (2003)	USA	1984–1997	SFA	Merged banks registered a greater improvement of profit efficiency. Further, a decrease in cost efficiency is greater in merged banks than those not involved in M&As

Source: Authors' elaboration

Note: (i) *DEA, SFA, DFA, TFA* and *EFA* are the acronyms for data envelopment analysis, stochastic frontier analysis, distribution free approach, thick frontier analysis and econometric frontier analysis, respectively studies conclude that efficiency gains from merger activities occur because (i) the larger banks resulting from consolidation may gain access to cost-saving technologies or spread their fixed costs over a larger base, thus reducing average costs, and (ii) of the exploitation of economies of scope. On the other hand, the most cited reasons of negative effects of M&As on bank efficiency are increased costs (e.g. consultant fees, severance pay, legal expenses) along with downsizing disruptions, the merging of organisational cultures and managerial turf battles. In sum, we can safely infer that the extant literature gives an inconclusive picture of the effects of M&As on the efficiency of acquiring banks. It is worth mentioning here that the contradictory findings may be due to the use of different methodologies and different time period being studied by the researchers in their studies.

4.6 Major Issues in Banking Efficiency Analyses

4.6.1 Selection of Inputs and Outputs

One of the major problems in bank efficiency studies is the choice of appropriate input and output variables. This problem is compounded by the fact that variable selection is often constrained by the paucity of data on relevant variables. The cost and output measurements in banking are especially difficult because many of the financial services are jointly produced and prices are typically assigned to a bundle of financial services. There has been long-standing disagreement among researchers over what banks produce. The most debatable issue relating to the definition of inputs and outputs is the role of deposits, i.e. is demand deposits an input or output? Two approaches dominate the banking theory literature: the production and intermediation approaches (Sealey and Lindley 1977).

The *production approach*, as pioneered by Benston (1965), emphasises the operational activity and treats banks as the providers of services to customers. The output under this approach represents the services provided to the customers and is best measured by the number and type of transactions, documents processed or specialised services provided over a given time period. However, in case of non-availability of detailed transaction flow data, they are substituted by the data on the number of deposits and loan accounts, as a surrogate for the level of services provided. In this approach, input includes physical variables (like labour, material, space or information systems) or their associated cost. This approach considers only operating costs and excludes the interest expenses paid on deposits since deposits are viewed as outputs. Berger and Humphrey (1997) suggested that the production approach is well suited for measuring branch level efficiency because branches primarily process customer documents for the institution as a whole and branch managers typically have little influence over bank funding and investment decisions.

The *intermediation approach* as proposed by Sealey and Lindley (1977) treats banks as financial intermediaries channeling funds between depositors and creditors. In this approach, banks produce intermediation services through the collection of deposits and other liabilities and their application in interest-earning assets, such as loans, securities and other investments. This approach includes both operating and interest expenses as inputs, whereas loans and other assets count as outputs. Berger and Humphrey (1997) suggested that the intermediation approach is best suited for analysing bank-level efficiency. This is because at a bank-level management will aim to reduce total costs and not just non-interest expenses. The debate on the identification of banking output further led to the establishment of the *asset*, the *user cost* and the *value-added* approaches, which can be seen as variants of the *intermediation approach*.

The *asset approach* is a reduced form modelling of the banking activity, focusing exclusively on the role of banks as financial intermediaries between depositors and final uses of bank assets. Deposits and other liabilities, together with real resources (labour and physical capital), are defined as inputs to the intermediation process, whereas the output vector includes earning assets such as loans and investments. This approach was first suggested by Sealey and Lindley (1977). The main criticism levelled at the intermediation and asset approaches is that they do not take into consideration the substantial amount of resources that the banks devote into acquiring deposit funds, particularly demand and savings deposits (Berger and Humphrey 1992).

The *user cost approach* determines whether a financial product is an input or an output on the basis of its net contribution to bank revenue. If the financial returns on an asset exceed the opportunity cost of the funds or alternately, if the financial costs of a liability are less than the opportunity cost, they are considered as outputs; otherwise, they are considered as inputs. Hancock (1985) was the first to apply the user cost approach to banking. This approach identifies the inputs of the production process in the banking industry as 'the net cost a bank must sustain in a given period of time in order to hold one unit of the financial instrument associated with the service'. In operational terms, user cost is calculated as the difference between all the revenues and all the costs (including the opportunity cost) generated by a financial instrument in the bank's portfolio. For example, the cost of using a bank loan can be approximated by the difference between the interest rate on a riskless security of equal amount (opportunity cost) and the expected yield of the loan. Here, deposits are included among output.

The *value-added approach*, as developed by Berger et al. (1987), differs from the asset and user cost approaches in that it considers all liability and asset categories to have some output characteristics rather than distinguishing inputs from outputs in a mutually exclusive way. This approach identifies any balance sheet item (assets or liabilities) as output if it contributes to the banks' value added (i.e. business associated with the consumption of real resources); otherwise, it is considered as an input or non-relevant output. Under this approach, the major categories of produced deposits (e.g. demand, term and saving deposits) and loans (e.g. mortgages and commercial loans) are viewed as important outputs because they form a significant proportion of value added.

In addition to the aforementioned approaches to specify inputs and outputs, Drake et al. (2006, 2009) proposed the use of a *profit/revenue approach* in which revenue components are defined as outputs and cost components as inputs. Berger and Mester (2003) argue that 'use of the profit approach may help take into account unmeasured changes in the quality of banking services by including higher revenues paid for the improved quality, and may help to capture the profit maximisation goal by including both the costs and revenues'. Also, the profit approach is considered to be the appropriate system to capture the diversity of strategic responses by financial firms in the face of dynamic changes in competitive and environmental conditions, such as in the case of the current financial crisis (Berger and Mester 2003). This approach analyses how each branch uses its resources (inputs) to generate revenues such as interest income and non-interest income from commissions.

On commenting these approaches for selecting inputs and outputs, Berger and Humphrey (1997) gave a final verdict by saying that *"neither of these two approaches is perfect because they cannot fully captures the dual roles of banks as (i) providing transactions/document processing services, and (ii) being financial intermediaries that transfer funds from the savers to investors"*. The imperfection is attributed to the dual role of deposits. Deposits have the input characteristics since they are raised by banks as the raw materials for loans and have the output characteristics because they are associated with a substantial amount of liquidity and payment services provided to depositors. However, Elyasiani and Mehdian (1990b) gave three advantages of using the intermediation approach. They argue that (a) it is more inclusive of the total banking cost as it does not exclude interest expense on deposits and other liabilities, (b) it appropriately categorises the deposits as inputs, and (c) it has an edge over other definitions for data quality considerations.

Table 4.8 lists out the input and output variables used in the studies on the efficiency and productivity of Indian banks. We note that there is no consensus on whether the deposits be included in input or output vector. Some researchers such as Bhattacharyya et al. (1997b), Saha and Ravisankar (2000) and Mukherjee et al. (2002) treat deposits as outputs, but Debnath and Shankar (2008), Rezvanian et al. (2008), Kumar and Gulati (2008a, b, 2009a), Ray (2007) and Das and Ghosh (2009) treat them as inputs, while the others such as Das and Ghosh (2006) and Chandrasekhar and Sonar (2008) treat them simultaneously as inputs and outputs. On the use of deposits as an input variable in a study aiming at analysing the impact of deregulation on bank efficiency, Ram Mohan and Ray (2004b) rightly remarked that 'using deposits and loans as outputs would have been appropriate in the nationalised era when maximizing these was indeed the objective of a bank but they are, perhaps, less appropriate in the reforms era. Banks are not simply maximizing deposits and loans; they are in the business of maximizing profits. If inputs are treated as pre-determined, this amounts to maximizing revenue'. It is important to note here that majority of the studies included in Table 4.8 have adopted an intermediation approach for selecting appropriate inputs and outputs.

Table 4.8 Input and output variables used in selected Indian studies on banking efficiency

Author (year)	Approach	Inputs	Outputs
Bhattacharyya et al. (1997a)	VA	1. Labour 2. Physical capital	1. Fixed deposits 2. Savings deposits 3. Current deposits 4. Investments 5. Loans and securities
Bhattacharyya et al. (1997b)	VA	1. Interest expense 2. Operating expense	1. Advances 2. Investments 3. Deposits
Saha and Ravisankar (2000)	n.s.	*Model A* 1. Branches 2. Staff 3. Establishment expenditure 4. Non-establishment expenditure	*Model A* 1. Deposits 2. Advances 3. Investments 4. Spread 5. Total income 6. Interest income 7. Non-interest income 8. Working funds
		Model B 1. Interest expenditure 2. Establishment expenditure 3. Non-establishment expenditure 4. Fixed assets	*Model B* 1. Deposits 2. Advances 3. Investments 4. Non-interest income 5. Spread 6. Total income
Mukherjee et al. (2002)	IA	1. Net worth 2. Borrowings 3. Operating expenses 4. Number of employees 5. Number of branches	1. Deposits 2. Net profit 3. Advances 4. Non-interest income 5. Interest spread
Sathye (2003)	IA	*Model A* 1. Interest expenses 2. Non-interest expenses *Model B* 1. Deposits 2. Staff	*Model A* 1. Net-interest income 2. Non-interest income *Model B* 1. Net loans 2. Non-interest income
Ram Mohan and Ray (2004b)	IA	1. Labour 2. Loanable funds	1. Net-interest margin 2. Commission, exchange, brokerage, etc.
Shanmugam and Das (2004)	IA	1. Deposits 2. Borrowings 3. Labour 4. Fixed assets	1. Net-interest margin 2. Non-interest income 3. Credits 4. Investments

(continued)

Table 4.8 (continued)

Author (year)	Approach	Inputs	Outputs
Das et al. (2005)	IA	1. Borrowed funds 2. Staff 3. Fixed assets 4. Equity	1. Investments 2. Performing loan assets 3. Other non-interest fee-based income
Chakrabarti and Chawla (2005)	Both PA and VA	*Model A* 1. Interest expenses 2. Operating expense *Model B* 1. Interest 2. Non-interest expenses	*Model A* 1. Advances 2. Investments 3. Deposits *Model B* 1. Interest income 2. Non-interest income
Galagedera and Edirisuriya (2005)	IA	1. Total deposits 2. Operating expenses	1. Loans 2. Other earning assets
Kumbhakar and Sarkar (2005)	VA	1. Labour 2. Capital	1. Deposits 2. Loans and advances 3. Investments 4. Number of branches
Ataullah and Le (2006)	IA	1. Operating expenses 2. Interest expenses	*Loan-based model* 1. Loans and advances 2. Investments *Income-based model* 1. Interest income 2. Non-interest income
Das and Ghosh (2006)	IA, VA and OA	*IA* 1. Demand deposits 2. Saving deposits 3. Fixed deposits 4. Labour 5. Capital-related operating expenses *VA and OA* 1. Labour 2. Capital-related operating expenses 3. Interest expenses	*IA* 1. Advances 2. Investments *VA* 1. Advances 2. Investments 3. Demand deposits 4. Fixed deposits 5. Saving deposits *OA* 1. Interest income 2. Non-interest income
Debasish (2006)	n.s.	1. Total deposits received 2. Total liabilities 3. Labour-related administrative costs 4. Capital-related administrative cost	1. Total loans extended 2. Total investments 3. Net profits 4. Interest and related revenues

(continued)

Table 4.8 (continued)

Author (year)	Approach	Inputs	Outputs
		5. Operating expenses	5. Non-interest income
		6. Fixed assets	6. Short-term securities issued by official sectors
		7. Total borrowings	7. Net-interest margin
		8. Net worth	
		9. Net NPA	
Sensarma (2006, 2008)	VA	1. Employees	1. Value of fixed deposits
		2. Fixed assets	2. Saving deposits
			3. Current deposits
			4. Investments
			5. Loans and advances
			6. Number of branches
Ray (2007)	IA	1. Borrowed funds	1. Credit
		2. Labour	2. Investments
		3. Physical capital	3. Other income
		4. Equity	
Chandrasekhar and Sonar (2008)	Both PA and IA	*PA*	*PA*
		1. Number of branches	1. Business mix (deposits plus advances)
		2. Number of automatic teller machines (ATMs)	
		3. Number of employees	
		4. IT investments	
		5. Fixed assets	
		IA	*IA*
		1. Deposits	1. Investments
		2. Number of branches	2. Advances (credit portfolio of banks)
		3. Number of ATMs	
		4. Number of employees	
		5. IT investments	
		6. Fixed assets	
Debnath and Shankar (2008)	IA	1. Total assets	1. Profit after taxes
		2. Deposits	2. Operating profit
			3. Interest income
			4. Total income
			5. Advances
			6. Net non-performing assets
Rezvanian et al. (2008)	IA	1. Borrowed funds	1. Advances
		2. Labour	2. Securities
		3. Fixed assets	3. Other earning assets
Das and Ghosh (2009)	IA	1. Deposits	1. Loans and advances
		2. Labour	2. Investments
		3. Capital	3. Other income
		4. Equity (quasi-fixed)	
Kumar and Gulati (2008a, b, 2009b)	IA	1. Physical capital	1. Net-interest income
		2. Labour	2. Non-interest income

(continued)

Table 4.8 (continued)

Author (year)	Approach	Inputs	Outputs
		3. Loanable funds (deposits plus borrowings)	
Ray and Das (2010)	IA	1. Funds (deposits plus borrowings)	1. Investments
		2. Labour	2. Earning advances
		3. Capital	3. Other income
		4. Equity (quasi-fixed)	
Zhao et al. (2010)	IA	1. Loanable funds	1. Book value of performing loans
		2. Non-interest operating costs	2. Other earning loans
			3. Fee-based income

Source: Authors' compilation
Notes: (i) *IA, PA* and *VA* stand for intermediation approach, production approach and value-added approach, respectively, and (ii) *n.s.* means 'not specified' by the authors

4.6.2 Choice of Estimation Methodology

As noted above, the literature on banking efficiency is very vast and contains a large number of articles. Besides using conventional financial ratios such as return to equity, return on assets and expense to income ratios, a number of alternative frontier efficiency measurement techniques have been used by the researcher for analysing the differences in efficiency across banks. Common frontier efficiency estimation techniques are the Data Envelopment Analysis (DEA), the Free Disposal Hull (FDH) analysis, the Stochastic Frontier Analysis (SFA), the Thick Frontier Analysis (TFA), the Recursive Thick Frontier Analysis (RTFA) and the Distribution Free Approach (DFA). The first two of these are non-parametric techniques, and the latter three are parametric methods. The availability of a variety of techniques led to another significant issue: whether to use SFA or DEA or TFA or DFA or FDH or RTFA in a particular banking efficiency analysis.

It is significant to note here that each frontier technique involves various models for deriving a measure of best practice for the sample of banks and then determine how closely individual banks lie relative to this standard. The best practice is usually in the form of an *efficient frontier* that is estimated using econometric or mathematical programming techniques. The frontier techniques summarise bank performance in a single statistic that controls for a difference among banks in a sophisticated multidimensional framework that has its roots in economic theory. Further, frontier efficiency measures dominate the traditional ratio analysis in terms of developing meaningful and reliable measures of bank performance. Owing to these features of frontier methodology, the conventional ratio analysis is becoming obsolete.

SFA is the most widely used parametric efficiency assessment method in the literature (Berger and Humphrey 1997). SFA evolved from Aigner and Chu (1968), Timmer (1971), Afrait (1972) and others. This approach specifies a function for cost, profit or production so as to determine the frontier and treats the residual as a composite error comprising: (a) random error with a symmetric distribution often normal and (b) inefficiency with an asymmetric distribution often a half-normal on the grounds that inefficiencies will never be a positive for production or profit or a negative for cost. A drawback of the SFA is that assumptions must be made about the shape of the frontier and the distribution of the inefficiency term. Some of the notable studies in banking that have utilised SFA include Ferrier and Lovell (1990), Chaffai (1997), Kumbhakar et al. (1998, 2001), Lang and Welzel (1999), Christopoulos and Tsionas (2001), Hao et al. (2001), Isik and Hassan (2002b), Hasan and Marton (2003), Weill (2003, 2004), Fan (2004), Bonin et al. (2005), Kwan (2006), Meso and Kaino (2008) and Fu and Heffernan (2009).

DFA has been developed by Berger (1993) and assumes that efficiencies are stable over time. Random errors are assumed to average out over time, thus requiring little to be assumed about the distributional form of the efficiency measure and random error. Some significant studies on the use of DFA are Berger (1993), Allen and Rai (1996), DeYoung (1997), Dietsch and Lozano-Vivas (2000), Rime and Stiroh (2003), Matousek and Taci (2004), Patti and Hardy (2005) and Weill (2007). In TFA, as developed by Berger and Humphrey (1992), instead of estimating a precise frontier bound, a cost function is estimated for the lowest average cost quartile of banks, which may be thought of as a 'thick frontier', where the firms exhibit an efficiency greater than the sample average. A cost function for the highest average cost quartile is also estimated. The difference between these two cost functions can be split into two factors. First is explained by market factors related to the available exogenous variables and the second factor cannot be explained, i.e. the 'inefficiency residual'. The researchers like Bauer et al. (1993), DeYoung (1994), Clark (1996), Lang and Welzel (1996, 1998), Humphrey and Pulley (1997) and Lozano-Vivas (1998) have applied TFA in their bank efficiency analyses. Recursive Thick Frontier Analysis (RTFA) developed by Wagenvoort and Schure (1999, 2006) does not require a distributional assumption on the inefficiency component of the error term. It allows technical inefficiency to vary over time and be dependent on the explanatory variables of the frontier model. Unlike some of the other panel data methods, RTFA works well even if the number of time periods in the panel data set is small. The application of RTFA in the measurement of banking efficiency is provided in Schure et al. (2004).

The most commonly used non-parametric frontier efficiency approaches are Data Envelopment Analysis (DEA) and its variant Free Disposal Hull (FDH) method. DEA originated with the seminal work of Charnes et al. (1978) is a mathematical programming-based technique and imposes no structure on the production process, so that the frontier is determined purely by data in the sample. Utilisation of linear programming generates a series of points of best practice observations, and the *efficient frontier* is derived as a series of piecewise linear combinations of these points. Thus, DEA is advantageous because it produces a true frontier from which relative efficiencies can be derived. However, DEA does not allow for random error in data. In other words, DEA assumes that there are no measurement errors, no inaccuracies associated with accounting data and no luck or chance that may temporarily give a bank better measured performance in the short-term (Berger and Humphrey 1997). If any of these errors is present in the data set, then that may be reflected as an ingredient of the measured inefficiency. Several studies have used DEA in assessing the relative efficiency of banks, for example, Rangan et al. (1988), Elyasiani and Mehdian (1990a), Berg et al. (1993), Bukh (1994), Schaffnit et al. (1997), Taylor et al. (1997), Ayadi (1998), Al-Shammari and Salimi (1998), Barr (2002), Manandhar and Tang (2002), Drake and Hall (2003), Luo (2003), Mercan et al. (2003), Halkos and Salamouris (2004), Ramanathan (2006), Mostafa (2007), Huang et al. (2008), Hsiao et al. (2010) and Fethi et al. (2011). FDH can be regarded as a generalisation of DEA variable returns-to-scale model. This model does not require the estimated frontier to be convex. Some important applications of FDH are the studies of Tulkens (1993) and Tulkens and Malnero (1994).

Further, there are few studies which applied both non-parametric and parametric techniques simultaneously (see, e.g. Ferrier and Lovell 1990; Resti 1998; Sturm and Williams 2004; Fiorentino et al. 2006; Kablan 2007; Figueira et al. 2009; Wezel 2010). It has been observed that though frontier methods (SFA, TFA, RTFA, DFA, DEA and FDH) are superior to financial accounting ratios analysis, yet no preferred efficiency frontier technique has emerged. Since both parametric and non-parametric frontier approaches have a range of advantages and disadvantages, which may influence the choice of methods in a particular application, the principal advantage of parametric frontier analysis is that it allows the test of hypothesis concerning the goodness of fit of the model. However, the major disadvantage is that it requires specification of a particular frontier function (like Cobb–Douglas or translog), which may be restrictive in most cases. Furthermore, the major advantage of the non-parametric frontier analysis is that it does not require the specification of a particular functional form for the technology. The main disadvantage is that it is not possible to estimate parameters for the model and, hence, impossible to test hypothesis concerning the performance of the model. However, no consensus has been reached in the literature about the appropriate and preferred estimation methodology (Staikouras et al. 2008).

Despite a dispute over the preferred methodology, an emerging view suggests that it is not necessary to have a consensus as to one single (best) frontier approach for measuring bank efficiency (Iqbal and Molyneux 2005). Instead, there should be a set of consistency conditions to be met for the efficiency measures derived from various approaches. If efficiency estimates are consistent across different methodologies, then these measures will be convincing and, therefore, valid (or believable) estimates. A technique is considered consistent if (i) it is distributionally comparable to other commonly used methods, (ii) it produces approximately the same ranking of institutions, (iii) it predominantly identifies the same best and worst banks, (iv) it predominantly produces the same relative ranking of banks over time, (v) its efficiency scores are consistent with 'competitive market conditions' and (vi) its measured efficiencies are consistent with prevailing measures of performance (Bauer et al. 1998). In sum, efficiency estimates derived from different approaches should be consistent by generating analogous efficiency levels and rankings concerning the identification of best and worst banks. These should also be consistent over time and in line with the competitive conditions of the market and also with standard non-frontier measures of performance. In the light of above-stated consistency conditions, methodological cross-checking is highly recommended for a banking efficiency analysis.

4.7 Conclusions

The main purpose of this chapter is to present a survey of empirical literature on bank efficiency. Four key research areas have been identified where most of the research efforts have been devoted in last two decades. The most prominent area which has been extensively explored by the researchers in recent years is the impact of financial deregulation on the efficiency of banking system. We note that contrary to conventional wisdom, the empirical evidences have shown that deregulation and financial liberalisation do not necessarily lead to an improvement in the efficiency of banks. It can either deteriorate or improve the efficiency and productivity of the banking sector, depending on industry conditions prior to or after deregulation. In particular, our survey shows that although the impact of deregulation on efficiency of banks has been mixed in the literature, the majority of studies, especially confined to banking sectors of developing countries, have shown a positive impact of liberalisation and deregulation on the relative efficiency of banks. In the Indian case too, the most of the studies focusing on the trends of efficiency concluded that banking reforms process since 1992 has had a positive impact on the efficiency of Indian banking industry as a whole and its distinct segments defined on the basis of ownership. Thus, an overwhelming majority of studies portrayed a positive impact of deregulatory policies on the efficiency and productivity of Indian banks.

An inspection of literature further highlights that the focus of large number of studies has been to explore the link between ownership structure and efficiency. It has been observed that the extant literature is inconclusive on the issue of efficiency differences between foreign and domestic banks. However, the broad conclusion which emerged from this survey is that foreign banks in developing countries are more efficient than domestic banks, while the opposite is true for developed economies. In Indian context, the mixed findings of the empirical investigations on the subject matter of ownership and banking efficiency are in line with the international experience, but present a very complicated picture since no clear dominance of a particular ownership group has emerged.

The third research area which received the large interest of the researchers is the cross-country comparisons of efficiency levels across countries. The studies on cross-country efficiency comparisons are mostly concentrated on the regions other than Asia. The reviewed studies offered a mixed bag of evidence on the effect of deregulation and liberalisation on efficiency across countries. The inclusion of the Indian banking sector in the reviewed literature is very scarce. The final research area focuses on the effects of M&As on the bank efficiency. It has been noted that though an overwhelming majority of studies reported the significant efficiency gains from bank mergers, a few studies also inferred that mergers may not have a beneficial effect in terms of X-efficiency of acquiring banks and the banking industry as a whole.

This chapter also discusses the two prominent issues in the banking efficiency literature. The first issue relates with the selection and specification of inputs and outputs in a study on the subject matter. The second issue is on the selection of appropriate frontier efficiency technique to measure bank efficiency. Regarding the first issue, we observed that though both intermediation and production approaches are not perfect to model the production process of banking firms, the intermediation approach dominates the production approach in the empirical applications because it is better suited to capture the decisions taken to minimise the cost of the financing mix. On the second issue, we note that a bank's efficiency score can differ completely due to the measurement technique, and there is virtually no consensus on the preferred estimation method of bank efficiency.

Chapter 5
Relevance of Non-traditional Activities on the Efficiency of Indian Banks

5.1 Introduction

Over the past three decades, financial liberalisation policies have been implemented widely in both the less developed and the relatively more advanced industrialised economies. These policies aimed at enhancing competition, improving resource allocation and acquiring more efficient financial institutions by making them less state directed and by exposing them to increased market competition (Barajas et al. 2000). India joined the financial liberalisation bandwagon in 1992 and adopted a gradualist, cautious and progressive approach to deregulate and liberalise the banking sector. The regulators have introduced a series of banking reforms measures like dismantling of administered interest rate structure, reduction in statutory pre-emptions, introduction of prudential norms in line with international best practices and liberal entry of *de novo* domestic private and foreign banks to improve the process of financial intermediation and foster better resource allocation in the banking system.

Consequent to the reform measures and rapid technological advances in information flows and communication infrastructure, Indian banking system has undergone significant transformations in the post-1992 period. The most prominent structural changes that have taken place in the Indian banking industry during the post-reforms years are (i) improvement in soundness of the banking system in terms of capital adequacy and asset quality; (ii) decline in the market share of public sector banks; (iii) strengthening of accounting, legal, supervisory and regulatory frameworks pertaining to the banking sector; (iv) decline in net-interest margin and intermediation cost due to heightened competition; (v) financial innovation; and (vi) a decline in traditional banking activities.[1] Among the aforementioned changes in the Indian banking industry, the decline in the traditional banking activities and

[1] The traditional banking business has been to make long-term loans and fund them by issuing short-dated deposits, a process which is commonly referred to as 'borrowing short and lending long' (Edwards and Mishkin 1995).

S. Kumar and R. Gulati, *Deregulation and Efficiency of Indian Banks*, India Studies in Business and Economics, DOI 10.1007/978-81-322-1545-5_5, © Springer India 2014

consequent increase in fee-producing non-traditional activities like leasing, merchant banking, investment banking, mutual funds, venture capital, securitisation, backup lines of credit, financial derivatives and stock broking has received considerable attention from bankers, regulators and academic researchers. Nachane and Ghosh (2002, 2007) are perhaps the first ones to recognise this change, and they have analysed the trends and determinants of off-balance sheet activities[2] in Indian banking industry.

Note here that the motivation for the banks to enter non-traditional areas include the need to have the profit centre, presence in diversified financial market services, broad-based customer access and the desire to have leading market positions in all financial services market (Ajit 1997). In the post-reforms years, the relative share of interest income emanating from traditional banking activities has declined and that of non-interest income originating from non-traditional activities which are not captured on the balance sheet has increased significantly. Hence, a remarkable shift in the sources of income of the Indian banks has been noticed, and non-interest income comprises a larger portion of commercial bank income today than in 1992 (see succeeding section for details).

The prevalent view in the extant literature on bank efficiency is that efficiency estimates obtained by not including off-balance sheet activities (so-called non-traditional activities) as one of the bank outputs may not provide accurate evaluation of a banks' condition (Siems and Clark 1997). It is significant to note here that majority of recent studies on bank efficiency in India have accounted for non-traditional activities by including non-interest income in the output vector as a proxy for these activities (see subsequent section on relevant literature review for details). However, to the best of our knowledge, none of these studies have investigated the impact of inclusion or exclusion of these activities on the efficiency estimates. Thus, a clear void exists in available literature since no study has been conducted to analyse how the entire distribution of efficiency scores differs when these activities are not considered. The present study is an endeavour in this direction and targeted to enrich the extant literature on the efficiency of Indian banks by providing a detailed analysis of this significantly understated and hitherto neglected aspect relating to the efficiency of Indian banks. In particular, we intend to see the differences in efficiency estimates with and without the inclusion of non-interest income as a proxy for non-traditional activities in the output specification. Further, in the literature on efficiency of banks in India, there exists no clear picture about the dominance of a particular ownership group over others (see again subsequent section on relevant literature review for details). In this chapter, we also focus on the issue that to what extent the relative rankings of distinct ownership groups are affected by the omission of this important variable in the output vector.

---

[2] Off-balance sheet activities involve trading financial instruments and generating income from fees and loans sales, activities that affect bank profit but do not appear on the bank balance sheet (Mishkin 2004). Therefore, we have used the terms off-balance sheet activities and non-traditional activities interchangeably in this chapter.

Delineation of this effect can throw new light not only on the effect of non-interest income in relative ownership group rankings but also provide guidance to future work on those factors that need to be concentrated upon to explain any remaining inconsistency in ownership group rankings.

The present study uses a non-parametric frontier efficiency measurement technique which is popularly known as the Data Envelopment Analysis (DEA) to estimate the relative cost, technical and allocative efficiency scores of Indian banks corresponding to two model specifications (one including a proxy for non-traditional activities in the output vector and other which omits this proxy). In recent years, there have been thousands of theoretical contributions and practical applications in various fields using DEA (Klimberg and Ratick 2008). The bibliographies compiled by Tavares (2002) and Emrouznejad et al. (2008) highlight that over the years, DEA has been applied in many diverse areas to analyse efficiency performance differentials. Its first application in banking industry appeared with the work of Sherman and Gold (1985). Since then, DEA has emerged as a very potent technique to measure the relative efficiency of financial institutions, particularly of commercial banks (see survey articles of Berger and Humphrey 1997; Ashton and Hardwick 2000; Fethi and Pasiouras 2010).

The empirical results highlight that the exclusion of non-interest income as a proxy for non-traditional activities in the output specification understates the cost efficiency of Indian banks and its impact seems to be more pronounced on technical efficiency rather than on allocative efficiency. Moreover, the omission of non-traditional activities in the definition of bank output also affects the relative rankings of ownership groups, especially of the foreign banks. Overall, the empirical findings reinforce the prevalent view in the recent literature and support the inclusion of non-traditional activities, as proxied by non-interest income, to analyse the efficiency of Indian banks more accurately.

The rest of the chapter is structured as follows. Section 5.2 provides the detailed account on the trends of non-traditional activities in Indian banking industry. Section 5.3 provides some empirical evidences on the subject matter. Section 5.4 outlines the conceptual framework for measuring the cost, technical and allocative efficiency scores using DEA approach. The sources of data and the specification of input and output variables are reported in Sect. 5.5. Section 5.6 presents the empirical results and discussion. The relevant conclusions and directions for future research are provided in the final section.

5.2 Non-traditional Activities in Indian Banking Industry

As noted above, there has been a significant shift in the sources of income of the Indian commercial banks since 1992. The relative share of income from traditional banking activities like advancing of loans has declined and that of non-traditional non-interest income sources – like guarantees, commitments, foreign exchange and stock index-related transactions, advisory, management and underwriting functions – has increased significantly. The decline in traditional banking activities occurred primarily due to emergence of deregulatory forces, financial innovations, heightened competition and stringent regulatory restrictions.

Tables 5.1 and 5.2 present the scenario in proper focus. We note that non-interest income in Indian commercial banking industry followed an uptrend with impressive growth rate of 16.3 % per annum during the period spanning from 1992–1993 to 2007–2008. Though the growth rates of non-interest income varied considerably across distinct ownership groups, all groups experienced remarkable growth with the rate above 10 %. In terms of the ordering of groups, the private banks (27.7 %) took the lead, followed by the foreign banks (18.2 %) and the public sector banks (13.7 %) (see Table 5.1).

Regarding the share of non-interest income in total income, we note that this share has increased consistently from 10.7 % in 1992–1993 to maximum of 21.62 % in 2003–2004 and then declined gently and reached to the level of 16.37 % in 2007–2008 (see Table 5.2). Overall, these figures reflect an increase in the level of non-traditional activities in Indian banking industry over the past decades. This phenomenon, however, has not necessarily been consistent across all the bank groups. Among bank groups, this share has been significantly higher for the foreign banks than the public and private sector banks, indicating the large size of off-balance sheet exposure of these banks. Further, the share of non-interest income in total income has increased sharply for the foreign banks from 7.71 % in 1992–1993 to 30.3 % in 2007–2008. On the other hand, the share of non-interest income in total income for the public and private sector banks has increased from 11.02 % and 10.76 % in 1992–1993 to 13.34 % and 19.33 % in 2007–2008, respectively. It is evident from these figures that the rise in the share of non-interest income in total income has been moderate for the public sector banks compared to the private banks.

Barring foreign banks, the ratio of non-interest income to total income for the public and private banks groups has undergone different phases during the period under consideration (Reserve Bank of India 2008c). Figure 5.1 clearly points out the trends and variations in the share of non-interest income in total income. In the Phase I (1992–1993 to 1995–1996), non-interest income as a percentage of total income for the public and private banks has increased slightly from 11.02 % and 10.76 % in 1992–1993 to 13.13 % and 14.46 % in 1995–1996, respectively. This was mainly due to buoyant primary capital market as banks were able to earn sizeable income from merchant banking activities. Phase II (1996–1997 to 2000–2001) witnessed that the rise in this ratio got stalled for the public sector banks because of the decline in fee and commission-based income due to the depressed capital market situations. However, the ratio showed wide fluctuations for the private banks. On the other hand, non-interest income to total income ratio for the foreign banks showed relatively less fluctuations.

In the Phase III (2001–2002 to 2003–2004), the ratio of non-interest income to total income rose sharply to 20.42 % and 22.96 % in the terminal year of this phase for the public and private sector banks, respectively. Further, this ratio reached at 30.91 % for the foreign banks in 2003–2004. The main reason for the sharp increase

Table 5.1 Growth of non-interest income in Indian banking industry

	Public sector banks		Private banks		Foreign banks		All banks	
Year	Nominal value (INR in millions)	Annual growth rate	Nominal value (INR in millions)	Annual growth rate	Nominal value (INR in millions)	Annual growth rate	Nominal value (INR in millions)	Annual growth rate
1992–1993	39,781.4	–	2,020.4	–	3,091.9	–	44,893.7	–
1993–1994	47,794.9	20.1	3,048.7	50.9	7,433.3	140.4	58,276.9	29.8
1994–1995	51,135.3	7.0	4,794.6	57.3	9,303.5	25.2	65,233.4	11.9
1995–1996	70,448.5	37.8	7,681.1	60.2	11,174.3	20.1	89,303.9	36.9
1996–1997	73,601.7	4.5	9,828.6	28.0	13,992.2	25.2	97,422.5	9.1
1997–1998	86,307.9	17.3	15,668.6	59.4	19,142.4	36.8	121,118.9	24.3
1998–1999	93,927.4	8.8	14,501.0	−7.5	18,625.7	−2.7	127,054.1	4.9
1999–2000	114,407.3	21.8	22,862.5	57.7	21,521.8	15.5	158,791.6	25.0
2000–2001	125,149.4	9.4	20,991.4	−8.2	25,130.3	16.8	171,271.1	7.9
2001–2002	165,272.0	32.1	42,687.1	103.4	32,602.8	29.7	240,561.9	40.5
2002–2003	212,715.6	28.7	72,322.9	69.4	30,714.1	−5.8	315,752.6	31.3
2003–2004	280,910.2	32.1	76,115.2	5.2	40,217.7	30.9	397,243.1	25.8
2004–2005	241,933.2	−13.9	63,671.7	−16.3	38,656.5	−3.9	344,261.4	−13.3
2005–2006	219,053.2	−9.5	80,912.5	27.1	53,712.3	38.9	353,678.0	2.7
2006–2007	208,715.8	−4.7	111,206.9	37.4	69,371.1	29.2	389,293.8	10.1
2007–2008	327,971.0	57.1	170,063.0	52.9	105,875.6	52.6	603,909.6	55.1
Average annual growth rate		13.7		27.7		18.2		16.3

Source: Statistical Tables Relating to Banks in India (various issues), RBI, Mumbai

Table 5.2 Share of non-interest income to total income (in percentage) in Indian banking industry

Year	Public sector banks	Private banks	Foreign banks	All banks
1992–1993	11.02	10.76	7.71	10.70
1993–1994	12.83	12.88	18.20	13.34
1994–1995	11.90	14.05	19.88	12.78
1995–1996	13.13	14.46	18.35	13.72
1996–1997	12.01	13.32	18.45	12.78
1997–1998	12.75	16.58	22.01	14.11
1998–1999	11.91	12.66	19.16	12.70
1999–2000	12.59	16.15	20.84	13.76
2000–2001	12.09	12.65	20.97	12.97
2001–2002	14.10	20.51	25.16	15.93
2002–2003	16.56	22.88	25.50	18.34
2003–2004	20.42	22.96	30.91	21.62
2004–2005	16.74	19.51	29.65	18.10
2005–2006	13.71	18.68	30.41	16.02
2006–2007	11.04	17.86	27.80	14.09
2007–2008	13.34	19.33	30.30	16.37

Source: Authors' calculations

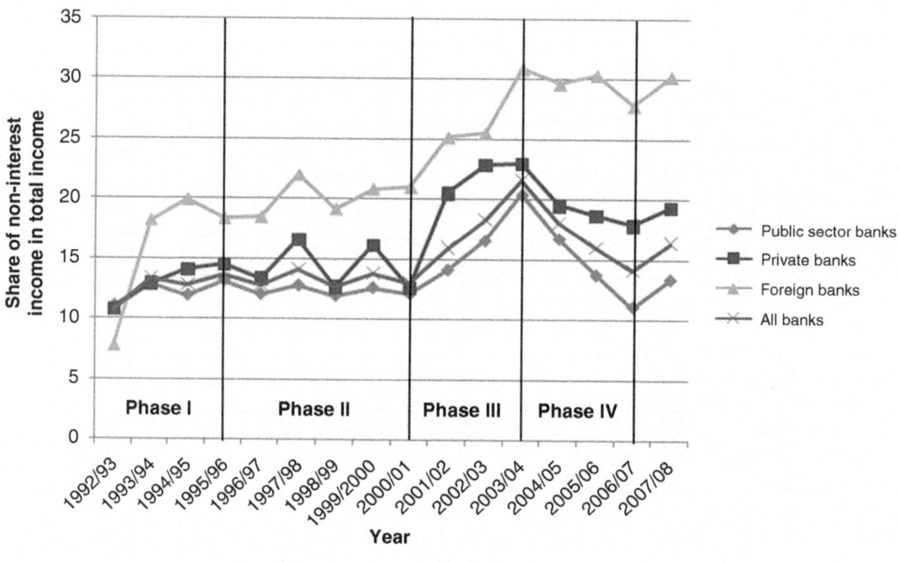

Fig. 5.1 Share of non-interest income in bank's total income (*Source*: Authors' elaboration)

in this ratio is that during this period, banks off-loaded high interest yielding government securities and earned large trading profits which lead to increased share of non-interest income. Phase IV (2004–2005 to 2006–2007) is characterised by a sharp decline in this ratio. At the end year of this phase, the ratio reached to the level of 11.04 % and 17.86 % for the public and private sector banks, respectively. This is due to the fact that banks incurred trading losses on government securities because of hardening of interest rates. In the year 2007–2008, the trend got reversed and the share of non-interest income in total income has gained momentum.

Above discussion illustrates the following important points. First, across-the-board growth of non-interest income of commercial banks suggests that non-traditional activities are becoming an important part of banking business strategies in India. Second, there has been significant increase in share of non-interest income in total income in the Indian banking industry during the period 1992–1993 to 2007–2008. Third, the increase in this share has been found to be more pronounced for the foreign banks, followed by the private and public sector banks. Fourth, there has been a modest rise in this share for the public sector banks relative to their counterparts. This indicates that there occurred no appreciable replacement of intermediation activities by the fee-producing activities in the public sector banks. Fifth, the ratio of non-interest income to total income for the foreign banks showed relatively less fluctuations as compared to the private and public sector banks.

5.3 Non-traditional Activities and Efficiency of Banks: Some Empirical Evidences

It is well established in literature that non-traditional activities captured by off-balance sheet items should be included in the model because these are often an effective substitute for directly issued loans, requiring similar information-gathering costs of origination (Berger and Mester 1997). The studies which examined the impact of non-traditional activities on the efficiency of US banks include Jagtiani et al. (1995), Siems and Clark (1997), Rogers (1998), Stiroh (2000) and Clark and Siems (2002), among others. The non-US studies on the subject matter comprise of Isik and Hassan (2003a) on Turkish banks, Tortosa-Ausina (2003) on Spanish banks, Rime and Stiroh (2003) on Swiss banks, Casu and Girardone (2005) on European banks, Sufian and Ibrahim (2005) on Malaysian banks, Lieu et al. (2005) and Huang and Chen (2006) on Taiwanese banks, Pasiouras (2008) on Greek banks, Sufian (2009b) and Sufian and Habibullah (2009) on Chinese banks, Budd (2009) on UAE banks and Lozano-Vivas and Pasiouras (2010) on banks belonging to 87 different countries (see Table A.2 for empirical findings of these studies).[3] In the aforementioned studies, the researchers have included either off-balance sheet (OBS) items or net non-interest income or any disaggregated component of OBS items as a proxy for non-traditional activities in the different model specifications. Except Jagtiani et al. (1995) and Pasiouras (2008), the overwhelming conclusion of these studies is that the exclusion of a proxy for non-traditional activities items might considerably understate the efficiency measures of

[3] Note that Table A.2 is given in the Appendix.

the banks that actively engaged in these types of activities. In particular, the neglect of non-traditional activities understates the bank efficiency and changes the ranking of individual banks. Thus, the prevalent view in the existing literature is that the failure to incorporate these activities would lead to biased conclusions.

Recognising the growing importance of the non-traditional activities in the recent years, most researchers in India have incorporated the non-interest income as a proxy for these activities in the output vector. The significant studies in this context are Mukherjee et al. (2002), Sathye (2003), Ram Mohan and Ray (2004b), Shanmugam and Das (2004), Chakrabarti and Chawla (2005), Das et al. (2005), Ataullah and Le (2006), Debasish (2006), Das and Ghosh (2009), Ray and Das (2010) and Zhao et al. (2008, 2010) (see Table 5.3 for details). However, to the best of our knowledge, the issue of the effects of inclusion or exclusion of non-traditional items in the output vector on the efficiency of banks is still unexplored for Indian banking sector.

From Table 5.3, we also note that Indian studies on bank efficiency often reach seemingly contradictory findings in terms of relative ranking of the different ownership groups and efficiency scores for individual banks because of the differences in specification of inputs and outputs, methods of estimation (like DEA and SFA), time period, functional forms, behavioural assumptions (production, cost, profit optimisation), etc. Further, the ordering of the bank groups is more or less influenced by the inclusion or exclusion of a proxy for non-traditional activities in the banks' output definition. In sum, there exists no clear picture about the dominance of a particular ownership group over others in Indian banking industry. In this chapter, we focus on the issue of relevance of non-interest income as a proxy for non-traditional activities in the output specification and try to analyse to what extent the relative rankings of individual banks and ownership groups are affected by the inclusion or exclusion of this important output variable.

5.4 Methodological Framework

5.4.1 Cost Efficiency and its Components: Concept and Measurement Approaches

A cost efficiency (CE) measure provides how close a bank's cost is to what a best-practice bank's cost would be for producing the same bundle of outputs (Weill 2004). Measuring cost efficiency requires the specification of an objective function and information on market prices of inputs. If the objective of the production unit is that of cost minimisation, then a measure of cost efficiency is provided by the ratio of minimum cost to observed cost (Lovell 1993). A methodological framework to measure cost efficiency of a firm dates back to the seminal work of Farrell (1957). In Farrell's framework, technical efficiency is just one component of cost

Table 5.3 Efficiency of Indian banks – a survey

Author (year)	Sample period	Inputs	Outputs	Efficiency measure	Ordering of the ownership group on the basis of efficiency
Panel A: Public > Private > Foreign					
Bhattacharyya et al. (1997b)	1986–1991	(i) Interest expense (ii) Operating expense	(i) Deposits (ii) Advances (iii) Investments	TE	Public > private > foreign
Das and Ghosh (2006)	1992–2002	Model 1 (i) Demand deposits (ii) Saving deposits (iii) Fixed deposits (iv) Labour Model 2 (i) Labour (ii) Capital-related operating expenses (iii) Interest expenses Model 3 (i) Labour (ii) Capital-related operating expenses (iii) Interest expenses	Model 1 (i) Advances (ii) Investments Model 2 (i) Advances (ii) Investments (iii) Demand deposits (iv) Fixed deposits (v) Saving deposits Model 3 (i) Interest income (ii) Non-interest income	TE, PTE, SE	Public > private > foreign
Sensarma (2008)	1986–2005	(i) Labour (ii) Physical capital	(i) Value of fixed deposits (ii) Saving deposits (iii) Current deposits (iv) Investments (v) Loans and advances (vi) Number of branches	APE, EFFCH, TECHCH, TFPCH	Public > private > foreign

(continued)

Table 5.3 (continued)

Author (year)	Sample period	Inputs	Outputs	Efficiency measure	Ordering of the ownership group on the basis of efficiency
Das and Ghosh (2009)	2003–2008	(i) Deposits (ii) Labour (iii) Capital (iv) Equity (quasi-fixed)	(i) Loans and advances (ii) Investments (iii) Other income	CE, SPE	Public > private > foreign
Mahesh and Rajeev (2009)	1985–2004	(i) Labour (ii) Capital (iii) Materials	(i) Deposits (ii) Advances (iii) Investments	Deposit (DE), advance (Ad. E), investment (IE) efficiencies	Public > private > foreign
Panel B: Public > Foreign > Private					
Ram Mohan and Ray (2004b)	1992–2000	(i) Labour (ii) Loanable funds	(i) Net-interest margin (ii) Commission, exchange, brokerage, etc.	TE, AE, RE	Public ≡ foreign > private (no significant difference between the efficiency of public and foreign banks)
Shanmugam and Das (2004)	1992–1999	(i) Deposits (ii) Borrowings	(i) Net-interest margin (ii) Non-interest income (iii) Credits (iv) Investments	TE	Public > foreign > private
Ray and Das (2010)	1997–2003	(i) Funds (ii) Labour (iii) Capital (iv) Equity (quasi-fixed)	(i) Investments (ii) Earning advances (iii) Other income	CE, SPE	Public > foreign > private
Panel C: Private > Public > Foreign					
Mukherjee et al. (2002)	1996–1999	(i) Net worth (ii) Borrowings (iii) Operating expenses (iv) Number of employees (v) Number of branches	(i) Deposits (ii) Net profit (iii) Advances (iv) Non-interest income (v) Interest spread	TE	Private > public > foreign

Sensarma (2006)	1986–2000	(i) Labour (ii) Capital	(i) Value of fixed deposits (ii) Saving deposits (iii) Current deposits (iv) Investments (v) Loans and advances (vi) Number of branches	CE, EFFCH, TECHCH, PECH, SECH, TFPCH	Private > public > foreign
Panel D: Private > Foreign > Public					
Zhao et al. (2010)	1992–2004	(i) Loanable funds (ii) Non-interest operating costs	(i) Performing loans (ii) Other earning assets (iii) Fee-based income	CE	Private > foreign > public
Panel E: Foreign > Private > Public					
Reddy (2004)	1996–2002	(i) Fixed assets (ii) Interest expended (iii) Wages	(i) Total income (ii) Liquid assets (iii) Total advances	TE, PTE, SE	Foreign > private > public
Chakrabarti and Chawla (2005)	1990–2002	Models A and B (i) Interest expenses (ii) Operating expense	Model A (i) Advances (ii) Investments (iii) Deposits Model B (i) Interest income (ii) Non-interest income	TE	Foreign > private > public
Das et al. (2005)	1997–2003	(i) Borrowed funds (ii) Number of employees (iii) Fixed assets (iv) Equity (quasi-fixed)	(i) Investments (ii) Performing loan assets (iii) Other non-interest fee-based income	TE, CE, RE, PE	Foreign > private > public
Debasish (2006)	1997–2004	(i) Total deposits received (ii) Total liabilities	(i) Total loans extended (ii) Total investments	TE	Foreign > private > public

(continued)

Table 5.3 (continued)

Author (year)	Sample period	Inputs	Outputs	Efficiency measure	Ordering of the ownership group on the basis of efficiency
		(iii) Labour-related administrative costs	(iii) Net profits		
		(iv) Capital-related administrative cost	(iv) Interest and related revenues		
		(v) Operating expenses	(v) Non-interest income		
		(vi) Fixed assets	(vi) Short-term securities issued by official sectors		
		(vii) Total borrowings	(vii) Net-interest margin		
		(viii) Net worth			
		(ix) Net NPAs			
Panel F: Foreign > Public > Private					
Zhao et al. (2008)	1992–2004	Models 1 and 2 (i) Total operating costs	Model 1 (i) Performing loans (ii) Other earning assets (iii) Fee-based income Model 2 (iv) Total loans (v) Other earning assets (vi) Fee-based income	TE, PTE, SE, EFFCH, TECHCH, PECH, SECH, TFPCH	Foreign > public > private
Panel G: Inconsistent results					
Sathye (2003)	Cross-sectional data for the year 1998	Model A (i) Interest expenses (ii) Non-interest expenses	Model A (i) Net-interest income (ii) Non-interest income	TE	Model A Public > foreign > private

		Model B	Model B	Model B
		(i) Deposits	(i) Net Loans	Foreign > public > private
		(ii) Staff	(ii) Non-interest income	
Ataullah and Le (2006)	1992–1998	Models A and B	Model A (loan-based model)	TE	Model A
		(i) Operating expenses	(i) Loans and advances	Public > foreign > private
		(ii) Interest expenses	(ii) Investments	
			Model B (income-based model)	Model B
			(i) Interest income	Foreign > public > private
			(ii) Non-interest income	

Source: Authors' compilation

Notes: (i) *DEA, SFA, DFA* and *TFA* are the acronyms for data envelopment analysis, stochastic frontier analysis, distribution free approach and thick frontier analysis, respectively; (ii) *TE, CE, RE, PE, APE, SPE, PTE* and *SE* stand for technical, cost, revenue, profit, alternative profit, standard profit, pure technical and scale efficiencies, respectively; (iii) *EFFCH, TECHCH, PECH, SECH* and *TFPCH* stand for efficiency change, technological change, pure technical efficiency change, scale efficiency change and total factor productivity change, respectively

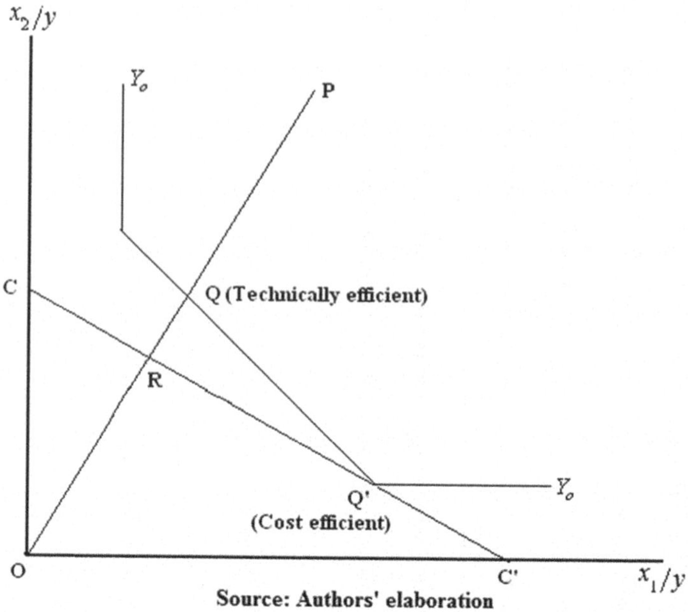

Fig. 5.2 Measurement of cost, technical and allocative efficiencies (*Source*: Authors' elaboration)

efficiency, and in order to be cost efficient, a bank must first be technically efficient. Technical efficiency (TE) refers to the ability of a bank to produce existing level of output with the minimum inputs (input-oriented) or to produce maximal output from a given set of inputs (output-oriented). However, another component of cost efficiency is allocative efficiency (AE), which reflects the ability of the bank to choose the inputs in optimal proportions, given their respective prices. AE describes whether the bank is using the right mix of inputs in light of the relative price of each input. It should be noted that allocative efficiency is interpreted as a residual component of the cost efficiency of the bank and obtained from the ratio of cost and technical efficiency scores. It is significant to note that a measure of cost efficiency corresponds to the behavioural goals[4] of the bank and a measure of technical efficiency ignores such goals.

An illustration of these efficiency measures as well as the way they are computed is given in Fig. 5.2.

In Fig. 5.2, it is assumed that the bank uses two inputs, x_1 and x_2, to produce output y. The bank's production frontier $y = f(x_1, x_2)$ is characterised by constant returns-to-scale, so that $1 = f(x_1/y,\ x_2/y)$, and the frontier is depicted by the efficient unit isoquant Y_oY_o. A bank is said to technically efficient if it is operating on Y_oY_o. However, technical inefficiency relates to an individual bank's failure to produce on

[4] In practice, the researchers identify three behavioural goals to be pursued by the banks, i.e. cost minimisation, revenue maximisation and profit maximisation.

Y_oY_o. Hence, Bank P in the figure is technically inefficient. Thus, for Bank P, the technical inefficiency can be represented by the distance QP. A Farrell's measure of TE is the ratio of the minimum possible inputs of the bank (i.e. inputs usage on the frontier, given its observed output level) to the bank's observed inputs. Accordingly, the level of TE for Bank P is defined by the ratio OQ/OP. It measures the proportion of inputs actually necessary to produce output. Allocative inefficiencies result from choosing the wrong input combinations given input prices. Now suppose that CC′ represents the ratio of input prices so that cost minimisation point is Q′. Since the cost at point R is the same as the cost at Q′, we measure the AE of the bank as OR/OQ, where the distance RQ is the reduction in production costs which could occur if production occurs at Q′. Finally, the cost efficiency of the bank is defined as OR/OP, which can be considered a composite measure efficiency that includes both technical and allocative efficiencies. In fact, the relationship between CE, TE and AE is expressed as

$$\begin{array}{ccccc} \text{CE} & = & \text{TE} & \times & \text{AE} \\ (\text{OR}/\text{OP}) & = & (\text{OQ}/\text{OP}) & \times & (\text{OR}/\text{OQ}). \end{array}$$

Most empirical analyses aiming at measuring the technical and cost-efficiencies of banking industry applied either parametric or non-parametric frontier efficiency measurement techniques. Common frontier efficiency estimation techniques are Data Envelopment Analysis (DEA), Free Disposal Hull (FDH), Stochastic Frontier Analysis (SFA), Thick Frontier Analysis (TFA) and Distribution Free Approach (DFA). The first two of these are non-parametric techniques, and the latter three are parametric methods. A typical frontier technique provides an overall, objectively determined, numerical efficiency value and ranking of firms that is not otherwise available in traditional financial accounting ratio analysis (Berger and Humphrey 1997). The basic tenet of frontier methodology is first to construct the efficiency frontier corresponding to a specific technical or behavioural goal and then to compute the bank-specific efficiency scores by working out the deviations from this frontier as inefficiency. Thus, a typical frontier efficiency measurement technique involves a two-step procedure to compute efficiency scores.

Both parametric and non-parametric approaches have a range of advantages and disadvantages, which may influence the choice of methods in a particular application. The principal advantage of parametric frontier analysis is that it allows the test of hypothesis concerning the goodness of fit of the model. However, the major disadvantage is that it requires specification of a particular frontier function (like Cobb–Douglas or translog), which may be restrictive in most cases. Furthermore, the major advantage of the non-parametric frontier analysis is that it does not require the specification of a particular functional form for the technology. The main disadvantage is that it is not possible to estimate parameters for the model and hence impossible to test hypothesis concerning the performance of the model. However, no consensus has been reached in the literature about the appropriate and preferred estimation methodology (Iqbal and Molyneux 2005; Staikouras et al. 2008).

5.4.2 DEA Models

As mentioned in the introductory section, this study uses Data Envelopment Analysis (DEA) to estimate empirically the cost, technical and allocative efficiency scores for individual banks. Using actual data for the banks under consideration, DEA employs linear programming technique to construct *efficient* or *best practice frontiers*. In fact, a large number of linear programming DEA models have been proposed in the literature to compute efficiency of individual banks corresponding to different technical or behavioural goals (see, e.g. Charnes et al. 1994; Cooper et al. 2007). In the present study, we employed the input-oriented DEA models corresponding to the assumptions of constant returns-to-scale[5] to compute cost, technical and allocative efficiency scores.

Let us suppose that there exist n banks ($j = 1, \ldots, n$) that produce a vector of s outputs $y = (y_1, \ldots, y_s) \in \Re_{s++}$ using a vector of m discretionary inputs $x^D = (x_1^D, \ldots, x_m^D) \in \Re_{m++}$, for which they pay prices $p = (p_1, \ldots, p_m) \in \Re_{m++}$ and l quasi-fixed inputs $x^{QF} = \left(x_1^{QF}, \ldots, x_l^{QF}\right) \in \Re_{l++}$ which do not have any associated input price vector. The technical efficiency for the case of bank 'o' can be calculated by solving the following linear programming problem:

$$\begin{aligned}
& TE_o^{CRS} = \min_{\theta,\lambda} \theta_o \\
& \text{subject to} \\
& \sum_{j=1}^{n} \lambda_j x_{ij}^D \le \theta_o x_{io}^D, && i = 1, \ldots, m \\
& \sum_{j=1}^{n} \lambda_j x_{kj}^{QF} \le x_{ko}^{QF}, && k = 1, \ldots, l \\
& \sum_{j=1}^{n} \lambda_j y_{rj} \ge y_{ro}, && r = 1, \ldots, s \\
& \lambda_j \ge 0, && j = 1, \ldots, n.
\end{aligned} \tag{5.1}$$

[5] Even though the true technology could be different from constant returns-to-scale (CRS), but we adopt the CRS specification of technology on account of the following reasons. First, given the small sample size like ours, one may get a distribution with many observations having efficiency score equal to 1 using variable returns-to-scale (VRS) specification. This implies that one may not get better discrimination of sampled units under VRS specification of technology in case of small sample size. Second, regarding the use of VRS specification of technology, Noulas (1997) stated that the assumption of CRS allows the comparison between small and large banks. In a sample where a few large banks are present, the use of VRS framework raises the possibility that these large banks will appear as being efficient for the simple reason that there are no truly efficient banks. Avkiran (1999) also mentions that under VRS each unit is compared only against other units of similar size, instead of against all units. Pasiouras et al. (2007) point out that the assumption of VRS is more suitable for large samples. The prominent studies that made use of CRS assumptions for measuring cost and technical efficiencies in banking system include Aly et al. (1990), Ariss et al. (2007), Hassan and Sanchez (2007), Pasiouras et al. (2007) and Rezvanian et al. (2008) among others.

The optimal value θ_o^* reflects the TE score of bank '*o*'. This efficiency score is within a range from zero to one, $0 < \theta_o^* \leq 1$, with a high score implying a higher efficiency. If $\theta_o^* = 1$, then the bank '*o*' is *Pareto-efficient*. Note that the model (5.1) measures the efficiency of single bank (i.e. bank '*o*'); it needs to be solved n times to obtain efficiency score of each bank in the sample.

Given the prices of inputs, the cost-minimising input quantities for bank '*o*' can be estimated by solving the following linear programming problem:

$$\begin{aligned} &\min_{\lambda, x^D} \sum_{i=1}^{m} p_i^o x_{io}^D \\ &\text{subject to} \\ &\sum_{j=1}^{n} \lambda_j x_{ij}^D \leq x_{io}^D, \qquad i = 1, \ldots, m \\ &\sum_{j=1}^{n} \lambda_j x_{kj}^{QF} \leq x_{ko}^{QF}, \qquad k = 1, \ldots, l \\ &\sum_{j=1}^{n} \lambda_j y_{rj} \geq y_{ro}, \qquad r = 1, \ldots, s \\ &\lambda_j \geq 0, \qquad j = 1, \ldots, n. \end{aligned} \tag{5.2}$$

From the solution to model (5.2), we get minimum costs as $\sum_{i=1}^{m} p_i^o x_{io}^{D^*}$, and the cost efficiency of bank '*o*' is then calculated as follows:

$$CE_o = \frac{\text{Minimum Cost}}{\text{Actual Cost}} = \frac{\sum_{i=1}^{m} p_i^o x_{io}^{D^*}}{\sum_{i=1}^{m} p_i^o x_i^D}.$$

Thus, the measure of allocative efficiency for bank '*o*' is obtained as

$$AE_o = \frac{CE_o}{TE_o}.$$

The frontier-based measures of cost, technical and allocative efficiencies always range between 0 and 1. Corresponding to these efficiency measures, the measures of inefficiency can be obtained as $(1 - CE_o)$, $(1 - TE_o)$ and $(1 - AE_o)$, respectively.

In the present study, instead of constructing a 'grand or intertemporal frontier'[6] as suggested by Tulkens and van den Eeckaut (1995) and implemented by Bhattacharyya et al. (1997b) for estimating the efficiency scores of individual banks, we followed Isik and Hassan (2002a), Pasiouras et al. (2007) and Kyj

[6] The 'grand frontier' envelops the pooled input–output data of all banks in all years.

and Isik (2008) and estimated separate annual *efficient frontiers* for obtaining year-by-year technical efficiency estimates. Isik and Hassan (2002a) pointed out the following two advantages of this approach. First, it is more flexible and, thus, more appropriate than estimating a single multiyear frontier for the banks in the sample. Second, it alleviates, at least to some extent, the problems related to the lack of random error in DEA by allowing an efficient bank in 1 year to be inefficient in another under the assumption that the errors owing to luck or data problems are not consistent over time.

5.5 Data and Measurement of Input and Output Variables

In computing the efficiency scores, the most challenging task that an analyst always encounters is to select the relevant inputs and outputs for modelling banks' behaviour. It is worth noting here that there is no consensus on what constitute the inputs and outputs of a bank and how to measure them (Casu and Girardone 2002; Sathye 2003). In the literature on banking efficiency, there are mainly two approaches for selecting the inputs and outputs for a bank: (i) the *production approach*, also called the *service provision* or *value-added approach*, and (ii) the *intermediation approach*, also called the *asset approach* (Humphrey 1985; Hjalmarsson et al. 2000). Both these approaches apply the traditional micro-economic theory of the firm to banking and differ only in the specification of banking activities. The production approach as pioneered by Benston (1965) treats banks as the providers of services to customers. The output under this approach represents the services provided to the customers and is best measured by the number and type of transactions, documents processed or specialised services provided over a given time period. However, in case of non-availability of detailed transaction flow data, they are substituted by the data on the number of deposits and loan accounts, as a surrogate for the level of services provided. In this approach, input includes physical variables (like labour, material, space or information systems) or their associated cost. This approach focuses only on operating cost and completely ignores interest expenses.

The intermediation approach as proposed by Sealey and Lindley (1977) treats banks as financial intermediaries channelling funds between depositors and creditors. In this approach, banks produce intermediation services through the collection of deposits and other liabilities and their application in interest-earning assets, such as loans, securities and other investments. This approach is distinguished from production approach by adding deposits to inputs, with consideration of both operating cost and interest cost. Berger and Humphrey (1997) pointed out that neither of these two approaches is perfect because they cannot fully capture the dual role of banks as providers of transactions/document processing services and being financial intermediaries. Nevertheless, they suggested that the intermediation approach is best suited for analysing bank-level efficiency, whereas the production approach is well suited for measuring branch-level efficiency. This is because, at the bank level, management will aim to reduce total costs and not just non-

Table 5.4 Input and output variables used in measurement of technical and cost-efficiencies

Model A	Model B
Inputs	
1. Physical capital	1. Physical capital
2. Labour	2. Labour
3. Loanable funds	3. Loanable funds
4. Equity (quasi-fixed)	4. Equity (quasi-fixed)
Outputs	
1. Advances	1. Advances
2. Investments	2. Investments
3. Non-interest income	

Source: Authors' elaboration

interest expenses, while at the branch level a large number of customer services processing take place, and bank funding and investment decisions are mostly not under the control of branches. Also, in practice, the availability of flow data required by the production approach is usually exceptional rather than in common.

Elyasiani and Mehdian (1990b) gave three distinct advantages of the intermediation approach over other approaches. They argue that (a) it is more inclusive of the total banking cost as it does not exclude interest expense on deposits and other liabilities, (b) it appropriately categorises the deposits as inputs and (c) it has an edge over other definitions for data quality considerations. Therefore, as in majority of the empirical literature, we adopted intermediation approach as opposed to the production approach for selecting input and output variables. In the present study, we establish Models A and B, respectively, with and without the inclusion of non-interest income as a proxy for non-traditional activities and compare the efficiency differences between them. Table 5.4 provides the details on input and output variables included in both the model specifications.

As seen in Table 5.4, Models A and B are based on the intermediation approach, but different inputs–outputs combinations are examined so as to explore the impact of non-traditional activities on bank efficiency. The two outputs of Model B are advances and investments. Hence, this is a standard specification in the intermediation approach which provides efficiency performance of the banks from the perspective of financial intermediation only and ignores the non-traditional activities which turned out to be a significant source of banks' income in the post-reforms period. In Model A, we introduce non-interest income as a proxy for non-traditional activities as an additional output to account for the fact that in recent years banks are heavily involved in fee-generating activities. In Models A and B, we include four variables in the input vector, i.e. (i) *physical capital*, (ii) *labour*, (iii) *loanable funds* and (iv) *equity* (see Table 5.5 for complete description of input and output variables).

It is worth noting here that we have taken the equity as quasi-fixed[7] variable without any associated price to account for both risk-based capital requirements and

[7] Like Ray and Das (2010), we treat equity as quasi-fixed input because compared to other inputs, the level of equity is much more difficult to alter, especially in the short run.

Table 5.5 Description of input and output variables

Variables	Description in the balance sheet	Unit of measurement
Input variables		
1. Physical capital (x_1)	Fixed assets	Lakh
2. Labour (x_2)	Staff (number of employees)	Number
3. Loanable funds (x_3)	Deposits + borrowings	Lakh
Output variables		
1. Advances (y_1)	Advances in India (= term loans + cash credits, overdrafts + bills purchased and discounted, etc.) + advances outside India	Lakh
2. Investments (y_2)	Investments in India (=investment in government securities + other approved securities + shares, debentures and bonds) + investments outside India	Lakh
3. Non-interest income (y_3)	Other income (=commission, exchange, brokerage, etc. + net profit (loss) on sales of investments + net profit (loss) on revaluation of investments + net profit (loss) on sale of land and other assets + net profit (loss) on exchange transactions + miscellaneous receipts)	Lakh
Quasi-fixed input variable		
4. Equity (x_4)	Capital + reserve and surpluses	Lakh
Input prices		
1. Price of physical capital (w_1)	(Rent, taxes and lighting + printing and stationary + depreciation on bank's property + repairs and maintenance + insurance)/physical capital	
2. Price of labour (w_2)	(Payment to and provisions for employees)/labour	
3. Price of loanable funds (w_3)	(Interest paid on deposits + interest paid on borrowings from RBI and other agencies)/loanable funds	

Source: Authors' elaboration
Note: 1 lakh = 100 thousands, and 10 lakh = 1 million

the risk-return trade-off that bank owners face. On commenting the inclusion of equity (so-called financial capital) in the input vector, Berger and Mester (1997) stated: '*A bank's insolvency risk depends on its equity (financial capital) available to absorb portfolio losses, as well as on the portfolio risk themselves. Insolvency risk affects bank costs and profits via risk premium the bank has to pay for uninsured debt, and through the intensity of risk management activities the bank undertakes*'. Maudos et al. (2002), Ram Mohan and Ray (2004b), Das et al. (2005) and Koutsomanoli-Filippaki et al. (2009b) have included the equity variable as one of the inputs while estimating the efficiency performance of banks. The prices of variable inputs are worked out as per unit price of physical capital, per employee wage bill and cost of loanable funds (see Table 5.5).

The required data on different set of input and output variables have been collected out from the various issues of (i) *Statistical Tables Relating to Banks in India*, an annual publication of Reserve Bank of India, (ii) *Performance Highlights of Public Sector Banks*, *Performance Highlights of Private Banks* and *Performance*

Highlights of Foreign Banks, annual publications of Indian Banks' Association. Our study is based on the secondary data spanning from the period 1992–1993 to 2007–2008. Following Barman (2007) and Roland (2008), we bifurcated the entire study period into two distinct subperiods: (i) first subperiod (1992–1993 to 1998–1999) and (ii) second subperiod (1999–2000 to 2007–2008). To compute cost, technical and allocative efficiency scores, the analysis has been carried out with real values of the variables (except labour) which have been obtained by deflating the nominal values by the implicit price deflator of gross domestic product at factor cost (base 1999–2000 = 100). Following Denizer et al. (2007), and Kumar and Gulati (2009b), we normalise all the input and output variables by dividing them by the number of branches of individual banks for the given year. The main purpose of using this normalisation procedure is that it reduces the effects of random noise due to measurement error in the inputs and outputs.

5.6 Empirical Results

This section delineates the impact of inclusion or exclusion of non-traditional activities on the cost efficiency and its distinct components, namely, technical and allocative efficiencies, in Indian banking industry during the period 1992–1993 to 2007–2008. For examining the relevance of including non-interest income emanating from non-traditional activities in the output specification to estimate bank efficiency in India, we followed a two-step approach. The first step examines the differences between the magnitude of efficiency estimates obtained from models with and without non-interest income and tests for differences between mean efficiency estimates when the non-interest income is first included and then excluded from the analysis. In the second step, ranking differences are investigated to identify the impact of the inclusion or exclusion of non-traditional activities on the individual banks and across distinct ownership groups.

5.6.1 Non-traditional Activities and Bank Efficiency

Table 5.6 provides year-wise mean cost, technical and allocative efficiency scores corresponding to Models A and B for Indian commercial banking industry. Recall that Model A includes non-interest income in the output vector as a proxy for non-traditional activities, whereas Model B excludes the same from the output vector. It is significant to note here that if the efficiency scores from Model A turn out to be higher than those have been obtained from Model B, then we can safely infer that the exclusion of non-traditional activities understates true efficiency of the banks. From Table 5.6, we note that mean CE measure corresponding to Model A varies from a minimum of 0.773 in 1995–1996 to a maximum of 0.872 in 1997–1998. Further, in the Model B, the same measure varies in the range between 0.736 in 1994–1995 and 0.842 in 1997–1998. The grand means of CE measure over banks

Table 5.6 Mean efficiency scores for Indian commercial banking industry: 1992–1993 to 2007–2008

Model specifications→		Model A (with non-interest income)			Model B (without non-interest income)		
Year↓	No. of banks	TE	AE	CE	TE	AE	CE
Panel A: Year-wise mean efficiency scores							
1992–1993	73	0.929	0.902	0.841	0.910	0.892	0.817
1993–1994	71	0.906	0.891	0.811	0.886	0.872	0.777
1994–1995	75	0.902	0.872	0.788	0.845	0.864	0.736
1995–1996	90	0.895	0.859	0.773	0.863	0.845	0.737
1996–1997	97	0.915	0.903	0.830	0.901	0.901	0.816
1997–1998	98	0.940	0.927	0.872	0.919	0.913	0.842
1998–1999	101	0.910	0.895	0.817	0.887	0.889	0.793
1999–2000	100	0.900	0.904	0.817	0.865	0.901	0.786
2000–2001	97	0.905	0.896	0.813	0.876	0.869	0.766
2001–2002	92	0.895	0.896	0.805	0.857	0.870	0.751
2002–2003	88	0.928	0.919	0.856	0.881	0.902	0.802
2003–2004	86	0.941	0.905	0.853	0.886	0.877	0.783
2004–2005	84	0.942	0.877	0.828	0.916	0.836	0.768
2005–2006	83	0.909	0.866	0.792	0.867	0.848	0.744
2006–2007	80	0.934	0.885	0.829	0.905	0.871	0.796
2007–2008	77	0.933	0.889	0.833	0.899	0.867	0.787
Panel B: Grand means							
Entire period		0.918	0.893	0.822	0.885	0.876	0.781
First subperiod		0.914	0.893	0.819	0.887	0.882	0.788
Second subperiod		0.921	0.893	0.825	0.884	0.871	0.776

Source: Authors' calculations

and time are 0.822 and 0.781 for Models A and B, respectively. Thus, the cost inefficiency figures corresponding to both the models are 17.8 % and 21.9 %,[8] respectively. These figures of cost inefficiency imply that Indian banks, in general, have not been successful in employing best practice production methods and achieving the maximum outputs from the minimum cost of inputs. Apparently, there exists substantial room for significant cost savings if Indian banks use and allocate their productive inputs more efficiently.

As noted in the Sect. 5.4 on methodological framework, technical and allocative efficiencies are two mutually exclusive components of cost efficiency. As a result, cost inefficiency stems from either technical inefficiency (i.e. wastage of inputs in producing a certain output bundle) and/or allocative inefficiency (i.e. failing to react optimally to relative prices of inputs). Further, technical inefficiency emanates from the inefficient functioning of the management in utilising inputs in the production process, while allocative inefficiency occurs due to stringent regulatory environment inhibiting the correct mix of inputs. Regulation is typically given as a major

[8] Cost inefficiency (%) = (1 − cost efficiency score) × 100.

source of allocative inefficiency, while technical inefficiency is attributed to a lack of strong competitive pressures, which allow bank managers to continue with less than optimal performance. Table 5.6 highlights that for both Models A and B, the grand mean of TE is greater than the grand mean of AE, indicating that cost inefficiency in Indian banking industry originates primarily due to allocative inefficiency rather than technical inefficiency.

For examining the impact of non-traditional activities, we make a comparison of the relative sizes of cost, technical and allocative efficiency levels across Models A and B. From Table 5.6, we further note that in each year, the mean CE, TE and AE scores obtained from Model A are consistently higher than those have been obtained from Model B. For the entire study period, the differences in the grand means of CE, TE and AE measures between the Models A and B have been noted to be 4.1 %, 3.3 % and 1.7 %, respectively. From the analysis for distinct subperiods, we again note the similar differences in the efficiency estimates derived from Models A and B. Thus, we observe that for an average bank, the exclusion of non-interest income as a proxy for non-traditional activities understates cost, technical and allocative efficiency measures. This suggests that the standard specification which omits non-traditional outputs understates efficiency levels of Indian banks. Peeping deep into the results, we also note that the inclusion of non-traditional activities impacts the most on technical efficiency rather than on allocative efficiency. This is because of the fact that any rise in the output given the inputs generally credited to managers' efforts rather than reduction in marginal cost.

From the above, we conclude that the estimated cost efficiency of banks in India would be biased when non-interest income is not included in the chosen model specification. Our results are completely in line with Berger and Mester (1997), Rogers (1998), Clark and Siems (2002), Isik and Hassan (2003a) and Lieu et al. (2005) and Budd (2009). In sum, our results convey that Indian banks enjoy a higher estimated cost efficiency when non-interest income is considered in the output vector, and for that reason, it would be erroneous to exclude the income stemming from non-traditional activities from the set of banks' output.

To test the statistical significance of the above-mentioned differences, we applied a battery of parametric and non-parametric statistical tests. Panel A of Table 5.7 presents the results of a series of paired *t*-test with the null hypothesis that the estimated mean CE, TE and AE are same for both output specifications. The null hypothesis of no difference in mean cost efficiency and its distinct components is rejected in all the instances. This indicates that the mean efficiency of banks is understated significantly when non-interest income is excluded in the output specification. This reinforces the view prevalent in the recent literature that the exclusion of non-traditional activities understates efficiency levels of the banks and may lead to biased conclusions. Panel B and C of the table provide the results of the sign test and Wilcoxon signed-ranks test which also support our inference that when we do not account for non-traditional activities, the cost efficiency of the average bank seem to decrease by 4.1 %.

Table 5.7 Hypothesis testing-efficiency differences across different model specifications in Indian commercial banking industry

Efficiency measure	TE	AE	CE
Panel A: Paired t-test			
H_o: Mean efficiency of Model A = mean efficiency of Model B			
t-statistics	10.263	6.498	10.851
p-value	<0.0001	<0.0001	<0.0001
Inference	Reject H_o	Reject H_o	Reject H_o
Panel B: Sign test			
H_o: Both efficiency samples are not different			
No. of positive differences	16	16	16
p-value	<0.0001	<0.0001	<0.0001
Inference	Reject H_o	Reject H_o	Reject H_o
Panel C: Wilcoxon signed-ranks test			
H_o: Both efficiency samples are not different			
t-statistics	136	136	136
p-value	0.000	0.000	0.000
Inference	Reject H_o	Reject H_o	Reject H_o

Source: Authors' calculations

5.6.2 *Non-traditional Activities and Ranking of Individual Banks*

To consider the impact of omitting non-interest income originating from the non-traditional activities on the ranking of individual banks, we analyse the ranking differences, that is, how much a bank betters (or worsen) its rank position under the two output specifications. For this, the Kendall rank correlation coefficient, commonly referred to as Kendall's tau (τ) coefficient, has been computed for measuring the degree of correspondence between the rankings of individual banks based on Models A and B. Although Spearman's rank correlation coefficient (r_s) is more popular than Kendall's τ statistic, yet we prefer the latter because it is actually a better estimate of the correlation, and we can draw more accurate generalisations from Kendall's statistic than from Spearman's (see Field 2005, for more details). The value of $\tau = 1$ implies that the agreement between two rankings is perfect, while $\tau = -1$ implies that one ranking is the reverse of the other.

Table 5.8 provides the year-wise Kendall's tau correlation coefficients between the efficiency scores of Models A and B. The perusal of table gives that for all efficiency measures, (i) there exists no perfect relationship between rankings of individual banks under Models A and B, and (ii) the probability of concordance between the rankings of banks varies from a moderate to high since the ranges of correlation coefficient have been observed to be 0.601–0.911 for CE, 0.514–0.854 for TE and 0.526–0.869 for AE. On the basis of the magnitude of correlation coefficients, we can safely infer that, in each year, the inclusion of non-traditional activities in the output specification has significantly affected the ranking of individual banks, but the extent differs. This implies that there was some relative

Table 5.8 Kendall's tau correlation coefficients between the efficiency scores of Models A and B (H_0: Efficiency scores of Models A and B are not correlated)

Year	TE	AE	CE
1992–1993	0.762*	0.844*	0.842*
1993–1994	0.793*	0.730*	0.798*
1994–1995	0.495*	0.811*	0.706*
1995–1996	0.796*	0.808*	0.795*
1996–1997	0.854*	0.869*	0.911*
1997–1998	0.780*	0.719*	0.776*
1998–1999	0.822*	0.846*	0.882*
1999–2000	0.762*	0.816*	0.833*
2000–2001	0.780*	0.607*	0.725*
2001–2002	0.730*	0.683*	0.730*
2002–2003	0.646*	0.648*	0.669*
2003–2004	0.514*	0.526*	0.601*
2004–2005	0.698*	0.610*	0.607*
2005–2006	0.733*	0.677*	0.717*
2006–2007	0.750*	0.765*	0.816*
2007–2008	0.710*	0.796*	0.789*

Source: Authors' calculations
Note: '*'indicates the significance at 5 % level

movement with regard to the rankings of banks between Models A and B. This outcome corresponds to Rogers (1998). In sum, the aforementioned analysis reveals that omitting non-traditional activities in the definition of bank output not only understates efficiency levels but also affects the relative ranking of individual banks.

5.6.3 *Non-traditional Activities and Efficiency of Ownership Groups*

In order to test the impact of inclusion or exclusion of non-traditional activities on the efficiency of distinct ownership groups in Indian commercial banking industry, we compare the grand means of efficiency scores obtained from Models A and B. From the Panel A of Table 5.9, we note that for the public sector banks' (PSBs) group, the grand means of CE, TE and AE for the entire study period have been observed to be 0.833, 0.925 and 0.898, respectively, for Model A, and 0.824, 0.920 and 0.892, respectively, for Model B. Thus, for an average bank belonging to this group, an ascent in CE, TE and AE with inclusion of non-interest income as a proxy for non-traditional activities is 0.9 %, 0.5 % and 0.6 %, respectively. These figures indicate that the insertion of non-traditional activities in the output specification does not bring any appreciable difference in the efficiency scores of an average bank belonging to this group. Similar conclusion holds for the analysis of distinct subperiods.

Panel B of Table 5.9 provides mean CE, TE and AE scores for the private banks' (PBs) group in each year of the study period. On comparing the mean efficiency scores between both the model specifications, we note that efficiency measures tend

Table 5.9 Mean efficiency scores across distinct ownership groups

Model specifications→		Model A (with non-interest income)			Model B (without non-interest income)		
Year↓	No. of banks	TE	AE	CE	TE	AE	CE
Panel A: Public sector banks (PSBs)							
1992–1993	27	0.941	0.890	0.838	0.937	0.889	0.834
1993–1994	27	0.894	0.846	0.760	0.882	0.836	0.741
1994–1995	27	0.879	0.838	0.740	0.853	0.842	0.723
1995–1996	27	0.923	0.839	0.778	0.918	0.841	0.776
1996–1997	27	0.944	0.918	0.867	0.943	0.915	0.864
1997–1998	27	0.949	0.904	0.861	0.949	0.902	0.858
1998–1999	27	0.897	0.890	0.799	0.896	0.886	0.794
1999–2000	27	0.905	0.918	0.835	0.905	0.911	0.828
2000–2001	27	0.896	0.874	0.786	0.896	0.861	0.774
2001–2002	27	0.901	0.883	0.798	0.900	0.879	0.793
2002–2003	27	0.941	0.949	0.896	0.939	0.944	0.888
2003–2004	27	0.935	0.936	0.877	0.923	0.909	0.840
2004–2005	27	0.954	0.911	0.870	0.953	0.900	0.859
2005–2006	27	0.928	0.904	0.841	0.927	0.896	0.832
2006–2007	28	0.958	0.926	0.888	0.953	0.926	0.883
2007–2008	28	0.953	0.941	0.897	0.951	0.939	0.895
Entire period	Grand means→	0.925	0.898	0.833	0.920	0.892	0.824
First subperiod		0.918	0.875	0.806	0.911	0.873	0.799
Second subperiod		0.930	0.916	0.854	0.927	0.907	0.844
Panel B: Private banks (PBs)							
1992–1993	23	0.874	0.847	0.742	0.861	0.849	0.734
1993–1994	23	0.865	0.882	0.763	0.847	0.853	0.724
1994–1995	23	0.857	0.900	0.770	0.837	0.905	0.755
1995–1996	33	0.874	0.871	0.763	0.861	0.857	0.739
1996–1997	33	0.905	0.922	0.835	0.902	0.924	0.834
1997–1998	34	0.922	0.947	0.874	0.914	0.931	0.853
1998–1999	33	0.891	0.913	0.814	0.887	0.908	0.807
1999–2000	32	0.898	0.918	0.826	0.889	0.914	0.813
2000–2001	31	0.876	0.908	0.798	0.871	0.897	0.784
2001–2002	30	0.884	0.912	0.809	0.857	0.884	0.760
2002–2003	30	0.915	0.933	0.857	0.887	0.907	0.807
2003–2004	30	0.915	0.892	0.818	0.866	0.885	0.767
2004–2005	29	0.906	0.851	0.773	0.904	0.845	0.766
2005–2006	28	0.893	0.851	0.762	0.890	0.839	0.748
2006–2007	25	0.914	0.880	0.806	0.914	0.879	0.806
2007–2008	23	0.895	0.874	0.783	0.889	0.869	0.772
Entire period	Grand means→	0.893	0.894	0.800	0.880	0.884	0.779
First subperiod		0.884	0.897	0.794	0.873	0.890	0.778
Second subperiod		0.900	0.891	0.804	0.885	0.880	0.780
Panel C: Foreign banks (FBs)							
1992–1993	23	0.970	0.971	0.943	0.928	0.937	0.880
1993–1994	21	0.965	0.959	0.927	0.935	0.940	0.880
1994–1995	25	0.968	0.884	0.855	0.844	0.848	0.732

(continued)

Table 5.9 (continued)

Model specifications→		Model A (with non-interest income)			Model B (without non-interest income)		
Year↓	No. of banks	TE	AE	CE	TE	AE	CE
1995–1996	30	0.891	0.863	0.779	0.816	0.836	0.700
1996–1997	37	0.903	0.876	0.798	0.871	0.870	0.764
1997–1998	37	0.949	0.924	0.878	0.900	0.903	0.821
1998–1999	41	0.933	0.885	0.830	0.881	0.877	0.783
1999–2000	41	0.897	0.885	0.798	0.819	0.884	0.738
2000–2001	39	0.933	0.902	0.845	0.865	0.852	0.746
2001–2002	35	0.899	0.891	0.807	0.824	0.852	0.711
2002–2003	31	0.930	0.879	0.821	0.824	0.861	0.723
2003–2004	29	0.973	0.890	0.868	0.873	0.840	0.748
2004–2005	28	0.967	0.870	0.844	0.891	0.763	0.683
2005–2006	28	0.906	0.846	0.773	0.787	0.812	0.653
2006–2007	27	0.927	0.848	0.790	0.847	0.807	0.697
2007–2008	26	0.947	0.847	0.808	0.853	0.787	0.683
Entire period	Grand means→	0.935	0.889	0.835	0.860	0.854	0.746
First subperiod		0.940	0.909	0.859	0.882	0.887	0.794
Second subperiod		0.931	0.873	0.817	0.843	0.829	0.709

Source: Authors' calculations

to rise when non-interest income is included in the output vector. This is evident from the fact that the grand means of CE, TE and AE in Model A are greater than those obtained from Model B for the entire period and distinct subperiods. In particular, the exclusion of non-traditional activities in the output specification has underestimated CE, TE and AE scores of an average private bank by 2.1 %, 1.3 % and 1.0 %, respectively.

The results for foreign banks (FBs) group are presented in Panel C. Like their domestic counterparts, the foreign banks have also exhibited an increase in mean CE, TE and AE scores when non-traditional activities have been accounted for in the output vector. Further, the differences in the grand means of CE, TE and AE of Models A and B are 8.9 %, 7.5 % and 3.5 %, respectively. Thus, the foreign banks are observed to be more efficient in the Model A.

Figure 5.3 provides a clear picture of the aforesaid results. We have plotted the grand means of CE, TE and AE measures obtained from Model A (with non-interest income) against those estimated from Model B (without non-interest income) for all the ownership groups. It is clear from the figure that Model B understates CE, TE and AE of all the ownership groups albeit with different magnitudes (see numerical value above each bar). Further, the cost efficiency of the FBs group rises to a large extent in comparison of the PBs and PSBs groups when non-interest income is included in the output specification. This indicates that the impact of inclusion or exclusion of a proxy for non-traditional activities is more pronounced in case of the FBs group. The most plausible reason of this finding is that the foreign banks earn a substantial part of their income from non-traditional activities rather than from traditional activities like advancing of loans and investments, and on the other hand,

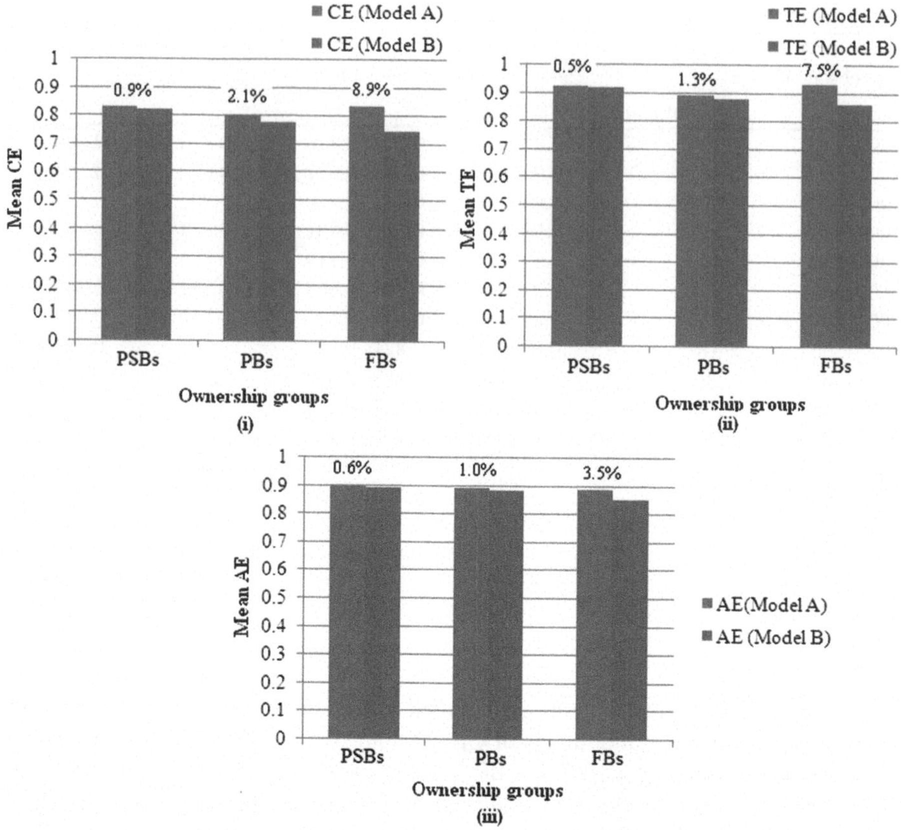

Fig. 5.3 Mean efficiency differences between Models A and B across ownership groups (*Source*: Authors' elaboration)

the public and private sector banks earn a large part of their income from traditional banking activities.

For testing the statistical significance of differences between efficiency scores of Models A and B in distinct ownership groups, we have again applied paired *t*-test, sign test and Wilcoxon signed-ranks test. Table 5.10 provides the results pertaining to these tests. We note that the null hypothesis is rejected in all the instances, indicating that the estimated mean efficiency of banks operating under different ownership patterns is undervalued when a proxy for non-traditional activities is not included in the output vector. In all, the above results highlight that (i) the cost efficiency of the foreign banks rises to a large extent in comparison to the public and private sector banks when non-interest income is included in the output specification and (ii) the exclusion of non-traditional activities impacts most the technical efficiency relative to allocative efficiency in all the ownership groups, and this impact is more pronounce in case of foreign banks group. Overall, the results

Table 5.10 Hypothesis testing-efficiency differences across different model specifications for distinct ownership groups

	Public sector banks (PSBs)			Private banks (PBs)			Foreign banks (FBs)		
Efficiency measure	TE	AE	CE	TE	AE	CE	TE	AE	CE
Panel A: Paired t-test									
(H_o: Mean efficiency of Model A = mean efficiency of Model B)									
t-statistics	2.653	3.097	4.152	4.015	3.638	4.651	10.377	5.378	9.989
p-value	0.018	0.007	0.001	0.001	0.002	0.000	<0.0001	<0.0001	<0.0001
Inference	Reject H_o	Reject H_o	Reject H_o	Reject H_o	Reject H_o	Reject H_o	Reject H_o	Reject H_o	Reject H_o
Panel B: Sign test									
(H_o: Both efficiency samples are not different)									
No. of positive differences	13	13	16	15	13	15	16	16	16
p-value	0.000	0.007	<0.0001	<0.0001	0.021	<0.0001	<0.0001	<0.0001	<0.0001
Inference	Reject H_o	Reject H_o	Reject H_o	Reject H_o	Reject H_o	Reject H_o	Reject H_o	Reject H_o	Reject H_o
Panel C: Wilcoxon signed-ranks test									
(H_o: Both efficiency samples are not different)									
t-statistics	130	123	136	135	125	135	136	136	136
p-value	0.001	0.004	0.000	0.001	0.003	0.000	0.000	0.000	0.000
Inference	Reject H_o	Reject H_o	Reject H_o	Reject H_o	Reject H_o	Reject H_o	Reject H_o	Reject H_o	Reject H_o

Source: Authors' calculations

suggest that the model which omits a proxy for non-traditional activities understates CE, TE and AE measures of distinct ownership groups albeit with different magnitudes.

5.6.4 Non-traditional Activities and Ranking of Ownership Groups

One of the most significant unsettled issues in the literature on the banking efficiency in India is: 'Are foreign banks always more efficient than their public and domestic private counterparts?' To settle this issue to a large extent, an attempt has also been made in this study. For this, we have made a comparison between the rankings of distinct ownership groups on the basis of grand means of CE, TE and AE scores obtained from Models A and B and also studied the changes in ranking in different phases of reforms. Table 5.11 provides the relevant results.

From the table, it has been observed that the exclusion of non-traditional activities in the output specification understates the ranking of FBs group in terms of cost- and technical efficiency measures. This is evident from the fact that FBs group always ranked at a higher place in Model A than where it was placed in Model B. This holds for both distinct subperiods and the entire study period. What is more, in case of the first subperiod, the ranking of foreign banks gets better in terms of AE measure when a proxy for non-traditional activities in the output vector is included. This amply reveals that the omission of non-traditional activities from the output specification understates efficiency of the foreign banks to a large extent and that changes its relative position in the group ranking. The main reason for this change is that the foreign banks earn a substantial part of their income from off-balance sheet activities rather than from the traditional activities like advancing of loans and investments.

Regarding the ranking of PSBs group, we further note that in Model B, the public sector banks emerge as relatively more cost, technical and allocative efficient than their counterparts, and by and large followed by the private and foreign banks. Barring a few exceptions, this holds for both distinct subperiods and the entire study period. Thus, our results highlight that the PSBs group emerges as more efficient than its counterparts if non-interest income is not included in the output vector. This is perhaps due to the fact that public sector banks earn a large part of their income from traditional banking activities. Further, the results clearly indicate that the PBs group generally gets the second place in the group ranking on the basis of Model B and usually attains third rank on the basis of Model A.

The above-mentioned results, thus, try to reconcile the conflicting evidences in the extant literature pertaining to the efficiency of foreign banks relative to domestic counterparts. We believe, on the basis of empirical results of the present study, that it is more likely that in any efficiency analysis of Indian banks covering the post-deregulation period, the foreign banks, on an average, may emerge as more efficient than the public and private banks if a proxy for non-traditional activities is

Table 5.11 Ranking of ownership groups under different model specifications

Period	Cost efficiency (CE)		Technical efficiency (TE)		Allocative efficiency (AE)	
	Model A (with non-interest income)	Model B (without non-interest income)	Model A (with non-interest income)	Model B (without non-interest income)	Model A (with non-interest income)	Model B (without non-interest income)
First subperiod	FBs > PSBs > PBs	PSBs > FBs > PBs	FBs > PSBs > PBs	PSBs > FBs > PBs	FBs > PBs > PSBs	PBs > FBs > PSBs
Second subperiod	PSBs > FBs > PBs	PSBs > PBs > FBs	FBs > PSBs > PBs	PSBs > PBs > FBs	PSBs > PBs > FBs	PSBs > PBs > FBs
Entire period	FBs > PSBs > PBs	PSBs > PBs > FBs	FBs > PSBs > PBs	PSBs > PBs > FBs	PSBs > PBs > FBs	PSBs > PBs > FBs

Source: Authors' calculations

included in the output vector. Nevertheless, the efficiency analysis of most recent years, particularly of late 1990s, gives somewhat different picture and shows the PSBs group as the most efficient group in the Indian banking industry. From Table 5.11, it is evident that though the ranking of bank groups remained unchanged between distinct subperiods in case of TE, they changed dramatically for CE and AE scores. In Model A, we note the ranking of groups in terms of CE measure as PSBs > FBs > PBs in the second subperiod against the ranking as FBs > PSBs > PBs in the first subperiod. Thus, it is clear that in recent years, the public sector banks overscored the foreign banks in terms of cost efficiency, and the foreign banks slipped the efficiency ladder and occupied second place. However, the private banks have consistently been the least cost efficient in both the subperiods.

It is important to note here that the dominance of PSBs group and its emergence as market leader in the recent years may be attributed to both internal and external factors. The most prominent internal factor is that in order to keep themselves intact in competitive environment and to improve their cost efficiency, the public sector banks focused on curtailing operating costs substantially and allocating loanable funds efficiently. In particular, they concentrated on (i) the rationalisation of the labour force and branching[9] and reduction in the cost of financial transactions, (ii) outsourcing of many routine activities, (iii) better recovery of nonperforming loans,[10] (iv) change in the orientation of public sector banks from social objectives towards an ascent on profitability, (v) imposition of capital market discipline and (vi) substantial increase in fee-based income. Thus, it is a highly impressive performance of the public sector banks on the front of reducing intermediation cost[11] that made the PSBs group as the most efficient group of the industry. The most significant external factor is relatively high intermediation cost of their counterparts, especially of the foreign banks in the banking operations. In the late 1990s, the private banks, especially new private banks, have invested large amounts on technology upgradation and expansion of branch network and infrastructure creation with a view to enhance efficiency and productive capacity in the long run. This has led to an increase in the intermediation cost in this segment of the industry.

---

[9] For making optimal use of labour force, these banks evolved policies aimed at 'rightsizing' and 'redeployment' of the surplus staff either by way of retraining them and giving them appropriate alternate employment or by introducing a 'voluntary retirement scheme (VRS)' with appropriate incentives. Consequently, the labour cost per unit of earning assets fell from 2.44 % in 1992–1993 to 0.95 % in 2007–2008.

[10] This is evident from the fact that in PSBs group, the quantum of net NPAs as percentage of net advances declined from 10.7 % in 1994–1995 to 1.0 % in 2007–2008.

[11] The intermediation cost is defined by operating costs as a percentage of total assets. It is believed that larger the cost–asset ratio, the lower is the level of efficiency. The cost–asset ratio for PSBs (PBs) group has declined from 2.64 % (2.71 %) in 1992–1993 to 1.77 % (2.06 %) in 2006–2007. However, the cost–asset ratio of FBs group has remained as high in 2006–2007 as it was in 1992–1993.

Due to this fact, the PBs group has failed to climb the efficiency ladder and ranked as least efficient.

Overall, the results suggest that the omission of non-traditional activities from the output specification understates the efficiency of foreign banks to a large extent and that changes their relative position in the group ranking. Moreover, the public sector banks emerge as more efficient than private and foreign banks if non-interest income is not included in the output vector. The results of present study, thus, try to reconcile the conflicting evidences relating with the efficiency of foreign banks relative to their domestic counterparts.

5.7 Conclusions

Since the advent of banking reforms in 1992, banks' responses to the changing nature of the operating environment have resulted in changes in the structure of their financial accounts and are mainly reflected in the increase of off-balance sheet activities. Using the non-parametric Data Envelopment Analysis (DEA) methodology, this chapter attempts to investigate not only the extent to which the inclusion of a proxy for non-traditional activities in the output definition of banks affects the estimated cost, technical and allocative efficiency scores but also examines how the relative ranking of distinct ownership groups varies in the Indian banking industry. The empirical results enable us to draw the following conclusions.

First, the omission of non-interest income as a proxy for non-traditional activities significantly understates cost, technical and allocative efficiencies of Indian banking industry. Second, the inclusion of non-traditional activities in the output specification has significantly affected the ranking of the individual banks in each year of the study period. Third, the model which omits non-traditional activities understates efficiency of distinct ownership groups albeit with different magnitudes. The efficiency of the foreign banks rises to a large extent in comparison of the public and private sector banks when non-interest income is included in the output specification. Fourth, from the analysis of ranking of ownership groups, we conclude that the public sector banks are more efficient than the private and foreign banks if non-interest income as a proxy for non-traditional activities is not included in the output vector. However, when this proxy is accounted for in the output specification, the foreign banks turn to be more efficient than the public and private sector banks. Thus, the inclusion of non-traditional activities not only improves the efficiency of foreign banks to a large extent but also changes their relative position in the group ranking.

Summing up, we observe that in contrast to the standard specification of intermediation approach, the efficiency of Indian banks rises significantly when non-traditional output is included in the output vector, and there exists a significant relative movement of banks and ownership groups with regard to rankings when non-traditional activities are accounted for. Thus, we can safely infer on the basis of empirical findings that non-traditional activities are totally relevant in an analysis of the efficiency of Indian banks, and these activities should be included as one of the outputs in the studies on banking efficiency, particularly aiming at the comparison of the performance among distinct ownership type institutions. Overall, the results of this study reinforce the prevailing view in the extant literature that the exclusion of non-traditional activities causes misspecification of banks' output and may distort the efficiency estimates.

Chapter 6
Financial Deregulation in the Indian Banking Industry: Has It Improved Cost Efficiency?

6.1 Introduction

Prior to the launching of financial deregulation programme in the year 1992, all the signs of financial repression such as excessively high-reserve requirements, credit controls, interest rate controls, strict entry barriers, operational restrictions and predominance of state-owned banks were present in the Indian banking system. The policy makers introduced an impressive array of reforms in the post-1992 period with the objectives to get rid of the regime of financial repression and to promote a diversified, efficient and competitive banking system. Deregulatory measures like lowering of statutory pre-emption, easing of directed credit rules, interest rates deregulation and lifting of entry barriers for *de novo* private and foreign banks were undertaken to induce efficiency and competition into the banking system. Prudential norms related to capital adequacy, asset classification and income recognition in line with international norms were also brought in place. For infusing sufficient financial strength to public sector banks, the government not only recapitalised these banks but also brought diversification in the ownership of these banks by allowing equity participation by private investors up to a limit of 49 %. Further, to impart a greater operational flexibility, the government backed off to a significant extent from behest lending and lending decisions were largely left to banks.

Given the broad sketch of deregulation programme portrayed above, one may ask whether the efficiency performance of Indian banks since 1992 has improved or not. This chapter explores this issue by providing a thorough investigation of intertemporal behaviour of cost efficiency and its components in Indian banking industry during the post-deregulation period (1992–1993 to 2007–2008). The chapter further investigates whether ownership structure plays an important role in efficiency levels. The understated issue of bank efficiency and bank size has also been addressed in this study. Our research efforts also focus on the hitherto neglected aspect of nature of returns-to-scale in Indian banking industry. As a methodological advance, the cost, technical and pure technical efficiency scores have been computed by DEA models with a quasi-fixed input.

S. Kumar and R. Gulati, *Deregulation and Efficiency of Indian Banks*, India Studies in Business and Economics, DOI 10.1007/978-81-322-1545-5_6, © Springer India 2014

The rest of the study is structured as follows. Section 6.2 provides the relevant literature review. Section 6.3 discusses the concept of cost efficiency and its components and outlines the non-parametric DEA methodology applied in this chapter. Specification of bank inputs and outputs, and data are presented in Sect. 6.4. Section 6.5 discusses the empirical findings of this chapter, and finally, Sect. 6.6 concludes the chapter.

6.2 Deregulation and Cost Efficiency: Relevant Literature Review

There has been a vast empirical literature concerning with the effect of deregulatory measures upon the cost efficiency of the banking industry in developed economies (see Grabowski et al. (1994) and Zaim (1995) for US banks; Sathye (2001) and Neal (2004) for Australian banks; Tortosa-Ausina (2002b), Maudos and Pastor (2003) for Spanish banks; Hasan and Marton (2003) for Hungarian banks; Girardone et al. (2004) for Italian banks; Gjirja (2004) for Swedish banks; Christopoulos and Tsionas (2001) and Chortareas et al. (2009) for Greek banks for a selection of examples). This literature is growing for developing economies, but is still relatively miniscule in volume. Note here that the empirical results are not always affirmative with the theoretical proposition that deregulation boosts competition in the banking industry which in turn improves efficiency.

Table 6.1 summarises the major findings of Indian studies. From the table, we note that the literature pertaining to the effect of deregulatory measures on cost efficiency of Indian banks is relatively scant and offers mixed results. Further, there exist substantial variations in the reported estimates of cost (in)efficiency for Indian banks. In addition, the literature provides no conclusive evidence on the dominant source of cost (in)efficiency in Indian banking industry. For example, Rezvanian et al. (2008) and Kumar (2013) found allocative efficiency as a main driver of cost efficiency in Indian banking industry, while Reserve Bank of India (2008c) found technical efficiency as a main source of cost efficiency. In addition, no consensus appears regarding the ranking of ownership groups.

Our study differs from earlier studies because we have undertaken a comprehensive analysis of intertemporal variations in cost efficiency across different ownership types and size classes using the data for larger time horizon (16 years). Earlier studies used relatively shorter time horizon. This can be confirmed from Table 6.1. In addition, we have incorporated the risk element in the efficiency appraisal of the Indian banks. Following Berger and Mester (1997), this is accomplished by including 'equity' as a quasi-fixed input variable in the input–output specification used for computing cost efficiency and its component measures. Using Fukushige and Miyara's (2005) approach, we thoroughly investigated the nature of returns-to-scale in Indian banking industry.

Table 6.1 Review of literature on cost efficiency of Indian banks

Author (year)	Period of study	No. of banks in the sample	Methodological framework	Effect of deregulation	Dominant source of CE	Cost-inefficiency (%)	Ranking of ownership groups
Kumbhakar and Sarkar (2005)	1986–2000	27 PSBs, 23 PBs	SFA	Negative	n.a.	25–31 %	PBs > PSBs
Das et al. (2005)	1997–2003	71 banks in 1996–1997 and 68 banks in 2002–2003	DEA	Positive	n.a.	2.9–9 %	FBs > PBs > PSBs
Sensarma (2005)	1986–2003	27 PSBs, 26 PBs, 25 FBs, 9 NPBs	SFA	Negative	n.a.	PSBs: 6.3–10.7 % PBs: 6.3–11.6 % FB: 42.8–78.7 % NPBs: 26.2–90.6 %	PSBs > PBs > FBs > NPBs
Rezvanian et al. (2008)	1998–2003	20 PSBs, 19 PBs, 16 FBs	DEA	Positive	AE	43.3–64.3 %	FBs > PBs > PSBs
Reserve Bank of India (2008c)	1992–2007	All banks	DEA	Negative	TE	29–58 %	SBI > NPBs > NBs > FBs > OPBs
Das and Ghosh (2009)	1992–2004	64 banks in 1992 and 71 banks in 2004	DEA	Negative	n.a.	12.6–23 %	PSBs > PBs > FBs

(continued)

Table 6.1 (continued)

Author (year)	Period of study	No. of banks in the sample	Methodological framework	Effect of deregulation	Dominant source of CE	Cost-inefficiency (%)	Ranking of ownership groups
Ray and Das (2010)	1997–2003	71 banks in 1996–1997 and 68 banks in 2002–2003	DEA	Positive	Both AE and TE	6.3–10.2 %	SBI > FBs > NB > PBs
Tabak and Tecles (2010)	2000–2006	67 banks	Bayesian SFA	Positive	n.a.	Model without OBS 12 %; Model with OBS 10 %	PSBs > PBs > FBs
Zhao et al. (2010)	1992–2004	27 PSBs, 20 PBs, 18 FBs	SFA	Positive	n.a.	4.8–16.6 %	PBs > FBs > PSBs
Kumar (2013)	1993–2008	27 PSBs	DEA	Positive	AE	20.4 %	SBI > NB

Source: Authors' elaboration

6.3 Methodological Framework

This study uses input-oriented DEA models to empirically estimate the cost, allocative, technical, pure technical and scale efficiencies for individual banks. The computational procedure used in this study to implement the DEA approach for the measurement of cost efficiency and its components is outlined as follows. Let us suppose that there exist n banks ($j = 1, \ldots, n$) that produce a vector of s outputs $y = (y_1, \ldots, y_s) \in \Re_{s++}$ using a vector of m discretionary inputs $x^D = \left(x_1^D, \ldots, x_m^D\right) \in \Re_{m++}$, for which they pay prices $p = (p_1, \ldots, p_m) \in \Re_{m++}$ and l quasi-fixed inputs $x^{QF} = \left(x_1^{QF}, \ldots, x_l^{QF}\right) \in \Re_{l++}$, which do not have any associated input price vector. The technical efficiency for the case of bank 'o' assuming constant returns-to-scale (CRS) can be calculated by solving the following linear programming problem:

$$
\begin{aligned}
& TE_o^{CRS} = \min_{\theta, \lambda} \theta_o \\
& \text{subject to} \\
& \sum_{j=1}^{n} \lambda_j x_{ij}^D \leq \theta_o x_{io}^D, && i = 1, \ldots, m \\
& \sum_{j=1}^{n} \lambda_j x_{kj}^{QF} \leq x_{ko}^{QF}, && k = 1, \ldots, l \\
& \sum_{j=1}^{n} \lambda_j y_{rj} \geq y_{ro}, && r = 1, \ldots, s \\
& \lambda_j \geq 0, && j = 1, \ldots, n.
\end{aligned}
\tag{6.1}
$$

The optimal value θ_o^* reflects the TE score of bank 'o'. This efficiency score is within a range from zero to one, $0 < \theta_o^* \leq 1$, with a high score implying a higher efficiency. If $\theta_o^* = 1$ then the bank 'o' is *Pareto efficient*. Note that the model (6.1) measures the TE of single bank (i.e. bank 'o'); it needs to be solved n times to obtain efficiency score of each bank in the sample.

The technical efficiency can be decomposed into pure technical efficiency (PTE) and scale efficiency (SE) since TE measures the inefficiencies due to the input-output configuration and as well as the size of operations (Avkiran 2006). The PTE measure for bank 'o' can be calculated by solving the following linear programming problem:

$$
\begin{aligned}
& PTE_o^{VRS} = \min_{\pi, \lambda} \pi_o \\
& \text{subject to} \\
& \sum_{j=1}^{n} \lambda_j x_{ij}^D \leq \pi_o x_{io}^D, && i = 1, \ldots, m \\
& \sum_{j=1}^{n} \lambda_j x_{kj}^{QF} \leq x_{ko}^{QF}, && k = 1, \ldots, l \\
& \sum_{j=1}^{n} \lambda_j y_{rj} \geq y_{ro}, && r = 1, \ldots, s \\
& \sum_{j=1}^{n} \lambda_j = 1, && j = 1, \ldots, n \\
& \lambda_j \geq 0.
\end{aligned}
\tag{6.2}
$$

The optimal value of the π_o (i.e. π_o^*) represents PTE which is a measure of efficiency without scale effects. It is important to note that the model (6.2) allows returns-to-scale to be variable (i.e. constant, increasing or decreasing). The convexity constraint $\sum_{j=1}^{n} \lambda_j = 1$ essentially ensures that an inefficient bank is only 'benchmarked' against banks of a similar size.

An optimal value of SE measure for bank 'o' as denoted by μ_o^* can be obtained as $\mu_o^* = \theta_o^* / \pi_o^*$. Since $\pi_o^* \geq \theta_o^*$ it follows that $\mu_o^* \leq 1$. If $\mu_o^* = 1$, then the bank 'o' is fully scale efficient. If $\mu_o^* < 1$, the bank is scale inefficient. There are two possible reasons for scale inefficiency. The bank could be operating under increasing returns-to-scale (IRS) and, therefore, be of suboptimal scale. Alternatively, the bank could be operating under decreasing returns-to-scale (DRS) and, therefore, be of supra-optimal scale. For ascertaining the nature of returns-to-scale for individual banks and industry as whole, we run two additional linear programming problems with nonincreasing returns-to-scale (NIRS) and nondecreasing returns-to-scale (NDRS) imposed. This is done by altering the model (6.2) and substituting the $\sum_{j=1}^{n} \lambda_j = 1$ restriction with $\sum_{j=1}^{n} \lambda_j \leq 1$ for NIRS and $\sum_{j=1}^{n} \lambda_j \geq 1$ for NDRS. The linear programming problems for estimating the technical efficiency scores under NIRS and NDRS assumptions are given as follows:

$$
\begin{array}{llll}
TE_o^{NIRS} = \min\limits_{\delta, \lambda} \delta_o & & TE_o^{NDRS} = \min\limits_{\omega, \lambda} \omega_o & \\
\text{subject to} & & \text{subject to} & \\
\sum_{j=1}^{n} \lambda_j x_{ij}^{D} \leq \delta_o x_{io}^{D}, & i = 1, \ldots, m & \sum_{j=1}^{n} \lambda_j x_{ij}^{D} \leq \omega_o x_{io}^{D}, & i = 1, \ldots, m \\
\sum_{j=1}^{n} \lambda_j x_{kj}^{QF} \leq x_{ko}^{QF}, & k = 1, \ldots, l & \sum_{j=1}^{n} \lambda_j x_{kj}^{QF} \leq x_{ko}^{QF}, & k = 1, \ldots, l \\
\sum_{j=1}^{n} \lambda_j y_{rj} \geq y_{ro}, & r = 1, \ldots, s & \sum_{j=1}^{n} \lambda_j y_{rj} \geq y_{ro}, & r = 1, \ldots, s \\
\sum_{j=1}^{n} \lambda_j \leq 1, & j = 1, \ldots, n & \sum_{j=1}^{n} \lambda_j \geq 1, & j = 1, \ldots, n \\
\lambda_j \geq 0. & & \lambda_j \geq 0. &
\end{array}
\tag{6.3}
$$

If $\mu_o^* < 1$ and $\theta_o^* = \delta_o^*$, then scale inefficiency is due to IRS and the bank is of suboptimal size. On the other hand, if $\mu_o^* < 1$ and $\theta_o^* < \delta_o^*$, then scale inefficiency is due to DRS and the bank is of supra-optimal size.

To get a concrete picture about the nature of returns-to-scale (RTS) at industry level, we applied hypothesis testing procedure suggested by Fukushige and Miyara (2005) procedure. The null and alternative hypotheses are stated as $H_o : \overline{TE}^{NIRS} = \overline{TE}^{NDRS}$ and $H_1 : \overline{TE}^{NDRS} > \overline{TE}^{NIRS}$ or $\overline{TE}^{NIRS} > \overline{TE}^{NDRS}$. Thus, we can apply either of the following two cases.

Case 1

$$H_o : \overline{TE}^{NIRS} = \overline{TE}^{NDRS} \text{ and } H_1 : \overline{TE}^{NDRS} > \overline{TE}^{NIRS}$$

The test statistic is

$$z = \frac{\Delta_1}{\sqrt{\frac{S^2_{TE^{NIRS}}}{n} + \frac{S^2_{TE^{NDRS}}}{n}}}$$

where $\Delta_1 = \overline{TE}^{NDRS} - \overline{TE}^{NIRS}$. If null hypothesis is rejected, we conclude that there exists increasing returns-to-scale in the banking industry.

Case 2

$$H_o : \overline{TE}^{NIRS} = \overline{TE}^{NDRS} \text{ and } H_1 : \overline{TE}^{NIRS} > \overline{TE}^{NDRS}$$

The test statistics is

$$z = \frac{\Delta_2}{\sqrt{\frac{S^2_{TE^{NIRS}}}{n} + \frac{S^2_{TE^{NDRS}}}{n}}}$$

where $\Delta_2 = \overline{TE}^{NIRS} - \overline{TE}^{NDRS}$. If null hypothesis is rejected, we conclude that there exists decreasing returns-to-scale in the banking industry. However, in both the cases, if null hypothesis is not rejected, we conclude that there exists constant returns-to-scale in the banking industry.

Given the prices of inputs, the cost minimising input quantities for bank 'o' can be estimated by solving the following linear programming problem:

$$\begin{aligned}
&\min_{\lambda,\, x^D} \sum_{i=1}^{m} p_i^o x_{io}^D \\
&\text{subject to} \\
&\sum_{j=1}^{n} \lambda_j x_{ij}^D \le x_{io}^D, && i = 1, \ldots, m \\
&\sum_{j=1}^{n} \lambda_j x_{kj}^{QF} \le x_{ko}^{QF}, && k = 1, \ldots, l \\
&\sum_{j=1}^{n} \lambda_j y_{rj} \ge y_{ro}, && r = 1, \ldots, s \\
&\lambda_j \ge 0, && j = 1, \ldots, n.
\end{aligned} \tag{6.4}$$

From the solution to model (6.4), we get minimum costs as $\sum_{i=1}^{m} p_i^o x_{io}^{D*}$, and the cost efficiency of bank 'o' is then calculated as follows:

$$CE_o = \frac{\text{Minimum Cost}}{\text{Actual Cost}} = \frac{\sum_{i=1}^{m} p_i^o x_{io}^{D*}}{\sum_{i=1}^{m} p_i^o x_i^D}.$$

Thus, the measure of allocative efficiency for bank '*o*' is obtained as

$$AE_o = \frac{CE_o}{TE_o}.$$

The CE, AE, TE, PTE and SE measures always range between 0 and 1. Corresponding to these efficiency measures, the measures of inefficiency can be obtained as $(1 - CE_o)$, $(1 - AE_o)$, $(1 - TE_o)$, $(1 - PTE_o)$ and $(1 - SE_o)$, respectively.

6.4 Data and Measurement of Input and Output Variables

Consistent with most of the recent literature on bank efficiency, this study uses a modified version of intermediation approach for selecting input and output variables. The input variables used for computing efficiency measures are (i) physical capital, (ii) labour, (iii) loanable funds and (iv) equity (as a quasi-fixed input), which are proxied by fixed assets, number of employees, deposits plus borrowings and capital plus reserves and surpluses, respectively. Correspondingly, the prices of these inputs are worked out as per unit price of physical capital, per employee wage bill and cost of loanable funds. It is worth mentioning here that we have considered the input variable 'equity' as a quasi-fixed variable without any associated price to account for both risk-based capital requirements and the risk-return trade-off that bank owners face. This adds a new dimension to the specification of input variables used for measuring the efficiency of Indian banks. The output vector contains three output variables: (i) advances, (ii) investments and (iii) non-interest income. The output variable 'non-interest income' accounts for income from fee-generating off-balance sheet items such as commission, exchange and brokerage. The inclusion of 'non-interest income' enables us to capture the recent changes in the production of services as Indian banks are increasingly engaging in non-traditional banking activities. As pointed out in the previous chapter, the failure to incorporate these types of activities may seriously understate bank's output, and thus, it is likely to have statistical and economic effects on estimated efficiency.

The present study is based on unbalanced data covering a 16-year period spanning from the financial year 1992–1993 to 2007–2008. The input and output data were collected from the various issues of (i) *Statistical Tables Relating to Banks in India*, an annual publication of Reserve Bank of India, and (ii) *Performance Highlights of Public Sector Banks*, *Performance Highlights of Private Banks* and *Performance Highlights of Foreign Banks*, annual publications of Indian Banks' Association. All data (except labour) were deflated using the GDP deflator using 1999–2000 as base year. Only banks with minimum of two branches were included in the sample. To reduce the effects of random noise due to measurement error in the inputs and outputs, we followed Denizer et al. (2007) and Kumar and Gulati (2009b) and normalised all the input and output variables by number of branches.

6.5 Empirical Results

6.5.1 Estimation Strategy

Having an access to panel data, two distinct approaches can, in principle, be adopted to estimate efficiency scores for individual banks. The first approach as suggested by Tulkens and van den Eeckaut (1995) aims to construct a 'grand or intertemporal frontier', which envelops the pooled input–output data of all banks in all years, for obtaining the efficiency scores of individual banks. The second approach is to estimate annual efficiency frontiers separately for obtaining year-by-year efficiency estimates. Isik and Hassan (2002a) pointed out the following two advantages of latter approach. First, it is more flexible and, thus, more appropriate than estimating a single multiyear frontier for the banks in the sample. Second, it alleviates, at least to some extent, the problems related to the lack of random error in DEA by allowing an efficient bank in 1 year to be inefficient in another under the assumption that the errors owing to luck or data problems are not consistent over time. In the present study, we went after Isik and Hassan (2002a), Pasiouras et al. (2007), Kyj and Isik (2008), Kumar and Gulati (2009b) and Burki and Niazi (2010), and adopted the latter approach to obtain the efficiency scores.

6.5.2 Trends in Cost (In)Efficiency at Industry Level

We begin by examining the trends in cost efficiency and its components in Indian banking industry during the post-reforms years. Table 6.2 provides the relevant results. We note that the mean CE scores ranged from a minimum of 0.773 in 1995–1996 to a maximum of 0.872 in 1997–1998, with the grand mean of 0.822. Accordingly, the Indian banking system exhibited significant cost inefficiency ranging between a minimum of 12.8 % and a maximum of 22.7 % during the 16-year period of evaluation. We further note from the figure of grand mean of CE scores that the average level of cost efficiency (inefficiency) in Indian banking industry was 82.2 % (17.8 %). This figure of cost efficiency implies that the typical bank in the sample could have produced the same level of outputs using only 82.2 % of the cost actually incurred, if it was producing on the cost frontier rather than at its current location. On the other hand, the figure of cost inefficiency implies that in each year of the study period, the typical bank needed 17.8 % more resources and, thus, incurred more cost to produce the same output relative to the best practice bank. This divulges that Indian banks, in general, have not been successful in employing best practice production methods and achieving the maximum outputs from the minimum cost of inputs. The apparent policy implication that can be derived from aforementioned analysis is that there is substantial room for significant cost savings if Indian banks use and allocate their productive inputs more efficiently. Interestingly, our estimates of average cost inefficiency in Indian banking are relatively low when compared to the inefficiencies in the banking systems of developing and emerging economies. For instance, the

Table 6.2 Mean cost, allocative, technical, pure technical and scale efficiency scores for Indian banking industry

Year↓	CE	AE	TE	PTE	SE
Panel A: Year-wise mean efficiency measures					
1992–1993	0.841	0.902	0.929	0.957	0.970
1993–1994	0.811	0.891	0.906	0.939	0.965
1994–1995	0.788	0.872	0.902	0.946	0.954
1995–1996	0.773	0.859	0.895	0.931	0.961
1996–1997	0.830	0.903	0.915	0.939	0.975
1997–1998	0.872	0.927	0.940	0.956	0.983
1998–1999	0.817	0.895	0.910	0.947	0.960
1999–2000	0.817	0.904	0.900	0.940	0.957
2000–2001	0.813	0.896	0.905	0.938	0.965
2001–2002	0.805	0.896	0.895	0.932	0.961
2002–2003	0.856	0.919	0.928	0.954	0.973
2003–2004	0.853	0.905	0.941	0.964	0.976
2004–2005	0.828	0.877	0.942	0.969	0.973
2005–2006	0.792	0.866	0.909	0.950	0.957
2006–2007	0.829	0.885	0.934	0.970	0.963
2007–2008	0.833	0.889	0.933	0.966	0.966
Panel B: Grand mean of efficiency measures					
Entire period	0.822	0.893	0.918	0.950	0.966
First subperiod	0.819	0.893	0.914	0.945	0.967
Second subperiod	0.825	0.893	0.921	0.954	0.966
Panel C: Average annual growth rates (%)					
Entire period	0.127	−0.034	0.161	0.161	0.004
First subperiod	0.259	0.391	−0.115	−0.136	0.021
Second subperiod	0.037	−0.325	0.350	0.364	−0.008
Acceleration (+)/Deceleration (−)	(−)	(−)	(+)	(+)	(−)

Source: Authors' calculations

estimated inefficiencies are 28 % for the Turkish banks (Isik and Hassan 2002a), 25.5 % for the Pakistani banks (Burki and Niazi 2010), 32.8 % for the Taiwanese banks (Chen 2004), 48 % for Kuwaiti banks (Darrat et al. 2002) and 48–59 % for Chinese banks (Fu and Heffernan 2007). Further, our estimate of cost inefficiency is lower than the world mean inefficiency of 27 % (Berger and Humphrey 1997) and mean inefficiency of 35 % for developing economies (Fu 2004).

Table 6.2 also provides the mean AE, TE, PTE and SE scores for Indian banks. It has been observed that, except 1998–1999 and 1999–2000, mean TE scores were consistently higher than mean AE scores, suggesting that allocative inefficiency (i.e. choosing the incorrect input combination given input prices) had greater significance than technical inefficiency (i.e. underutilisation or wasting of inputs) as a source of cost inefficiency within all inefficient banks. This is also evident from the fact that of 17.8 % of average cost inefficiency, 10.7 % was caused by inappropriate selection of the optimal combinations of inputs given their prices and technology, and the remaining was due to wastage of inputs in the production process. In sum, the observed cost inefficiency in Indian banking industry originated primarily due to regulatory environment in which banks were operating rather than managerial problems in using the resources. This finding suggests that the managers of Indian banks on average were doing better job in utilising all factor inputs rather than choosing the proper input mix given the prices.

Furthermore, except 2 years 2006–2007 and 2007–2008, the mean SE scores for Indian banks for the remaining years under evaluation were found to be persistently higher than that of PTE scores over the period. In addition, the figures of grand mean for PTE and SE scores provide that the average level of pure technical inefficiency was about 5 %, while scale inefficiency was about 3.4 %. Thus, the major source of the overall technical inefficiency for Indian banks is pure technical inefficiency (input related) and not scale inefficiency (output related). This finding implies that technical inefficiency emanates primarily due to managerial underperformance in controlling the waste of inputs in production process rather than failure to operate at optimum scale size. In all, the results suggest that there is more opportunity for TE gains from better utilisation of existing resources by the management than from taking advantage of scale economies.

To assess whether the efficiency of Indian banking industry improved with the augmentation of intensity of reforms since 1997–1998, we carried out a comparative analysis of the mean efficiency scores between the subperiods, and the relevant results are reported in Panel B of Table 6.2. We note that the average CE of Indian banks improved by a meagre amount of less than 1 % between the distinct subperiods. This implies that the cost inefficiency declined paltry during the second subperiod relative to the first one (18.1 % vs. 17.5 %). A similar behaviour has been observed for TE levels. In particular, the technical inefficiency declined by about 0.7 % in the second subperiod from the level that has been observed in the first subperiod. Regarding AE, we note that an ascent in the intensity of reforms did not bring any significant change in its level. Thus, the observed ascent in CE between the subperiods was contributed solely by increase in TE. In addition, the comparative analysis of mean PTE and SE between subperiods offers that (i) PTE improved by 0.9 % in the second phase relative to first phase (0.954 vs. 0.945) and (ii) SE remained almost unaltered.

To ascertain a more concrete picture, we estimated average annual growth rates of efficiency estimates for the entire study period and distinct subperiods (see Panel C of Table 6.2).[1] We note that CE of Indian banking industry grew at a diminutive rate of

[1] For computing the average annual growth rate of efficiency scores for the entire study period, we estimated a log-linear trend equation: $\ln E_t = \alpha + \beta t + \varepsilon_t$, where E_t is mean efficiency score in the year t ($t = 1,2,\ldots,T$) and ε_t denotes stochastic error term. Following Boyce (1986), a kinked exponential model has been used for estimating the growth rates for the subperiods. The regression equation in kinked exponential model takes the form $\ln E_t = \alpha + \beta_1(Dt + (1 - D)k) + \beta_2(1 - D)(t - k) + \varepsilon_t$, where D is a dummy variable ($D = 1$ for first subperiod and 0 for second subperiod) and k is the midpoint of the two discontinuous series ($k = 7.5$ in the present study). The OLS estimates of β_1 and β_2 (i.e. $\hat{\beta}_1$ and $\hat{\beta}_2$) give the growth rates for the first and second subperiods, respectively. Further, a temporal pattern of growth may have a tendency to either accelerate or decelerate. To explore such possibilities, we estimated the log quadratic equation: $\ln E_t = a + bt + ct^2 + u_t$. A significantly positive value of c indicates acceleration in the growth rate of efficiency; a significantly negative value indicates a deceleration. It is worth mentioning here that the inclusion of time squares on the right-hand side of the aforementioned equation introduces a multicollinearity problem. This is solved by normalising time in mean deviation form. That is, it is set to zero on the midpoint of the time series. For more detailed discussion, interested parties can refer to Majumdar (1998).

0.127 % per annum over the entire study period. Further, it exhibited a positive trend in both the subperiods albeit the growth rates were marginal. Overall, CE of Indian banks propagated at a very modest rate during the post-deregulation years. The growth rates' analysis of the sources of CE reveals that TE of Indian banking industry followed an uptrend, while AE followed a path of deceleration. We further note that (i) the AE experienced an inverted U-shaped behaviour, with a negative trend during the second subperiod relative to a positive trend during the first subperiod; (ii) a significant improvement has taken in the growth of TE during the second subperiod relative to first one; and (iii) the sources of CE moved in opposite directions, and they were counterbalancing in nature. The analysis of the growth rates for PTE and SE scores of Indian banks reveals that both the measures had shown only a marginal growth. Further, we observed a U-turn and an inverted U-turn in the temporal behaviour of PTE and SE, respectively during the most recent years of the sampled period. It is interesting to note that CE, AE and SE measures had a tendency to decelerate, while TE and PTE measures had a tendency to accelerate over time.

From the aforementioned results, it seems that deregulation process did have a positive impact in improving the cost efficiency levels on average for the overall Indian banking sector. However, the observed declining trend in AE is a serious concern. One of the most plausible reasons for increasing allocative inefficiency might be high fluctuations and instability in factor prices due to chronic inflation in the country in the recent years. If bank managers are uncertain about prices, they are likely to make inefficient decisions (Isik and Hassan 2002a). Another plausible reason could be the idle capacity and staff redundancies of some state-owned banks. Even when the management recognises the need to choose a different mix of inputs in light of given prices, it might feel constrained from doing so due to, for example, political and social resistance to lay off staff (Havrylchyk 2006). Deterioration in allocative efficiency during the study period may also be occurred due to an introduction of stringent regulatory restrictions primarily in the area of maintaining capital adequacy ratio as per Basel norms during the post-reforms years. From no norm of capital adequacy in the pre-reforms period, Indian banking system is implementing Basel I and II norms in a phased manner during the post-reforms years. Further, in more recent years, domestic banks have increasingly used equity market to raise funds. This exposed banks to the consequences of the imperfections inherent in this market. This may have led to distortions in the process of allocating resources in Indian banks. Overall, the analysis manifests that the declining trend in the allocative efficiency offsetted the uptrend in the technical efficiency and, thus, found to be responsible for the modest growth of cost efficiency in Indian banking industry.

6.5.3 Comparison of Efficiency Across Distinct Ownership Groups

Any analysis of bank efficiency seems incomplete if no attempt is made to examine the performance differential across the entire spectrum of ownership groups in the banking system. This subsection tries to study the differences in efficiency measures across public, private and foreign bank groups operating in India. Although these groups of banks operate in the same market, each group faces a different set of regulations and have different business strategies. In the light of this, we expect to find variations in the performance, both across ownership groups and over time. Here, we try to quantify and explain the anticipated variations in their performance. This task would also enable us to verify the issue of economic linkage of ownership vis-à-vis efficiency performance in the light of *property right hypothesis, principal agent framework* (Alchian 1965; De Alessi 1980) and *public choice theory* (Niskanen 1975; Levy 1987). As per property right hypothesis, private banks should perform more efficiently than public counterparts, because of strong linkage between markets for corporate control and efficiency of private banks.

The relevant results are reported in Table 6.3. We note that (i) on average, there appeared CE differences across ownership groups, but these differences were not fairly large; (ii) private banks were underperformer relative to public and foreign banks; and (iii) on year-to-year basis, foreign banks outperformed the peers by a good margin. Our results suggest that public sector banks performed better than private banks, but not strikingly different from foreign banks. Thus, the ranking of ownership groups in Indian banking industry seems to be PSBs = FBs > PBs. The similar ordering of the banks' groups also holds broadly for the components of CE. Our finding pertaining to the ordering of ownership groups seems completely in consonance with Ram Mohan and Ray (2004b) and in line with Tabak and Tecles (2010) who reported the better performance of PSBs relative to their counterparts in terms of CE. It has been argued by Tabak and Tecles (2010) that PSBs benefited from the increased competition in the country enhancing their cost efficiency, while private and foreign banks were concerned in service quality improvements which involve huge costs. This is evident from the fact that, in 2006–2007, the estimated ratio of operating cost to total assets is lower for PSBs (1.77) relative to private (2.06) and foreign (2.78) banks (Reserve Bank of India 2008c). In fact, PSBs had managed their operating expenses in more aggressive manner than their counterparts during the last couple of years and, thus, experienced substantial cost efficiency gains.

The aforementioned empirical evidence vividly indicates that contrary to general belief, PSBs outperformed relative to their counterparts during the post-reforms years. We feel that some discussion on what derived the better efficiency performance of these banks is warranted here. In this context, the most significant factor is the heightened competition in the Indian banking sector during the post-reforms period due to relaxed entry norms for *de novo* private domestic and foreign banks. To keep their survival intact in the highly competitive environment, the PSBs, especially the weak ones, started allocating resources efficiently, and changed their behavioural attitude and business strategies. Further, in their drive to achieve higher levels of operating efficiency, Indian PSBs during the post-reforms years primarily concentrated on the rationalisation of the labour force and branching, and reduction in the cost of financial transactions. For making optimal use of labour force, these banks evolved policies aimed at 'rightsizing' and 'redeployment' of the surplus staff either

Table 6.3 Mean cost, allocative, technical, pure technical and scale efficiency scores of banks across ownership groups

Bank group	Public sector banks					Private banks					Foreign banks				
Year↓	CE	AE	TE	PTE	SE	CE	AE	TE	PTE	SE	CE	AE	TE	PTE	SE
Panel A: Year-wise mean efficiency scores															
1992–1993	0.838	0.890	0.941	0.962	0.979	0.742	0.847	0.874	0.936	0.933	0.943	0.971	0.970	0.972	0.997
1993–1994	0.760	0.846	0.894	0.926	0.966	0.763	0.882	0.865	0.929	0.932	0.927	0.959	0.965	0.965	1.000
1994–1995	0.740	0.838	0.879	0.913	0.963	0.770	0.900	0.857	0.942	0.911	0.855	0.884	0.968	0.986	0.982
1995–1996	0.778	0.839	0.923	0.937	0.985	0.763	0.871	0.874	0.925	0.945	0.779	0.863	0.891	0.933	0.956
1996–1997	0.867	0.918	0.944	0.951	0.992	0.835	0.922	0.905	0.943	0.961	0.798	0.876	0.903	0.927	0.974
1997–1998	0.861	0.904	0.949	0.955	0.994	0.874	0.947	0.922	0.955	0.965	0.878	0.924	0.949	0.958	0.991
1998–1999	0.799	0.890	0.897	0.926	0.969	0.814	0.913	0.891	0.948	0.941	0.830	0.885	0.933	0.961	0.969
1999–2000	0.835	0.918	0.905	0.936	0.966	0.826	0.918	0.898	0.950	0.946	0.798	0.885	0.897	0.935	0.959
2000–2001	0.786	0.874	0.896	0.931	0.963	0.798	0.908	0.876	0.936	0.938	0.845	0.902	0.933	0.945	0.987
2001–2002	0.798	0.883	0.901	0.939	0.959	0.809	0.912	0.884	0.936	0.947	0.807	0.891	0.899	0.922	0.974
2002–2003	0.896	0.949	0.941	0.965	0.976	0.857	0.933	0.915	0.947	0.967	0.821	0.879	0.930	0.950	0.977
2003–2004	0.877	0.936	0.935	0.959	0.975	0.818	0.892	0.915	0.955	0.960	0.868	0.890	0.973	0.979	0.994
2004–2005	0.870	0.911	0.954	0.964	0.993	0.773	0.851	0.906	0.962	0.942	0.844	0.870	0.967	0.980	0.985
2005–2006	0.841	0.904	0.928	0.963	0.964	0.762	0.851	0.893	0.964	0.927	0.773	0.846	0.906	0.923	0.980
2006–2007	0.888	0.926	0.958	0.979	0.979	0.806	0.880	0.914	0.971	0.943	0.790	0.848	0.927	0.959	0.964
2007–2008	0.897	0.941	0.953	0.974	0.978	0.783	0.874	0.895	0.955	0.939	0.808	0.847	0.947	0.967	0.978
Panel B: Grand mean of efficiency scores															
Entire period	0.833	0.898	0.925	0.949	0.975	0.800	0.894	0.893	0.947	0.944	0.835	0.889	0.935	0.954	0.979
First subperiod	0.806	0.875	0.918	0.939	0.978	0.794	0.897	0.884	0.940	0.941	0.859	0.909	0.940	0.957	0.981
Second subperiod	0.854	0.916	0.930	0.957	0.973	0.804	0.891	0.900	0.953	0.945	0.817	0.873	0.931	0.951	0.978

Panel C: Average annual growth rates (%)															
Entire period	0.833	0.572	0.276	0.279	−0.001	0.228	−0.007	0.270	0.217	0.063	−0.765	−0.613	−0.168	−0.123	−0.060
First subperiod	0.589	0.762	−0.182	−0.120	−0.071	1.815	1.189	0.593	0.175	0.437	−1.453	−0.790	−0.714	−0.429	−0.290
Second subperiod	1.001	0.442	0.590	0.553	0.048	−0.940	−0.990	0.049	0.246	−0.194	−0.294	−0.492	0.206	0.086	0.098
Acceleration (+)/ Deceleration (−)	(+)	(−)	(+)	(+)	(+)	(−)	(−)	(−)	(+)	(−)	(+)	(+)	(+)	(+)	(+)

Panel D: Hypothesis testing – differences in annual mean efficiency across pairwise ownership groups

Ownership categories	Public versus private					Private versus foreign					Public versus foreign				
ANOVA test	4.619*	0.127	15.755**	0.078	45.596**	5.284*	0.814	23.112**	1.196	52.549**	0.014	0.532	1.061	0.515	0.901
	(0.040)	(0.724)	(0.000)	(0.782)	(<0.0001)	(0.029)	(0.671)	(<0.0001)	(0.283)	(<0.0001)	(0.908)	(0.472)	(0.311)	(0.479)	(0.350)
Mann–Whitney test	1.960*	0.396	3.148**	0.491	4.373**	−2.017*	0.773	−3.582**	−1.000	−4.448**	0.113	0.999	−1.018	−0.622	−0.943
	(0.050)	(0.692)	(0.002)	(0.623)	(<0.0001)	(0.044)	(0.440)	(0.000)	(0.318)	(<0.0001)	(0.910)	(0.318)	(0.309)	(0.534)	(0.346)
Kruskal–Wallis test	3.843*	0.157	9.911**	0.241	19.124**	4.070*	0.597	12.831**	0.999	19.782**	0.013	0.999	1.036	0.387	0.889
	(0.050)	(0.692)	(0.002)	(0.623)	(<0.0001)	(0.044)	(0.440)	(0.000)	(0.318)	(<0.0001)	(0.910)	(0.318)	(0.309)	(0.534)	(0.346)
Kolmogorov–Smirnov test	0.438***	0.188	0.625**	0.250	0.813**	0.313	0.313	0.688**	0.375	0.813**	0.188	0.375	0.313	0.188	0.250
	(0.065)	(0.912)	(0.002)	(0.631)	(<0.0001)	(0.347)	(0.347)	(0.000)	(0.162)	(<0.0001)	(0.912)	(0.347)	(0.347)	(0.912)	(0.631)

Source: Authors' calculations

Notes: (i) The figures in parentheses are the *p*-values, and (ii) '***', '**', and '*' indicates statistical significance at 1 %, 5 %, and 10 % level of significance, respectively

by way of retraining them and giving them appropriate alternate employment or by introducing a 'voluntary retirement scheme (VRS)' with appropriate incentives. Consequently, the labour cost per unit of earning assets fell from 2.44 % in 1992–1993 to 0.95 % in 2007–2008. With the objectives of cutting the cost of day-to-day banking operations in the long run, and retaining their existing customers and attracting new ones by providing new technology-based delivery channels (like internet banking, mobile banking and card-based funds transactions), PSBs made a heavy investment in information technology during the post-reforms years. Between September 1999 and March 2008, PSBs incurred an expenditure of INR 150 billion on computerisation and development of communication networks (Reserve Bank of India 2006b). The computerisation of branches and installation of ATMs are two major areas in which the use of technology is clearly visible. By end-March 2008, about 93.7 % branches of PSBs were fully computerised, of which 67.7 % branches of nationalised banks and 95 % of SBI and its associates were under core banking solutions. The number of both on-site and off-site ATMs by PSBs increased from 3,473 at the end of March 2003 to 34,789 at the end of March 2008. On the whole, the post-reforms period witnessed an enhanced level of IT usage by PSBs which might have contributed to efficiency improvement.

Another major influential factor that contributed to high levels of cost efficiency is that due to profound changes in the regulatory and legal frameworks, there has been a better recovery of nonperforming loans which led to an improvement in the assets quality of the PSBs. This is evident from the fact that in public sector banking segment, the quantum of net NPAs as a percentage of net advances declined from 10.7 % in 1994–1995 to 0.99 % in 2005–2006. Among the various channels of recovery available to banks for dealing with bad loans, SARFAESI Act[2] and the Debt Recovery Tribunals (DRTs) have been the most effective in terms of the amount recovered (Reserve Bank of India 2008c). Due to better recovery of NPAs, the share of net-interest income in total income of PSBs has increased significantly. Further, in the Indian banking industry, the off-balance sheet activities business has soared during the post-reforms years. This has led to increase in 'other income' of the PSBs. The improvement in efficiency could also be attributable to the fact that there has been a change in the orientation of PSBs from social objectives towards an ascent on profitability, particularly given that with the dilution of the government equity in most of these banks, a stake of private investors is involved. The capital market discipline imposed on PSBs since 1992–1993 when these banks were allowed to raise capital from the stock market has also led to significant efficiency gains. Another plausible explanation of relatively higher efficiency of Indian PSBs is that the government ownership facilitated recapitalisation of these banks at the onset of reforms, and this provided the depositors the implicit guarantee of 'too-big-to-fail' (Das and Ghosh 2006). Due to customers' perception that in troubled times,

[2] The Securitisation and Reconstruction of Financial Assets and Enforcement of Security Interest Act, 2002 (SARFAESI), empowers banks to recover their non-performing assets without the intervention of the court.

the public sector banks act as safe havens, these banks attracted large volume of funds by paying lower rates of interest than private banks. This in turn saved the considerable sums of money of PSBs and as a consequence improved their cost efficiency. Moreover, the loan approvals and extensions of PSBs are generally less prudential because of government intervention. This loose lending policy boosted loan production and other bank outputs per unit of input in the PSBs. From the above discussion, we may infer that higher cost efficiency levels in Indian public sector banking during the post-reforms years not only stemmed due to cost-curtailing measures adopted by PSBs but also occurred due to measures aiming at augmenting income-generating capacity of banks.

The subperiod analysis reveals that the efficiency gaps between the banks in distinct ownership groups were more pronounced during the first phase of reforms relative to second one. In particular, the foreign banks exhibited higher level of efficiency estimates than their public and private counterparts during the first subperiod. It is striking to note here that the reforms measures undertaken during the second subperiod have not only reduced the efficiency gaps across ownership groups but also affected their ranking. An ascent in cost efficiency of PSBs has been noted during the second phase of reforms (1999–2000 to 2007–2008). This period coincides with the period of the aftermath of South East Asian Financial Crisis of 1997–1998. The ordering of ownership groups in terms of CE reshuffled to PSBs > FBs > PBs. In addition, this ranking also holds for AE, TE, PTE and SE measures because of all-round improvement in efficiency (particularly of the AE) during the second phase of reforms.

From the growth rates for efficiency measures, we note that the CE, TE, AE and PTE of public sector banks followed an uptrend during the post-reforms period, while the SE experienced a downtrend. On the other hand, the CE of private banks also grew over the entire study period, and both TE and AE of private banks moved in the opposite direction. In particular, TE grew and AE declined. Also, the growth in TE was mainly due to growth in PTE rather than SE. Further, the CE of foreign banks dropped off significantly over the study period because the declining trend in the AE was strong enough to offset the uptrend in the TE. Moreover, the CE of public and foreign banks showed a tendency to accelerate in the long run, and that of private banks had a tendency to decelerate. Regarding the sources of cost inefficiency, we broadly found that there existed a trade-off between one source of inefficiency against another.

To answer the question 'Does ownership matter in Indian banking industry?', we made use of a battery of parametric and non-parametric tests to find out the statistical significance of observed efficiency differentials across ownership categories. The results are reported in Panel D of Table 6.3. We note that (i) no significant difference between efficiency measures of public and foreign banks appeared in Indian banking industry; (ii) the difference between CE, TE and SE of public and private banks was observed to be statistically significant; and (iii) the CE, TE and SE differences between private and foreign banks were also found to be statistically significant. Thus, the aforementioned findings suggest that there exist significant efficiency differentials across public and private banks, and private and foreign banks, but not in public and foreign banks' groups. Thus, the results broadly suggest that there are significant differences in the efficiency performance of banks belonging to distinct ownership groups. In sum, this hypothesis testing exercise facilitates us to safely conclude that ownership matters in case of Indian banking industry.[3]

An efficiency analysis in Indian banking industry seems inadequate if the records of efficiency performance of *de novo* private banks are not detailed. This is because the entry of these banks completely changed the landscape of Indian banking industry by infusing greater price and non-price competition, a thing which was completely missing in the pre-reforms years. In the post-reforms years, PSBs and old private banks got fierce competition from these banks and faced with a fall in their market shares. In addition, *de novo* private banks brought in with the state-of-the-art banking technologies, adequate capital resources, well-trained and professional manpower and lean organisational system. The estimates of CE and its components for two groups of domestic private banking segment are reported in Table 6.4. We note that the *de novo* private banks were more cost efficient than old private banks. The main source of cost inefficiency in old private banks was technical inefficiency, and in new private banks, it was driven by allocative inefficiency. Further, managerial inefficiency emerged as a main culprit for technical inefficiency in *de novo* private banks. However, technical inefficiency of old private banks stemmed largely from scale inefficiency.

The most plausible reason for the better performance of *de novo* private banks is that due to their late entry into the industry, they had the advantage of not carrying any baggage from the past, as was the case with the other groups operating in Indian banking industry. Therefore, new private banks have successfully managed their business at lower operating costs than the other groups (Sensarma 2006). Further, this is not surprising because employees and managers of *de novo* private banks are more trained and qualified than those of old private banks. In addition, new private banks evolved a rewarding incentive schemes for their employees and managers to put their best foot forward. This is what is missing in old private banks.

To explore which bank group dominates in the formation of *cost efficient frontier* for the Indian banking industry, we constructed the frequency distribution of CE scores for each bank group in all the sample years and reported the results in Table 6.5. For the analytical purpose, we categorised the number of banks in five distinct categories: (i) $0 \leq CE < 0.45$, (ii) $0.45 \leq CE < 0.60$, (iii) $0.60 \leq CE < 0.75$, (iv) $0.75 \leq CE < 0.90$ and (v) $0.90 \leq CE \leq 1$. We note that leaving aside a few exceptions, majority of public, private and foreign banks had CE score above 60 % in each year of the study period. Further, in each year, a greater proportion of public and private banks fell in the class interval $0.75 \leq CE < 0.90$ relative to foreign banks and, thus, had CE level between 75 % and 90 %. In

[3] This result is complemented by the rejection of null hypothesis of no difference in efficiency score across distinct ownership groups in majority of the sample years under consideration, particularly in the most recent years. The detailed results are available upon request to the authors.

Table 6.4 Mean cost, allocative, technical, pure technical and scale efficiency scores for old and new private banks

	Old private banks					New private banks				
Year↓	CE	AE	TE	PTE	SE	CE	AE	TE	PTE	SE
Panel A: Year-wise mean efficiency scores										
1992–1993	0.742	0.847	0.874	0.936	0.933	–	–	–	–	–
1993–1994	0.763	0.882	0.865	0.929	0.932	–	–	–	–	–
1994–1995	0.770	0.900	0.857	0.942	0.911	–	–	–	–	–
1995–1996	0.783	0.870	0.897	0.939	0.956	0.711	0.874	0.814	0.888	0.917
1996–1997	0.828	0.920	0.899	0.945	0.953	0.856	0.926	0.924	0.935	0.988
1997–1998	0.857	0.940	0.912	0.954	0.955	0.919	0.965	0.949	0.956	0.993
1998–1999	0.799	0.919	0.867	0.939	0.926	0.855	0.896	0.954	0.971	0.982
1999–2000	0.806	0.915	0.880	0.945	0.933	0.886	0.929	0.953	0.965	0.986
2000–2001	0.789	0.911	0.862	0.935	0.925	0.825	0.899	0.915	0.940	0.974
2001–2002	0.808	0.924	0.870	0.939	0.930	0.811	0.878	0.920	0.927	0.992
2002–2003	0.845	0.935	0.900	0.944	0.955	0.884	0.929	0.950	0.955	0.994
2003–2004	0.819	0.914	0.894	0.949	0.944	0.814	0.840	0.965	0.969	0.996
2004–2005	0.792	0.884	0.892	0.964	0.926	0.722	0.762	0.942	0.957	0.985
2005–2006	0.746	0.858	0.865	0.957	0.906	0.813	0.830	0.976	0.986	0.990
2006–2007	0.780	0.876	0.888	0.965	0.922	0.875	0.889	0.982	0.985	0.997
2007–2008	0.767	0.881	0.869	0.952	0.916	0.818	0.859	0.954	0.961	0.992
Panel B: Grand mean of efficiency measures										
Entire period	0.793	0.899	0.881	0.946	0.933	0.830	0.883	0.938	0.953	0.984
First subperiod	0.792	0.897	0.882	0.941	0.938	0.835	0.915	0.910	0.938	0.970
Second subperiod	0.795	0.900	0.880	0.950	0.929	0.828	0.868	0.951	0.961	0.990
Panel C: Average annual growth rates (%)										
Entire period	0.115	0.109	0.028	0.165	−0.121	−0.081	−0.860	0.766	0.461	0.305
First subperiod	1.549	1.282	0.229	0.089	0.175	0.496	−0.604	1.060	0.556	0.497
Second subperiod	−0.962	−0.864	−0.110	0.218	−0.325	−0.711	−1.140	0.444	0.357	0.095
Acceleration (+)/Deceleration (−)	(−)	(−)	(−)	(−)	(−)	(−)	(−)	(−)	(−)	(−)

Source: Authors' calculations

Table 6.5 Frequency distribution of cost efficiency scores for public, private and foreign banks

	Categories					
	I	II	III	IV	V	
Year↓	$0 \leq CE < 0.45$	$0.45 \leq CE < 0.60$	$0.60 \leq CE < 0.75$	$0.75 \leq CE < 0.90$	$0.90 \leq CE \leq 1$	No. of cost efficient banks
Panel A: Public sector banks						
1992–1993 (N = 27)	0 (0 %)	0 (0 %)	4 (14.8 %)	17 (63.0 %)	6 (22.2 %)	2 (7.4 %)
1993–1994 (N = 27)	0 (0 %)	1 (3.7 %)	14 (51.9 %)	7 (25.9 %)	5 (18.5 %)	3 (11.1 %)
1994–1995 (N = 27)	0 (0 %)	4 (14.8 %)	11 (40.7 %)	8 (29.6 %)	4 (14.8 %)	3 (11.1 %)
1995–1996 (N = 27)	0 (0 %)	1 (3.7 %)	13 (48.1 %)	6 (22.2 %)	7 (25.9 %)	4 (14.8 %)
1996–1997 (N = 27)	0 (0 %)	0 (0 %)	3 (11.1 %)	15 (55.6 %)	9 (33.3 %)	3 (11.1 %)
1997–1998 (N = 27)	0 (0 %)	0 (0 %)	5 (18.5 %)	11 (40.7 %)	11 (40.7 %)	1 (3.7 %)
1998–1999 (N = 27)	0 (0 %)	0 (0 %)	8 (29.6 %)	15 (55.6 %)	4 (14.8 %)	1 (3.7 %)
1999–2000 (N = 27)	0 (0 %)	1 (3.7 %)	6 (22.2 %)	12 (44.4 %)	8 (29.6 %)	6 (22.2 %)
2000–2001 (N = 27)	0 (0 %)	0 (0 %)	12 (44.4 %)	10 (37 %)	5 (18.5 %)	2 (7.4 %)
2001–2002 (N = 27)	0 (0 %)	0 (0 %)	7 (25.9 %)	16 (59.3 %)	4 (14.8 %)	2 (7.4 %)
2002–2003 (N = 27)	0 (0 %)	0 (0 %)	2 (7.4 %)	13 (48.1 %)	12 (44.4 %)	7 (25.9 %)
2003–2004 (N = 27)	0 (0 %)	0 (0 %)	1 (3.7 %)	16 (59.3 %)	10 (37 %)	3 (11.1 %)
2004–2005 (N = 27)	0 (0 %)	0 (0 %)	1 (3.7 %)	17 (63 %)	9 (33.3 %)	3 (11.1 %)
2005–2006 (N = 27)	0 (0 %)	0 (0 %)	7 (25.9 %)	13 (48.1 %)	7 (25.9 %)	3 (11.1 %)
2006–2007 (N = 28)	0 (0 %)	0 (0 %)	1 (3.6 %)	14 (50 %)	13 (33.3 %)	3 (10.7 %)
2007–2008 (N = 28)	0 (0 %)	0 (0 %)	0 (0 %)	15 (53.6 %)	13 (46.4 %)	4 (14.3 %)
Panel B: Private banks						
1992–1993 (N = 23)	0 (0 %)	1 (4.3 %)	11(47.8 %)	9 (39.1 %)	2 (8.7 %)	1 (4.3 %)
1993–1994 (N = 23)	0 (0 %)	3 (13 %)	6 (26.1 %)	12 (52.2 %)	2 (8.7 %)	1 (4.3 %)
1994–1995 (N = 23)	0 (0 %)	0 (0 %)	8 (34.8 %)	15 (65.2 %)	0 (0 %)	0 (0 %)
1995–1996 (N = 33)	0 (0 %)	4 (12.1 %)	12 (36.4 %)	11 (33.3 %)	6 (18.2 %)	2 (6.1 %)
1996–1997 (N = 33)	0 (0 %)	0 (0 %)	6 (18.2 %)	20 (60.6 %)	7 (21.2 %)	3 (9.1 %)
1997–1998 (N = 34)	0 (0 %)	0 (0 %)	3 (8.8 %)	19 (55.9 %)	12 (35.3 %)	6 (17.6 %)
1998–1999 (N = 33)	0 (0 %)	0 (0 %)	10 (30.3 %)	16 (48.5 %)	7 (21.2 %)	4 (12.1 %)

1999–2000 (N = 32)	0 (0 %)	0 (0 %)	8 (25 %)	15 (46.9 %)	9 (28.1 %)	3 (9.4 %)
2000–2001 (N = 31)	0 (0 %)	2 (6.5 %)	9 (29 %)	14 (45.2 %)	6 (19.4 %)	3 (9.7 %)
2001–2002 (N = 30)	0 (0 %)	2 (6.7 %)	7 (23.3 %)	14 (46.7 %)	7 (23.3 %)	4 (13.3 %)
2002–2003 (N = 30)	0 (0 %)	2 (6.7 %)	3 (10 %)	12 (40 %)	13 (43.3 %)	6 (20 %)
2003–2004 (N = 30)	0 (0 %)	1 (3.3 %)	7 (23.3 %)	14 (46.7 %)	8 (26.7 %)	4 (13.3 %)
2004–2005 (N = 29)	0 (0 %)	3 (10.3 %)	9 (31 %)	12 (41.4 %)	5 (17.2 %)	2 (6.9 %)
2005–2006 (N = 28)	0 (0 %)	3 (10.7 %)	9 (32 %)	13 (46.4 %)	3 (10.7 %)	3 (10.7 %)
2006–2007 (N = 25)	0 (0 %)	3 (12 %)	3 (12 %)	15 (60 %)	4 (16 %)	2 (8 %)
2007–2008 (N = 23)	0 (0 %)	1 (4.3 %)	6 (26.1 %)	16 (69.6 %)	0 (0 %)	0 (0 %)
Panel C: Foreign banks						
1992–1993 (N = 23)	0 (0 %)	0 (0 %)	2 (8.7 %)	4 (17.4 %)	17 (73.9 %)	15 (65.2 %)
1993–1994 (N = 21)	0 (0 %)	0 (0 %)	2 (9.5 %)	4 (19 %)	15 (71.4 %)	10 (47.6 %)
1994–1995 (N = 25)	2 (8 %)	0 (0 %)	3 (12 %)	5 (20 %)	15 (60 %)	9 (36.0 %)
1995–1996 (N = 30)	4 (13.3 %)	2 (6.7 %)	3 (10 %)	9 (30 %)	12 (40 %)	8 (26.7 %)
1996–1997 (N = 37)	3 (8.1 %)	3 (8.1 %)	6 (16.2 %)	11 (29.7 %)	14 (37.8 %)	9 (24.3 %)
1997–1998 (N = 37)	1 (2.7 %)	1 (2.7 %)	6 (16.2 %)	10 (27 %)	19 (51.4 %)	12 (32.4 %)
1998–1999 (N = 41)	2 (4.9 %)	3 (7.3 %)	5 (12.2 %)	14 (34.1 %)	17 (41.5 %)	11 (26.8 %)
1999–2000 (N = 41)	3 (7.3 %)	2 (4.9 %)	9 (22 %)	15 (36.6 %)	12 (29.3 %)	10 (24.4 %)
2000–2001 (N = 39)	1 (2.6 %)	3 (7.7 %)	4 (10.3 %)	13 (33.3 %)	18 (46.2 %)	11 (28.2 %)
2001–2002 (N = 35)	2 (5.7 %)	5 (14.3 %)	4 (11.4 %)	10 (28.6 %)	14 (40 %)	11 (31.4 %)
2002–2003 (N = 31)	2 (6.5 %)	1 (14.3 %)	4 (12.9 %)	12 (38.7 %)	12 (38.7 %)	9 (29.0 %)
2003–2004 (N = 29)	2 (6.9 %)	1 (3.4 %)	3 (10.3 %)	3 (10.3 %)	20 (69 %)	9 (31.0 %)
2004–2005 (N = 28)	3 (10.7 %)	0 (0 %)	4 (14.3 %)	6 (21.4 %)	15 (53.6 %)	12 (42.9 %)
2005–2006 (N = 28)	3 (10.7 %)	3 (10.7 %)	7 (25 %)	3 (10.7 %)	12 (42.9 %)	12 (42.9 %)
2006–2007 (N = 27)	0 (0 %)	8 (29.6 %)	2 (7.4 %)	6 (22.2 %)	11 (40.7 %)	10 (37.0 %)
2007–2008 (N = 26)	2 (7.7 %)	2 (7.7 %)	6 (23.1 %)	5 (19.2 %)	11 (42.3 %)	8 (30.8 %)

Source: Authors' calculations
Note: Figures in parentheses are the percentages

contrast, majority of the foreign banks had CE level greater than 90 %. This finding clearly indicates that there is a large scope for public and private banks to curtail their cost of operations while still maintaining the same level of output.

Looking at the number of cost efficient banks in each ownership type, we note that the percentage of banks lying on the *cost efficient frontier* was far more in foreign banks' group than the public and private banks' groups in each sample year. For instance, of 18 banks that together constructed the best practice frontier of Indian banking industry in the year 1992–1993, the number of public, private and foreign banks were 2, 1 and 15, respectively. The figures in table for the remaining years also confirmed the dominance of foreign banks in constructing the *efficient frontier* of Indian banking industry.

In all, the results of this study contradict the *property rights hypothesis* and *public choice theory* since PSBs shared the place on the podium along with foreign banks and were more efficient than private banks. Further, while foreign banks were mostly defining the grand technological frontier of the Indian banking system, PSBs closely pursued the frontier to stay competitive. In the post-reforms years, almost all the PSBs computerised their branches and introduced core banking solutions and made heavy investments in IT solutions. Although this push up the cost in the initial years, but operating cost declined substantially in the subsequent years. The reflection in the decline in operating cost can be seen from the improvement in cost efficiency of these banks during the most recent years.

6.5.4 Comparison of Efficiency in Domestic and Foreign Banks

Next, we move to empirically investigate the impact of foreign ownership on bank performance in India. In particular, we intend to test the validity of either the *home field advantage hypothesis* or the *global advantage hypothesis* in the Indian banking industry. Both the hypotheses are developed by Berger et al. (2000). The former hypothesis argues that foreign banks may have lower efficiency than domestic banks due to the cross-border disadvantages. This might be due to the liability of foreignness[4] which imposes costs on foreign banks such that the domestic banks are more efficient than foreign banks (Sturm and Williams 2004). On the other hand, the global advantage hypothesis suggests that some foreign banks overcome the diseconomies of cross-border operations and have higher efficiencies than domestic banks (Ersoy 2009).

Table 6.6 provides the relevant results. We note that foreign banks had higher average CE, TE, PTE and SE levels than domestic banks. Thus, empirical evidences

---

[4] The liability of foreignness is the costs borne by banks operating away from their home market; such costs include monitoring, staff turnover, diseconomies of scale for retail operations and factors such as culture, language and market structure acting as barriers to entry (Miller and Parkhe 2002).

Table 6.6 Mean cost, allocative, technical, pure technical and scale efficiency scores for domestic and foreign banks

	Domestic banks					Foreign banks				
Year↓	CE	AE	TE	PTE	SE	CE	AE	TE	PTE	SE
Panel A: Year-wise mean efficiency measures										
1992–1993	0.794	0.870	0.911	0.950	0.958	0.943	0.971	0.970	0.972	0.997
1993–1994	0.762	0.862	0.881	0.928	0.950	0.927	0.959	0.965	0.965	1.000
1994–1995	0.754	0.866	0.869	0.926	0.939	0.855	0.884	0.968	0.986	0.982
1995–1996	0.770	0.856	0.896	0.931	0.963	0.779	0.863	0.891	0.933	0.956
1996–1997	0.849	0.920	0.922	0.947	0.975	0.798	0.876	0.903	0.927	0.974
1997–1998	0.868	0.928	0.934	0.955	0.978	0.878	0.924	0.949	0.958	0.991
1998–1999	0.808	0.903	0.894	0.938	0.954	0.830	0.885	0.933	0.961	0.969
1999–2000	0.830	0.918	0.902	0.944	0.955	0.798	0.885	0.897	0.935	0.959
2000–2001	0.792	0.892	0.885	0.934	0.949	0.845	0.902	0.933	0.945	0.987
2001–2002	0.803	0.898	0.892	0.937	0.953	0.807	0.891	0.899	0.922	0.974
2002–2003	0.875	0.941	0.927	0.956	0.971	0.821	0.879	0.930	0.950	0.977
2003–2004	0.846	0.913	0.925	0.957	0.967	0.868	0.890	0.973	0.979	0.994
2004–2005	0.820	0.880	0.929	0.963	0.967	0.844	0.870	0.967	0.980	0.985
2005–2006	0.801	0.877	0.910	0.963	0.945	0.773	0.846	0.906	0.923	0.980
2006–2007	0.850	0.904	0.938	0.975	0.962	0.790	0.848	0.927	0.959	0.964
2007–2008	0.845	0.911	0.927	0.966	0.960	0.808	0.847	0.947	0.967	0.978
Panel B: Grand mean of efficiency measure										
Entire period	0.817	0.896	0.909	0.948	0.959	0.835	0.889	0.935	0.954	0.979
First subperiod	0.801	0.886	0.901	0.939	0.960	0.859	0.909	0.940	0.957	0.981
Second subperiod	0.829	0.904	0.915	0.955	0.959	0.817	0.873	0.931	0.951	0.978
Panel C: Average annual growth rates (%)										
Entire period	0.520	0.245	0.275	0.249	0.029	−0.765	−0.613	−0.168	−0.123	−0.060
First subperiod	1.124	0.991	0.137	0.029	0.124	−1.453	−0.790	−0.714	−0.429	−0.290
Second subperiod	0.106	−0.266	0.369	0.400	−0.036	−0.294	−0.492	0.206	0.086	0.098

Source: Authors' calculations

are in favour of the *global advantage hypothesis* in Indian banking industry since foreign banks outperformed their domestic counterparts. The better efficiency performance of foreign banks in India might be because of their superior investment strategies, managerial services and provision of better-quality services to their customers. Moreover, market conditions in India may have presented opportunities for foreign banks to exploit their comparative advantages, resulting in higher efficiencies. Furthermore, domestic banks found to be more allocatively efficient. This might be due to the fact that domestic banks face less expensive input prices, particularly of labour input. The aforementioned findings are further supported by the rejection of the null hypothesis of no difference in efficiency levels across domestic and foreign banks in majority of the sample years under consideration.[5]

In order to study the impact of reforms on the relative ranking of the foreign and domestic banks, we compared the efficiency performance across distinct subperiods. We observe that foreign banks were more efficient than domestic banks during the first subperiod. However, as a reflection of deregulation and liberalisation policies, the scene began to change. Domestic banks' performance exceeded those of the foreign banks in terms of CE, AE and PTE in the second subperiod. This is mainly due to the efforts of the GOI and RBI which restructured the domestic banking industry, and overcome the setbacks being faced by these banks before 1990s. Moreover, domestic banks have also invested heavily in technological upgradation like ATMs, mobile banking and internet banking, which boosted up their performance. Thus, efficiency gaps between foreign and domestic banks narrowed down with the increase in the pace of reforms. In sum, we can infer that though a strong presence of *global advantage hypothesis* has been observed in Indian banking industry from the analysis of sample period, this presence lost its sheen and was appearing in somewhat weak form during the most recent years. All in all, the results thus favour the existing policy of opening up the Indian banking sector, with liberalisation of foreign entry by way of setting up a wholly owned banking subsidiary (WOS) or conversion of the existing branches into a WOS. We expect that the liberal entry of foreign banks will also really push the domestic banks closer to global best practices, and would improve their performance and service quality.

6.5.5 Bank Size and Efficiency

As pointed out in the literature on banking efficiency, the relationship between cost structure and size has important policy implications regarding the optimal structure of the banking industry. Thus, an effort has also been made in the present study to shed light on the temporal pattern of efficiency of Indian banks across different size classes. Since the categorisation of banks on the basis of size is always arbitrary, we categorised the Indian banks into four distinct categories on the basis of quartile

---

[5] The detailed results are available upon request to the authors.

value of total assets: (i) micro banks (with total assets less than first quartile), (ii) small banks (with total assets lie between first quartile and median), (iii) medium banks (with total assets lie between median and third quartile) and (iv) large banks (with total assets greater than third quartile). A similar grouping is done by Tecles and Tabak (2010) for Brazilian banks.

The mean efficiency scores for four asset size groupings of Indian banks are presented in Table 6.7. Our results suggest that medium banks outperformed the banks belonging to other size classes in terms of cost efficiency and its components. The dominance of medium banks (containing the most of *de novo* private and foreign banks) in terms of efficiency performance has also been noted in the first and second subperiods. The most plausible reason for higher efficiency performance of medium banks is that these banks have leaner organisational structure that allows them to take prompt strategic actions to exploit emerging market opportunities and to create a niche market position for themselves. Further, recent advances in technology, increased competition and deregulation have reduced the minimum efficient scale of technology, thereby making medium-sized banks more efficient. However, higher inefficiency in larger banks (containing the most of public sector banks) may be simply due to their presence in rural markets, where the population density is low, which make delivery systems more costly. This finding of our study is in line with Das and Ghosh (2006) for Indian banks and Reda and Isik (2006) for Egyptian banks.

For seeking the answer of the question Does size really matter in Indian banking industry?, we made use of both parametric and non-parametric tests for hypothesis testing and reported the relevant results in Table 6.8. We note that leaving aside PTE measures, the efficiency differences between two specific size classes were generally significant in Indian banking industry. The results suggest that there exist significant differentials in CE, AE and SE of banks belonging to different size classes. However, the relationship between bank size and TE measure found to be not too strong. In sum, our analysis suggests that size really matters in explaining the cost- and allocative efficiency differences in Indian banking industry.

6.5.6 Returns-to-Scale

This subsection provides the empirical evidence pertaining to nature of returns-to-scale in Indian banking industry. For examining the predominant form of scale economies in Indian banking industry, we determine the number and percentage of banks operating under constant, increasing and decreasing returns-to-scale. We also computed a López-Cortés and Snowden's (1998) scale deficiency index (hereafter called as LCS's deficiency index) which is the proportion of banks that are characterised by decreasing returns-to-scale to the total number of scale-deficient banks.[6] If the value of deficiency index is greater than 0.5, then a larger number of

[6] LCS's scale deficiency index = Banks with DRS/(Banks with IRS + Banks with DRS).

Table 6.7 Mean cost, allocative, technical, pure technical and scale efficiency scores for distinct size categories

Size category→	Micro banks					Small banks				
Year↓	CE	AE	TE	PTE	SE	CE	AE	TE	PTE	SE
1992–1993	0.834	0.904	0.918	0.957	0.959	0.807	0.893	0.898	0.938	0.957
1993–1994	0.807	0.896	0.898	0.952	0.943	0.856	0.944	0.903	0.931	0.970
1994–1995	0.781	0.841	0.932	0.990	0.942	0.840	0.937	0.896	0.950	0.942
1995–1996	0.745	0.833	0.879	0.952	0.924	0.777	0.881	0.881	0.909	0.968
1996–1997	0.741	0.844	0.872	0.914	0.955	0.875	0.937	0.932	0.959	0.973
1997–1998	0.860	0.906	0.948	0.962	0.985	0.899	0.960	0.936	0.960	0.975
1998–1999	0.802	0.854	0.933	0.973	0.957	0.838	0.929	0.899	0.950	0.948
1999–2000	0.780	0.862	0.896	0.951	0.942	0.803	0.921	0.872	0.923	0.945
2000–2001	0.800	0.861	0.926	0.964	0.960	0.827	0.930	0.885	0.923	0.960
2001–2002	0.748	0.857	0.869	0.909	0.958	0.832	0.922	0.898	0.944	0.953
2002–2003	0.753	0.840	0.896	0.934	0.961	0.881	0.939	0.933	0.958	0.972
2003–2004	0.791	0.849	0.930	0.964	0.966	0.840	0.898	0.934	0.957	0.976
2004–2005	0.751	0.818	0.915	0.963	0.950	0.829	0.875	0.944	0.975	0.968
2005–2006	0.683	0.790	0.860	0.906	0.951	0.805	0.876	0.915	0.965	0.947
2006–2007	0.685	0.780	0.880	0.939	0.938	0.868	0.917	0.943	0.986	0.956
2007–2008	0.720	0.809	0.886	0.949	0.935	0.850	0.901	0.943	0.972	0.971
Grand mean										
Entire period	0.767	0.846	0.902	0.949	0.952	0.839	0.916	0.913	0.950	0.961
First subperiod	0.796	0.868	0.912	0.957	0.952	0.842	0.926	0.906	0.942	0.962
Second subperiod	0.746	0.829	0.895	0.942	0.951	0.837	0.909	0.919	0.956	0.961
Size category→	Medium banks					Large banks				
	CE	AE	TE	PTE	SE	CE	AE	TE	PTE	SE
1992–1993	0.869	0.903	0.962	0.976	0.985	0.854	0.908	0.938	0.957	0.980
1993–1994	0.849	0.894	0.945	0.964	0.979	0.725	0.827	0.875	0.905	0.967
1994–1995	0.811	0.879	0.919	0.947	0.970	0.715	0.829	0.860	0.895	0.960
1995–1996	0.806	0.884	0.911	0.942	0.968	0.764	0.837	0.908	0.921	0.984
1996–1997	0.848	0.916	0.924	0.939	0.983	0.853	0.914	0.932	0.944	0.987
1997–1998	0.875	0.938	0.930	0.952	0.978	0.854	0.903	0.944	0.950	0.993
1998–1999	0.832	0.903	0.921	0.950	0.968	0.795	0.895	0.886	0.917	0.967
1999–2000	0.865	0.927	0.933	0.952	0.979	0.820	0.910	0.897	0.933	0.960
2000–2001	0.851	0.921	0.919	0.943	0.974	0.776	0.870	0.889	0.922	0.964
2001–2002	0.843	0.922	0.912	0.940	0.969	0.796	0.882	0.899	0.933	0.964
2002–2003	0.910	0.958	0.949	0.963	0.985	0.880	0.939	0.934	0.959	0.974
2003–2004	0.928	0.950	0.976	0.985	0.991	0.853	0.924	0.922	0.950	0.971
2004–2005	0.898	0.938	0.956	0.972	0.984	0.834	0.876	0.952	0.965	0.989
2005–2006	0.858	0.912	0.939	0.976	0.962	0.837	0.899	0.929	0.955	0.973
2006–2007	0.889	0.923	0.963	0.981	0.981	0.875	0.920	0.950	0.974	0.975
2007–2008	0.892	0.930	0.959	0.978	0.980	0.868	0.917	0.946	0.965	0.980
Grand mean										
Entire period	0.864	0.919	0.939	0.960	0.977	0.819	0.891	0.916	0.940	0.974
First subperiod	0.841	0.902	0.930	0.953	0.976	0.794	0.873	0.906	0.927	0.977
Second subperiod	0.882	0.931	0.945	0.966	0.978	0.838	0.904	0.924	0.951	0.972

Source: Authors' calculations

Table 6.8 Hypothesis testing for pairwise differences in efficiency measures across size classes

Size categories	Micro versus small	Micro versus medium	Micro versus large	Small versus medium	Small versus large	Medium versus large
Panel A: ANOVA test						
CE	23.918*	41.957*	8.238*	4.508**	1.810	8.578*
	(<0.0001)	(<0.0001)	(0.007)	(0.042)	(0.189)	(0.006)
AE	38.720*	45.483*	12.320*	0.077	5.617**	7.423**
	(<0.0001)	(<0.0001)	(0.001)	(0.783)	(0.024)	(0.011)
TE	1.427	18.394*	1.990	10.104*	0.104	6.342**
	(0.242)	(0.000)	(0.169)	(0.003)	(0.749)	(0.017)
PTE	0.028	2.543	1.038	2.280	1.536	7.765*
	(0.868)	(0.121)	(0.316)	(0.142)	(0.225)	(0.009)
SE	14.371**	38.886*	25.980*	20.304*	10.921*	0.838
	(0.045)	(<0.0001)	(<0.0001)	(<0.0001)	(0.002)	(0.367)
Panel B: Mann–Whitney test						
CE	−3.788*	−4.372*	−2.507**	−2.036**	0.905	2.319**
	(0.000)	(<0.0001)	(0.012)	(0.042)	(0.365)	(0.020)
AE	−4.222*	−4.335*	−2.902*	−0.207	2.055**	2.375**
	(<0.0001)	(<0.0001)	(0.004)	(0.836)	(0.040)	(0.018)
TE	−1.472	−3.280*	−1.565	−2.583*	−0.490	1.998**
	(0.141)	(0.001)	(0.118)	(0.010)	(0.624)	(0.046)
PTE	−0.038	−1.208	0.924	−1.264	1.189	2.188**
	(0.970)	(0.227)	(0.356)	(0.206)	(0.234)	(0.029)
SE	−1.999**	−4.262*	−4.073*	−3.490*	−2.584*	0.943
	(0.046)	(<0.0001)	(<0.0001)	(0.000)	(0.010)	(0.346)
Panel C: Kruskal–Wallis test						
CE	14.352*	19.114*	6.285**	4.144**	0.819	5.375**
	(0.000)	(<0.0001)	(0.012)	(0.042)	(0.365)	(0.020)
AE	17.821*	18.792*	8.422*	0.043	4.222**	5.643**
	(<0.0001)	(<0.0001)	(0.004)	(0.836)	(0.040)	(0.018)
TE	2.166	10.759*	2.448	6.670*	0.240	3.991**
	(0.141)	(0.001)	(0.118)	(0.010)	(0.624)	(0.046)
PTE	0.001	1.459	0.854	1.596	1.414	4.785**
	(0.970)	(0.227)	(0.356)	(0.206)	(0.234)	(0.029)
SE	3.995**	18.161*	16.593*	12.183*	6.679*	0.890
	(0.046)	(<0.0001)	(<0.0001)	(0.000)	(0.010)	(0.346)
Panel D: Kolmogorov–Smirnov test						
CE	0.750*	0.813*	0.500**	0.438***	0.313	0.375
	(<0.0001)	(<0.0001)	(0.023)	(0.065)	(0.347)	(0.162)
AE	0.813*	0.813*	0.625*	0.188	0.438***	0.438***
	(<0.0001)	(<0.0001)	(0.002)	(0.912)	(0.065)	(0.065)
TE	0.250	0.563*	0.313	0.500**	0.188	0.438***
	(0.631)	(0.007)	(0.347)	(0.023)	(0.912)	(0.065)
PTE	0.125	0.250	0.250	0.313	0.250	0.438***
	(0.999)	(0.631)	(0.631)	(0.347)	(0.631)	(0.065)
SE	0.438***	0.875*	0.750*	0.625*	0.438***	0.313
	(0.065)	(<0.0001)	(<0.0001)	(0.002)	(0.065)	(0.347)

Source: Authors' calculations

Notes: (i) The figures in parentheses are the *p*-values, and (ii) '***', '**' and '*' indicates statistical significance at 1 %, 5 % and 10 % level of significance, respectively

Table 6.9 Returns-to-scale

Year	CRS	IRS	DRS	LCS's scale deficiency index[a]
1992–1993 (N = 73)	27 (37.0 %)	44 (60.3 %)	2 (2.7 %)	0.043
1993–1994 (N = 71)	27 (38.0 %)	34 (47.9 %)	10 (14.1 %)	0.227
1994–1995 (N = 75)	21 (28.0 %)	46 (61.3 %)	8 (10.7 %)	0.148
1995–1996 (N = 90)	28 (31.1 %)	49 (54.4 %)	13 (14.4 %)	0.210
1996–1997 (N = 97)	30 (30.9 %)	46 (47.4 %)	21 (21.6 %)	0.313
1997–1998 (N = 98)	46 (46.9 %)	37 (37.8 %)	15 (15.3 %)	0.288
1998–1999 (N = 101)	31 (30.7 %)	48 (47.5 %)	22 (21.8 %)	0.314
1999–2000 (N = 100)	30 (30.0 %)	47 (47.0 %)	23 (23.0 %)	0.329
2000–2001 (N = 97)	30 (30.9 %)	47 (48.5 %)	20 (20.6 %)	0.299
2001–2002 (N = 92)	24 (26.1 %)	45 (48.9 %)	23 (25.0 %)	0.338
2002–2003 (N = 88)	35 (39.8 %)	38 (43.2 %)	15 (17.0 %)	0.283
2003–2004 (N = 86)	38 (44.2 %)	40 (46.5 %)	8 (9.3 %)	0.167
2004–2005 (N = 84)	33 (39.3 %)	47 (56.0 %)	4 (4.8 %)	0.078
2005–2006 (N = 83)	25 (30.1 %)	47 (56.6 %)	11 (13.3 %)	0.190
2006–2007 (N = 80)	32 (40.0 %)	43 (53.8 %)	5 (6.3 %)	0.104
2007–2008 (N = 77)	23 (29.9 %)	44 (57.1 %)	10 (13.0 %)	0.185
Total (%)	480 (34.5 %)	702 (50.4 %)	210 (15.1 %)	0.230

Source: Authors' calculations
Note: [a]stands for López-Cortés and Snowden's (1998) scale deficiency index

scale-deficient banks experience DRS, while a value less than 0.5 indicates that a larger number of banks experience IRS, in any specific year. The results are summarised in Table 6.9.

From the table, we note that the percentage of banks experiencing IRS was about three times the percentage of banks experiencing DRS. Moreover, in majority of years under consideration, the share of banks showing IRS was higher than the share of the banks experiencing DRS or CRS. Further, we observe that in no year, the value of LCS's deficiency index was greater than 0.5, indicating that a large number of scale-deficient banks were operating in the zone of IRS and, thus, had suboptimal size. The straightforward implication of this finding is that a typical bank in Indian banking industry is too small to achieve economies of scale. Thus, to reap the benefits of economies of scale, most of the Indian banks need to enhance their scale of operations.

To get a more concrete picture about the nature of returns-to-scale in the Indian banking industry as a whole, we applied Fukushige and Miyara's (2005) procedure for testing the statistical significance of returns-to-scale at aggregate (or industry) level. Table 6.10 provides the relevant results. We note that the alternative hypothesis $H_1 : \overline{TE}^{NIRS} > \overline{TE}^{NDRS}$ was accepted in all the years under evaluation. This signifies the existence of increasing returns-to-scale across the Indian banking industry. In all, the results statistically confirm that majority of Indian banks are

Table 6.10 Hypothesis testing for the nature of returns-to-scale

Year (number of banks)	Test statistics	$H_o : \overline{TE}^{NIRS} = \overline{TE}^{NDRS}$ $H_1 : \overline{TE}^{NIRS} > \overline{TE}^{NDRS}$	Nature of returns-to-scale
1992–1993 (N = 73)	z-value	−2.327 (0.989)	IRS
	Inference	Accept H_O	
1993–1994 (N = 71)	z-value	−2.248 (0.987)	IRS
	Inference	Accept H_O	
1994–1995 (N = 75)	z-value	−2.552(0.994)	IRS
	Inference	Accept H_O	
1995–1996 (N = 90)	z-value	−0.601(0.726)	IRS
	Inference	Accept H_O	
1996–1997 (N = 97)	z-value	0.112(0.455)	IRS
	Inference	Accept H_O	
1997–1998 (N = 98)	z-value	−0.826(0.795)	IRS
	Inference	Accept H_O	
1998–1999 (N = 101)	z-value	−0.759(0.776)	IRS
	Inference	Accept H_O	
1999–2000 (N = 100)	z-value	−0.832(0.797)	IRS
	Inference	Accept H_O	
2000–2001 (N = 97)	z-value	−1.916(0.972)	IRS
	Inference	Accept H_O	
2001–2002 (N = 92)	z-value	−1.214(0.887)	IRS
	Inference	Accept H_O	
2002–2003 (N = 88)	z-value	−1.432(0.923)	IRS
	Inference	Accept H_O	
2003–2004 (N = 86)	z-value	−1.930(0.972)	IRS
	Inference	Accept H_O	
2004–2005 (N = 84)	z-value	−2.319(0.989)	IRS
	Inference	Accept H_O	
2005–2006 (N = 83)	z-value	−2.036(0.978)	IRS
	Inference	Accept H_O	
2006–2007 (N = 80)	z-value	−2.119(0.982)	IRS
	Inference	Accept H_O	
2007–2008 (N = 77)	z-value	−2.430(0.992)	IRS
	Inference	Accept H_O	

Source: Authors' calculations

operating in the zone of IRS and, thus, operate below the optimal scale of operations (i.e. at the declining portion of the long-run average cost curve). The results suggest that substantial reduction in average costs could be achieved in the Indian banking sector either by internal growth or consolidation since most of the Indian banks operate in the IRS portion of their production functions. Our results are consistent with those observed by Reda and Isik (2006), Rezvanian et al. (2008) and Burki and Niazi (2010) who found a strong evidence of economies of scale in Egyptian, Indian and Pakistani banking systems, respectively. The policy implication of aforementioned findings is that the GOI and RBI could possibly encourage the Indian banks to enhance their efficiency performance either by setting policies to support the more liberal entry and expansion of *de novo* private and foreign banks, or to buoy up mergers and acquisitions (M&As) among banks operating in the industry.

6.5.7 Factors Explaining Interbank Variations in Efficiency Measures

This subsection presents the results of the post-DEA analysis in which panel data Tobit model has been applied to explore the factors explaining the interbank variations in efficiency. Note here that panel data Tobit model is an appropriate method since the dependent variable, the calculated efficiency measure, falls between the interval 0 and 1, and thus, censored at 1. Some of the notable studies that applied the panel data Tobit analysis for explaining the interbank variations in efficiency include Pasiouras (2008) for Greek banks, Awdeh and El Moussawi (2009) for Lebanese banks, Tochkov and Nenovsky (2009) for Bulgarian banks, Sufian (2009a) for Malaysian banks, Staub et al. (2010) for Brazilian banks and Burki and Niazi (2010) for Pakistani banks, among others.

In the post-DEA regression analysis, the choice of the explanatory variables is always problematic. In fact, the issue of what independent variables to be included in the model is complicated due to the fact that theory does not offer such guidance (Ariff and Can 2008). In the absence of a theoretical rationale for determinants of efficiency of banks, we, therefore, used previous research in this area as a yardstick. In particular, we estimated the following regression models for distinct efficiency measures:

$$\begin{aligned} &\text{Model 1}: \ \text{Efficiency} = f(\text{ROA}, \text{OFF\_BALANCE}, \text{SIZE}, \text{NPA}) \\ &\text{Model 2}: \ \text{Efficiency} = f(\text{ROA}, \text{OFF\_BALANCE}, \text{SIZE}, \text{NPA}, \text{D}_{\text{PUBLIC}}, \text{D}_{\text{PRIVATE}}) \end{aligned}$$

The first regressor included in our second-stage DEA analysis is SIZE, which is measured by the logarithm of total assets. In the literature on the bank efficiency, there is an ambiguity in the relationship between bank size and efficiency. The positive and significant coefficient of SIZE may be considered as an indication of significant economies of scale in the production process. It is contended that large banks may be able to hire a better management team; utilise better technology; be located in larger, more diversified loan portfolios; and thus, succeed in their attempts to establish scale economies (Kyj and Isik 2008). The studies of Berger et al. (1993b), Miller and Noulas (1996), Yildirim (2002), Ray and Das (2010) and Burki and Niazi (2010) found a significant positive relationship between bank size and efficiency. On the other hand, Hermalin and Wallace (1994), Kaparakis et al. (1994), DeYoung and Nolle (1996), Ataullah et al. (2004), Girardone et al. (2004) and Kumar and Gulati (2008b) reported a significant negative relationship. However, there are also a few studies that reported no significant relationship between bank size and efficiency (see, for instance, Aly et al. 1990; Cebenoyan et al. 1993; Mester 1993, 1996; Pi and Timme 1993; Berger and Hannan 1998;

Berger and Mester 1997; Chang et al. 1998; Havrylchyk 2006). Since previous empirical work does not provide any clear evidence, no a priori expectation is formed regarding the sign of relationship between bank size and efficiency.

The second predictor used in the analysis is ROA, which is an indicator of profitability of banks. It is hypothesised that more profitable banks are also more efficient. Therefore, we expect a positive relationship between ROA and efficiency measures. Earlier studies that reported a positive relationship between profitability and bank efficiency include Jackson and Fethi (2000), Pasiouras (2008), Havrylchyk (2006), Sufian and Majid (2007) and Sufian (2009a). In recent years, banks have made larger exposure to off-balance sheet activities with the objective to generate more non-interest revenues. The effect of this exposure is expected to be translated positively in their operating efficiency to generate incomes. Thus, we expect a positive relationship between the predictor OFF_BALANCE and efficiency measure. OFF_BALANCE is measured as a ratio of non-interest income to total assets. Sufian (2009a), and Kumar and Gulati (2009a) confirmed a positive relationship between the exposure to off-balance sheet activities and bank efficiency in their empirical works.

The ratio of nonperforming loans to total advances (NPAs) is a good indicator of asset quality of banks. The conventional wisdom favours a strict negative relationship between NPAs and efficiency measure since the lower of this ratio would facilitate higher efficiency in the banking operations. Thus, we expect a negative and significant coefficient of the predictor NPA in our post-DEA analysis, which would confirm the presence of *bad management* and *bad luck hypotheses* proposed by Berger and DeYoung (1997) in the Indian banking industry. The *bad management hypothesis* posits that nonperforming loans are generally caused by controllable (i.e. endogenous) factors such as poor bank management quality. Banks with poor managers do not adequately monitor and control operational expenses and problem loans which lead to cost inefficiency. On the other hand, the *bad luck hypothesis* asserts that problem loans are generally caused by uncontrollable (i.e. exogenous) factors such as adverse weather conditions for a bank operating in a rustic area. Thus, the measured CE of banks might be fallaciously low because low cost efficiency may reflect the high operating cost of managing problem loans (additional management effort, loan workout arrangements, etc.). Finally, to control for the effects of ownership status of banks, we introduced two dummy variables, namely, D_PUBLIC and D_PRIVATE for public and private banks, respectively, and use foreign banks as base category in our regression models. It is worth noting here that we expect no a priori relationship between ownership dummies and efficiency measures.

Table 6.11 reports the post-DEA results. We note that in both the model specifications, i.e. Model 1 (without ownership dummies) and Model 2 (with ownership dummies), except ROA, all the regressors bear the sign consistent with a priori expectations. The explanatory variable OFF_BALANCE has had a significant positive impact on efficiency measures, indicating that the larger the exposure of banks to off-balance sheet activities, the higher is the level of efficiency. With respect to asset quality of banks, we note that there exists a significant negative relationship between NPAs and cost and allocative efficiencies, i.e. the lower the

Table 6.11 Results of the post-DEA analysis

Model specifications	Model 1 (without ownership dummies)					Model 2 (with ownership dummies)				
	CE	AE	TE	PTE	SE	CE	AE	TE	PTE	SE
Panel A: Independent variables										
Constant	0.4981*	0.6510*	0.8369*	1.0429*	0.8987*	0.4911*	0.6483*	0.8255*	1.0766*	0.8563*
	(10.65)	(17.79)	(21.98)	(23.92)	(40.63)	(8.84)	(14.83)	(0.000)	(20.30)	(33.60)
ROA	−0.0162**	−0.0147*	−0.0017	−0.0045	0.00004	−0.0185*	−0.0152*	−0.0053	−0.0052	−0.0033
	(−2.40)	(−2.82)	(−0.31)	(−0.69)	(0.01)	(−2.73)	(−2.89)	(−0.93)	(−0.78)	(−1.03)
OFF_BALANCE	0.0635*	0.0421*	0.0483*	0.362*	0.0281*	0.0622*	0.0418*	0.0471*	0.0382*	0.0255*
	(10.79)	(9.40)	(8.36)	(5.62)	(8.09)	(10.34)	(0.000)	(7.82)	(5.60)	(7.41)
SIZE	0.0191*	0.0151*	0.0024	−0.0065**	0.0025***	0.0219*	0.0159*	0.0064***	−0.0094**	0.0093*
	(6.09)	(6.19)	(0.96)	(−2.26)	(1.69)	(4.89)	(4.52)	(1.73)	(−2.19)	(4.49)
NPA	−0.0025*	−0.0022*	−0.0004	−0.0013***	0.0005	−0.0026*	−0.0022*	−0.0005	−0.0014***	0.0004
	(−2.98)	(−3.23)	(−0.64)	(−1.70)	(1.21)	(−3.07)	(−3.26)	(−0.84)	(−1.80)	(1.19)
D_PUBLIC						−0.0227	−0.0059	−0.0348***	0.0169	−0.0521*
						(−1.01)	(−0.34)	(−1.91)	(0.81)	(−5.03)
D_PRIVATE						−0.0502*	−0.0117	−0.0694*	−0.0075	−0.0684*
						(−2.96)	(−0.88)	(−5.20)	(−0.49)	(−8.96)
Panel B: Test statistics										
No. of observations	687	687	687	687	687	687	687	687	687	687
Log likelihood	121.73	269.43	142.99	10.61	393.45	126.84	269.87	158.67	11.91	433.64
Wald χ^2	176.85*	149.16*	82.48*	40.74*	78.64*	186.71*	149.62*	108.38*	41.08*	156.58*
		(0.000)	(0.000)	(0.000)	(0.000)	(0.000)	(0.000)	(0.000)	(0.000)	(0.000)

Source: Authors' calculations

Notes: (i) In Panel A, the figures in parentheses are the *t*-values; (ii) in Panel B, the figures in parentheses are the *p*-values; and (iii) '***', '**' and '*' indicate significance at 1 %, 5 % and 10 % level of significance, respectively

ratio of nonperforming loans to total advances, the higher is the efficiency of banks in reducing costs of banking operations and choosing the optimal mix of inputs. Additionally, it bears the sign according to a priori expectation with TE, PTE and SE, but coefficient is statistically significant only for PTE. The observed negative relationship between asset quality and efficiency may be an indication of poor management (*bad management*) or a direct consequence of adverse factors outside the management control (*bad luck*). Whether exogenously or endogenously determined, this negative relationship reflects the high operating cost of managing nonperforming loans. Thus, it is not clear whether the results support *bad luck* or *bad management* hypotheses, but it is clear that the results do not support the *skimping* hypothesis[7] in case of Indian banking industry. Our results are in line with those of Isik and Hassan (2003b) for Turkish banks.

The predictor SIZE seems to have a positive and statistically significant relation with CE, AE and SE measures. The possible explanation of this finding is that larger banks tend to be more efficient indicating that there are significant economies of scale. Thus, the larger is the size of the bank, the more is the possibility of managing its input costs efficiently. However, the same bears a strong negative relation with PTE measure. Our results, thus, suggest that bank size is inversely related to managerial efficiency in case of Indian banking industry. The decline in managerial efficiency of the large banks, particularly of PSBs, could be due to their complex and politically determined bureaucratic organisational structure that impeded their ability to keep up with smaller private domestic and foreign banks, which were quicker to adopt new financial technology (e.g. ATMs and e-banking) and to introduce new financial products (e.g. car financing and credit cards). This finding is consistent with Ataullah et al. (2004) for India and Pakistan, and opposed to Yildirim (2002) who find a positive relationship between size and managerial efficiency of Turkish banks.

We further note that ROA as an indicator of profitability has a significant negative coefficient in both the models. Most probably this is the outcome of the problem of multicollinearity. However, we have a valid and logical explanation for the observed opposing results regarding the relationship between profitability and cost efficiency. The negative effect of profitability on cost efficiency and its components may be stemmed from the fact that most of cost efficient banks have invested heavily on IT in their drive to provide better customer services at low transaction cost which inversely affected their margins. On the other hand, the cost-inefficient banks enjoy higher profitability due to high margins charged by those banks. This is a pointer towards the prevalence of '*quite life*' hypothesis in the Indian banking industry. According to Berger and Hannan (1998), in more concentrated markets, efficiency of banks worsen because the absence of

[7] The skimping hypothesis maintains that the high volume of problem loans may be a conscious decision of a bank because its management might be trading off between short-term operating costs and long-run profitability. Management might rationally decide to reduce short-term expenses by skimping on resources allocated to loan origination and monitoring, at the expense of greater problem loans and costs in the future.

competitive pressures results in lessened effort by managers to minimise costs. Managers can simply have a '*quiet life*', translating higher inefficiencies in higher prices. Our results are line with those observed by Awdeh and El Moussawi (2009) for Lebanese banks and Turati (2001) for European banks.

Finally, the banks with private ownership are underperforming relative to public and foreign banks in terms of CE. This is evidenced by the negative and significant coefficient of the dummy variable D_PRIVATE. The negative and statistically significant coefficients of ownership dummy variables in case of TE and SE measures suggest that on average, foreign banks are more technically and scale efficient than private and public banks. Thus, we can safely infer that private banks are less cost efficient than their foreign and public counterparts. The regression results reiterate our earlier finding that public and foreign banks share the same place on the podium and are definitely more cost efficient than private banks. It has also been observed that the ownership does not have a strong link with the allocative efficiency of Indian banks.

All in all, the regression results suggest that ownership effects are significant in explaining cost variations in Indian banking industry. In a nutshell, we can conclude that (i) private banks are less cost efficient than public and foreign banks; (ii) the negative relationship between NPA and efficiency measures supports the bad luck or bad management hypotheses instead of the skimping hypothesis in case of Indian banking industry; (iii) larger banks are more cost efficient, indicating the existence of significant economies of scale; and (iv) higher levels of efficiency are explained significantly by the greater exposure of banks to off-balance sheet activities in the Indian context.

6.6 Conclusions

The Indian banking industry has been substantially deregulated over the last two decades, with entry restrictions for *de novo* private and foreign banks greatly relaxed, and the industry has followed interest rates deregulation, lowering of statutory pre-emption, easing of directed credit rules and diversification in the ownership of public sector banks. By employing DEA models that incorporate the quasi-fixed inputs, this study examines how the cost efficiency performance of the banking industry has been affected by these deregulatory changes. In particular, we empirically tested the basic underlined hypothesis that the cost efficiency of Indian banks will rise in the more liberal and competitive environment. The main finding of our empirical analysis is that typical bank in the Indian banking industry wastes about 17.8 % of its costs relative to the best practice bank. Interestingly, our estimate of 17.8 % average cost inefficiency is considerably lower than that of the world's average of 27 % cited in the extensive survey of Berger and Humphrey (1997). It seems from the results that allocative inefficiency is the main culprit behind cost inefficiency in the Indian banking sector. Further, technical inefficiency is primarily due to managerial underperformance in controlling the waste of inputs in the production process rather than failure to operate at optimum scale size.

The results pertaining to trends of cost efficiency indicate that the financial deregulation process initialised in the early 1990s has had a positive impact on the cost efficiency of Indian banks, and the observed increase in cost efficiency (albeit modest) is entirely due to improvements in technical efficiency. Our most striking result is that allocative efficiency in the banking industry worsened during the post-reforms period. The most likely explanation for this is that high fluctuations and instability in factor prices due to chronic inflation in the country in the recent years constrained the bank managers to take rational decision regarding input mix. The most interesting finding of our study that makes India's approach of deregulation a success story is that CE of public sector banks followed an increasing trend over the entire study period and distinct sub-periods. In addition, technical and allocative efficiencies followed an uptrend. Another striking finding of our study is that public sector banks that pursue not only profit maximization objective but are also concerned with social justice in the allocation of credit have been observed to be more efficient than private banks. In particular, we get the ranking of ownership groups in Indian banking industry as PSBs = FBs > PBs.

Our results also show that the magnitude of the deregulation impact varies among the different forms of ownership. The cost efficiency of public and private banks grew, but declined in case of foreign banks during the post-reforms years. A grim aspect relating to the cost efficiency performance of private and foreign banks is that allocative efficiency of these banks dropped off significantly during the 16-year period under evaluation. Other significant finding of this study is that in a majority of years, foreign banks were dominating in defining the production frontier of the Indian banking system. This result may indicate that foreign banks in India have succeeded in using their superior technology and managerial expertise and experience, and this in turn has offsetted potential cross-border disadvantages, e.g. lack of knowledge about the local market and barriers of culture and regulations. Thus, the empirical evidence is in favour of the prevalence of the *global advantage hypothesis* in Indian banking industry.

It has also been observed that medium banks outperformed the banks belonging to other size classes in terms of cost efficiency and its components. Regarding the nature of returns-to-scale, we note that the banking industry in India experienced increasing returns-to-scale. This suggests that Indian banks should focus on augmenting their size to meet the market demand through either internal growth or M&As. Finally, the results of second-stage DEA analysis reveal that (i) private banks are less cost efficient than public and foreign banks; (ii) the negative relationship between NPA and efficiency measures supports the bad luck or bad management hypotheses instead of the skimping hypothesis in the case of Indian banking industry; (iii) larger banks are more cost efficient, indicating the existence of significant economies of scale in Indian banking industry; and (iv) higher levels of efficiency are explained significantly by the greater exposure to off-balance sheet activities.

The aforementioned findings help us to draw a broad conclusion that to a large extent, the financial deregulation programme seems to be successful in achieving the cost efficiency gains in the Indian banking industry, and public sector banks tend to have benefited most from liberalisation and deregulation. The results explicitly signal that the approach of cautious and gradual banking reforms adopted by Indian policy makers has started bearing fruit in terms of the creation of an efficient banking system, which is immune to any sort of financial crisis and resilient to both internal and external shocks. The Indian banks have not experienced the kinds of losses and write-downs that even venerable banks and financial institutions in the Western world have faced after the global financial meltdown of 2008. Indian banks have shown resilience, as they have a buffer well over the required capital adequacy ratio of 9 %. The cautious approach of Reserve Bank of India in the early 2000s advising banks to go slow on their exposure to sensitive sectors like real estate and capital market has also helped the banking system to get insulated from the worst of effects of global financial crisis. All this is a pointer towards the overall effectiveness of banking reforms process in India. In sum, the banking reforms process that initiated in 1992 provided strong economic incentives to the banks, especially PSBs, to organise their inputs in the cost-effective manner. Overall, the financial deregulation programme in India has achieved the desired results in terms of efficiency performance. In the light of empirical findings of this study, we suggest that the future reforms in the banking sector should be directed towards strengthening competitive and market-oriented policies.

Chapter 7
Sources of Productivity Gains in Indian Banking Industry: Is It Efficiency Improvement or Technological Progress?

7.1 Introduction

The key objective of this chapter is to assess the efficacy of India's financial deregulation programme by analysing the developments in total factor productivity (TFP) growth across different ownership groups in Indian banking sector over the post-deregulation years. In particular, the research question which we have addressed in this chapter is as follows: Did financial deregulation spur total factor productivity growth of Indian banks? The findings of this research work may provide some important insights to the policy makers in designing and refashioning the strategies for the banks. The study has been carried out against the backdrop of a comprehensive financial deregulation and liberalisation programme which has embarked upon in the year 1992. The programme aimed at getting rid of the regime of financial repression that has surfaced in the Indian banking industry owing to the factors like virtually no competition among banks, high pre-emption of lendable resources, massive political interference, and poor banking regulation and supervisory framework. The abysmally low levels of profitability and high proportion of bad loans on the books of Indian banks at the beginning of 1990s gave alarming signals to the policy makers for the need of introducing wide ranging reforms in the banking sector. Consequent to the policy actions that were recommended by many high-powered committees and implemented by the policy makers during the post-1992 years, the Indian banking industry witnessed a transformation from a financially repressed industry to a high competitive industry. Now, the public, private and foreign banks are investing heavily in the state-of-the-art banking technology and competing fiercely for providing the innovative financial products and services to their customers at a competitive pricing.

We differ from existing studies that have taken a look at the productivity growth of Indian banks during the post-reforms period in several ways. Unlike the previous studies (e.g. Ram Mohan and Ray 2004a, Rezvanian et al. 2008 and Zhao et al. 2008) that estimated bank productivity using radial Malmquist productivity index (MPI), we made use of input-oriented non-radial MPI approach for obtaining more robust

S. Kumar and R. Gulati, *Deregulation and Efficiency of Indian Banks*, India Studies in Business and Economics, DOI 10.1007/978-81-322-1545-5_7, © Springer India 2014

estimates of TFP growth for Indian banks over the period 1992–1993 to 2007–2008. In particular, we used Esmaeili's (2009) slack-based measure (SBM) model for exogenously fixed inputs to compute input-oriented distance functions that are required for computing MPI. The main advantage of using SBM-based MPI approach is that in contrast to the radial MPI approach, which is based on a proportional reduction in input vector or an increase in output vectors without taking slacks into account, our input-oriented SBM-based MPI deals directly with input excesses (slacks) when estimating the distance functions. Further, the sample period in the existing studies is insufficient to analyse the full impact of deregulation programme. Also, to the best of our knowledge, none of the available study has made a comprehensive comparative analysis of developments of TFP growth and its distinct sources between the underlined phases of the process of financial deregulation. In addition to this, the previous studies that employed MPI approach used balanced panel data sets for the sake of convenience and consequently completely ignored the effect of entry and exit of banking firms on the estimates of productivity growth. In contrast, our study has used an unbalanced panel data set for a longer sample period of 16 years and has carried out a detailed analysis of the trends of TFP growth between first and second phase of banking reforms to see whether deepening of reforms process augmented the TFP of banks or not. In addition, we have included the 'equity' (i.e. financial capital) directly in the linear programming problem as an exogenously fixed input to control for the bank's risk profile. The inclusion of equity as an input variable is completely in the lines suggested by Mester (1996) who argued that it is important to account for differences in the risk profiles across banks while assessing the performance of banks.

The rest of the chapter is structured as follows. The following section reviews the state-of-the-art literature and provides existing gaps in it. Section 7.3 presents the methodological framework used for measuring and decomposing TFP growth. Specification of input and output variables and database used in this chapter are presented in Sect. 7.4. Section 7.5 discusses the empirical findings and, finally, Sect. 7.6 concludes the chapter and highlights the policy lessons learnt from this exercise.

7.2 Relevant Literature Review

During the last few decades, the wind of deregulation in the banking systems swept across many parts of the world. Proponents of deregulation policies believe that deregulation boosts efficiency through operational savings and thus leading to a surge in productivity growth. Nevertheless, an excellent literature review by Berger and Humphrey (1997) on the subject matter, which now requires an updation, highlights that the studies aiming at analysing the impact of financial deregulation on the efficiency and productivity have contradictory implications regarding the effects of deregulation.

7.2.1 *Deregulation and Productivity Change: International Experience*

One strand of the empirical literature provides the evidence in favour of deregulatory policies and highlights a positive effect of introducing deregulation and liberalisation policies on the productivity of the banking system. Furthermore, leaving aside a few studies, most of the studies reported technological progress as the dominant source of observed TFP growth in the banking system. The studies which offer the broad inference that productivity gains are driven primarily by technological progress (frontier-shift effect) rather efficiency change (catch-up effect) include Fukuyama (1995) for Japanese banks; Noulas (1997) for Hellenic banks; Gilbert and Wilson (1998) for Korean banks; Leightner and Lovell (1998) for Thai banks; Elyasiani and Mehdian (1990a) and Mukherjee et al. (2001) for US banks; Avkiran (1999), Worthington (1999), Sturm and Williams (2004) and Neal (2004) for Australian banks; Casu et al. (2004) for European banks; Rebelo and Mendes (2000) for Portuguese banks; Jackson et al. (1998) for Turkish banks; Tsionas et al. (2003), Athanasoglou et al. (2009) and Chortareas et al. (2009) for Greek banks; Asmild et al. (2004) for Canadian banks; Kirikal (2005) for Estonian banks; Lin et al. (2007) and Liu (2010) for Taiwanese banks; Guzmán and Reverte (2008) for Spanish banks; Heffernan and Fu (2009), Matthews and Zhang (2010) and Chang et al. (2012) for Chinese banks; Fethi et al. (2011) for Egyptian banks; Majid et al. (2011) for Malaysian banks; Hadad et al. (2011) for Indonesian banks; Lee et al. (2010) for Singaporean banks; and Seelanatha (2007) for Sri Lankan banks. The studies that found a strong productivity growth due to the catch-up effect after deregulation include Berg et al. (1992) for Norwegian banks; Isik and Hassan (2003c) for Turkish banks; Deng et al. (2011) for Malaysian banks and Sufian (2009b) for Chinese banks.

The other strand of empirical literature presents the studies that reported a negative effect or no discernible effect of deregulation and liberalisation measures on the productivity growth of the banking industry. Humphrey (1991, 1993) and Wheelock and Wilson (1999) for US banks found a general drop in average productivity caused by failure to catch up. However, Alam (2001) found that the deregulation resulted in a productivity surge in the first half of the 1980s followed by a productivity regress in the second half for US banks. Outside the USA, Mahadevan and Kim (2001) for Korean banks, Rizvi (2001) for Pakistani banks, Fukuyama and Weber (2002) for Japanese banks, Sathye (2002) for Australian banks and Sufian (2011) for Malaysian banks found that deregulation has led to deterioration in productivity driven mainly by the technological regress, while the studies by Hao et al. (2001) for Korean banks and Dogan and Fausten (2003) for Malaysian banks found a little or no effect of liberalisation on the productivity estimates.

7.2.2 *Deregulation and Productivity Change: The Indian Experience*

The literature pertaining to the effects of deregulatory measures on TFP growth of Indian banks is very scant. Table 7.1 summarises the main findings of the empirical studies. We note that the existing studies on the productivity growth of Indian banks has reached to a broad agreement that deregulation programme has had a positive impact on the productivity of Indian banks, and this impact prevails across all ownership categories. We also note that no consensus appears regarding the ranking of ownership groups on the basis of productivity performance; nevertheless, many of the studies found that the productivity gains in the public sector banks are larger than what have been noted for the domestic private and foreign banks. Further, there exists a substantial variation in the estimates of TFP growth, and the findings are quite sensitive to the choice of inputs and outputs and also to the estimation methodology.

The extant literature on the effects of deregulation programme on the productivity growth of Indian banks suffers from a number of shortcomings. The two prominent shortcomings are (i) the use of relatively short time period for seeking the impact of regulatory changes on productivity growth of banks and (ii) the use of balanced panel data in most of the studies for estimating productivity growth rates and thus ignoring the effect of entry and exit in the industry on the productivity performance. As mentioned in the introductory section, the present study intends to contribute significantly to the current literature by using the longer sample period (1992–2008) and making use of an unbalanced panel data set. For obtaining more robust productivity estimates, we made use of input-oriented non-radial MPI model with a exogenously fixed input.

7.3 Methodological Framework

As noted above, input-oriented[1] non-radial MPI with an exogenously fixed input has been used for measuring productivity growth of Indian banks. The MPI is first initiated by Caves et al. (1982a, b) and further developed by Färe (1988) and Färe et al. (1994a). The selection of MPI in this study over that of two other best known productivity indices, namely, the Törnqvist and Fisher indices, is based upon the fact that only the MPI (i) allows the decomposition of productivity change into two mutually exclusive components, namely, efficiency change and technological change; (ii) does not require price data, thereby avoiding problems associated

[1] In DEA literature, SBM models can be defined by input-oriented, output-oriented and non-oriented structures. We use input-oriented structure in the present study because a great majority of studies in banking obtain the efficiency estimates under this approach. Moreover, we feel that input orientation is more plausible in an efficiency analysis pertaining to developing country like India because given the higher control over inputs (e.g. personnel, expenses) rather than outputs (e.g. loans, income), the bank managers usually adopt the policy to curtail the use of inputs to achieve the same level of bank outputs. In addition, the use of input orientation facilitates a direct and meaningful comparison of the results of our study with other studies on productivity change.

Table 7.1 Estimates of total factor productivity growth in the Indian banking sector

Author (year)	Period of the study	Panel type (no. of banks in the sample)	Methodology	Effect of deregulation	Main driver of productivity growth (loss)	% TFP growth (loss)	Ranking of ownership groups
Bhattacharyya et al. (1997a)	1970–1992	Balanced panel (27 PSBs)	SFA (cost frontier)	Positive	Efficiency improvement	SBI = 3.86 %, NBs = 2.83 % All banks = 2.05 %	SBI > NBs
Kumbhakar and Sarkar (2003)	1985–1996	Balanced panel (27 PSBs, 23 PBs)	SFA (cost frontier)	Negative	Technological regress	PSBs = 2.56 %, PBs = 2.97 %	PBs > PSBs
Ram Mohan and Ray (2004)	1992–2000	Balanced panel (27 PSBs, 20 PBs, 11 FBs)	Törnqvist index and DEA-based MPI	Positive	Technological progress	Törnqvist index: PSBs = 0.77 %, PBs = 0.49 %, FBs = −3.07 % MPI: PSBs = 0.80 %, PBs = −1.76 %, FBs = 9.22 %	Törnqvist index PSBs > PBs MPI FBs > PSBs
Galagedera and Edirisuriya (2005)	1995–2002	Balanced panel (20 PSBs, 23 PBs)	DEA-based MPI	Positive	Efficiency improvement	PSBs = 1.3 %, PBs = 0 %, All banks = 0.6 %	PSBs > PBs
Reddy (2005a)	1996–2002	Balanced panel (27 PSBs, 21 OPBs, 6 NPBs, 26 FBs)	DEA-based MPI	Positive	Efficiency improvement	PSBs = 2.2 %, OPBs = 0.2 % NPBs = −5.3 %, FBs = −3.7 % All banks = −0.8 %	PSBs > OPBs
Sensarma (2006)	1986–2000	Balanced panel (27 PSBs, 25 PBs, 22 FBs)	SFA (cost frontier)	Positive	Technological progress	PSBs = varies from 0 % to 38.4 % PBs = varies from 0 % to 44.9 % FBs = −8.02 % to 32.8 %	PBs > PSBs > FBs

(continued)

Table 7.1 (continued)

Author (year)	Period of the study	Panel type (no. of banks in the sample)	Methodology	Effect of deregulation	Main driver of productivity growth (loss)	% TFP growth (loss)	Ranking of ownership groups
Rezvanian et al. (2008)	1998–2003	Balanced panel (20 PSBs, 19 PBs, 16 FBs)	DEA-based MPI	Positive	Technological progress	PSBs = 11.7 %, PBs = 11.1 %, FBs = 65.9 %, all banks = 26.1 %	FBs > PSBs > PBs
Zhao et al. (2008)	1992–2004	Balanced panel (27 PSBs, 20 PBs, 18 FBs)	DEA-based MPI	Positive	Technological progress	PSBs = 5.9 %, PBs = 4.1 %, FBs = 5 %, all banks = 5.1 %	PSBs > FBs > PBs
Das and Kumbhakar (2012)	1996–2005	Panel of 948 banks	Input distance function approach	Positive	Efficiency improvement	PSBs = 4.9 %, PBs = 2.2 %, FBs = 3.7 %, all banks = 3.5 %	PSBs > FBs > PBs

Source: Authors' elaboration

with unavailability or distortions of price information; (iii) allows for the use of multiple-inputs and/or multiple-outputs without being concerned about aggregation problems; and (iv) does not require a prespecified optimising criterion such as cost minimisation or profit maximisation (Grifell-Tatjé and Lovell 1996). However, the main disadvantage of the MPI is the lack of a stochastic specification, thus, making it sensitive to any random shocks or data measurement errors (Leung 1998).

A non-radial MPI is defined using distance functions. Let $x^t = (x_1{}^t, \ldots, x_m{}^t)$ denote a vector of m discretionary inputs at time t, $z^t = (z_1{}^t, \ldots, z_l{}^t)$ be a vector of l non-discretionary (or 'exogenously fixed') inputs at time t and $y^t = (y_1{}^t, \ldots, y_s{}^t)$ be a vector of s outputs at time t.[2] The slack variables for the ith discretionary input and k^{th} non-discretionary input are represented by s_i^- and s_k^-, respectively, which indicate input excesses. The input-oriented distance function of bank 'o' for the period t in relation to the constant returns to scale(CRS) technology in that period can be calculated by solving the following SBM model dealing with both discretionary and non-discretionary input variables, which is developed by Esmaeili (2009) as an extension of SBM model of Tone (2001).

$$\left[\hat{D}_I^t(y_o^t, x_o^t, z_o^t)|CRS\right]^{-1} = \tilde{\theta}_o^t(y_o^t, x_o^t, z_o^t) = \min_{\lambda_j, s_i^-} 1 - \frac{1}{m}\sum_{i=1}^{m} s_i^- / x_{io}^t$$

subject to

$$\begin{aligned} &\sum_{j=1}^{n} \lambda_j x_{ij}^t + s_i^- = x_{io}^t && (i = 1, \ldots, m) \\ &\sum_{j=1}^{n} \lambda_j z_{kj}^t + s_k^- = z_{ko}^t && (k = 1, \ldots, l) \\ &\sum_{j=1}^{n} \lambda_j y_{rj}^t \geq y_{ro}^t && (r = 1, \ldots, s) \\ &\lambda_j \geq 0 && (j = 1, \ldots, n) \\ &s_i^-, s_k^- \geq 0. \end{aligned} \tag{7.1}$$

Here, n is the number of banks; x_{ij}, z_{kj} and y_{rj} are the levels of the ith discretionary input, k^{th} non-discretionary input and r^{th} output, respectively, for the jth bank; and λ_j is the weight of the jth bank. Note here that only the discretionary input excesses enter

[2] DEA literature categorises input and output variables into two broad categories: discretionary and non-discretionary. Discretionary variables are those variables that can be controlled by the management of each decision making unit (DMU) and varied at its discretion. Non-discretionary variables are exogenously fixed inputs or outputs that are beyond the control of a DMU's management. Some examples of non-discretionary factors in the DEA literature are the number of competitors in the branches of a restaurant chain, soil characteristics and topography in different farms, age of facilities in different universities, the populations of wards in evaluating the relative efficiency of public libraries, snowfall or weather in evaluating the efficiency of maintenance units, local unemployment rates which affect the ability to attract recruits by different US Army recruitment stations and the number of transactions (for a purely gratis service) in library performance (Esmaeili 2009).

into the objective function. A bank is called SBM efficient if and only if $\widetilde{\theta}_o^{t*}(y^t, x_o^t, z_o^t) = 1$. It is worth noting here that efficiency score is equivalent to the inverse of input-oriented distance function, i.e. $\widetilde{\theta}_o^t(y^t, x_o^t, z_o^t) = 1/\hat{D}_I^t(y_o^t, x_o^t, z_o^t)$. The above-stated SBM model has many desirable features which may explain why we are interested in using it to investigate the efficiency of converting multiple-inputs into multiple-outputs. These characteristics include the following: (i) this scalar measure deals directly with the input excesses of the banks concerned, and (ii) it is unit invariant and monotonically decreasing with respect to input excess.

Assume two time periods t and $t + 1$, and taking time period t as the reference period, the input-oriented MPI can be expressed in terms of distance functions as follows:

$$MPI_I(y^{t+1}, x^{t+1}, z^{t+1}, y^t, x^t, z^t) = \underbrace{\frac{D_I^{t+1}(y^{t+1}, x^{t+1}, z^{t+1}|CRS)}{D_I^t(y^t, x^t, z^t|CRS)}}_{EFFCH} \times \underbrace{\sqrt{\frac{D_I^t(y^{t+1}, x^{t+1}, z^{t+1}|CRS)}{D_I^{t+1}(y^{t+1}, x^{t+1}, z^{t+1}|CRS)} \frac{D_I^t(y^t, x^t, z^t|CRS)}{D_I^{t+1}(y^t, x^t, z^t|CRS)}}}_{TECH} \tag{7.2}$$

From (7.2), we note that the MPI is, thus, defined as the product of efficiency change (EFFCH), which is how much closer a bank gets to the *efficient frontier* (*catching-up effect* or *falling behind*), and technical change (TECH), which is how much the benchmark production frontier shifts at each bank's observed input mix (*technical progress* or *regress*). A MPI > 1 (<1) implies total factor productivity growth (regress), and similar interpretation holds for technical efficiency change and technical change.

As described in (7.2), in order to calculate the MPI for the bank 'o', four distance functions, $D_I^t(y^t, x^t, z^t|CRS)$, $D_I^{t+1}(y^{t+1}, x^{t+1}, z^{t+1}|CRS)$, $D_I^{t+1}(y^t, x^t, z^t|CRS)$ and $D_I^t(y^{t+1}, x^{t+1}, z^{t+1}|CRS)$, are required to compute. These distance functions can be computed by the following four linear programming problems.

$$\left[\hat{D}_I^{t+q}(y_o^{t+q}, x_o^{t+q}, z_o^{t+q})|CRS\right]^{-1} = \widetilde{\theta}_o^{t+q}(y_o^{t+q}, x_o^{t+q}, z_o^{t+q}) = \min_{\lambda_j, s_i^-} 1 - \frac{1}{m}\sum_{i=1}^{m} s_i^- / x_{io}^{t+q}$$

$$\begin{aligned}
&\text{subject to} \\
&\sum_{j=1}^{n} \lambda_j x_{ij}^{t+q} + s_i^- = x_{io}^{t+p} && (i = 1, \ldots, m) \\
&\sum_{j=1}^{n} \lambda_j z_{kj}^{t+q} + s_k^- = z_{ko}^{t+p} && (k = 1, \ldots, l) \\
&\sum_{j=1}^{n} \lambda_j y_{rj}^{t+q} \geq y_{ro}^{t+p} && (r = 1, \ldots, s) \\
&\lambda_j \geq 0 && (j = 1, \ldots, n) \\
&s_i^-, s_k^- \geq 0
\end{aligned} \tag{7.3}$$

Where

$(p,q) = (0,0)$ for solving for $[D_I^t(y^t, x^t, z^t|CRS)]^{-1}$;
$(p,q) = (1,1)$ for solving for $[D_I^{t+1}(y^{t+1}, x^{t+1}, z^{t+1}|CRS)]^{-1}$;
$(p,q) = (0,1)$ for solving for $[D_I^{t+1}(y^t, x^t, z^t|CRS)]^{-1}$; and
$(p,q) = (1,0)$ for solving for $[D_I^t(y^{t+1}, x^{t+1}, z^{t+1}|CRS)]^{-1}$.

Note here that we consider the estimation of non-radial MPI in terms of distance functions using CRS assumption. The issue of whether to use CRS or variable returns to scale (VRS) assumption to estimate MPI is widely discussed. Färe et al. (1994a) proposed an 'enhanced decomposition', which takes the efficiency change component calculated relative to the CRS technology and further decomposed into a 'pure technical efficiency change' component (calculated relative to the VRS technology) and a residual 'scale efficiency' component, which captures changes in the deviation between the VRS and CRS technologies. The decomposition by Färe et al. (1994a) has been criticised by Ray and Desli (1997) by contending that there may be confusion in the simultaneous use of CRS and VRS technologies within the same decomposition of the MPI. Since then there have been a host of proposed alternate decompositions of the MPI under VRS assumption, including Ray and Desli (1997), Simar and Wilson (1998), Grifell-Tatjé and Lovell (1999) and Balk (2001). These alternative ways to decompose the MPI may lead to different conclusions about the sources of productivity change in an empirical application. As pointed out by Grifell-Tatjé and Lovell (1995), a MPI may not be a correct measure of TFP changes when VRS are assumed for the technology. Coelli and Rao (2005) state that it is important that CRS be imposed upon any technology that is used to estimate distance functions for the calculation of a MPI applicable to both firm-level and aggregate data; otherwise, the resulting measures may not properly reflect the TFP gains or losses resulting from scale economies. In order to avoid this controversy, the CRS assumption is maintained in the present study.

7.4 Database, Input–Output Variables and Empirical Setting for TFP Measurement

Consistent with most of the recent literature on banking efficiency, we follow the intermediation approach (Sealey and Lindley 1977) and employ a four-input, three-output specification. The input variables used for computing MPI are physical capital, labour, loanable funds and equity, which are proxied by fixed assets, staff, deposits plus borrowings and capital plus reserves and surpluses, respectively. On commenting the inclusion of equity (so-called financial capital) in the input vector, Berger and Mester (1997) stated "A bank's insolvency risk depends on its equity (financial capital) available to absorb portfolio losses, as well as on the portfolio risk themselves. Insolvency risk affects bank costs and profits via risk premium the bank has to pay for uninsured debt and through the intensity of risk management activities the bank undertakes". Maudos et al. (2002), Ram Mohan and Ray (2004b), Das et al. (2005) and Koutsomanoli-Filippaki et al. (2009b) have included the equity variable as one of the inputs while estimating the efficiency performance of banks. Compared with the other three inputs, the level of equity is difficult to alter especially in the short run. For this reason, we treat equity as a non-discretionary (or exogenously fixed) input.

The three outputs are advances, investments and non-interest income. The inclusion of 'non-interest income' along with the advances and investments as the earning assets enables us to capture the recent changes in the production of services as Indian banks are increasingly engaging in nontraditional banking activities. As pointed out by Siems and Clark (1997), the failure to incorporate these types of activities may seriously understate bank output, and this is likely to have statistical and economic effects on estimated efficiency. Some notable banking efficiency analyses that include 'non-interest income' as an output variable are Isik and Hassan (2002a), Drake and Hall (2003), Sufian (2006), Sufian and Majid (2007) and Hahn (2007), among others. In Indian context, Gulati and Kumar (2011) found that the exclusion of 'non-interest income' as a proxy for nontraditional activities causes misspecification of banks' output and distorts the efficiency estimates.

The required data for public, private and foreign banks have been culled out from the various issues of 'Statistical Tables Relating to Banks in India', an annual publication of Reserve Bank of India. All data except staff were deflated by the implicit GDP deflator with 1993–1994 as the base year. Following Barman (2007) and Roland (2008), we bifurcated the entire study period (1992–1993 to 2007–2008) into distinct subperiods: (i) first phase of banking reforms (1992–1993 to 1998–1999) and (ii) second phase of banking reforms (1999–2000 to 2007–2008). To reduce the effects of random noise due to measurement error in the inputs and outputs, we followed Denizer et al. (2007) and Kumar and Gulati (2009b) and normalised all the input and output variables by dividing them by the number of branches of individual banks for the given year.

The number of banks ranges from 73 to 99 in different years of the periods from 1992–1993 to 2007–2008. For obtaining more reliable efficiency estimates, we removed the banks that have been identified as outliers in accordance of the procedure suggested by Banker and Gifford (1988). The first step in the Banker and Gifford method identifies the outliers. The outliers are those observations whose super-efficiency score exceeds a pre-specified screen level. In the second step, the observations identified as outliers are removed, and a conventional DEA model is estimated with the remaining observations. This study adopts the Andersen and Petersen's (1993) super-efficiency model to identify outliers in the data rather than the ranking the efficient banks. Following Avkiran (2006), any bank having super-efficiency score above value of 2 has been considered as an outlier in the sample and has been dropped from the sample. In order to avoid potential biases due to unbalanced panel data, MPI computations were performed separately for each 2-year sequential period using in each case a balanced panel of banks.

7.5 Empirical Results

7.5.1 Level of Technical Efficiency

Since an input distance function is reciprocally associated with the input-oriented Farrell's (1957) measure of technical efficiency, we begin our analysis with a discussion of technical efficiency estimates. Table 7.2 displays the annual means of the technical efficiency under CRS technology for the Indian banking industry and its distinct ownership groups over the study period. We note that the grand average of TE measure over the banks and time is 81.2 %, suggesting that average technical inefficiencies (i.e. average dispersion of banks from the best practice banks) are 18.8 %. This figure of technical inefficiency suggests that if Indian banks were technically efficient, they would use about 20 % less resources to produce the same amount of outputs during this period. In addition, no statistically significant change in average technical efficiency has been observed between the distinct subperiods.

We further note that foreign banks are 14.2 % more technically efficient than private banks and outperformed public sector banks by a margin of 8.7 %. The results of the Kruskal–Wallis test confirm that efficiency differences across

Table 7.2 Year-wise estimates of mean technical efficiency scores for Indian banking industry and its distinct segments

Year	Public	Private	Foreign	All banks
Panel A: Year-wise mean TE scores				
1993–1994	0.733	0.767	0.940	0.809
1994–1995	0.719	0.763	0.936	0.801
1995–1996	0.787	0.705	0.890	0.796
1996–1997	0.854	0.756	0.850	0.817
1997–1998	0.876	0.811	0.892	0.859
1998–1999	0.760	0.736	0.870	0.794
1999–2000	0.797	0.767	0.830	0.801
2000–2001	0.747	0.695	0.882	0.785
2001–2002	0.696	0.693	0.839	0.747
2002–2003	0.837	0.802	0.858	0.832
2003–2004	0.844	0.799	0.939	0.861
2004–2005	0.825	0.721	0.929	0.824
2005–2006	0.834	0.745	0.862	0.813
2006–2007	0.869	0.770	0.884	0.842
2007–2008	0.821	0.651	0.904	0.798
Panel B: Grand mean of TE scores				
First subperiod	0.788	0.756	0.896	0.813
Second subperiod	0.808	0.738	0.881	0.811
Entire period	0.800	0.745	0.887	0.812

Source: Authors' calculations

ownership groups are statistically significant.[3] On the whole, this also implies that foreign banks fared better than domestic banks. Thus, the empirical evidence is in favour of the presence of *global advantage hypothesis* rather than *home field advantage hypothesis* in Indian banking sector. This finding of ours is consistent with those found by Kraft and Tirtiroglu (1998) for Crotia, Isik and Hassan (2002a) for Turkey, Grigorian and Manole (2006) for 17 European transition countries, Hasan and Marton (2003) for Hungary, Weill (2003) for Czech Republic and Poland, Sturm and Williams (2004) for Australia, Havrylchyk (2006) for Poland, Bhattacharyya et al. (1997b) and Debasish (2006) for India, Sufian (2010) for Malaysia, Akhtar (2010) for Pakistan, Fang et al. (2011) for six transition countries and so on.

It has also been observed that the above ranking of ownership groups in terms of technical efficiency also prevails in the two subperiods. In addition, the average efficiency level for PSBs has increased by 2 % in the second phase of reforms than what has been observed in the first phase. This indicates that the steps undertaken by the policy makers to curtail the waste of resources involved in the banking operations seems to be somewhat successful for Indian public sector banking segment. The result should not be surprising because at the time of introduction of second phase of banking reforms, the PSBs had almost fully adjusted to liberalisation, enhanced competition and new prudential regulations of the banking sector. On the other hand, a decline in average efficiency levels has been observed for domestic private and foreign banks in the second phase of reforms relative to the levels that have attained in the first phase.

7.5.2 TFP Growth in Indian Banking Industry

Table 7.3 reports the estimated yearly indices of EFFCH, TECH and TFPCH for the sample years and the geometric means of these indices for the entire study period as well as for the two subperiods. As can be seen from the table, during the sample years, the TFPCH index attained a value above unity in nine instances, exhibiting a productivity gain, and a value below unity in six instances, indicating a productivity regress. Thus, the productivity growth in Indian banking industry showed some volatility which may be due to the changes in macroeconomic environment of Indian economy. Nonetheless, the banking industry in India registered a modest productivity growth at an average annual growth rate of 1.3 % over the entire study period. As the table displays, the observed productivity growth seems to have been brought about by technological change, which has been growing modestly (1.2 % per annum). Further, the technical efficiency change has been observed to be relatively flat over the study period.

[3] Results of the Kruskal–Wallis test are omitted for the sake of brevity. However, full results are available upon request to the authors.

Table 7.3 Year-wise indices of TFPCH, EFFCH and TECH for Indian banking industry

		Indices		
Year ↓	No. of banks	EFFCH	TECH	TFPCH
Panel A: Year-wise geometric means				
1993–1994	73	1.011	0.933	0.944
1994–1995	73	0.994	0.976	0.970
1995–1996	75	0.996	0.923	0.919
1996–1997	90	1.059	1.001	1.060
1997–1998	98	1.079	0.942	1.016
1998–1999	98	0.917	1.140	1.046
1999–2000	99	1.009	1.082	1.091
2000–2001	97	0.955	1.117	1.066
2001–2002	90	0.955	1.133	1.081
2002–2003	86	1.120	0.913	1.023
2003–2004	87	1.030	1.015	1.046
2004–2005	82	0.946	1.023	0.968
2005–2006	82	0.985	0.977	0.962
2006–2007	78	1.032	0.954	0.985
2007–2008	77	0.936	1.101	1.031
Panel B: Geometric means				
First subperiod		1.008	0.983	0.991
Second subperiod		0.995	1.032	1.027
Entire period		1.001	1.012	1.013

Source: Authors' calculations

Notes: (i) *EFFCH, TECH* and *TFPCH* refer to efficiency change, technological change and total factor productivity change, respectively, and (ii) the financial year 1992–1993 is taken as a base year

Our estimate of TFP growth is lower than those provided by the majority of the studies on productivity growth of Indian banking industry (see Table 7.1 for the perusal of TFP estimates by different studies). However, we assert that our estimates are more robust than that reported in Table 7.1 because (i) the MPI model used in this study deals directly with the input slacks, (ii) the dataset used is more informative due to its unbalanced nature, and (iii) outliers distorting the TFP estimates have been removed from the data set in the final run. Now, we move towards a comparative analysis of our TFP estimates with that obtained for other developing countries. This would help us to gauge the efficacy of India's approach of liberalising and deregulating the banking sector. Table 7.4 facilitates this sort of comparison. From the table, we note that the banking industries of other developing countries experienced higher productivity growth during the post-liberalisation period than what has been observed for Indian banking industry. We are aware that such a cross-country comparisons of productivity are not much valuable in terms of providing future directions for banking reforms, yet our comparative analysis emanates a clear message that more policy actions are needed to enhance the productivity growth in Indian banking industry.

Turning to the subperiod analysis, we note that technological regress has been the key factor responsible for observed productivity regress in the first phase of

Table 7.4 Average annual TFP growth rates in selected developing countries

Author(s) (year)	Country	Sample period	Average annual TFP growth rate in the post-deregulation period (%)
Leightner and Lovell (1998)	Thailand	1989–1994	9
Isik and Hassan (2003a)	Turkey	1981–1990	7.1
Howcroft and Ataullah (2006)	Pakistan	1992–1998	3.7 (loan-based model) 2.9 (income-based model)
Seelanatha (2007)	Sri Lanka	1989–2004	3.4
Heffernan and Fu (2009)	China	2000–2007	4.0 (DEA-based MPI) 2.8 (SFA-based divisia)
Fethi et al. (2011)	Egypt	1985–2002	7.9
Majid et al. (2011)	Malaysia	1996–2002	2.4
Deng et al. (2011)	Malaysia	2001–2008	1.4
Chang et al. (2012)	China	2002–2009	3.85

Source: Authors' compilation

reforms. However, the deepening of the reforms process yielded some positive results in terms of productivity growth since a striking rebound has taken place in the second subperiod when productivity grew at the rate of 2.7 % per annum against the background of a productivity regress in the first phase. In addition, the observed U-turn in the productivity behaviour of Indian banks during the latter phase of deregulation was due to a strong 'frontier-shift' effect. The most depressing development that has emerged in this phase was that despite the progress of technology at a decent rate of 3.2 % per annum, the TFP of Indian banking industry did not grew at a considerable pace owing to adverse technical efficiency change. In fact, the installed technology in the Indian banks was not utilised fully by their employees to the extent necessary to start the process of catching-up among banks.

Our results convey that Indian banks had an initial period of adjustment to the new operational environment characterised with the introduction of prudential policies and the relaxed entry norms, during which they concentrated into improving their efficiency within the more traditional technological framework. Only after a few years of initial adjustments, into the later years of the reforms, technological change really starts to take-off, pushing the frontier inwards; a higher frontier is more difficult to reach, which explains no efficiency change; the sector overall experienced a positive TFP changes of 1.3 % per annum. It is significant to note that during the second phase of reforms, there has been a strategic push towards technology adoption in Indian banking industry. Both public and private banks have realised that technology alone could enable them to trim costs, achieve efficiency and survive in a highly competitive environment. Consequently, they invested heavily in the IT with the objective to provide state-of-the-art technology-based services (like ATMs, net banking, mobile banking, Electronic Funds Transfer at Point of Sale terminals (EFTPOS), debit cards, and telephone banking) to their customers.

7.5.3 TFP Growth Across Distinct Ownership Groups

Now we investigate the magnitude and sources of TFP changes within each ownership group. Table 7.5 presents the relevant results. We note that there are differences in the productivity performance of banks arising from different ownership status. Over the entire sample period, PSBs experienced productivity growth at an annual rate of 2.7 %, on average. Private banks came next with an annual average growth rate of 0.8 %, and foreign banks were the slowest in productivity growth with an annual average rate of 0.5 %. Thus, PSBs seem to be outperformed on the productivity front relative to their counterparts. Further, the main contributor to the observed productivity growth in all the ownership groups is the technological progress. The analysis of subperiods reveals a U-turn in the productivity behaviour of private and foreign banks during the second phase of reforms. In addition, the main cause of observed productivity gains was considerable technological progress, which even offset the impact of negative catching-up effect. On the other hand, an acceleration in productivity growth has been noted in the group of PSBs during the second phase of reforms, which occurred due to improvement in technical efficiency (0.8 % per annum) coexisting with almost constant rate of technological progress (2.1 % per annum).

Any analysis of productivity growth in Indian banking industry seems incomplete if the developments in productivity of *de novo* private banks are not detailed. This is because the entry of these banks completely changed the landscape of Indian banking industry by infusing greater price and non-price competition, a thing which was completely missing in the pre-reforms years. In the post-reforms years, PSBs and old private banks got fierce competition from these banks and are faced with a fall in their market shares. In addition, *de novo* private banks brought in with state-of-the art banking technologies, adequate capital resources, well-trained and professional manpower and lean organisational system. We report the estimates of EFFCH, TECH and TFPCH for two groups of domestic private banking segment in Table 7.6. The *de novo* private banks made more steady progress in productivity, on average by 5.9 % per year, which was entirely contributed by sweeping technological advances. On the other hand, old private banks experienced a flat TFP growth. Thus, the poor productivity performance of the old private banks can be held responsible for the very moderate productivity growth in the domestic private banking segment. Another interesting finding is that the catching-up effect was missing in both new and old private banks since the installed technology was not utilised fully by their employees to the extent necessary to break through.

The aforementioned analysis facilitates that the ranking of ownership groups in Indian banking industry is sensitive to the level of aggregation at which the researcher is explaining the outcomes of his empirical investigation. In particular, if the level of aggregation is high and only three ownership groups are being considered, then the ranking in terms of productivity performance is that productivity increases in PSBs were the fastest (2.7 % per annum), followed by private banks (0.8 % per annum) and foreign banks (0.5 % per annum). However, when the

Table 7.5 TFP change and its components in distinct ownership groups

Ownership type	Public sector banks				Private banks				Foreign banks			
Year	No. of banks	EFFCH	TECH	TFPCH	No. of banks	EFFCH	TECH	TFPCH	No. of banks	EFFCH	TECH	TFPCH
Panel A: Year-wise geometric means												
1993–1994	27	0.940	1.000	0.939	23	1.086	0.904	0.982	23	1.026	0.888	0.912
1994–1995	27	0.981	1.012	0.993	23	1.005	1.003	1.008	23	0.999	0.910	0.909
1995–1996	27	1.106	0.879	0.972	23	0.909	0.896	0.814	25	0.967	0.999	0.967
1996–1997	27	1.101	1.006	1.108	33	1.077	0.991	1.067	30	1.004	1.008	1.012
1997–1998	27	1.037	0.983	1.019	34	1.095	1.000	1.095	37	1.096	0.864	0.947
1998–1999	27	0.858	1.298	1.114	33	0.901	1.156	1.041	38	0.977	1.028	1.005
1999–2000	27	1.046	1.076	1.126	32	1.029	1.100	1.131	40	0.968	1.072	1.038
2000–2001	27	0.941	1.149	1.082	31	0.893	1.153	1.030	39	1.016	1.067	1.084
2001–2002	27	0.930	1.160	1.079	30	0.988	1.125	1.111	33	0.945	1.118	1.056
2002–2003	27	1.209	0.881	1.065	29	1.176	0.875	1.028	30	0.998	0.983	0.981
2003–2004	27	1.013	1.010	1.023	30	0.990	1.020	1.010	30	1.089	1.015	1.105
2004–2005	27	0.971	0.996	0.968	28	0.897	1.031	0.925	27	0.974	1.043	1.015
2005–2006	27	1.010	0.898	0.907	28	1.036	0.965	0.999	27	0.913	1.076	0.982
2006–2007	27	1.046	0.949	0.993	25	1.017	0.972	0.988	26	1.033	0.943	0.974
2007–2008	28	0.935	1.116	1.043	23	0.843	1.104	0.931	26	1.029	1.082	1.114
Panel B: Geometric mean												
First subperiod		1.000	1.022	1.022		1.009	0.988	0.997		1.011	0.947	0.958
Second subperiod		1.008	1.021	1.030		0.981	1.035	1.015		0.995	1.043	1.038
Entire period		1.005	1.022	1.027		0.992	1.016	1.008		1.001	1.004	1.005

Source: Authors' calculations

Notes: (i) *EFFCH, TECH* and *TFPCH* refer to efficiency change, technological change and total factor productivity change, respectively, and (ii) the financial year 1992–1993 is taken as a base year

Table 7.6 TFP change and its components in old and new private banks

Bank groups→	Old private banks			New private banks		
Year↓	EFFCH	TECH	TFPCH	EFFCH	TECH	TFPCH
Panel A: Year-wise geometric means						
1993–1994	1.086	0.904	0.982	–	–	–
1994–1995	1.005	1.003	1.008	–	–	–
1995–1996	0.909	0.896	0.814	–	–	–
1996–1997	1.086	0.986	1.071	1.053	1.003	1.056
1997–1998	1.083	0.956	1.035	1.129	1.134	1.280
1998–1999	0.884	1.144	1.012	0.946	1.186	1.121
1999–2000	1.024	1.053	1.079	1.043	1.251	1.306
2000–2001	0.932	1.100	1.025	0.790	1.323	1.045
2001–2002	0.991	1.124	1.113	0.980	1.128	1.105
2002–2003	1.165	0.888	1.034	1.204	0.841	1.013
2003–2004	0.977	1.026	1.003	1.021	1.007	1.028
2004–2005	0.912	1.040	0.948	0.856	1.004	0.860
2005–2006	1.006	0.954	0.959	1.129	0.999	1.128
2006–2007	1.005	0.973	0.977	1.050	0.969	1.017
2007–2008	0.874	1.111	0.972	0.776	1.087	0.843
Panel B: Geometric mean						
First subperiod	1.005	0.978	0.983	–	–	–
Second subperiod	0.984	1.027	1.011			
Entire period	0.993	1.007	1.000	0.989	1.070	1.059

Source: Authors' calculations

Notes: (i) *EFFCH, TECH* and *TFPCH* refer to efficiency change, technological change and total factor productivity change, respectively, and (ii) the financial year 1992–1993 is taken as a base year

ownership groups are further disaggregated, then the ranking turns out be different and holds as follows: productivity improvements in *de novo* private bankers were the fastest (5.9 % per annum), followed by PSBs (2.7 % per annum), as well as foreign banks (0.5 % per annum) and old private banks (no growth).

7.5.4 TFP Growth in Domestic and Foreign Banks

We next turn to compare the productivity performance of domestic and foreign banks operating in India. Table 7.7 summarises the relevant results. As can be seen from the values in the table, domestic banks experienced productivity growth at the rate of 1.8 % per annum, while foreign banks' productivity grew at a rate of 0.5 % per annum. Thus, domestic banks outperformed foreign banks in terms of TFP growth over the entire study period. Further, the observed productivity growth in both domestic and foreign banks was largely attributable to the technological progress, with domestic banks fared better than foreign banks (1.9 % vs. 0.4 % per annum). The analysis of subperiods reveals that domestic banks experienced

Table 7.7 TFP change and its components in domestic and foreign banks

Bank groups→	Domestic banks			Foreign banks		
Year↓	EFFCH	TECH	TFPCH	EFFCH	TECH	TFPCH
Panel A: Year-wise geometric means						
1993–1994	1.005	0.955	0.959	1.026	0.888	0.912
1994–1995	0.992	1.008	1.000	0.999	0.910	0.909
1995–1996	1.010	0.887	0.896	0.967	0.999	0.967
1996–1997	1.088	0.998	1.085	1.004	1.008	1.012
1997–1998	1.069	0.993	1.061	1.096	0.864	0.947
1998–1999	0.881	1.217	1.073	0.977	1.028	1.005
1999–2000	1.037	1.089	1.129	0.968	1.072	1.038
2000–2001	0.915	1.151	1.054	1.016	1.067	1.084
2001–2002	0.960	1.141	1.096	0.945	1.118	1.056
2002–2003	1.192	0.877	1.046	0.998	0.983	0.981
2003–2004	1.001	1.015	1.016	1.089	1.015	1.105
2004–2005	0.933	1.014	0.946	0.974	1.043	1.015
2005–2006	1.023	0.932	0.953	0.913	1.076	0.982
2006–2007	1.032	0.960	0.991	1.033	0.943	0.974
2007–2008	0.892	1.110	0.991	1.029	1.082	1.114
Panel B: Geometric mean						
First subperiod	1.005	1.005	1.010	1.011	0.947	0.958
Second subperiod	0.995	1.028	1.023	0.995	1.043	1.038
Entire period	0.999	1.019	1.018	1.001	1.004	1.005

Source: Authors' calculations

Notes: (i) *EFFCH, TECH* and *TFPCH* refer to efficiency change, technological change and total factor productivity change, respectively, and (ii) the financial year 1992–1993 is taken as a base year

productivity gains in both the subperiods, yet the pace of productivity growth was higher in second phase of reforms relative to first one (2.3 % vs. 1 % per annum). However, foreign banks enjoyed productivity gains only during the second subperiod. Further, the improvement in technological progress contributed to TFP growth of domestic and foreign banks, with foreign banks exhibited better productivity performance than their domestic counterparts during the second phase of reforms relative to what has been observed in first phase. Despite the increase in TECH during the latter phase, the decline in the foreign banks' TECH during the earlier years resulted a gradual increase during the entire study period.

On explaining the raison d'être of the poor performance of foreign banks on the productivity front, Sensarma (2006) noted that these banks incurred a lot of expenses in acquiring top-end customers and new technology, and also the pressure on foreign banks to contain costs is less as compared to other bank groups. Thus, their high cost practices adversely affected their productivity. In addition, foreign banks do not understand local markets as well as the domestic banks do, which impairs their productivity. Small and medium entrepreneurs and often even Indian corporate entities are loathe to approaching foreign banks since they are given more flexibilities by domestic banks and also feel more comfortable in banking with the domestic banks. The sluggish growth performance of foreign banks might also be due to the fact that they are already operating at a high level of technical efficiency and thus leaving a little scope for the further improvement. Thus, it appears that the post-liberalisation period has not been favourable to the foreign banks. However, the better performance of domestic banks is due to the fact that these banks incurred much of expenditure to undertake not only the innovation to accommodate e-banking operations but also build wide network of on-site and off-site ATMs. In particular, number of ATMs for domestic (foreign) banks increased from 11,745 (797) in 2004–2005 to 42,497 (1,054) in 2008–2009. Therefore, following Dacanay III (2007b) and Sensarma (2006), we conclude that foreign banks are not necessarily always better in terms of technology compared to domestic banks.

All in all, the results suggest that the deregulatory policies have been found to be effective in bringing improvements in the productivity performance of banks across distinct ownership groups, especially PSBs. Further, the majority of gains in productivity are in the second phase of reforms. A few possible reasons of the observed productivity gains in PSBs include the efforts of PSBs to rationalise the input usage particularly of the labour input,[4] to introduce new technology-based products and services, to implement a stricter monitoring and control mechanism on lending and to improve management and corporate governance. Concomitantly, the successful introduction of *de novo* private and foreign banks has induced the greater competition to PSBs. Despite strong growth in the balance sheets of the *de novo* private banks, the PSBs have exhibited remarkable stability. Although there have been a few instances of weaknesses in a few *de novo* private banks, pre-emptive measures in the form of the mergers of such banks with the stronger banks or the infusion of new capital and change in ownership, on a voluntary or involuntary basis, have contributed to the strength of the PSBs, engendered confidence in the depositors and enabled the maintenance of overall financial stability. This finding of our study is completely in consonance with those reported by Ram Mohan and Ray (2004a), Rezvanian et al. (2008), Reserve Bank of India (2008c) and Zhao et al. (2008).

Although the above analysis portrays a strict ranking of ownership groups with regard to TFP growth at a first glance, the application of the Kruskal–Wallis test on yearly basis confirms that only in four years of the study period, productivity growth rates across ownership types have been established as statistically significant.[5] This serve as a pointer towards the fact that there seems to be a convergence in the productivity levels of banks belonging to different ownership groups.

---

[4] In November 1999, Voluntary Retirement Scheme (VRS) in Public Sector Banks was formally taken up by the Government of India with a view to right size the over staffed banks. PSBs incurred large expenditures under voluntary premature retirement of nearly 12% of their staff strength as a concrete effort to minimise the critical waste of labour inputs (Acharya and Mohan 2010).

[5] Results of Kruskal–Wallis test are omitted for the sake of brevity. However, full results are available upon request to the authors.

7.5.5 TFP Growth Across Distinct Size Classes

An examination of TFP growth differentials across different size classes carries significant importance because of the fact that it is often put forward that enhanced competition triggered by the deregulation and liberalisation in the banking sector affects small, medium and large banks asymmetrically, given that the markets in which small banks operate and the characteristics of customers they serve are considerably different from those of medium and large banks. For example, relative to medium and large banks, small and micro banks may have (a) less access to the expanded financial opportunities that globalisation and deregulation have created and (b) less access to the financial resources necessary to take full advantage of technological advances (Mehdian et al. 2007). In the post-deregulation period, a huge amount of money has been invested by Indian banks either in distribution channels or in computer and software systems. As a result, Indian banks could be able to produce new services and increase the quality of their productive and organisational systems, with a corresponding effect on productivity and production costs. These changes in the Indian banking industry may have offered greater expanded opportunities to medium and large banks than for small and micro banks. Against this background, we expect larger productivity gains for medium and large banks than for small and micro banks.

We followed Tabak and Tecles (2010) to categorise the Indian banks into four distinct size categories based on their total assets: (i) micro banks (total assets less than Q_1), (ii) small banks (total assets lie between Q_1 and median), (iii) medium banks (total assets lie between median and Q_3) and (iv) large banks (total assets greater than Q_3). Table 7.8 provides the year-wise estimates of EFFCH, TECH and TFPCH indices for distinct size classes. We note that medium banks experienced the highest productivity growth (2.5 % per annum), followed by large banks (2 % per annum), small banks (0.4 % per annum) and micro banks (0.3 % per annum). In case of medium banks, both efficiency improvement and technical progress components have observed a surge during the post-reforms years, while the latter has turned out to be the more dominant source of TFP growth. However, in case of large banks, technical efficiency followed a downtrend, and the progress in technology was even more impressive than medium banks. The results thus clearly indicate that phenomenon of 'frontier shift' has occurred in the large and medium banks' groups. The presence of 'frontier-shift' effect in the medium and large banks is the outcome of heavy investments made by these groups in information and communication technology (ICT) during the post-deregulation years. In addition, the 'frontier-shift' effect was more pronounced in large and medium banks relative to small and micro banks. We further note that technical efficiency fell in small and large banks during the study period, while the same improved slightly in micro and medium banks. The connotation of this finding is that phenomenon of 'catching-up' was completely absent in small and large banks and was present but not very pervasive in micro and medium banks. Thus, the resource utilisation process in micro and medium banks has improved moderately over the deregulation years. On

Table 7.8 TFP change and its components by size categories in Indian banking industry

Size categories→	Micro banks			Small banks			Medium banks			Large banks		
Year↓	EFFCH	TECH	TFPCH	EFFCH	TECH	TFPCH	EFFCH	TECH	TFPCH	EFFCH	TECH	TFPCH
Panel A: Year-wise geometric means												
1993–1994	0.997	0.907	0.905	1.132	0.905	1.024	1.006	0.937	0.942	0.915	0.987	0.904
1994–1995	1.075	0.970	1.043	0.976	0.956	0.932	0.970	0.973	0.943	0.961	1.007	0.968
1995–1996	0.997	0.976	0.973	0.912	0.909	0.830	0.982	0.911	0.895	1.108	0.895	0.992
1996–1997	1.037	0.977	1.013	1.054	1.007	1.062	1.041	1.005	1.047	1.108	1.015	1.125
1997–1998	1.104	0.852	0.941	1.059	0.968	1.025	1.108	0.972	1.078	1.045	0.984	1.028
1998–1999	0.995	0.979	0.974	0.889	1.168	1.038	0.938	1.128	1.058	0.854	1.317	1.125
1999–2000	0.938	1.093	1.026	1.016	1.045	1.062	1.043	1.132	1.180	1.042	1.058	1.102
2000–2001	1.007	1.074	1.081	0.956	1.099	1.051	0.915	1.156	1.058	0.942	1.140	1.075
2001–2002	0.963	1.129	1.087	0.970	1.093	1.059	0.924	1.173	1.084	0.964	1.136	1.095
2002–2003	0.992	1.008	0.999	1.148	0.882	1.013	1.181	0.889	1.050	1.175	0.876	1.029
2003–2004	1.088	0.971	1.056	0.946	1.035	0.978	1.103	1.031	1.138	0.991	1.026	1.017
2004–2005	0.944	1.067	1.008	0.934	1.053	0.984	0.938	0.992	0.930	0.970	0.982	0.953
2005–2006	0.927	1.058	0.981	0.999	0.992	0.991	1.011	0.940	0.949	1.009	0.921	0.929
2006–2007	1.003	0.950	0.953	1.052	0.963	1.013	1.043	0.958	0.999	1.032	0.948	0.979
2007–2008	0.977	1.044	1.020	0.916	1.127	1.032	0.955	1.115	1.065	0.901	1.117	1.006
Panel B: Geometric mean												
First subperiod	1.033	0.942	0.974	1.000	0.982	0.982	1.006	0.985	0.991	0.994	1.027	1.020
Second subperiod	0.981	1.042	1.023	0.991	1.029	1.020	1.009	1.038	1.048	1.000	1.019	1.019
Entire period	1.002	1.001	1.003	0.994	1.010	1.004	1.008	1.017	1.025	0.998	1.022	1.020

Source: Authors' calculations

the whole, medium banks responded more positively to the changes in the landscape of Indian banking industry than micro and small banks.

The subperiod analysis reveals that the behaviour of productivity change in micro, small and medium banks observed a U-turn in the second subperiod relative to the first subperiod (see Panel B of Table 7.8). However, in case of large banks, productivity growth remained more or less invariant in both the subperiods. The figures in the table also reveal that the speed of productivity growth in medium banks during the second subperiod was almost double than what was observed in micro, small and large banks. Further, technological progress was the dominant source of observed U-turn in the TFP growth across all size classes. Moreover, the phenomenon of 'frontier shift' was more pronounced in micro and medium banks during the second subperiod. This is because, in the wake of competition, many micro banks, especially those belonging to foreign and new private banks segments, adopted latest banking technology.

To test whether the observed differences in the productivity growth across distinct size classes are statistically significant or not, we applied a Kruskal–Wallis test. We note that the pairwise differences in annual TFP growth are insignificant. This indicates that no significant differences exist in productivity growth across the banks belonging to distinct size categories. In order to complement our analysis, we also tested the null hypothesis of no difference in productivity performance of micro, small, medium and large banks in each year of the study period. We note that barring a few years, the null hypothesis of no difference in the annual TFP growth of different sized banks is not rejected.[6] All in all, we conclude that the relationship between banks' size and productivity appears in a weak form in Indian banking industry.

7.5.6 *Technological Innovators*

In this subsection, we identify the number of innovator banks in each year of the study period. The innovator banks are those banks that actually shift the *best-practice* production frontier. In order to determine whether a particular bank is an innovator or not, we followed the criteria proposed by Färe et al. (1994b). According to these criteria, the bank 'o' is said to be an innovator if (i) technological change index is greater than 1, (ii) technical efficiency in the period $t + 1$ with respect to the technology of the period t is greater than 1 and (iii) technical efficiency in the period $t + 1$ is equal to 1, i.e.

[6] Results of the Kruskal–Wallis test are omitted for the sake of brevity. However, full results are available upon request to the authors.

Table 7.9 Technological innovators by year and ownership type

Year	Public sector banks	Private banks	Foreign banks	Total
1993–1994	1	1	7	9
1994–1995	1	0	7	8
1995–1996	0	4	8	8
1996–1997	4	5	3	11
1997–1998	4	4	6	14
1998–1999	3	5	4	12
1999–2000	7	7	9	23
2000–2001	3	3	14	20
2001–2002	3	3	11	17
2002–2003	3	0	7	10
2003–2004	2	3	8	13
2004–2005	2	2	14	18
2005–2006	2	2	9	13
2006–2007	0	1	6	7
2007–2008	3	0	8	11

Source: Authors' calculations

$$TECH > 1 \quad \text{(i)}$$
$$\widetilde{\theta}_o^{\,t}(y^{t+1}, x^{t+1}, z^{t+1}) > 1 \quad \text{(ii)}$$
$$\widetilde{\theta}_o^{\,t+1}(y^{t+1}, x^{t+1}, z^{t+1}) = 1 \quad \text{(iii)}.$$

The first condition ensures that the innovator banks exhibit technical advancement; second one implies that these banks after the technical change operate beyond the frontier of the previous period; while the last condition implies that after the technical change they become technically efficient (Galanopoulos et al. 2004). Banks satisfying the aforementioned three conditions can be regarded as having contributed to a shift in the frontier between period t and $t + 1$. Table 7.9 shows the number of banks that emerged as innovators in each year of the study period. We note that there exists a wide variation in the number of innovators in each year, with the year 2006–2007 having only 7 banks and the year 1999–2000 having as many as 23 banks. Further, foreign banks appear as prime innovators in introducing new banking technology in the Indian banking industry. This finding delineates the significant role that foreign ownership plays in the Indian banking industry during the deregulation process.

7.5.7 Factors Affecting TFP Growth

To investigate the factors that affect the productivity growth of Indian banks, we performed a second-stage panel data regression analysis. In the present study, we used two panel data models: fixed-effect (FE) and random-effect (RE) models, on the following model specifications.

$$\begin{aligned}\text{Model 1}: \text{TFPCH/EFFCH/TECH} &= f(\text{NPA, SIZE, OFF\_BALANCE, ROA})\\ \text{Model 2}: \text{TFPCH/EFFCH/TECH} &= f(\text{NPA, SIZE, OFF\_BALANCE, ROA,}\\ &\qquad \text{D\_PUBLIC, D\_PRIVATE})\end{aligned}$$

The description of each of the explanatory variables and the expected sign of their relationship with productivity indices are as follow. The ratio of net non-performing assets to net advances (NPA) is used as a proxy for the asset quality of a bank; the logarithm of total assets (SIZE) captures bank size; the ratio of total non-interest income to total assets (OFF_BALANCE) is used as a proxy for the bank's exposure to off-balance sheet activities; (ROA) is a proxy measure for bank profitability calculated as the ratio of net profit to total assets. The ownership dummies for public and private banks, i.e. D_PUBLIC and D_PRIVATE, are introduced in the regression models to examine the impact of ownership on the productivity levels. We hypothesise that larger profitability (ROA) and exposure to off-balance sheet activities (OFF_BALANCE) have a positive effect, and the poor asset quality (NPA) has a negative effect on the productivity of the Indian banks. However, we are not ascertained about the effect of size and ownership on the productivity levels. Thus, barring the predictors SIZE, D_PUBLIC and D_PRIVATE, all the remaining predictors in the regression model bear a unidirectional relationship with the productivity indices.

The estimated results are reported in Table 7.10. We note that in both the model specifications, i.e. Model 1 (without ownership dummies) and Model 2 (with ownership dummies), Hausman test statistic favours the use of random-effects model. Further, the explanatory power of the models is reasonably high since the values of Wald χ^2 statistic for all the regression equations are statistically significant. The figures in the table reveal that in both the models, OFF_BALANCE is the only variable which has had a significant positive impact on productivity indices. Thus, we can safely infer that the exposure of banks to off-balance sheet activities is the most influential factor affecting the productivity growth of banks operating in India. Besides, the SIZE appears to have negative relation with productivity indices, but the same is significant only for technological change in the Model 1. This indicates that larger banks are not necessarily more involved in innovation activities. As far as the effect of ownership on the productivity growth is concerned, we note that D_PUBLIC and D_PRIVATE variables bear insignificant regression coefficients. Thus, the regression results suggest that ownership effects are not significant in explaining TFP growth variations in Indian banking industry. In a nutshell, we can conclude that (i) the exposure to off-balance activities is the most influential factor explaining the interbank variations in productivity growth and its sources, and (ii) larger banks are not always more productive and embrace technological advances.

Table 7.10 Factors affecting productivity growth and its components

	Model 1 (without ownership dummies)						Model 2 (with ownership dummies)					
Dependent variable→	EFFCH		TECH		TFPCH		EFFCH		TECH		TFPCH	
Model specifications	Fixed effects	Random effects	Fixed effects	Random effects	Fixed effects	Random effects	Fixed effects	Random effects	Fixed effects	Random effects	Fixed effects	Random effects
Panel A: Independent variables												
Constant	0.913*	0.913*	1.090*	1.088*	0.995*	0.994*	0.913*	0.914*	1.094*	1.092*	0.996*	1.004*
	(18.91)	(18.06)	(22.94)	(20.82)	(16.93)	(16.80)	(15.89)	(15.04)	(19.35)	(18.04)	(14.25)	(14.38)
ROA	0.0039	0.0042	−0.0031	−0.0031	0.0027	0.0032	0.0038	0.0039	−0.0031	−0.0032	0.0024	0.0032
	(1.16)	(1.21)	(−0.93)	(−0.94)	(0.65)	(0.75)	(1.11)	(1.14)	(−0.93)	(−0.94)	(0.58)	(0.75)
OFF_BALANCE	0.0101**	0.0103**	0.0161*	0.0161*	0.0274*	0.0281*	0.0095**	0.0097**	0.0162*	0.0162*	0.0266*	0.0279*
	(2.29)	(2.34)	(3.73)	(3.71)	(5.14)	(5.27)	(2.12)	(2.17)	(3.67)	(3.65)	(4.87)	(5.11)
SIZE	0.0051	0.0050	−0.0053***	−0.0054***	−0.00097	−0.0013	0.0056	0.0055	−0.0058	−0.0058	−0.0002	−0.0016
	(1.53)	(1.52)	(−1.65)	(−1.66)	(−0.24)	(−0.33)	(1.22)	(1.19)	(−1.28)	(−1.29)	(−0.03)	(−0.29)
NPA	0.0008	0.0009	−0.0011	−0.001	0.0003	0.0009	0.0008	0.0009	−0.0011	−0.0010	0.00024	0.0014
	(0.91)	(0.98)	(−1.18)	(−1.09)	(0.25)	(0.87)	(0.89)	(0.93)	(−1.18)	(−1.09)	(0.22)	(1.28)
D_PUBLIC							−0.0047	−0.0038	0.0032	0.0032	−0.0068	−0.0004
							(−0.20)	(−0.16)	(0.14)	(0.14)	(−0.24)	(−0.02)
D_PRIVATE							−0.0142	−0.0134	0.0015	0.0013	−0.0234	−0.0203
							(−0.79)	(−0.75)	(0.09)	(0.08)	(−1.07)	(−0.93)

(continued)

Table 7.10 (continued)

	Model 1 (without ownership dummies)						Model 2 (with ownership dummies)					
Dependent variable→	EFFCH		TECH		TFPCH		EFFCH		TECH		TFPCH	
Model specifications	Fixed effects	Random effects	Fixed effects	Random effects	Fixed effects	Random effects	Fixed effects	Random effects	Fixed effects	Random effects	Fixed effects	Random effects
Panel B: Test statistics												
R^2	0.0187	0.0188	0.0240	0.0244	0.0546	0.0562	0.0189	0.0191	0.0240	0.0244	0.0564	0.0585
F-statistic/Wald	2.47^{**}	10.43^{**}	5.32^{*}	21.05^{*}	8.65^{*}	37.73^{*}	1.78	10.97^{***}	3.54^{*}	21.00^{*}	6.01^{*}	41.73^{*}
χ^2 (p-value)	(0.043)	(0.033)	(0.0003)	(0.0003)	(0.000)	(0.000)	(0.101)	(0.089)	(0.0019)	(0.002)	(0.000)	(0.000)
No. of observations	679	679	679	679	679	679	679	679	679	679	679	679
Panel C: Choice of model on the basis of Hausman test												
Chi (χ^2)	−1.40		1.75		5.77		1.42		0.93		9.32	
			(0.782)		(0.217)		(0.964)		(0.988)		(0.156)	
Preferred specification	Not defined		Random effects		Random effects		Random effects		Random effects		Random effects	

Source: Authors' calculations

Notes: (i) In Panel A, the figures in parentheses are the t-values associated with the relative test; (ii) in Panel B and C, the figures in parentheses are the p-values associated with the relative test; and (iii) '***', '**', and '*' indicate significance at 1 %, 5 % and 10 % level of significance, respectively

7.6 Conclusions

By applying a non-radial Malmquist productivity index (MPI) approach, this paper attempts to investigate the pattern and the sources of total factor productivity (TFP) growth across different ownership groups in Indian banking industry during the post-deregulation period spanning from 1992–1993 to 2007–2008. The empirical results of this study highlights that the productivity of Indian banks recorded a moderate improvement at a rate of 1.3 % per annum in the post-deregulation period. Further, larger productivity gains have been observed during the second phase of reforms. This period coincides with the period of the aftermath of South East Asian Financial Crisis of 1997–1998. Significant improvement in the productivity performance of Indian banks explicitly signals that the approach of cautious and gradual banking reforms adopted by Indian policy makers has started bearing fruit in terms of the creation of a productive banking system which is immune to any sort of financial crisis and resilient to both internal and external shocks. Overall, the empirical results are in favour of conventional wisdom that financial deregulation exerts a positive influence on the productivity growth of banks.

Analysis of the sources of productivity growth reveals that the observed productivity growth in Indian banking industry was almost single-handedly generated from technology advances, because technical efficiency change was almost stagnant. This suggests that the reform measures targeting to lead efficiency improvements are likely to have a little impact on the sustainable growth of the banking system relative to the policies that foster the adoption of the latest technologies. In the context of India, the policy interventions aiming to enhance the contribution of efficiency change in TFP are needed. Invariant level of technical efficiency can be the consequence of either structural rigidities that create principal–agent problems or the rigidities associated with labour markets or both. The efforts towards better manpower planning, diversification towards nontraditional activities, improvement in the bank management's flexibility in decision making, creation of a conducive environment for market-driven mergers/amalgamations, high recovery rate of bad loans, etc., can augur higher level of efficiency for domestic banks especially old private and public sector banks.

Another striking finding of this study is that although banks' ownership structure per se does not seem to have an impact on bank productivity, the public sector banks seem to have made more steady progress in productivity relative to old domestic private and foreign banks. The policy implication of this finding is that dominance of public ownership of banks is not a hindrance for the future growth of Indian banking industry. Thus, our research offers a silver lining for other developing and emerging economies that have the dominance of public sector banks and are in the process of carrying out the banking reforms. Further, the productivity of *de novo* private banks grew at the impressive rate of 5.9 % per annum since their entry. In addition, domestic banks outperformed the foreign banks in terms of productivity growth during the entire study period. Our empirical results also reflect the enormous relevance of foreign ownership in Indian banking industry since foreign banks have emerged as the leading technological innovators in the banking system.

Further, the nature of observed productivity surge across distinct ownership groups has been observed to be technology-driven, supporting the hypothesis that a diversity of market participants playing on a level field could act as a stimulant to innovation in response to greater competition. The results also suggest that the banks should focus on extension of nontraditional activities in their drive for achieving higher productivity levels.

Finally, the banking industries of other developing countries seem to have fared better than Indian banking industry during the post-deregulation years, suggesting the need for more efforts by the Indian policy makers for augmenting the productivity growth. The raison d'être for modest productivity growth in Indian banking industry during the post-reforms years is that despite the advances in banking technologies in terms of methodologies, procedures and techniques during the post-reform years, there has been little or slow catching-up or diffusion of new technologies probably due to low skill level of the workforce in the banking industry to adopt these technologies in a more efficient manner. Since the onset of reforms, the RBI has laid an emphasis to invest in new banking technologies (e.g. establishment of ATMs, smart cards, credit cards, phone banking and internet and intranet banking) but without upgrading the commensurate management and organisational skills needed to use these best practice technologies. In the light of this, a big push is needed to develop a strong training system in banks with the objective to upgrade the skills of manpower. This would be helpful not only in using the new technologies and, consequently, in improving the technical efficiency but also in measuring, controlling and monitoring credit risk.

Chapter 8
Major Conclusions, Policy Implications and Some Areas for Future Research

8.1 Introduction

Over the last 20 years, the Indian banking system has experienced a significant transformation from a financially repressed system to a sound and efficient system which has the resilience to withstand the force of a financial crisis. From the early 1970s through the late 1980s, the role of market forces in the Indian banking system was almost missing, and excess regulation in terms of high liquidity requirements and state interventions in allocating credit and determining the prices of financial products resulted in serious financial repression. Realising the presence of the signs of financial repression and to seek an escape from any potential crisis in the banking sector, the Government of India (GOI) embarked on a comprehensive banking reforms plan in 1992 with the objective of creating a more diversified, profitable, efficient and resilient banking system. The reform measures were sequenced to create an enabling environment for banks to overcome the external constraints and operate with greater flexibility. The main agenda of the reform process was to focus on key areas: (i) restructuring of public sector banks (PSBs) by imparting more autonomy in decision making and by infusing fresh capital through recapitalisation and partial privatisation, (ii) creating contestable markets by removing entry barriers for *de novo* domestic private and foreign banks, (iii) improving the regulatory and supervisory framework, and (iv) strengthening the banking system through consolidation. To meet the agenda of banking reforms programme, the policy makers heralded an episode of interest rates deregulation, standardised minimum capital requirements as per Basel norms, prudential norms relating to income recognition, assets classification and provisioning for bad loans and changes in the legal and supervisory environment.

Bearing the aforementioned developments in mind, the main objective of this study is to analyse the impact of financial deregulation and liberalisation measures introduced since 1992 on the efficiency and productivity growth of the Indian banking industry at aggregate and disaggregate levels. To this end, we studied the evolution of cost efficiency and total factor productivity (TFP) growth across distinct

S. Kumar and R. Gulati, *Deregulation and Efficiency of Indian Banks*, India Studies in Business and Economics, DOI 10.1007/978-81-322-1545-5_8, © Springer India 2014

ownership groups and size classes over the period spanning from 1992–1993 to 2007–2008. We used an input–output specification which incorporates 'equity' as a quasi-fixed input. Our input–output specification is broadly consistent with popularly used intermediation approach. We employed Data Envelopment Analysis (DEA) models to estimate the cost efficiency and its component measures for Indian banks. Moreover, DEA-based non-radial Malmquist productivity index (MPI) approach has been used to compute the yearly indices of TFP growth, technical efficiency change and technical change.

8.2 Major Conclusions

The main inferences that have been drawn from the empirical results can be summarised as follows. In order to reach at the best-specification of inputs and outputs, we made a comparison of the estimates of cost, technical and allocative efficiencies with and without the non-interest income as a proxy for non-traditional activities in the output vector. Our results show that the omission of non-interest income from the list of banks' outputs significantly understated the cost, technical and allocative efficiencies of the Indian banking industry. Further, the exclusion of these activities in the output specification has significantly affected the ranking of the individual banks and ownership groups in each year of the study period. In particular, we note that the PSBs were more efficient than the private and foreign banks if non-interest income as a proxy for non-traditional activities was not included in the output vector. However, when this proxy accounted for in the output specification, the foreign banks turned to be more efficient than their counterparts. Thus, the inclusion of a proxy for non-traditional activities has not only improved the efficiency level of foreign banks to a large extent but also changed their relative position in the groups' ranking. Therefore, we can safely infer on the basis of empirical findings that non-traditional activities are totally relevant in an analysis of the efficiency of Indian banks, and a proxy for these activities should be included as one of the outputs in the studies on bank efficiency, particularly aiming at the comparison of the performance among distinct ownership type institutions. Overall, the results of this study reinforced the prevailing view in the extant literature that the exclusion of non-traditional activities causes misspecification of banks' output and may distort the efficiency estimates, and therefore, a better-specification must include a proxy for non-traditional activities.

The analysis of evolution of cost efficiency in Indian banking industry shows that typical bank operating in Indian banking industry, on average, has exhibited the degree of cost inefficiency in tune of 17.8% in each year of the study period. The observed level of X-inefficiency in Indian banking industry is slightly lower than that of the world's average of 27% cited in the extensive survey of Berger and Humphrey (1997). Further, the main source of observed cost inefficiency was allocative in nature rather than technical, indicating that Indian banks were doing a better job technically rather than allocatively. In addition, the observed technical inefficiency in the Indian banking system was primarily due to managerial underperformance in controlling the waste of inputs in the production process rather than failure to operate at optimum scale size. Our results further suggest that the deepening of the reforms process has had a positive impact on the cost efficiency of Indian banks. The analysis of growth rates revealed that that cost efficiency of Indian banks grew at a very moderate rate of 0.127% per annum over the sample years, and its trend was positive in both the subperiods. The moderate rate of cost efficiency was mainly due to negative growth in allocative efficiency since technical efficiency followed an uptrend. The observed negative growth of allocative efficiency may be because of high fluctuations and instability in factor prices, idle capacity and staff redundancies.

The empirical findings on the basis of cost efficiency of distinct ownership groups indicate that PSBs were more cost efficient along with the foreign banks than private banks. Further, the study points out that cost efficiency of PSBs has observed an improvement (though at a moderate rate) during the entire study period, and most of the observed efficiency gains have emanated after few years of launching the reforms process, i.e. from 1998 to 1999 onwards. This improvement in cost efficiency of PSBs was mainly attributed to technical efficiency, since the managers of PSBs operate relatively not efficient with respect to the optimal combination of inputs given their prices and technology. The results suggest that the PSBs have benefited more significantly from the reform process than other banks – something which might be expected given that government policy had a particular focus on the efficiency improvement of these banks.

The study also finds that cost efficiency of private banks grew at a modest rate, and intensification of reforms failed to impart to a positive impact on the cost efficiency performance of these banks. Further, new private banks outperformed old private banks in the post-reforms years since these banks have successfully managed their business at lower operating costs and did not carry any baggage from the past. During the post-reforms period, the cost efficiency performance of old private banks was lackadaisical, resulting in a pulling down of the overall performance of the private banking segment below the level that has been observed by public and foreign banks. Regarding the foreign banks, it has been observed that cost efficiency of these banks exhibited a negative trend during the entire study period and distinct subperiods. The empirical results also reveal that (i) in the majority of years, foreign banks were dominating in defining the grand technological frontier of the Indian banking system, and (ii) foreign banks were more cost efficient than their domestic counterparts. This finding suggests that foreign banks in the Indian banking system have succeeded in using their superior technology and managerial expertise and experience, and this in turn has offset potential cross-border disadvantages, e.g. lack of knowledge about the local market and barriers of culture and regulations. Thus, the empirical evidence is in favour of the prevalence of the *global advantage hypothesis* in Indian banking industry.

The analysis of returns-to-scale provides that most of Indian banks were facing substantial scale problems, especially due to increasing returns-to-scale. This suggests that substantial efficiency gains could be obtained by altering the scale via either internal growth or consolidation in the sector. An analysis of the relationship between bank size and efficiency exhibits that medium banks were more cost efficient than small, followed by large and micro banks. This indicates that recent advances in technology, increased competition and deregulation have reduced the minimum efficient scale of technology, thereby making medium-sized banks more efficient.

In this study, we also explored the issue of what determine the interbank variations in bank efficiency. In particular, the impact of environmental factors like ownership status, size, profitability and asset quality has been examined on the efficiency levels of banks. Our results show that private banks were less cost efficient than public and foreign banks. In addition, the relationship between efficiency and profitability has been observed to be positive. Another important result is that the bad luck or bad management hypothesis instead of the skimping hypothesis is prevalent in the Indian banking industry. Moreover, we find that size matters in explaining the interbank variations in cost efficiency. Furthermore, the banks with extensive exposure to off-balance sheet activities are more efficient.

The analysis of total factor productivity (TFP) growth in Indian banking industry reveals that the productivity performance of Indian banks recorded a moderate improvement after the introduction of deregulatory policies, whereas their technical efficiency has not improved as expected. In general, the productivity growth in Indian banking industry was mainly attributable to the technological progress rather than the improvement in efficiency. Our results suggest that innovation in banking technology made a greater contribution in achieving the productivity growth rate of 1.3% per annum during the post-deregulation period. Thus, technical progress was the key driver of productivity growth in Indian banking industry. Further, deepening of the reforms process yielded positive results in terms of productivity growth. After productivity regress in the first phase of liberalisation and deregulation, a striking rebound has taken place in the second subperiod, when productivity grew at the rate of 2.7% per annum in the second phase. Further, the observed U-turn in the productivity behaviour of Indian banks during the latter phase of deregulation was due to a strong ‘frontier-shift’ effect. The most depressing development that has emerged in this phase was that the gains from technical change were reduced by adverse technical efficiency change. In fact, the installed technology in the Indian banks was not utilised fully by their staff to the extent necessary to start the process of catching-up among banks.

Another significant finding of our analysis is that the PSBs made steadier progress in productivity relative to domestic private and foreign banks. In particular, productivity growth within PSBs was the fastest (2.7% per annum), followed by private banks (0.8% per annum) and foreign banks (0.5% per annum). Further, the nature of the observed productivity surge across these ownership groups was technology driven, supporting the hypothesis that a diversity of market participants playing on a level field could act as a stimulant to innovation in response to greater competition. Further, PSBs had a significantly higher average productivity growth in the first phase of reforms, but foreign banks were ranked the best in the second phase. The reshuffle of ranking between public and foreign banks can be explained as the result of increased competition to create a niche in the market place. Moreover, in the second phase of reforms, the group of PSBs was the only one that succeeded in enhancing efficiency, but all categories of banks experienced technological progress. There were sweeping technological advances in foreign banks.

The study also finds that domestic banks outperformed the foreign banks in terms of productivity growth during the entire study period. However, there was a reshuffling in the ranking between domestic and foreign banks during the second phase. Foreign banks emerged as the best performer in terms of productivity growth due to their exceptional performance in introducing technical innovations. In addition, foreign banks emerged as the leading innovators in the Indian banking industry. This reflects the enormous relevance of foreign ownership in Indian banking industry.

Regarding the temporal behaviour of TFP growth across size classes, it has been observed that the productivity growth in medium and large banks was the speediest throughout the entire period. Small and micro banks also had productivity gains during the sample period, but those gains were too meagre. Further, in both medium and large banks, TFP growth was largely contributed by technological progress, suggesting that these banks are the leaders in adopting more sophisticated and advanced banking technology.

The panel data regression analysis provides that the exposure of banks to off-balance sheet activities is the most significant factor explaining the interbank variations in productivity growth and its sources. This suggests that the banks having more involvement in non-traditional activities experience larger productivity gains. Further, profitability of banks has a direct relationship with the productivity growth, and larger banks are not necessarily those experience larger productivity gains. Furthermore, ownership per se does not exert any significant influence on the productivity growth of Indian banks.

8.3 Policy Implications

The empirical findings of the present study shed light on the potential direction of future banking reforms in India and also on the issue of how banks might go about increasing the cost efficiency of their operations. The following significant policy implications can be gleaned from the aforementioned empirical results.

First, given the evidence that public sector banks were more cost efficient and experienced higher TFP growth than domestic private banks, we can say with a great confidence that private ownership by itself may not be sufficient to ensure that Indian banks operate efficiently. This is also a pointer towards the fact that dominance of public ownership of banks is not a hindrance for the future growth of the banking industry, in particular, and the economy, in general. Moreover, we find that (i) foreign banks were more efficient than domestic private banks, (ii) foreign banks were dominating in defining the yearly efficient frontiers of the Indian banking system and (iii) foreign banks were leading technological innovators of the industry. These findings indicate the relevance of foreign bank entry in the Indian banking system and suggest that the relaxations in the entry of foreign banks would make an important contribution towards improving overall bank efficiency. All in all, our study thus favours the existing policy of opening-up the Indian banking sector, with the liberalisation of foreign entry by way of setting up a wholly owned banking subsidiary (WOS) or conversion of the existing branches into a WOS. We expect that this will really push the domestic banks closer to the global best practices and would improve their performance and service quality.

Second, the empirical evidence highlights that the key driver of the observed productivity growth in Indian banking industry is technological progress. In the post-deregulation years, increased application of technology played an important role in improving cost efficiency and productivity of banks. This justifies the RBI's focus on the use of information technology in the banking sector on the large scale. Beginning with the magnetic ink character recognition (MICR) cheque clearing system, the Indian retail payment system got a major boost during the post-reforms period with the introduction of technologically advanced and secured systems such as the electronic fund transfer, electronic clearing system, the special National Electronics Funds Transfer System (NEFT) and card-based systems that greatly enhanced efficiency levels in banking operations. The introduction of Real Time Gross Settlement (RTGS) improved the cash management by banks. Another technology induced cost effective initiative was the introduction of virtual banking services through the establishment of ATMs and shared ATM networks, smart cards, stored-value cards, phone banking and ultimately the internet and intranet banking. The RBI also operationalised the Very Small Aperture Terminal (VSAT) network to provide reliable communication backbone to the financial sector. To facilitate connectivity within the banking sector, the RBI, public sector banks and Institute for Development and Research in Banking Technology (IDRBT) collectively set up the Indian Financial Network (INFINET) based on satellite communication. Such technological initiatives promoted by the RBI produced a strong 'frontier-shift' effect in the Indian banking industry during the post-deregulation period.

Third, the banking industries of other developing countries seem to have fared better than Indian banking industry during the post-deregulation years, suggesting the need for more efforts by the Indian policy makers for augmenting the productivity growth. The raison d'être for modest productivity growth in Indian banking industry during the post-reforms years is that despite the advances in banking technologies in terms of methodologies, procedures and techniques during the post-reform years, there has been little or slow catching-up or diffusion of new technologies probably due to low skill level of the workforce in the banking industry to adopt these technologies in a more efficient manner. Since the onset of reforms, the RBI has laid an emphasis to invest in new banking technologies but without upgrading the commensurate management and organisational skills needed to use these best practice technologies. In the light of this, a big push is needed to develop a strong training system in banks with the objective to upgrade the skills of manpower. This would not only be helpful in using the new technologies and, consequently, in improving the technical efficiency but also in measuring, controlling and monitoring credit risk.

Fourth, our empirical findings indicate that (i) medium and large banks exhibited the higher efficiency than the small and micro banks and (ii) most of the banks were operating in the zone of increasing returns-to-scale. These findings suggest that in general, Indian banks could improve their cost efficiency by growing in size, perhaps by using mergers and acquisitions (M&As). Simply, substantial cost efficiency gains may perhaps be obtained from altering the scale of operations via either internal growth or consolidation in the sector.

Finally, the future reforms in the banking sector should be directed towards strengthening competitive and market-oriented policies. In particular, the government should continually introduce reform measures to improve risk management, transparency and corporate governance in Indian banks. This is because the empirical findings of the present study are in favour of conventional wisdom that financial deregulation exerts a positive influence on the efficiency and productivity of banks. Our findings suggest that banking reforms programme initiated in 1992 provided the anticipated banking efficiency gains, especially across public sector banks. This reflects that the banking reforms process in India has achieved the desired results to a large extent and, thus, offers a success story that may be emulated by other developing economies that are undergoing banking reforms not only because an ascent in the efficiency has been observed in the majority of banks but also significant technological progress has taken place over time. The empirical results implicitly signal the effective working of monetary policy in India since the early 1990s. During the post-reforms period, the policy makers gradually reduced the level of statutory pre-emption (by lowering CRR and SLR) which in turn increased the banks' lending capacity. Increase in the banks' credit creating capacity not only wiped out the signs of repression in the banking system but also enhanced the interest income of the banks. The increase in interest income contributed positively to the banks' output and was well mirrored in the improvement of the cost efficiency of banks.

8.4 Some Areas for Future Research

Our study has some limitations, and these suggest potential directions for future work. The first shortcoming of the present study is that we only investigated the cost efficiency of Indian banks. Cost efficiency gives a measure of how close a bank's costs are to those of the best banking practice after controlling for comparative output levels. However, a measure of profit efficiency which assesses how close a bank comes to generate the maximum possible profit given the levels of input and output prices (quantities) and other exogenous conditions could capture inefficiencies on the output side as well as those on the input side. Thus, further research into investigating the profit efficiency of Indian banks would be a valuable addition to the extant literature. The second shortcoming of this study is that it employs the only Data Envelopment Analysis (DEA) methodology for computing cost, allocative, technical, pure technical and scale efficiency scores for individual banks. An interesting direction for further research would be to employ Stochastic Frontier Approach (SFA) along with DEA to estimate the relative efficiency of Indian banks. This would lead to methodological cross-checking and help to assess the robustness of empirically estimated efficiency levels. Another potential direction for future research is that one could also investigate the impact of inclusion or exclusion of a proxy for non-traditional activities in the output specification on the total factor productivity (TFP) growth and its components in Indian banking industry.

Appendix

S. Kumar and R. Gulati, *Deregulation and Efficiency of Indian Banks*, India Studies in Business and Economics, DOI 10.1007/978-81-322-1545-5, © Springer India 2014

Table A.1 Recommendations of major committees and working groups

S. no.	Financial year	Committee/report/working group	Chairman	Purpose	Major recommendations
Panel A: Pre-reforms era					
1	1975	Working Group on Customer Services in Banks	R.K. Talwar	Improvement in providing services to customer	(i) The bank should assess and reassess on continuous basis the customers' perception about banks' services (ii) To formulate strategies to appraise and improve the customer services
2	1977	PEP (Productivity, Efficiency and Profitability) Committee on Banking	J.C. Lathur	To assess the performance of commercial banks on four major aspects, viz. productivity, social objectives (spatial and sectoral) and profitability	Recommended to examine the aspects like planning, budgeting marketing, management information system (MIS), annual accounts, audit systems, procedures, cash remittance and currency chests
3	1985	Committee to Review the Working of the Monetary System	S. Chakravarty	To upgrade monetary system of India	(i) To improve productivity of banking operations (ii) Shifting to 'monetary targeting' as a basic framework of monetary policy (iii) Emphasis on the objectives of price policy and economic growth (iv) Coordination between monetary and fiscal policy (v) Suggestion of scheme of interest rates in accordance with valid economic criteria

4	1985	Working Group to Review the System of Inspection of Banks	Pendharkar	To review systems and procedures relating to inspection in order to meet the emerging supervisory concerns	(i) To conduct financial inspection of banks offices for making detailed assessment of all the aspects of banking operations (ii) To introduce annual financial reviews in respect of public sector banks
5	1987	Working Group on the Money Markets	N. Vaghul	Development of money market	(i) To free inter-bank call money rates from ceiling stipulation (ii) Setting up of Discount and Finance House to impart greater liquidity in secondary markets (iii) Issuance of commercial paper having good dividend record
6	1990	Committee on Customer Services	M.N. Goiporia	To improve customer services in Indian banking	(i) Enlarging the scope of teller machines, extending banking hours for non-cash transactions, etc. (ii) Opening of specialised branches focusing on international banking, industrial finance and small-scale industries (iii) Compensating customers for delay in collection of cheques, payment of mail transfer, telegraphic transfer, etc. (iv) Making bank employees more responsive and customer friendly (v) Technology upgradation and continuous review of system in tune with changing needs of customers

(continued)

Table A.1 (continued)

S. no.	Financial year	Committee/report/working group	Chairman	Purpose	Major recommendations
Panel B: Post-reforms era					
7	1991	Committee on Frauds and Malpractices in Banks	A. Ghosh	To enquire into the aspects of frauds and malpractices in banks	(i) Joint custody and dual responsibility of cash and other valuables (ii) Transactions in currency chests to be reported to RBI on the same day (iii) All the transactions to be recorded in full details
8	1991–1992	Committee on Bank Accounts	A. Ghosh	To examine the advisability of greater or fuller disclosure in the published accounts of banks	To change the formats of balance sheet, and profit and loss accounts of bank
9	1992	Committee on the Financial System	M. Narasimham	To review the financial system	(i) Reduction in statuary pre-emptions like statutory liquidity ratio (SLR) and cash reserve ratio (CRR) in a phased manner (ii) Deregulation of administered interest rates so as to reflect emerging market conditions (iii) Phasing out of directed credit programmes and redefinition of the priority sector lending (iv) Improved prudential norms relating to capital adequacy, asset classification and income recognition in line with the international standards (v) Removal of branch licensing (vi) Relaxing the entry regulations for *de novo* private and foreign banks

10	1992	Committee to Enquire into Securities Transactions of Banks and Financial Institutions	R. Janakiraman	To investigate irregularities in fund management in commercial banks and financial institutions	(i) Introduction of proper control system (ii) Removal of lacunae in the existing systems and procedures to prevent stock scam in future (iii) Examination of entire securities transactions of banks and financial institutions (iv) Strengthening of monitoring mechanism
11	1992	Working Group on Security Equipments	Rashid Jilani	To draw up standard specifications for security equipments like cash safes, vaults, etc.	Member banks need to procure only those security instruments that bear the relevant ISI mark
12	1994	Committee on Technology Issues	W.S. Saraf	To improve payment system with the help of technology	(i) To brought changes relating to payment system, cheque clearing, securities settlements, technology and training in technology for the banking system (ii) Promotion of credit card culture (iii) A delivery versus payment system for Subsidiary General Ledger transactions in government securities
13	1995	Working Group on Internal Control Systems of Banks	Rashid Jilani	To review efficacy and adequacy of the internal control, inspection and audit system in banks with a view to strengthening the supervisory system and reliability of data	(i) Fraudulent transactions to be reported to vigilance chief of inspection (ii) Appropriate control measures should be devised and documented to prevent the computer system from attack of unscrupulous elements

(continued)

Table A.1 (continued)

S. no.	Financial year	Committee/report/working group	Chairman	Purpose	Major recommendations
					(iii) Regular checking by inspectors and auditors to verify correctness of information regarding asset classification, income recognition and provisioning
14	1996	Working Group on On-Site Supervision of Banks	S. Padmanabhan	To make recommendations on on-site supervision	(i) To introduce rating methodology for banks on the line of the CAMELS[a] model with appropriate modifications to suit Indian conditions (ii) Change in approach relating to targeted appraisals of major portfolios, control systems and statutory inspections (iii) Focused approach to follow up on inspection reports and for supervisory interventions
15	1996	Committee for Proposing Legislation on Electronic Funds Transfer and other Electronic Payments	K.S. Shere	To propose legislation on Electronic Funds Transfer (EFT) and other electronic payments	(i) An EFT system may be started with the RBI assuming the role of a service provider as well as the regulator (ii) The scope of EFT should extend to any credit transfer in India (iii) To define the responsibilities and liabilities of participants and bank customers (iv) To adopt security procedures involving electronic authentication, and provisions against computer misuse, frauds, etc.

16	1997	Committee on Banking Education	Kannan	To revise and modify the examination system for the banks which is being administered by the Indian Institute of Bankers'(IIB), Mumbai	(i) Introduction of Junior Associate Diploma and Certificated Associate Examinations (ii) Employees of finance companies should also be covered by the IIB examinations (iii) Increase the level of specialisation at senior level
17	1997	Working Group on Harmonizing Development Financial Institutions (DFIs) and Banks	S.H. Khan	To review the role, structure and operations of DFIs and commercial banks in emerging market environment	(i) To reduce the statutory pre-emption applicable to DFIs and commercial banks in a phased manner (ii) Merger of State Financial Corporations (SFCs) and State Industrial Development Corporations (SIDCs) in each state into a single entity, namely, State level Financial Institutes (SFIs) (iii) The supervisory framework of DFIs and banks has to be risk based with focus on macro-management and consolidated supervision by bank supervisor
18	1998	Committee on the Banking Sector Reforms	M. Narasimham	To review the progress of financial reforms to-date and chart out a programme on banking sector reforms necessary to strengthen India's banking system and make it internationally competitive	(i) To increase the minimum capital adequacy ratio from the existing level of 8–10% in a phased manner, viz. 9% by 2000 and 10% by 2002 (ii) An asset is classified as doubtful if it is in the substandard category for 18 months in the first instance and eventually for 12 months and loss if it has been so identified but not written off

(continued)

Table A.1 (continued)

S. no.	Financial year	Committee/report/working group	Chairman	Purpose	Major recommendations
					(iii) The rehabilitation of weak public sector banks which have accumulated a high percentage of nonpaying assets (NPAs) (iv) Modernization and technology upgradation, the pace and reach of computerisation process in public sector banks (v) To reduce the average level of net NPAs for all banks to below 5% by the year 2000 and to 3% by 2002 (vi) The share of priority sector in the total bank credit has to be reduced from the existing level of 40–10% (vii) To review and amend the provisions of RBI Act, Banking Regulation Act, State Bank of India Act, Bank Nationalisation Act, etc., so as to bring them in the line with the current needs of the banking industry
19	1999	Working Group on Restructuring Weak Public Sector Banks	M. S. Verma	To suggest measures for revival of weak public sector bank	(i) To identify weak public sector banks on the basis of seven parameters like capital adequacy ratio, coverage ratio, return on assets, net interest margin, ratio of operating profit to average working funds, ratio of cost to income and ratio of staff cost to net interest income (NII) plus all other income

					(ii) Restructuring of weak banks should be done in two phases. In the first phase, focus should be on operational and financial restructuring aimed at restoring competitive efficiency, and second phase opts for privatisation merger
20	1999	Committee on Technology Upgradation in the Banking Sector	A. Vasudevan	To upgrade the existing technology in the banking sector	(i) Usage of INFINET network based on VSAT should get a high priority for performing inter- and intra-bank operations (ii) The technology should be allowed to improve standards based on solution for multi-vendor, heterogeneous environment, working co-operatively and collectively for EFTPOs (iii) Task force may be set up by the IBA system to explore feasible methodology for working out a unique identification system for individual customer at banks (iv) RBI to appoint IDRBT as a certification agency for security management
21	1999	Working Group on International Banking Statistics	N.K. Puri	To efficiently monitor the coverage of data on international claims and liabilities of the banking sector	(i) Establishment of Central Database Management System (CDBMS) at the RBI with the access of all user departments

(continued)

Table A.1 (continued)

S. no.	Financial year	Committee/report/working group	Chairman	Purpose	Major recommendations
					(ii) Data collection activity of RBI with the help of Locational Banking Statistics and Consolidated Banking Statistics would get operationalised in 1999–2000
22	2000	Report of Advisory Group on Transparency in Monetary and Financial Policies	M. Narasimham	To study the status of applicability, relevance and compliance of the global standards and codes in Indian financial system	(i) Various duties and responsibilities of the central bank should be clearly defined on single document so as to provide transparency in this context (ii) Changes in the setting of monetary policy instruments should be publicly announced and explained in a timely manner (iii) The framework, instruments used and targets which are prescribed to pursue the objectives of monetary policy should be described, explained and publicly disclosed
23	2001	Report on Internet Banking	S. R. Mittal	To examine different aspects of internet banking from regulatory and supervisory perspective	(i) Logical access controls should be implemented on data, systems, application software, utilities, telecommunication lines, libraries, system software, etc. (ii) Banks should use the proxy server type of firewall so that there is no direct connection between the Internet and the bank's system

					(iii) All unnecessary services on the application server such as ftp, telnet should be disabled (iv) The bank should have a proper infrastructure and schedules for backing up data (v) The banks should acquire tools for monitoring systems and the networks against intrusions and attacks (vi) The banks should review their security infrastructure and security policies regularly and optimise them in the light of their own experiences and changing technologies
24	2001	Expert Committee on Legal Aspects of Bank Frauds	N.L. Mitra	To inspect issues related to bank fraud	(i) To investigate serious financial frauds with the help multidimensional investigative agency and to be tried in a fast track special court (ii) A systemic adjustment including making of necessary legal compliance report and attaching certain functional responsibilities to the financial auditors
25	2002	Report of the Consultative Group of Directors of Banks/Financial Institutions	A.S. Ganguly	To review the supervisory role of Boards of banks and financial institutions and to obtain feedback on the functioning of the Boards vis-à-vis compliance,	(i) Due diligence of the directors of all banks should be done in regard to their suitability for the post by way of qualifications and technical expertise

(continued)

Table A.1 (continued)

S. no.	Financial year	Committee/report/working group	Chairman	Purpose	Major recommendations
				transparency, disclosures, audit committees, etc.	(ii) For assessing integrity and suitability, factors such as criminal records, financial position, civil actions undertaken to pursue personal debts and previous questionable business practices should be considered (iii) Government should follow some norms like BIS for judging the suitability of directors for appointment on Board of Directors of Public Sector Banks (iv) There could be a Supervisory Committee of the Board in all banks, be they public or private sector, which will work on collective trust and at the same time, without diluting the overall responsibility of the Board
26	2002	Standing Committee on International Financial Standards and Codes	Y. V. Reddy	To facilitate positioning of international financial standards and codes in relevant areas of the financial system in India	(i) To identify and monitor developments in global standards and codes being evolved especially in the context of International Financial Architecture (ii) To consider all the aspects of applicability of standards and codes to Indian financial system, and chalk out a road map for aligning India's standards in the light of international standards

					(iii) To review periodically the status and progress in regards to the codes and practices
27	2002	Report of the Review Group on the Working of the Local Area Bank Scheme	G. Ramachandran	To examine whether the scheme of Local Area Banks (LABs) has fulfilled its objectives, and whether the LABs licensed so far have served the purpose for which they were set up	(i) To highlight various constraints faced by LABs, viz. resources available to these banks, chances for diversification of business, pattern relating to risks faced by LABs, etc., and draw attention of regulatory authority to take suitable measures (ii) LABs should not be permitted to engage the services of agents and quasi agents for achieving their business outreach (iii) LABs need to be treated like any other commercial bank and therefore, regulation and supervision should be entrusted to the same wing of the RBI which is responsible for Regulation and Supervision of the commercial banks
28	2004	Working Group on Banking Arrangements for Implementation of Value Added Tax	Usha Thorat	To assess the likely impact of introduction of VAT in terms of volume of transactions and to suggest changes required in terms of technology	(i) Collection of taxes must pass through banking channel so as to enable the department to track the flow of funds (ii) A technology intensive and superior option can be found in the use of electronic payment systems through payment gateways

(continued)

Table A.1 (continued)

S. no.	Financial year	Committee/report/working group	Chairman	Purpose	Major recommendations
					(iii) Usage of a unique identification number (comparable to PAN for Income Tax) to facilitate assesses to pay taxes at any bank branch in the country
29	2006	Working Group to Formulate a Scheme for Ensuring Reasonableness of Bank Charges	N. Sadasivan	To ensure reasonableness of bank charges and to incorporate the same in Fair Practices Code	(i) To examine the issue with reference to the users of the services, the nature of transactions and the value of transactions (ii) A distinctly different and liberalised approach in pricing the services to the middle and lower segments should be adopted (iii) To scan the list of services available to individuals from banks in addition to banking services like deposits, remittances etc.
30	2009	Committee on Financial Sector Reforms	Raghuram G. Rajan	To identify the emerging challenges in meeting the financing needs of the Indian economy and to identify real sector reforms that would allow those needs to be more easily met by the financial sector	(i) Liberalise the banking correspondent regulation so that a wide range of local agents can serve to extend financial services (ii) Allow banks that undershoot their priority sector obligations to buy the PSLC and submit it towards fulfilment of their target (iii) Liberalise the interest rate that institutions can charge, ensuring credit reaches the poor

					(iv) Be more liberal in allowing takeovers and mergers, including by domestically incorporated subsidiaries of foreign banks (v) Free banks to set up branches and ATMs anywhere (vi) Supervision of all deposit taking institutions must come under the RBI
31	2009	Committee on Financial Sector Assessment	Rakesh Mohan	(i) To assess the stability and resilience of financial systems	(i) Branch licensing policy could be broadly structured on the lines of that followed in new private sector banks, consistent with the country's WTO commitments, but licensing of branches would continue to be based on reciprocity
				(ii) To assess the status and implementation of international financial standards and codes	(ii) Introduction of LAF has been a major step as regards money market operations
				(iii) To take up legal, infrastructural and market development issues	(iii) To monitor and address the international interaction and consistency of emergency arrangements and responses being put in place to address the current financial crisis (iv) To put in place a mechanism whereby banks can report developments affecting operational risk to the Reserve Bank

(continued)

Table A.1 (continued)

S. no.	Financial year	Committee/report/working group	Chairman	Purpose	Major recommendations
					(v) As regards improvements in the governance of PSBs, appropriate care requires to be taken in ensuring proper quality of directors, and improving flexibility in decision making, unhindered by government interference
32	2009	Committee to Review Lead Bank Scheme	Usha Thorat	(i) For a comprehensive review of the Lead Bank Scheme[b]	(i) To focus on addressing the 'enablers' and 'impeders' in achieving greater financial inclusion and flow of credit to priority sectors, while continuing to monitor subsidy linked government sponsored schemes
				(ii) To focus on financial inclusion and recent developments in the banking sector	(ii) To enable banks and State Governments to work together for inclusive growth
					(ii) Lead banks are expected to open a Financial Literacy and Credit Counselling Centre (FLCC) in every district where they have lead responsibility

Source: Authors' elaboration

[a]The group recommended six rating factors for public and private banks, namely, capital adequacy, asset quality, management, earnings, liquidity, systems and controls. However, for foreign banks four rating factors have been suggested, namely, capital adequacy, asset quality, liquidity compliance and systems (i.e. CACLS)

[b]The Lead Bank Scheme (LBS) was introduced by Reserve Bank in 1969 when designated banks were made key instruments for local development and entrusted with the responsibility of identifying growth centres, assessing deposit potential and credit gaps and evolving a coordinated approach for credit deployment in each district, in concert with other banks and other agencies. The LBS underwent significant transformation in 1989 when the service area approach was dovetailed into the scheme

Table A.2 Impact of non-traditional activities on the banking efficiency: an international experience

Author (year)	Country (sample period)	Methodology (efficiency measures)	Inputs	Outputs (model in which they are included)	Major findings
Jagtiani et al. (1995)	USA (quarterly data 1988–1990)	Translog cost function (CE)	*Models a, b, c, d, e, f, g and h* (i) Labour (ii) Physical capital (iii) Financial capital	(i) Earning assets *(Models a, b, c, d, g and h)* (ii) Deposits *(Models b, e, f, g and h)* (iii) OBS guarantees *(Models d, f and h)* (iv) OBS foreign currency *(Models d, f and h)* (v) OBS interest rate *(Models d, f and h)* (vi) Aggregate OBS items *(Models c, e and g)*	Off-balance sheet (OBS) products have little or no significant effect on the scale economies. Further, no evidence of cost complementarities in the production process with the inclusion of OBS products has been noted
Siems and Clark (1997)	USA (cross-sectional data for the year 1995)	TFA (PE)	*Models 1 and 2* (i) Labour (ii) Premises and fixed assets (iii) Funds	(i) Sum of commercial and industrial loans, agricultural loans, direct leasing, foreign loans and loans to financial institutions *(Models 1 and 2)* (ii) Sum of consumer and real estate loans *(Models 1 and 2)* (iii) Sum of demand deposits, savings deposits and retail time deposits *(Models 1 and 2)* (iv)Off-balance sheet activities *(Model 2)*	Exclusion of OBS activities as an output in the profit function has not been supported statistically and may distort profit efficiency computations

(continued)

Table A.2 (continued)

Author (year)	Country (sample period)	Methodology (efficiency measures)	Inputs	Outputs (model in which they are included)	Major findings
Rogers (1998)	USA (1991–1995)	DFA (CE, RE, PE)	*Models unrestricted and restricted* (i) Labour (ii) Physical capital (iii) Time and savings deposits (iv) Purchased funds	(i) Demand deposits *(Models unrestricted and restricted)* (ii) Time and savings deposits *(Models unrestricted and restricted)* (iii) Real estate loans *(Models unrestricted and restricted)* (iv) Other loans *(Models unrestricted and restricted)* (v) Net non-interest income *(Model unrestricted)*	Omission of non-traditional activities proxied by net non-interest income understates the banks' cost- and profit efficiency
Stiroh (2000)	USA (1991–1997)	SFA (CE, APE)	(i) Purchased funds *(Models 1, 2, 3 and 4)* (ii) Core deposits *(Models 1, 2, 3 and 4)* (iii) Labour *(Models 1, 2, 3 and 4)*	(i) Business loans *(Models 1, 2, 3 and 4)* (ii) Consumer loans *(Models 1, 2, 3 and 4)* (iii) Securities *(Models 1, 2, 3 and 4)* (iv) Net non-interest income *(Model 2)* (v) Off-balance sheet items *(Model 3)* *Fixed netputs* (i) Off-balance sheet items *(Model 4)* (ii) Physical capital *(Models 1, 2, 3 and 4)* (iii) Equity capital *(Models 1, 2, 3 and 4)*	The efficiency estimates of US bank holding companies are sensitive to output specification and failure to account for OBS items understates the level of profit efficiency

Clark and Siems (2002)	USA (1992–1997)	SFA and DFA (CE, PE)	*Models 1 and 2* (i) Labour (ii) Premises and equipments (iii) Funds (iv) Equity capital (netput)	(i) Commercial loans, direct leasing, foreign loans and loans to financial institutions *(Models 1 and 2)* (ii) Consumer and real estate loans *(Models 1 and 2)* (iii) Other on-balance sheet assets *(Models 1 and 2)* (iv) Commitments, lines of credit and credit guarantees *(Model 2)* (v) Derivatives activities *(Model 2)*	Cost and production X-efficiency estimates increase with the inclusion of the OBS measure, while profit X-efficiency estimates are unaffected
Isik and Hassan (2003a)	Turkey (1981–1990)	DEA-based Malmquist productivity index (TE, PTE, SE, TECHCH, EFFCH, PECH,SECH, TFPCH)	*Models 1 and 2:* (i) Labour (ii) Capital (iii) Loanable funds	(i) Short-term loans *(Models 1 and 2)* (ii) Long-term loans *(Models 1 and 2)* (iii) Other earning assets *(Models 1 and 2)* (iv) Risk-adjusted off-balance sheet items *(Model 2)*	Exclusion of OBS items significantly deteriorates the average efficiency and productivity scores of the Turkish banking industry
Tortosa-Ausina (2003)	Spain (1986–1997)	DEA (CE)	*Models unrestricted and restricted:* (i) Labour (ii) Physical capital (iii) Loanable funds	(i) Loans *(Models unrestricted and restricted)* (ii) Other earning assets *(Models unrestricted and restricted)* (iii) Fee-generating income *(Model unrestricted)*	Average cost efficiency of Spanish banks has enhanced when fee-generating income as a proxy for non-traditional activities is accounted in the output vector

(continued)

Table A.2 (continued)

Author (year)	Country (sample period)	Methodology (efficiency measures)	Inputs	Outputs (model in which they are included)	Major findings
Rime and Stiroh (2003)	Switzerland (1996–1999)	DFA (CE, APE)	*Models 1, 2 and 3* (i) Labour (ii) Deposits	(i) Money market claims *(Models 1, 2 and 3)* (ii) Bank loans *(Models 1, 2 and 3)* (iii) Mortgage loans *(Models 1, 2 and 3)* (iv) Securities *(Models 2 and 3)* (v) Trading assets *(Model 3)* (vi) Amount of securities accounts *(Model 3)* *Netputs* (i) Equity capital *(Model 1)* (ii) Physical capital *(Model 1)* (iii) OBS commitments *(Model 2)* (iv) Derivatives *(Model 3)*	Failure to account for OBS items leads cost- and profit efficiency to be dramatically understated
Casu and Girardone (2005)	European Banks (1994–2000)	DEA-based Malmquist productivity index (EFFCH, TECHCH, TFPCH)	*Models A and B* (i) Deposits (ii) Labour (iii) Physical capital	(i) Total loans *(Models A and B)* (ii) Other earning assets *(Models A and B)* (iii) Nominal value of OBS *(Model B)*	Inclusion of OBS items results in an increase in the estimated productivity levels of the European countries (France, Germany, Italy, Spain and UK) under study. Further, the impact seems to be bigger on technological change rather than efficiency change

Lieu et al. (2005)	Taiwan (1998–2001)	SFA (CE)	*Models A1, A2 and B* (i) Funds (ii) Capital (iii) Labour	(i) Real investment *(Models A1, A2 and B)* (ii) Real loans *(Models A1, A2 and B)* (iii) Nominal value of OBS *(Model A1)* (iv) Non-interest income *(Model A2)*	Exclusion of OBS items as output leads to underestimation of cost efficiency of Taiwanese banks by 5%. The banks with higher OBS output gain higher cost efficiency
Sufian and Ibrahim (2005)	Malaysia (2001–2003)	DEA-based Malmquist productivity index (TECHCH, EFFCH, PECH, SECH, TFPCH)	*Models 1, 2 and 3* (i) Labour (ii) Fixed assets (iii) Deposits	(i) Total loans *(Models 1, 2 and 3)* (ii) Investments and dealing securities *(Models 1, 2 and 3)* (iii) Off-balance sheet items *(Model 2)* (iv) Non-interest income *(Model 3)*	Inclusion of OBS items results in an increase in productivity of Malaysian banks. Moreover, it has more effect on technological change rather than efficiency change
Huang and Chen (2006)	Taiwan (1992–2004)	DEA (CE)	(i) Financial activity costs (ii) Operating cost	(i) Interest income (ii) Non-interest income (trading revenue, fee income, non-fee income, income from fiduciary activities	Inclusion of non-interest income has positive impact on the cost efficiency of Taiwanese banks
Pasiouras (2008)	Greece (2000–2004)	DEA (TE, PTE, SE)	(i) Fixed assets *(Models 1, 2, 3 and 4)* (ii) Customer deposits and short-term funding *(Models 1, 2, 3 and 4)*	(i) Loans *(Models 1, 2, 3 and 4)* (ii) Other earning assets *(Models 1, 2, 3 and 4)*	Inclusion of off-balance sheet items in the output vector does not have an impact on the efficiency scores of Greek banks, while inclusion of loan loss provisions in the input vector contributes to highest efficiency scores

(continued)

Table A.2 (continued)

Author (year)	Country (sample period)	Methodology (efficiency measures)	Inputs	Outputs (model in which they are included)	Major findings
			(iii) Number of employees *(Models 1, 2, 3 and 4)*	(iii) Off-balance sheet items *(Models 2 and 4)*	
			(iv) Loan loss provisions *(Models 3, 4 and 5)*	(iv) Net-interest income *(Model 5)*	
			(v) Employee expenses *(Model 5)*	(v) Net commission income *(Model 5)*	
			(vi) Non-interest expenses *(Model 5)*	(vi) Other income *(Model 5)*	
Budd (2009)	UAE (2001–2005)	DEA-based Malmquist productivity index (TE, AE, CE, PTE, SE, EFFCH, TECHCH, PECH, SECH, TFPCH)	*Models 1 and 2* (i) Labour (ii) Capital (iii) Deposits	(i) Loans *(Models 1 and 2)* (ii) Investments *(Models 1 and 2)* (iii) Off-balance sheet items *(Model 2)*	The inclusion of OBS items increases efficiency scores and estimated productivity levels of UAE banks
Sufian (2009b)	China (2000–2005)	DEA-based Malmquist productivity index (EFFCH, TECHCH, PECH, SECH, TFPCH)	*Models 1 and 2* (i) Total deposits (ii) Fixed assets	(i) Total loans *(Models 1 and 2)* (ii) Investments *(Models 1 and 2)* (iii) Off-balance sheet items *(Model 2)*	Inclusion of OBS items has positive impact on the efficiency change, while it has negative impact on total factor productivity of the China's banking industry

Sufian and Habibullah (2009)	China (2000–2005)	DEA (TE, PTE, SE)	*Models 1 and 2* (i) Total deposits (ii) Fixed assets	(i) Total loans *(Models 1 and 2)* (ii) Investments *(Models 1 and 2)* (iii) Off-balance sheet items *(Model 2)*	Inclusion of OBS items improves the technical, pure technical and scale efficiencies of Chinese banks
Lozano-Vivas and Pasiouras (2010)	87 countries (1999–2006)	SFA (CE, APE)	*Models A1, A2 and A3* (i) Loanable funds (ii) Fixed assets (iii) Labour	(i) Loans *(Models A1, A2 and A3)* (ii) Other earning assets *(Models A1, A2 and A3)* (iii) Off-balance sheet items *(Model A2)* (iv) Non-interest income *(Model A3)*	There is an increase in the average cost efficiency of banks when off-balance sheet or non-interest income is accounted for in the output vector. However, the inclusion of OBS does not have any significant impact on profit efficiency

Source: Authors' compilation

Notes: (i) *DEA, SFA, DFA* and *TFA* are the acronyms for data envelopment analysis, stochastic frontier analysis, distribution free approach and thick frontier analysis, respectively; (ii) *TE, CE, RE, PE, APE, SPE, PTE* and *SE* stand for technical, cost, revenue, profit, alternative profit, standard profit, pure technical and scale efficiencies, respectively; (iii) *EFFCH, TECHCH, PECH, SECH* and *TFPCH* stand for efficiency change, technological change, pure technical efficiency change, scale efficiency change and total factor productivity change, respectively

References

Acharya S, Mohan R (eds) (2010) India's economy performances and challenges. Oxford University Press, New Delhi

Afrait SN (1972) Efficiency estimation of production functions. Int Econ Rev 13(3):568–598

Agarwal P (2000) Regulation and reform of the financial sector in India: an analysis of the underlying incentives. In: Kahkonen S, Lanyi A (eds) Institute, incentives and economic reforms in India. Sage, New Delhi

Aigner DJ, Chu SF (1968) On estimating the industry production function. Am Econ Rev 58(4):826–839

Aigner DJ, Lovell CAK, Schmidt P (1977) Formulation and estimation of stochastic frontier production function models. J Econom 6(1):21–37

Ajit D (1997) Para banking in India: some issues. Econ Polit Wkly 32(42):2677–2686

Akhavein JD, Berger AN, Humphrey DB (1997) The effects of bank megamergers on efficiency and prices: evidence from a bank profit function. Rev Ind Organ 12(1):95–139

Akhtar MH (2010) X-efficiency analysis of Pakistani commercial banks. Int Manage Rev 6(1):12–24

Alam ISM (2001) A non-parametric approach for assessing productivity dynamics of large US banks. J Money Credit Bank 33(1):121–139

Alchian AA (1965) Some economics of property rights. II Politico 30(4):816–829

Ali AI, Gstach D (2000) The impact of deregulation during 1990–1997 on banking in Austria. Empirica 27(3):265–281

Ali AI, Seiford LM (1993) The mathematical programming approach to efficiency analysis. In: Fried HO, Lovell CAK, Schmidt SS (eds) The measurement of productive efficiency. Oxford University Press, New York, pp 120–159

Allen L, Rai A (1996) Operational efficiency in banking: an international comparison. J Bank Financ 20(4):655–672

Al-Shammari M, Salimi A (1998) Modeling the operating efficiency of banks: a nonparametric methodology. Log Inf Manage 11(1):5–17

Altunbas Y, Evans L, Molyneux P (2001) Bank ownership and efficiency. J Money Credit Bank 33(4):926–954

Aly HY, Grabowski R, Pasurka C, Rangan N (1990) Technical, scale, and allocative efficiencies in U.S. banking: an empirical investigation. Rev Econ Stat 72(2):211–218

Andersen P, Petersen NC (1993) A procedure for ranking efficient units in DEA. Manage Sci 39(10):1261–1264

Ariff M, Can L (2008) Cost and profit efficiency of Chinese banks: a non-parametric analysis. China Econ Rev 19(2):260–273

Ariss RT (2008) Financial liberalization and bank efficiency: evidence from post-war Lebanon. Appl Financ Econ 18(11):931–946

S. Kumar and R. Gulati, *Deregulation and Efficiency of Indian Banks*, India Studies in Business and Economics, DOI 10.1007/978-81-322-1545-5, © Springer India 2014

Ariss RT, Rezvanian R, Mehdian SM (2007) Cost efficiency, technological progress and productivity growth of banks in GCC countries. Int J Bus 12(4):471–491

Arun TG, Turner JD (2002) Financial sector reforms in developing countries: the Indian experience. World Econ 25(3):429–445

Asaftei G, Kumbhakar SC (2008) Regulation and efficiency in transition: the case of Romanian banks. J Regul Econ 33(3):253–282

Ashton JK, Hardwick P (2000) Estimating inefficiencies in banking. J Interdiscip Econ 11(1):1–33

Asmild M, Paradi JC, Aggarwall V, Schaffnit C (2004) Combining DEA window analysis with the malmquist index approach in a study of the Canadian banking industry. J Prod Anal 21(1):67–89

Ataullah A, Le H (2006) Economic reforms and bank efficiency in developing countries: the case of the Indian banking industry. Appl Financ Econ 16(9):653–663

Ataullah A, Cockerill T, Le H (2004) Financial liberalization and bank efficiency: a comparative analysis of India and Pakistan. Appl Econ 36(17):1915–1924

Athanasoglou PP, Georgioua EA, Staikouras CC (2009) Assessing output and productivity growth in the banking industry. Q Rev Econ Finan 49(4):1317–1340

Avkiran NK (1999) The evidence on efficiency gains: the role of mergers and the benefits to the public. J Bank Financ 23(7):991–1013

Avkiran NK (2000) Rising productivity of Australian trading banks under deregulation 1986–1995. J Econ Financ 24(2):122–140

Avkiran NK (2006) Productivity analysis in the services sector with data envelopment analysis, 3rd edn. University of Queensland Business School, The University of Queensland, Brisbane

Avkiran NC, Rowlands T (2008) How to better identify the true managerial performance: state of the art using DEA. Omega Int J Manage Sci 36(2):317–324

Awdeh A, El Moussawi C (2009) Bank efficiency and foreign ownership in the Lebanese banking sector. Rev Middle East Econ Financ 5(2):1–22

Ayadi OF (1998) Bank performance measurement in a developing economy: an application of data envelopment analysis. Manage Financ 24(7):5–16

Baker RC, Talluri S (1997) A closer look at the use of data envelopment analysis for technology selection. Comp Ind Eng 32(1):101–108

Balk B (2001) Scale efficiency and productivity change. J Prod Anal 15(3):159–183

Banker RD (1993) Maximum likelihood, consistency and data envelopment analysis: a statistical foundation. Manage Sci 39(10):1265–1273

Banker RD, Morey R (1986) Efficiency analysis for exogenously fixed inputs and outputs. Oper Res 34(4):513–521

Banker RD, Charnes A, Cooper WW (1984) Some models for estimating technical and scale inefficiencies in DEA. Manage Sci 30(9):1078–1092

Banker RD, Chang H, Lee SY (2010) Differential impact of Korean banking system reforms on bank productivity. J Bank Financ 34(7):1450–1460

Banker RD, Gifford JL (1988) A relative efficiency model for the evaluation of public health nurse productivity. Mellon University Mimeo, Carnegie

Barajas A, Steiner R, Salazar N (2000) The impact of liberalization and foreign investment in Colombia's financial sector. J Dev Econ 63(1):157–197

Barman RB (2007) Determinants of profitability of banks in India. In: Presidential address delivered at the 43rd annual conference of The Indian Econometric Society (TIES) held on 5th–7th January, Indian Institute of Technology, Mumbai

Barr RS (2002) Evaluating the productive efficiency and performance of U.S. commercial banks. Manage Financ 28(8):3–25

Barros CP, Mascarenhas MJ (2005) Technical and allocative efficiency in a chain of small hotels. Int J Hosp Manage 24(3):415–436

Barry TA, Dacanay SJ, Lepetit L, Tarazi A (2008) Ownership and banking efficiency in the Asia Pacific region. Available via DIALOG. http://ssrn.com/abstract=1244163

Battese GE, Coelli TJ (1988) Prediction of firm-level technical efficiencies with a generalized frontier production function and panel data. J Econom 38(3):387–399

Battese GE, Coelli TJ (1992) Frontier production functions, technical efficiency and panel data: with application to paddy farmers in India. J Prod Anal 3(1–2):153–169

Battese GE, Coelli TJ (1995) A model for technical inefficiency effects in a stochastic frontier production function for panel data. Empir Econ 20(2):325–332

Bauer PW, Berger AN, Humphrey DB (1993) Efficiency and productivity growth in U.S. banking. In: Fried HO, Lovell CAK, Schmidt SS (eds) The measurement of productive efficiency. Oxford University Press, New York, pp 318–413

Bauer PW, Berger AN, Ferrier GD, Humphrey DB (1998) Consistency conditions for regulator analysis of financial institutions: a comparison of frontier efficiency methods. J Econ Bus 50(2):85–114

Benston GJ (1965) Branch banking and economies of scale. J Financ 20(2):312–331

Berg SA, Forsund FR, Jansen ES (1992) Malmquist indices of productivity growth during the deregulation of Norwegian banking: 1980–89. Scand J Econ 94(Suppl):S211–S228

Berg SA, Forsund F, Hjalmarsson L, Suominen M (1993) Banking efficiency in the Nordic countries. J Bank Financ 17(2–3):371–388

Berger A (1993) Distribution free estimates of efficiency in the U.S. banking industry and tests of the standard distributional assumptions. J Prod Anal 4(3):261–292

Berger AN (2007) International comparisons of banking efficiency. Financ Mark Inst Instrum 16(3):119–144

Berger AN, DeYoung R (1997) Problem loans and cost efficiency in commercial banking. J Bank Financ 21(6):849–870

Berger AN, Hannan TH (1998) The efficiency cost of market power in the banking industry: a test of the 'quiet life' and related hypotheses. Rev Econ Stat 80(3):454–465

Berger AN, Humphrey DB (1991) The dominance of inefficiencies over scale and product mix economies in banking. J Monet Econ 28(1):117–148

Berger AN, Humphrey DB (1992) Measurement and efficiency issues in commercial banking. In: Griliches Z (ed) Output measurement in the service sectors. University of Chicago Press, Chicago, pp 245–279

Berger AN, Humphrey DB (1997) Efficiency of financial institutions: international survey and directions for future research. Eur J Oper Res 98(2):175–212

Berger A, Mester L (1997) Inside the black box: what explains differences in the efficiency of financial institutions? J Bank Financ 21(7):895–947

Berger A, Mester LJ (2003) Explaining the dramatic changes in performance of US banks: technological change, deregulation, and dynamic changes in competition. J Financ Intermed 12(1):57–95

Berger AN, Hanweck GA, Humphrey DB (1987) Competitive viability in banking: scale, scope, and product mix economies. J Monet Econ 20(3):501–520

Berger AN, Hancock D, Humphrey DB (1993a) Bank efficiency derived from the profit function. J Bank Financ 17(2–3):317–347

Berger AN, Hunter W, Timme S (1993b) The efficiency of financial institutions: a review and preview of research past, present and future. J Bank Financ 17(2–3):221–249

Berger AN, DeYoung R, Genay H, Udell GF (2000) Globalization of financial institutions: evidence from cross-border banking performance. Brookings-Wharton Papers on Financial Services, 3, p 23–158

Berger AN, Hasan I, Zhou M (2005) Ownership, financial liberalization, and efficiency of Chinese banks. Available via DIALOG. http://www.fma.org/Chicago/Papers/Chinabankeff_forown_fma 2005.pdf

Berger AN, Hasan I, Zhou M (2009) Bank ownership and efficiency in China: what lies ahead in the world's largest nation? J Bank Financ 33(1):113–130

Bertrand M, Schoar A, Thesmar D (2007) Banking deregulation and industry structure: evidence from the French banking reforms of 1985. J Financ 62(2):597–628

Bhattacharyya S, Patel UR (2003) Reforms strategies in the Indian financial sector. A paper presented at conference on 'India's and China's experience with reform and growth, National Council of Applied Economic Research, 15th–16th November, New Delhi

Bhattacharyya A, Bhattacharyya A, Kumbhakar SC (1997a) Changes in economic regime and productivity growth: a study of Indian public sector banks. J Comp Econ 25(2):196–219

Bhattacharyya A, Lovell CAK, Sahay P (1997b) The impact of liberalization on the productive efficiency of Indian commercial banks. Eur J Oper Res 98(2):332–345

Bhaumik SK, Dimova R (2004) How important is ownership in a market with a level playing field? The Indian banking sector revisited. J Comp Econ 32(1):165–180

Bhaumik SK, Mukherjee P (2001) The Indian banking industry: a commentary. Discussion paper no.17, Centre for New and Emerging Markets, London Business School, London

Bhide MG, Prasad A, Ghosh S (2002) Banking sector reforms: a critical overview. Econ Polit Wkly 37(5):399–408

Bogetoft P, Hougaard JL (2004) Super efficiency evaluations based on potential slack. Eur J Oper Res 152(1):14–21

Bonin JP, Hasan I, Wachtel P (2005) Bank performance, efficiency and ownership in transition countries. J Bank Financ 29(1):31–53

Bos JWB, Schmiedel H (2007) Is there a single frontier in a single European banking market? J Bank Financ 31(7):2081–2102

Boyce JK (1986) Kinked exponential models for growth rate estimation. Oxford B Econ Stat 48(4):385–391

Brissimis SN, Delis MD, Papanikolaou NI (2008) Exploring the nexus between banking sector reform and performance: evidence from newly acceded EU countries. J Bank Financ 32(12):2674–2683

Budd BQ (2009) The consideration of off-balance sheet activities on banking efficiency and productivity performances within the UAE. Int J Bus Emerg Mark 1(4):315–340

Bukh PN (1994) Efficiency loss in the Danish banking sector: a data envelopment approach. IFV working paper 1994-2, University of Aarhus, Denmark

Burki AA, Niazi GSK (2010) Impact of financial reforms on efficiency of state-owned, private and foreign banks in Pakistan. Appl Econ 42(24):3147–3160

Canhoto A, Dermine J (2003) A note on banking efficiency in Portugal, new vs. old banks. J Bank Financ 27(11):2087–2098

Casu B, Girardone C (2002) A comparative study of the cost efficiency of Italian bank conglomerates. Manage Financ 28(9):3–23

Casu B, Girardone C (2005) An analysis of the relevance of off-balance sheet items in explaining productivity change in European banking. Appl Financ Econ 15(15):1053–1061

Casu B, Molyneux P (2003) A comparative study of efficiency in European banking. Appl Econ 35(17):1865–1876

Casu B, Girardone C, Molyneux P (2004) Productivity change in European banking: a comparison of parametric and non-parametric approaches. J Bank Financ 28(10):2521–2540

Caves D, Christensen L, Diewert WE (1982a) The economic theory of index numbers and the measurement of input, output, and productivity. Econometrica 50(6):1393–1414

Caves D, Christensen L, Diewert WE (1982b) Multilateral comparisons of output, input, and productivity using superlative index numbers. Econ J 92(365):73–86

Cebenoyan AS, Cooperman ES, Register CA (1993) Firm inefficiency and the regulatory closure of S&Ls: an empirical investigation. Rev Econ Stat 75(3):540–545

Chaffai M (1997) Estimating input-specific technical inefficiency: the case of Tunisian banking industry. Eur J Oper Res 98(2):314–331

Chaffai ME, Dietsch M, Lozano-Vivas A (2001) Technological and environmental differences in the European banking industries. J Financ Serv Res 19(2–3):147–162

Chakrabarti R (2005) Banking in India–reforms and reorganization. Available via DIALOG. http://ssrn.com/abstract=649855

Chakrabarti R, Chawla G (2005) Banking efficiency in India since the reforms: an assessment. Money Financ 9(2):31–47
Chandrasekhar M, Sonar RM (2008) Impact of information technology on the efficiency and total factor productivity of Indian banks. S Asia J Manage 15(3):74–95
Chang CC, Luh YH (2000) Efficiency change and growth in productivity: the Asian growth experience. J Asia Econ 10(4):551–570
Chang CE, Hasan I, Hunter WC (1998) Efficiency of multinational banks: an empirical investigation. Appl Financ Econ 8(6):1–8
Chang TP, Hu JL, Chou RY, Sun L (2012) The sources of bank productivity growth in China during 2002–2009: a disaggregation view. J Bank Financ 36(7):1997–2006
Chantapong S, Menkhoff L (2005) Cost efficiency of domestic and foreign banks in Thailand: evidence from panel data. A paper presented at Xth Spring Meeting of Young Economists at HEI, Geneva, 22–24 April 2005. Available via DIALOG. http://econstor.eu/bitstream/10419/19802/1/Chantapong.pdf
Charnes A, Cooper WW (1962) Programming with linear fractional functional. Nav Res Log Q 9(3–4):181–185
Charnes A, Cooper WW, Rhodes E (1978) Measuring the efficiency of decision making units. Eur J Oper Res 2(6):429–444
Charnes A, Cooper WW, Seiford L, Stutz J (1982) A multiplicative model of efficiency analysis. Socio Econ Plan Sci 16(5):223–224
Charnes A, Clark CT, Cooper WW, Golany B (1985) A developmental study of data envelopment analysis in measuring the efficiency of maintenance units in the US Air Forces. Ann Oper Res 2(1):95–112
Charnes A, Cooper WW, Lewin AY, Seiford LM (eds) (1994) Data envelopment analysis: theory, methodology and applications. Kluwer Academic, Boston
Chatterjee G (2006) Is inefficiency of banks in India a cause for concern? evidence from the post-reforms era. J Emerg Mark Financ 5(2):151–182
Chatterjee B, Sinha RP (2006) Cost efficiency and commercial bank lending: some empirical results. Indian Econ J 54(1):145–165
Chen TY (2004) A study of cost efficiency and privatisation in Taiwan's banks: the impact of the Asian financial crisis. T Serv Ind J 24(5):137–151
Chen C (2009) Bank efficiency in sub-saharan African middle-income countries. IMF working paper no 09/14
Chen X, Skully M, Brown K (2005) Banking efficiency in China: application of DEA to pre- and post-deregulation eras (1993–2000). China Econ Rev 16(3):229–245
Chortareas GE, Girardone C, Ventouri A (2009) Efficiency and productivity of Greek banks in the EMU era. Appl Financ Econ 19(16):1317–1328
Christopoulos DK, Tsionas EG (2001) Banking economic efficiency in the deregulation period: results from heteroscedastic stochastic frontier models. Manch Sch 69(6):656–676
Claessens S, Demirgüç-Kunt A, Huizinga H (2001) How does foreign entry affect the domestic banking market? J Bank Financ 25(5):891–911
Clark J (1996) Economic cost, scale efficiency and competitive viability in banking. J Money Credit Bank 28(3):342–364
Clark JA, Siems TF (2002) X-efficiency in banking: looking beyond the balance sheet. J Money Credit Bank 34(4):987–1013
Coelli T (2000) On the econometric estimation of the distance function representation of a production technology. Working paper 2000/42, CORE, Catholic University of Louvain, Louvain-la-Neuve
Coelli T, Perelman S (1999) A comparison of parametric and non-parametric distance functions: with application to European railways. Eur J Oper Res 117(2):326–339
Coelli TJ, Rao DSP (2005) Total factor productivity growth in agriculture: a Malmquist index analysis of 93 countries: 1980–2000. Agric Econ Int Assoc Agric Econ 32(1):115–134

Coelli TJ, Estache A, Perelman S, Trujillo L (2003) A primer on efficiency measurement for utilities and transport regulators. The World Bank, Washington, DC

Coelli T, Prasada Rao DS, O'Donnell CJ, Battese GE (2005) An introduction to efficiency and productivity analysis, 2nd edn. Springer, New York

Cook WD, Hababou M, Roberts GS (2001) The effect of financial liberalization on the Tunisian banking industry: a non-parametric approach. Topics in Middle Eastern and North African Economies, Electronic Journal 3, Middle East Economic Association and Loyola University, Chicago. Available via DIALOG. http://www.luc.edu/orgs/meea/volume3/Hababou.pdf

Cooper WW, Seiford LM, Zhu J (2004) Handbook on data envelopment analysis. Kluwer Academic, New York

Cooper WW, Seiford LM, Tone K (2007) Data envelopment analysis: a comprehensive text with models, applications, references and DEA-solver software, 2nd edn. Springer, New York

Cornwell C, Schmidt P (1996) Production frontiers and efficiency measurement. In: Matyas L, Sevestre P (eds) The econometrics of panel data: a handbook of the theory with applications. Kluwer Academic, Boston

Cornwell C, Schmidt P, Sickles RC (1990) Production frontiers with cross-sectional and time-series variations in efficiency levels. J Econom 46(1–2):185–200

Cuesta R (2000) A production model with firm specific temporal variation in technical efficiency: with application to Spanish dairy farms. J Prod Anal 13(2):139–158

Cuesta RA, Orea L (2002) Mergers and technical efficiency in Spanish savings banks: a stochastic distance function approach. J Bank Financ 26(12):2231–2247

Dacanay SJO III (2007a) Profit and cost efficiency of Philippine commercial banks under periods of liberalization, crisis and consolidation. T Bus Rev 7(2):315–322

Dacanay SJO III (2007b) Malmquist index and technical efficiency of Philippine commercial banks in the post-Asian financial crisis period. Philipp Manage Rev 14(3):93–114

Darrat AF, Topuz C, Yousf T (2002) Assessing cost and technical efficiency of banks in Kuwait. A Paper presented at ERF's 8th annual conference, January, Cairo

Das A, Ghosh S (2006) Financial deregulation and efficiency: an empirical analysis of Indian banks during post-reforms period. Rev Financ Econ 15(3):193–221

Das A, Ghosh S (2009) Financial deregulation and profit efficiency: a nonparametric analysis of Indian banks. J Econ Bus 61(6):509–528

Das A, Kumbhakar SC (2012) Productivity and efficiency dynamics in Indian banking: an input distance function approach incorporating quality of inputs and outputs. J Appl Econom 27(2):205–234

Das A, Nag A, Ray SC (2005) Liberalization, ownership and efficiency in Indian banking: a nonparametric analysis. Econ Polit Wkly 40(12):1190–1197

De Alessi L (1980) The economics of property rights: a review of the evidence. In: Richard OZ (ed) Research in law and economics: a research annual, vol 2. Jai Press, Greenwich, pp 1–47

De Guevara JF, Maudos J (2007) Explanatory factors of market power in the banking system. Manch Sch 75(3):275–296

Debasish SS (2006) Efficiency performance in Indian banking-use of data envelopment analysis. Global Bus Rev 7(2):325–333

Debnath RM, Shankar R (2008) Measuring performance of Indian banks: an application of data envelopment analysis. Int J Bus Perform Manage 10(1):57–85

Delis MD, Koutsomanoli-Fillipaki A, Staikouras CK, Katerina G (2009) Evaluating cost and profit efficiency: a comparison of parametric and non-parametric methodologies. Appl Financ Econ 19(3):191–202

Deng Q, Wong WP, Wooi HC, Xiong CM (2011) An engineering method to measure the bank productivity effect in Malaysia during 2001–2008. Syst Eng Procedia 2(1):1–11

Denizer CA, Dinc M, Tarimcilar M (2000) Measuring banking efficiency in the pre- and post-liberalization environment: evidence from the Turkish banking system. World Bank Policy Research working paper no 2476

Denizer CA, Dinc M, Tarimcilar M (2007) Financial liberalization and banking efficiency: evidence from Turkey. J Prod Anal 27(3):177–195

Deprins D, Simar L, Tulkens H (1984) Measuring labor efficiency in post offices. In: Marchand M, Pestieau P, Tulkens H (eds) The performance of public enterprises: concepts and measurement. North-Holland, Amsterdam, pp 243–267

DeYoung R (1994) Fee-based services and cost efficiency in commercial banks. In: Proceedings: conference on bank structure and competition, Federal Reserve Bank of Chicago, Chicago, pp 501–520

DeYoung R (1997) A diagnostic test for the distribution-free efficiency estimator: an example using U.S. commercial bank data. Eur J Oper Res 98(2):243–249

DeYoung R (1998) Management quality and X-efficiency in national banks. J Financ Serv Res 13 (1):5–22

DeYoung R, Hasan I (1998) The performance of de novo commercial banks: a profit efficiency approach. J Bank Financ 22(5):565–587

DeYoung N, Nolle DE (1996) Foreign-owned banks in the United States: earning market share or buying it? J Money Credit Bank 28(4):622–636

DeYoung R, Evanoff D, Molyneux P (2009) Mergers and acquisitions of financial institutions: a review of the post-2000 literature. J Financ Serv Res 36(2):87–110

Dietsch M, Lozano-Vivas A (2000) How the environment determines banking efficiency: a comparison between French and Spanish industries. J Bank Financ 24(6):985–1004

Dogan E, Fausten DK (2003) Productivity and technical change in Malaysian banking: 1989–1998. Asia Pac Financ Mark 10(2–3):205–237

Doyle J, Green R (1994) Efficiency and cross efficiency in DEA: derivations, meanings and the uses. J Oper Res Soc 45(5):567–578

Drake L, Hall MJB (2003) Efficiency in Japanese banking: an empirical analysis. J Bank Financ 27(5):891–917

Drake L, Hall MJB, Simper R (2006) The impact of macroeconomic and regulatory factors on bank efficiency: a non-parametric analysis of Hong Kong's banking system. J Bank Financ 30(5):1443–1466

Drake L, Hall MJB, Simper R (2009) Bank modeling methodologies: a comparative nonparametric analysis of efficiency in the Japanese banking sector. J Int Financ Mark Inst Money 19(1):1–15

Dulá JH, Hickman BL (1997) Effects of excluding the column being scored from the DEA envelopment LP technology matrix. J Oper Res Soc 48(10):1001–1012

Edwards FR, FS Mishkin (1995) The decline of traditional banking: implication for financial stability and regulatory policy, NBER working paper series, working paper no 4993, National Bureau of Economic Research

Elyasiani E, Mehdian SM (1990a) A nonparametric approach to measurement of efficiency and technological change: the case of large US banks. J Financ Serv Res 4(2):157–168

Elyasiani E, Mehdian SM (1990b) Efficiency in the commercial banking industry: a production frontier approach. Appl Econ 22(4):539–551

Elyasiani E, Mehdian S (1995) The comparative efficiency performance of small and large U.S. commercial banks in the pre- and post-deregulation eras. Appl Econ 27(11):1069–1079

Emrouznejad A, Parker B, Tavares G (2008) Evaluation of research in efficiency and productivity: a survey and analysis of the first 30 years of scholarly literature in DEA. J Soc Econ Plan Sci 42(3):151–157

Ersoy I (2009) The impact of the global financial crisis on the efficiency of foreign banks in Turkey. Available via DIALOG. http://www.opf.slu.cz/kfi/icfb/proc2009/pdf/08_Ersoy1.pdf

Esmaeili M (2009) A slack-based measure of efficiency for the case of exogenously fixed factors. Expert Syst Appl 36(3):4822–4825

Espitia-Escuer M, Garcia-Cebrian LI (2004) Determinants of the productive efficiency for the bank systems in the European Union countries. Int J Prod Perform Manage 53(3):435–446

Fan L (2004) Efficiency versus risk in large domestic US banks. Manage Financ 30(9):1–19

Fang Y, Hasan I, Marton K (2011) Bank efficiency in transition economies: recent evidence from South-Eastern Europe. Bank of Finland Research discussion papers 5

Färe R (1988) Fundamentals of production theory. Springer, Berlin

Färe R, Grosskopf S, Lovell CAK (1985) The measurement of efficiency of production. Kluwer-Nijhoff, Boston

Färe R, Grosskopf S, Lovell CAK (1994) Production frontiers. Cambridge University Press, New York

Färe R, Grosskopf S, Norris M, Zhang Z (1994) Productivity growth, technical progress and efficiency changes in industrialized countries. Am Econ Rev 84(1):66–83

Färe R, Grifell-Tatjé E, Grosskopf S, Lovell CAK (1997) Biased technical change and the Malmquist productivity index. Scand J Econ 99(1):119–127

Farrell MJ (1957) The measurement of productive efficiency. J R Stat Soc Ser A 120(3):253–290

Ferrier GD, Lovell CAK (1990) Measuring cost efficiency in banking: econometrics and linear programming evidence. J Econom 46(1–2):229–245

Fethi MD, Pasiouras F (2010) Assessing bank efficiency and performance with operational research and artificial intelligence techniques: a survey. Eur J Oper Res 204(2):189–198

Fethi MD, Shaban M, Weyman-Jones T (2011) Liberalization, privatization and the efficiency and productivity of Egyptian banks: a non-parametric approach. T Serv Ind J 31(7):1143–1163

Field A (2005) Discovering statistics with SPSS. Sage, London

Figueira C, Nellis J (2007) Banking efficiency in non-core EU countries: a comparative analysis of Portugal and Spain, Cranfield School of Management, Research paper series no RP 2/07, Cranfield University, Cranfield

Figueira C, Nellis J, Parker D (2006) Does ownership affect the efficiency of African banks? J Dev Area 40(1):38–63

Figueira C, Nellis J, Parker D (2009) The effects of ownership on bank efficiency in Latin America. Appl Econ 41(18):2353–2368

Fiorentino E, Karmann A, Koetter M (2006) The cost efficiency of German banks: a comparison of SFA and DEA, discussion paper series 2, banking and financial studies, no 10, Deutsche Bundesbank. Available via DIALOG. http://www.bundesbank.de/download/bankenaufsicht/dkp/200610dkp_b.pdf

Fixler DJ, Zieschang KD (1993) An index number approach to measuring bank efficiency: an application to mergers. J Bank Financ 17(2–3):437–450

Forsund FR, Lovell CAK, Schmidt P (1980) A survey of frontier production functions and of their relationship to efficiency measurement. J Econom 13(1):5–25

Fried HO, Lovell CAK, Schmidt SS, Yaisawarng S (2002) Accounting for environmental effects and statistical noise in data envelopment analysis. J Prod Anal 17(1–2):157–174

Fried HO, Lovell CAK, Schmidt S (2008) The measurement of productive efficiency and productivity growth. Oxford University Press, New York

Fries S, Taci A (2005) Cost efficiency of banks in transition: evidence from 289 banks in 15 post-communist countries. J Bank Financ 29(1):55–81

Fu X (2004) Efficiency and competition in China's banking sector. A Ph.D. thesis- Cass Business School, City University, London

Fu X, Heffernan S (2007) Cost X-efficiency in China's banking sector. China Econ Rev 18(1):35–53

Fu X, Heffernan S (2009) The effects of reform on China's bank structure and performance. J Bank Financ 33(1):39–52

Fuentes R, Vergara M (2007) Is ownership structure a determinant of bank efficiency? Central Bank of Chile working paper no 456. Available via DIALOG. http://www.bcentral.cl/estudios/documentos-trabajo/pdf/dtbc456.pdf

Fukushige M, Miyara I (2005) Statistical hypothesis testing for returns to scale using data envelopment analysis. Available via DIALOG. http://www.mssanz.org.au/MODSIM03/Volume_03/B15/03_Fukushige.pdf

Fukuyama H (1995) Measuring efficiency and productivity growth in Japanese banking: a nonparametric frontier approach. Appl Financ Econ 5(2):95–107
Fukuyama H, Weber WL (2002) Estimating output allocative efficiency and productivity change: application to Japanese banks. Eur J Oper Res 137(1):177–190
Fung MKY, Wan KKH, Hui YV, Law JS (2008) Productivity changes in Chinese airports: 1995–2004. Transp Res Part E 44(3):521–542
Gaganis C, Pasiouras F (2009) Efficiency in the Greek banking industry: a comparison of foreign and domestic banks. Int J Econ Bus 16(2):221–237
Galagedera DUA, Edirisuriya P (2005) Performance of Indian commercial banks (1995–2002). S Asia J Manage 12(4):52–74
Galanopoulos K, Karagiannis G, Koutroumanidis T (2004) Malmquist productivity index estimates for European agriculture in the 1990s. Ope Res Int J 4(1):73–91
Garden K, Ralston D (1999) The X-efficiency and allocative efficiency effects of credit unions mergers. J Int Financ Mark Inst Money 9(3):285–301
Gilbert RA, Wilson PW (1998) Effects of deregulation on the productivity of Korean banks. J Econ Bus 50(2):133–155
Girardone C, Molyneux P, Gardener EPM (2004) Analyzing the determinants of bank efficiency: the case of Italian banks. Appl Econ 36(3):215–227
Gjirja M (2004) Decomposing efficiency and productivity in Swedish banking: an empirical investigation. In efficiency and productivity in Swedish banking, a published Ph.D. thesis, Göteborg University, Göteborg
Gourlay A, Ravishankar G, Weyman-Jones T (2006) Non-parametric analysis of efficiency gains from bank mergers in India, Working paper 2006-17, Department of Economics, Loughborough University. Available via DIALOG. http://www.lboro.ac.uk/departments/sbe/RePEc/lbo/lbowps/Gourlay_Ravishankar_Weyman_Jones_Indian_Banks.pdf
Grabowski R, Rangan N, Rezvanian R (1994) The effect of deregulation on the efficiency of US banking firms. J Econ Bus 46(1):39–54
Greene WH (1980) Maximum likelihood estimation of econometric frontier functions. J Econom 13(1):27–56
Greene WH (1990) A gamma-distributed stochastic frontier model. J Econom 46(1–2):141–163
Greene WH (1993) The econometric approach to efficiency analysis. In: Fried HO, Lovell CAK, Schmidt SS (eds) The measurement of productive efficiency: techniques and applications. Oxford University Press, Oxford, pp 68–119
Grifell-Tatjé E, Lovell CAK (1995) A note on the Malmquist productivity index. Econ Lett 47(2):169–175
Grifell-Tatjé E, Lovell CAK (1996) Deregulation and productivity decline: the case of Spanish saving banks. Eur Econ Rev 40(6):1281–1303
Grifell-Tatjé E, Lovell CAK (1999) Profits and productivity. Manage Sci 45(9):1177–1193
Grigorian DA, Manole V (2006) Determinants of commercial bank performance in transition: an application of data envelopment analysis. Comp Econ Stud 48(3):497–522
Gulati R, Kumar S (2011) Impact of non-traditional activities on the efficiency of Indian banks: a non-parametric approach. Macroecon Financ Emerg Mark Econ 4(1):125–166
Guzmán I, Reverte C (2008) Productivity and efficiency change and shareholder value: evidence from the Spanish banking sector. Appl Econ 40(15):2037–2044
Hadad MD, Hall MJB, Kenjegalieva K, Santoso W, Satria R, Simper R (2008) Efficiency in Indonesian banking: recent evidence, Department of Economics, working paper no. 2008-13, Loughborough University
Hadad MD, Hall MJB, Kenjegalieva KA, Santoso W, Simper R (2011) Productivity changes and risk management in Indonesian banking: a Malmquist analysis. Appl Financ Econ 21(12):847–861
Hahn FJ (2007) Environmental determinants of banking efficiency in Austria. Empirica 34(3):231–245

Halkos GE, Salamouris DS (2004) Efficiency measurement of the Greek commercial banks with the use of financial ratios: a data envelopment analysis approach. Manage Account Res 15(2):201–224

Hancock D (1985) Bank profitability, interest rates and monetary policy. J Money Credit Bank 17(2):189–202

Hanson JA (2005) Improving performance of the Indian banks. In: Basu P (ed) India's financial sector: recent reforms, future challenges. Macmillan, New Delhi

Hanson JA, Kathuria S (1999) India: a financial sector for the twenty-first century. Oxford University Press, New Delhi

Hao J, Hunter WC, Yang WK (2001) Deregulation and efficiency: the case of private Korean banks. J Econ Bus 53(2–3):237–254

Hasan I, Marton K (2003) Development and efficiency of the banking sector in a transitional economy: Hungarian experience. J Bank Financ 27(12):2249–2271

Hassan KM, Sanchez B (2007) Efficiency determinants and dynamic efficiency changes in Latin American banking industries, Working paper-32, Networks Financial Institute, Indiana State University. Available via DIALOG. http://papers.ssrn.com/sol3/papers.cfm?abstract_id=1087045

Hauner D, Peiris SJ (2005) Bank efficiency and competition in low-income countries: the case of Uganda, IMF working paper no WP/05/240. Available via DIALOG. www.imf.org/external/pubs/ft/wp/2005/wp05240.pdf

Hausman JA (1978) Specification tests in econometrics. Econometrica 46(6):1251–1271

Hausman JA, Taylor WE (1981) Panel data and unobservable individual effects. Econometrica 49(6):1377–1398

Havrylchyk O (2006) Efficiency of the Polish banking industry: foreign versus domestic banks. J Bank Financ 30(7):1975–1996

Heffernan S, Fu X (2009) Bank productivity changes in two Asian giants. In: A paper presented at UKEPAN conference, Leicester, November 2009. Received from Available via DIALOG. http://www.cass.city.ac.uk/__data/assets/pdf_file/0005/77801/CBR_WP01-10.pdf

Hermalin BE, Wallace NE (1994) The determinants of efficiency and solvency in savings and loans. Rand J Econ 25(3):361–381

Hermes N, Lensink R (2008) Does financial liberalization influence saving, investment and economic growth? Evidence from 25 emerging market economies, 1973–1996. In: Guha-Khasnobis B, Mavrotas G (eds) Financial development, institutions, growth and poverty reduction. Palgrave MacMillan, Basingstoke, pp 164–189

Hermes N, Nhung VTH (2010) The impact of financial liberalization on bank efficiency: evidence from Latin America and Asia. Appl Econ 42(26):3351–3365

Hjalmarsson L, Andersson I, Mlima A, (2000) Swedish banking efficiency and productivity in an international perspective. Estocolmo: Supplement no. 28 to the Government Inquiry on the International Competitiveness of the Swedish Financial Sector, Stockholm

Ho D (2004) Bank branch profitability and productivity: a domestic and international study using DEA, A masters' thesis submitted to Department of Chemical Engineering and Applied Chemistry, University of Toronto

Horrace WC, Schmidt P (1996) Confidence statements for efficiency estimates from stochastic frontier models. J Prod Anal 7(2&3):257–282

Howcroft B, Ataullah A (2006) Total factor productivity change: an examination of the commercial banking industry in India and Pakistan. T Serv Ind J 26(2):189–202

Hsiao HC, Chang H, Anna M, Cianci AM, Huang LH (2010) First financial restructuring and operating efficiency: evidence from Taiwanese commercial banks. J Bank Financ 34 (7):1461–1471

Huang LW, Chen YK (2006) Does bank performance benefit from non-traditional activities? A case of non-interest income in Taiwan commercial banks. Asia J Manage Humanit Sci 1(3):359–378

Huang LH, Hsiao HC, Cheng MA, Chang SJ (2008) Effects of financial reform on productivity change. Ind Manage Data Syst 108(7):867–886

Humphrey DB (1985) Costs and scale economies in bank intermediation. In: Aspinwall RC, Eisenbeis RA (eds) Handbook for banking strategy. Wiley, New York

Humphrey DB (1991) Productivity in banking and effects from deregulation. Econ Rev 77(1):16–28

Humphrey DB (1993) Cost and technological change: effects from bank deregulation. J Prod Anal 4(1–2):9–34

Humphrey DB, Pulley LB (1997) Banks' responses to deregulation: profits, technology, and efficiency. J Money Credit Bank 29(1):73–93

Humphrey DB, Vale B (2004) Scale economies, bank mergers, and electronic payments: a spline function approach. J Bank Financ 28(7):1671–1696

Iqbal M, Molyneux P (2005) Thirty years of Islamic banking: history, performance and prospects. Palgrave Macmillan, New York

Isik I (2007) Bank ownership and productivity developments: evidence from Turkey. Stud Econ Financ 24(2):115–139

Isik I (2008) Productivity, technology and efficiency of de novo banks: a counter evidence from Turkey. J Multinatl Financ Manage 18(5):427–442

Isik I, Hassan MK (2002a) Technical, scale and allocative efficiencies of Turkish banking industry. J Bank Financ 26(4):719–766

Isik I, Hassan MK (2002b) Cost and profit efficiency of Turkish banking industry: an empirical investigation. Financ Rev 37(2):257–280

Isik I, Hassan K (2003a) Efficiency, ownership and market structure, corporate control and governance in the Turkish banking industry. J Bus Financ Acc 30(9–10):1363–1421

Isik I, Hassan MK (2003b) Financial deregulation and total factor productivity change: an empirical study of Turkish commercial banks. J Bank Financ 27(8):1455–1485

Isik I, Hassan MK (2003c) Financial disruption and bank productivity: the 1994 experience of Turkish banks. Q Rev Econ Financ 43(2):291–320

Jackson PM, Fethi MD (2000) Evaluating the technical efficiency of Turkish commercial banks: an application of DEA and Tobit analysis. A paper presented at the international DEA symposium, University of Queensland, Brisbane, 2–4 July 2000

Jackson PM, Fethi MD, Inal G (1998) Efficiency and productivity growth in Turkish commercial banking sector: a non-parametric approach. A paper presented at the European symposium on: Data envelopment analysis – recent developments and applications, Wernigerode, 16–18 October. Available via DIALOG. https://lra.le.ac.uk/bitstream/2381/367/1/dpno1.pdf

Jacobs R (2000) Alternative methods to examine hospital efficiency: data envelopment analysis and stochastic frontier analysis, discussion paper no 177, University of York, Centre for Health Economics. Available via DIALOG http://www.york.ac.uk/inst/che/pdf/DP177.pdf

Jaffry S, Ghulam Y, Pascoe S, Cox J (2007) Regulatory changes and productivity of the banking sector in the Indian sub-continent. J Asia Econ 18(3):415–438

Jagirdar B (1996) Capital adequacy: some issues. Econ Polit Wkly 31(12):731–739

Jagtiani J, Nathan A, Sick G (1995) Scale economies and cost complementarities in commercial banks: on and off-balance sheet activities. J Bank Financ 19(7):1175–1189

Jemric I, Vujcic B (2002) Efficiency of banks in Croatia: a DEA approach. Comp Econ Stud 44(2–3):69–193

Jiang C, Yao S, Zhang Z (2009) The effects of governance changes on bank efficiency in China: a stochastic distance function approach. China Econ Rev 20(4):717–731

Jondrow J, Lovell C, Materov I, Schmidt P (1982) On the estimation of technical efficiency in the stochastic frontier production function model. J Econom 19(2–3):233–238

Joshi V, Little IMD (1996) India's economic reforms 1991–2001. Clarendon Press Oxford, New York

Kablan S (2007) Measuring bank efficiency in developing countries: the case of WAEMU (West African Economic Monetary Union), African Economic conference, November 2007. Available via DIALOG. http://www.afdb.org/fileadmin/uploads/afdb/Documents/Knowledge/25038351-EN-MESURE-DE-LA-PERFORMANCE-DES-BANQUES-UEMOA.PDF

Kaparakis E, Miller S, Noulos A (1994) Short-run cost inefficiency of commercial banks: a flexible stochastic frontier approach. J Money Credit Bank 26(4):875–893

Karas A, Schoors K, Weill L (2008) Are private banks more efficient than public banks? Evidence from Russia. BOFIT discussion papers no. 3/2008, BOFIT-Institute for Economies in Transition, Bank of Finland. Available via DIALOG http://lnweb90.worldbank.org/Caw/CawDocLib.nsf/0/6B26415F1873B0B485257432004834FC/$file/DP0308.pdf

Ketkar KW (1993) Public sector banking, efficiency and economic growth in India. World Dev 21(10):1685–1697

Ketkar KH, Ketkar SL (1992) Bank nationalisation, financial savings and economic development–a case study. J Dev Areas 27(1):69–84

Kirikal LY (2005) Productivity, the malmquist index and the empirical study of banks in Estonia. A Ph.D. thesis, School of Economics and Business Administration, Tallinn University of Technology, Tallinn

Kittelsen S (1999) Monte carlo simulations of DEA efficiency measures and hypothesis test. Memorandum no. 09/99, Department of Economics, University of Oslo

Klimberg RK, Ratick SJ (2008) Modeling data envelopment analysis (DEA) efficient location/allocation decisions. Comput Oper Res 35(2):457–474

Klopp GA (1985) The analysis of the efficiency of production system with multiple inputs and outputs. A Ph.D. dissertation, University of Illinois at Chicago, Industrial and System Engineering College

Koenker RW, Bassett GW (1978) Regression quantiles. Econometrica 46(1):33–50

Kochar A (2005) Social banking and poverty: a micro-empirical analysis of the Indian experience. Working paper, Stanford Cent Int Dev, Stanford University

Kondeas AG, Caudill SB, Gropper DM, Raymond JE (2008) Deregulation and productivity changes in banking: evidence from European unification. Appl Financ Econ Lett 4(3):193–197

Košak M, Zajc P, Zorić J (2009) Bank efficiency differences in the new EU member states. Baltic J Econ 9(2):67–90

Koutsomanoli-Filippaki A, Mamatzakis E, Staikouras C (2009a) Structural reforms and banking efficiency in the new EU States. J Policy Model 31(1):17–21

Koutsomanoli-Filippaki A, Margaritis D, Staikouras C (2009b) Efficiency and productivity growth in the banking industry of Central and Eastern Europe. J Bank Financ 33(3):557–567

Kraft E, Tirtiroglu D (1998) Bank efficiency in Croatia: a stochastic-frontier analysis. J Comp Econ 26(2):282–300

Kraft E, Hofler R, Payne J (2006) Privatization, foreign bank entry and bank efficiency in Croatia: a fourier-flexible function stochastic cost frontier analysis. Appl Econ 38(17):2075–2088

Krishnasamy G, Ridzwa AH, Perumal V (2003) Malaysian post merger banks' productivity: application of Malmquist productivity index. Manage Financ 30(4):63–74

Kumar S (2013) Banking reforms and the evolution of cost efficiency in Indian public sector banks. Econ Change Restruct 46(2):143–182

Kumar S, Gulati R (2008a) Evaluation of technical efficiency and ranking of public sector banks in India: an analysis from cross-sectional perspective. Int J Prod Perform Manage 57(7):540–568

Kumar S, Gulati R (2008b) An examination of technical, pure technical, and scale efficiencies in Indian public sector banks using data envelopment analysis. Eurasian J Bus Econ 1(2):33–69

Kumar S, Gulati R (2009a) Technical efficiency and its determinants in the Indian domestic banking industry: an application of DEA and Tobit analysis. Am J Financ Acc 1(3):256–296

Kumar S, Gulati R (2009b) Did efficiency of Indian public sector banks converge with banking reforms? Int Rev Econ 56(1):47–84

Kumar S, Gulati R (2010) Dynamics of cost efficiency in Indian public sector banks: a post-deregulation experience, A paper presented in the 12th annual conference on money and

finance in the Indian economy, 11th–12th Mar 2010. Available via DIALOG. http://www.igidr.ac.in/~money/mfc-12/Dynamics%20of%20cost% 20efficiency_sunil%20kumar.pdf
Kumbhakar SC (1987) The specification of technical and allocative inefficiency of multi-product firms in stochastic production and profit frontiers. J Quant Econ 3(2):213–223
Kumbhakar SC (1990) Production frontiers, panel data and time-varying technical inefficiency. J Econom 46(1–2):201–211
Kumbhakar S, Hjalmarsson L (1995) Labor use efficiency in Swedish social insurance offices. J Appl Econom 10(1):33–47
Kumbhakar SC, Lovell CAK (2000) Stochastic frontier analysis. Cambridge University Press, New York
Kumbhakar SC, Lozano-Vivas A (2005) Deregulation and productivity: the case of Spanish banks. J Regul Econ 27(3):331–351
Kumbhakar SC, Sarkar S (2003) Deregulation, ownership and productivity growth in the banking industry: evidence from India. J Money Credit Bank 35(3):403–424
Kumbhakar SC, Sarkar S (2005) Deregulation, ownership, and efficiency change in Indian banking: an application of stochastic frontier analysis. In: Ghosh R, Neogi C (eds) Theory and application of productivity and efficiency: econometric and DEA approach. Macmillan India, New Delhi
Kumbhakar SC, Wang D (2007) Economic reforms, efficiency and productivity in Chinese banking. J Regul Econ 32(2):105–129
Kumbhakar S, Hesmati A, Hjalmarsson L (1998) How fast do banks adjust? A dynamic model of labour-use with an application to Swedish banks. J Prod Anal 18(1):79–102
Kumbhakar SC, Lozano-Vivas A, Lovell CAK, Hasan I (2001) The effects of deregulation on the performance of financial institutions: the case of Spanish savings banks. J Money Credit Bank 33(1):101–120
Kwan SH (2003) Operating performance of banks among Asian economies: an international and time series comparison. J Bank Financ 27(3):471–489
Kwan SH (2006) The X-efficiency of commercial banks in Hong Kong. J Bank Financ 30(4):1127–1147
Kyj L, Isik I (2008) Bank X-efficiency in Ukraine: an analysis of service characteristics and ownership. J Econ Bus 60(4):369–393
Lang G, Welzel P (1996) Efficiency and technical progress in banking empirical results for a panel of German co-operative banks. J Bank Financ 20(6):1003–1023
Lang G, Welzel P (1998) Technology and cost efficiency in universal banking: a thick frontier analysis of the German banking industry. J Prod Anal 10(1):63–84
Lang G, Welzel P (1999) Mergers among German cooperative banks: a panel-based stochastic frontier analysis. Small Bus Econ 13(4):273–286
Lee L (1983) A test for distributional assumptions for the stochastic frontier function. J Econom 22(3):245–267
Lee Y, Schmidt P (1993) A production frontier model with flexible temporal variation in technical efficiency. In: Fried HO, Lovell CAK, Schmidt SS (eds) The measurement of productive efficiency. Oxford University Press, Oxford
Lee BL, Worthington AC, Leong WH (2010) Malmquist indices of pre- and post-deregulation productivity, efficiency and technological change in the Singaporean banking sector. Singapore Econ Rev 55(4):599–618
Leeladhar V (2008) Consolidation in the Indian financial sector, address at the international banking & finance conference, 2008, organized by the Indian Merchants' Chamber, Mumbai, BIS Review 46/2008. Available via DIALOG. http://www.bis.org/review/r080421d.pdf?frames=0
Leightner JE, Lovell CAK (1998) The impact of financial liberalization on the performance of Thai banks. J Econ Bus 50(2):115–131
Lensink R, Meesters A, Naaborg I (2008) Bank efficiency and foreign ownership: do good institutions matter? J Bank Financ 32(5):834–844
Leung HM (1998) Productivity of Singapore's manufacturing sector: an industry level nonparametric study. Asia Pac J Manage 15(1):19–31

Levy B (1987) A theory of public enterprise behavior. J Econ Behav Organ 8(1):75–96

Liang L, Wu J, Cook WD, Zhu J (2008) Alternative secondary goals in DEA cross-efficiency evaluation. Int J Prod Econ 113(2):1025–1030

Lieu P, Yeh T, Chiu Y (2005) Off-balance sheet activities and cost inefficiency in Taiwan's banks. Serv Ind J 25(7):925–944

Lin YH, Hsu GJY, Hsiao CK (2007) Measuring efficiency of domestic banks in Taiwan: application of data envelopment analysis and Malmquist index. Appl Econ Lett 14(11):821–827

Liu ST (2010) Measuring and categorizing technical efficiency and productivity change of commercial banks in Taiwan. Expert Sys Appl 37(4):2783–2789

Liu B, Tripe D (2002) New Zealand bank mergers and efficiency gains. J Asia Pac Bus 4(4):61–81

López-Cortés GC (1997) An efficiency analysis of Mexico's commercial banks before, during and after financial liberalization. International Business Resource Group, discussion paper no EC5/97, pp 1–36, Lancaster University, Lancaster

López-Cortés G, Snowden PN (1998) The Mexican banking industry through privatization to intervention: a DEA perspective 1982–1996. International Business Resource Group (IBRG), discussion paper no EC8/98, Department of Economics, The Management School, Lancaster University, Lancaster

Lovell CAK (1993) Production frontiers and productive efficiency. In: Fried H, Lovell CAK, Schmidt S (eds) The measurement of productive efficiency. Oxford University Press, New York, pp 3–67

Lovell CAK, Rouse APB (2003) Equivalent standard DEA models to provide super-efficiency scores. J Oper Res Soc 54(1):101–108

Lozano-Vivas A (1998) Efficiency and technical change for Spanish banks. Appl Financ Econ 8(3):289–300

Lozano-Vivas A, Pasiouras F (2010) The impact of non-traditional activities on the estimation of bank efficiency: international evidence. J Bank Financ 34(7):1436–1449

Lozano-Vivas A, Pastor JT, Hasan I (2001) European bank performance beyond country borders: what really matters? Eur Financ Rev 5(1–2):141–165

Lozano-Vivas A, Pastor JT, Pastor JM (2002) An efficiency comparison of European banking systems operating under different environmental conditions. J Prod Anal 18(1):59–78

Luo X (2003) Evaluating the profitability and marketability efficiency of large banks: an application of data envelopment analysis. J Bus Res 56(8):627–635

Maghyereh A (2004) The effect of financial liberalization on the efficiency of financial institutions: the case of Jordanian commercial banks. J Transnatl Manage Dev 9(2–3):71–106

Mahadevan R, Kim S (2001) Did financial deregulation since 1980s prior to 1997 affect the efficiency performance of Korean banks. Indian J Quant Econ 16(1):81–100

Mahesh HP, Bhide S (2008) Do financial sector reforms make commercial banks more efficient? a parametric exploration of the Indian case. Margin J Appl Econ Res 2(4):415–441

Mahesh HP, Rajeev M (2009) Producing financial services: an efficiency analysis of Indian commercial banks. J Serv Res 8(2):7–29

Majid M, Saal DS, Battisti G (2011) The impact of Islamic banking on the cost efficiency and productivity change of Malaysian commercial banks. Appl Econ 43(16):2033–2054

Majumdar SK (1998) Assessing comparative efficiency of the state-owned mixed and private sectors in Indian industry. Pubic Choice 96(1–2):1–24

Majumdar SK, Chang H (1996) Scale efficiencies in US telecommunications: an empirical investigation. Manage Decis Econ 17(3):303–318

Malmquist S (1953) Index numbers and indifference surfaces. Trabajos de Estatistica 4(2):209–242

Manandhar R, Tang JCS (2002) The evaluation of bank branch performance using data envelopment analysis: a framework. J High Technol Manage Res 13(1):1–17

Matousek R, Taci A (2004) Efficiency in banking: empirical evidence from the Czech Republic. Econ Plan 37(3):225–244

Matousek R, Dasci S, Sergi BS (2008) The efficiency of the Turkish banking system during 2000–2005. Int J Econ Policy Emerg Econ 1(4):341–355

Matthews K, Ismail M (2006) Efficiency and productivity growth of domestic and foreign commercial banks in Malaysia. Cardiff economics working papers no 2006/02, Cardiff Business School, Cardiff University, Cardiff

Matthews K, Zhang NX (2010) Bank productivity in China 1997–2007: measurement and convergence. China Econ Rev 21(4):617–628

Maudos J, Pastor JM (2003) Cost and profit efficiency in the Spanish banking sector (1985–1996): a non-parametric approach. Appl Financ Econ 13(1):1–12

Maudos J, Pastor JM, Pérez F, Quesada J (2002) Cost and profit efficiency in European banks. J Int Financ Mark Inst Money 12(1):33–58

Meeusen W, van den Broeck J (1977) Efficiency estimation from Cobb–Douglas production functions with composed error. Int Econ Rev 18(2):435–444

Mehdian SM, Perry MJ, Rezvanian R (2007) The effect of globalization on efficiency change, technological progress and the productivity growth of U.S. small and large banks. North Am J Financ Bank Res 1(1):1–21

Mercan M, Reisman A, Yolalan R, Emel AB (2003) The effect of scale and mode of ownership on the financial performance of the Turkish banking sector: results of a DEA-based analysis. Socio Econ Plan Sci 37(3):185–202

Meso BW, Kaino DK (2008) Financial liberalization and bank efficiency: the case of commercial banks in Kenya. ICFAI J Appl Econ 8(3):7–22

Mester LJ (1993) Efficiency in the savings and loan industry. J Bank Financ 17(2–3):267–286

Mester IJ (1996) A study of bank efficiency taking into account risk preferences. J Bank Financ 20(6):1025–1045

Miller SM, Noulas AG (1996) The technical efficiency of large bank production. J Bank Financ 20(3):495–509

Miller SR, Parkhe A (2002) Is there a liability of foreignness in global banking? An empirical test of banks X-efficiency. Strateg Manage J 23(1):55–75

Ministry of Finance (1998) Report of the committee on banking sector reforms. (Chairman: M. Narasimham), New Delhi

Mirmirani S, Li HC, Ilacqua JA (2008) Health care efficiency in transition economies: an application data envelopment analysis. Int Bus Econ Res J 7(2):47–56

Mishkin FS (2004) The economics of money, banking and financial markets. Pearson Addison-Wesley, Boston

Mohan R (2007) India's financial sector reforms: fostering growth while containing risk. Address at Yale University, New Haven, 3 Dec 2007. Available via DIALOG. http://www.bis.org/review/r071207e.pdf?frames=0

Mohan R, Prasad A (2005) India's experience with financial sector development. In: Basu P (ed) India's financial sector: recent reforms, future challenges. Macmillan India, New Delhi

Mostafa M (2007) Modeling the efficiency of GCC banks: a data envelopment analysis approach. Int J Prod Perform Manage 56(7):623–643

Mukherjee K, Ray SC, Miller SM (2001) Productivity growth in large US commercial banks: the initial post-deregulation experience. J Bank Financ 25(5):913–939

Mukherjee A, Nath P, Pal M (2002) Performance benchmarking and strategic homogeneity of Indian banks. Int J Bank Mark 20(3):122–139

Musonda A (2008) An investigation into the determinants of cost efficiency in the Zambian banking sector. A paper presented at 13th Annual African econometrics society (AES) conference, University of Pretoria, South Africa, 9th–11th July, 2008. Available via DIALOG. http://www.africametrics.org/documents/conference08/day2/session6/musonda.pdf

Mylonidis N, Kelnikola I (2005) Merging activity in the Greek banking system: a financial accounting perspective. S East Eur J Econ 3(1):121–144

Nachane DM, Ghosh S (2002) Determinants of off-balance sheet activities: an empirical analysis of public sector banks. Econ Polit Wkly 37(5):421–427

Nachane DM, Ghosh S (2007) An empirical analysis of the off-balance sheet activities of Indian banks. J Emerg Mark Financ 6(1):39–59

Neal P (2004) X-efficiency and productivity change in Australian banking. Aust Econ Pap 43(2):174–191

Nguyen N, Williams J (2005) Liberalization, ownership and efficiency issues: a comparative study of South East Asian banking. A paper presented at conference on globalization and financial services in emerging economics held at The World Bank, Washington, DC, 20th–21st June 2005. Available via DIALOG. http://siteresources.worldbank.org/INTFR/Resources/475459-1107978088492/Liberalisation_ownership.pdf

Nikiel EM, Opiela TP (2002) Customer type and bank efficiency in Poland implication for emerging market banking. Contemp Econ Policy 20(3):255–271

Niskanen W (1975) Bureaucrats and politicians. J Law Econ 18(3):617–643

Njie M (2007) Impact of financial liberalization on the productive efficiency of the banking industry in Malaysia. Bank J Malays 131(1):49–67

Noulas AG (1997) Productivity growth in the Hellenic banking industry: state versus private banks. Appl Financ Econ 7(3):223–228

Noulas A (2001) Deregulation and operating efficiency: the case of the Greek banks. Manage Financ 27(8):35–47

Odeck J (2008) The effect of mergers on efficiency and productivity of public transport services. Transp Res Part A 42(4):696–708

Oral M, Kettani O, Lang P (1991) A methodology for collective evaluation and selection of industrial R&D projects. Manage Sci 37(7):871–883

Ozcan YA (2008) Health care benchmarking and performance evaluation: an assessment using Data Envelopment Analysis (DEA). Springer, New York

Ozdincer B, Ozyildirim C (2008) Determining the factors of bank performance with a focus on risk and technical efficiency. A paper presented at 2nd WSEAS international conference on management, marketing and finances (MMF'08), Harvard, 24–26 Mar 2008

Ozkan-Gunay EN, Tektas A (2006) Efficiency analysis of the Turkish banking sector in pre-crisis and crisis period: a DEA approach. Contemp Econ Policy 24(3):418–431

Park KH, Weber WL (2006) A note on efficiency and productivity growth in the Korean banking industry: 1992–2002. J Bank Financ 30(8):2371–2386

Pasiouras F (2008) Estimating the technical and scale efficiency of Greek commercial banks: the impact of credit risk, off-balance sheet activities, and international operations. Res Int Bus Financ 22(3):301–318

Pasiouras F, Sifodaskalakis E, Zopounidis C (2007) Estimating and analyzing the cost efficiency of Greek co-operative banks: an application of two-stage data envelopment analysis. Working paper no 12, School of Management, University of Bath, Bath

Pasricha ASK (2007) On financial sector reform in emerging markets: enhancing creditors' rights and securitizing non-performing loans in the Indian banking sector – an elephant's tale. Buffalo Law Rev 55(1):325–382

Patti EB, Hardy DC (2005) Financial sector liberalization, bank privatization, and efficiency: evidence from Pakistan. J Bank Financ 29(8–9):2381–2406

Peng YH, Wang K (2004) Cost efficiency and the effect of mergers on the Taiwanese banking industry. T Serv Ind J 24(4):21–39

Perera S, Skully M, Wickramanayake J (2007) Cost efficiency in South Asian banking: the impact of bank size, state ownership and stock exchange listings. Int Rev Financ 7(1–2):35–60

Peristiani S (1997) Do mergers improve the X-efficiency and scale efficiency of U.S. banks? Evidence from the 1980s. J Money Credit Bank 29(3):326–337

Pi L, Timme SG (1993) Corporate control and bank efficiency. J Bank Financ 17(2–3):515–530

Pitt MM, Lee LF (1981) The measurement and sources of technical inefficiency in the Indonesian weaving industry. J Dev Econ 9(1):43–64

Poghosyan T, Poghosyan A (2010) Foreign bank entry, bank efficiency and market power in Central and Eastern European countries. Econ Transit 18(3):571–598

Rajan RG (2009) A hundred small steps: report of the Committee on Financial Sector Reforms. Planning Commission, Government of India, Sage Publications, New Delhi

Rajan RG, Zingales L (1998) Financial dependence and growth. T Am Econ Rev 88(3):559–586

Ram Mohan TT, Ray S (2004a) Productivity growth and efficiency in Indian banking: a comparison of public, private and foreign banks. Department of Economics, working paper no 2004/27, University of Connecticut, Connecticut. Available via DIALOG. http://digitalcommons.uconn.edu/econ wpapers/200427

Ram Mohan TT, Ray SC (2004b) Comparing performance of public and private sector banks: a revenue maximization efficiency approach. Econ Polit Wkly 39(12):1271–1275

Ramanathan R (2006) Performance of banks in countries of the Gulf Cooperation Council. Int J Prod Perform Manage 56(2):137–154

Rangan N, Grabowski R, Aly H, Pasurka C (1988) The technical efficiency of U.S. banks. Econ Lett 28(2):169–175

Rangarajan C (2007) The Indian banking system–challenges ahead. First R.K. Talwar Memorial Lecture- 2007, Indian Institute of Banking and Finance, July 31. Available via DIALOG. www.iibf.org.in/portal/documents/crangarajan_Lecture.doc

Ray SC (2004) Data envelopment analysis: theory and techniques for economics and operations research. Cambridge University Press, Cambridge, UK

Ray SC (2007) Are some Indian banks too large? an examination of size efficiency in Indian banking. J Prod Anal 27(1):41–56

Ray S, Das A (2010) Distribution of cost and profit efficiency: evidence from Indian banking. Eur J Oper Res 201(1):297–307

Ray S, Desli E (1997) Productivity growth, technical progress and efficiency change in industrialized countries: comment. Am Econ Rev 87(5):1033–1039

Rebelo J, Mendes V (2000) Malmquist indices of productivity change in Portuguese banking: the deregulation period. Int Adv Econ Res 6(3):531–543

Reda M, Isik I (2006) Efficiency and productivity change of Egyptian commercial banks (1995–2003). In: Selected papers from the thirteenth anual conference, Economic Research Forum, Cairo, pp 87–136

Reddy AA (2004) Banking sector liberalization and efficiency of Indian banks. ICFAI J Bank Manage 3(2):37–53, 844

Reddy AA (2005a) Banking sector deregulation and productivity change decomposition of Indian banks. Financ India 19(3):983–1001, 846

Reddy YV (1998) RBI and banking sector reforms. Reserve Bank India Bulletin, December, pp 99–1008

Reddy YV (2005b) Banking sector reforms in India: an overview. Reserve Bank India Bulletin, June, pp 577–583

Reddy YV (2007) India-perspective for growth with stability. BIS Rev 54/2007. Available via DIALOG. http://www.bis.org/review/r070529d.pdf

Reserve Bank of India (1975) Report of the working group on customer services in banks. (Chairman: R.K. Talwar), Mumbai

Reserve Bank of India (1977) Report of the productivity, efficiency & profitability committee on banking. (Chairman: J.C. Lathur), Mumbai

Reserve Bank of India (1985a) Report of the committee to review the working of the monetary system. (Chairman: S. Chakravarty), Mumbai

Reserve Bank of India (1985b) Report of the working group to review the system of inspection of banks. (Chairman: Pendharkar), Mumbai

Reserve Bank of India (1987) Report of the working group on the money markets. (Chairman: N. Vaghul), Mumbai

Reserve Bank of India (1990) Report of the committee on customer services in banks. (Chairman: M.N. Goiporia), Mumbai

Reserve Bank of India (1991) Report of the committee on frauds and malpractices in banks. (Chairman: A. Ghosh), Mumbai

Reserve Bank of India (1991–1992) Report of the committee on bank accounts. (Chairman: A. Ghosh), Mumbai

Reserve Bank of India (1992a) Report of the committee on the financial system. (Chairman: M. Narasimham), Mumbai
Reserve Bank of India (1992b) Report of the committee to enquire into securities transactions of banks and financial institutions. (Chairman: A. Janakiraman), Mumbai
Reserve Bank of India (1992c) Report of the working group on security equipments. (Chairman: R. Jilani), Mumbai
Reserve Bank of India (1993) Report on trend and progress of banking in India: 1992–1993, Mumbai
Reserve Bank of India (1994a) Report of the committee on technology issues. (Chairman: W.S. Saraf), Mumbai
Reserve Bank of India (1994b) Report on trend and progress of banking in India: 1993–1994, Mumbai
Reserve Bank of India (1995a) Report of the working group on internal control systems of banks. (Chairman: R. Jilani), Mumbai
Reserve Bank of India (1995b) Report on trend and progress of banking in India: 1994–1995, Mumbai
Reserve Bank of India (1996a) Report of the committee for proposing legislation on electronic funds transfer and other electronic payments. (Chairman: K.S. Shere), Mumbai
Reserve Bank of India (1996b) Report of the working group on on-site supervision of banks. (Chairman: S. Padmanabhan), Mumbai
Reserve Bank of India (1996c) Report on trend and progress of banking in India: 1995–1996, Mumbai
Reserve Bank of India (1997a) Report of the committee on banking education. (Chairman: R. Kannan), Mumbai
Reserve Bank of India (1997b) Report of the Working Group on harmonizing Development Financial Institutions (DFIs) and banks. (Chairman: S.H. Khan), Mumbai
Reserve Bank of India (1997c) Report on trend and progress of banking in India: 1996–1997, Mumbai
Reserve Bank of India (1997d) Report on trend and progress of banking in India: 1997–1998, Mumbai
Reserve Bank of India (1999a) Report of the committee on technology upgradation in the banking sector. (Chairman: A. Vasudevan), Mumbai
Reserve Bank of India (1999b) Report of the Working Group on international banking statistics. (Chairman: N.K. Puri), Mumbai
Reserve Bank of India (1999c) Report of the Working Group on restructuring weak public sector banks. (Chairman: M.S. Verma), Mumbai
Reserve Bank of India (1999d) Report on trend and progress of banking in India: 1998–1999, Mumbai
Reserve Bank of India (2000a) Report of advisory group on transparency in monetary and financial policies. (Chairman: M. Narasimham), Mumbai
Reserve Bank of India (2000b) Report on trend and progress of banking in India: 1999–2000, Mumbai
Reserve Bank of India (2001a) Report of the expert committee on legal aspects of bank frauds. (Chairman: N.L. Mitra), Mumbai
Reserve Bank of India (2001b) Report on internet banking. (Chairman: S.R. Mittal), Mumbai
Reserve Bank of India (2001c) Report on trend and progress of banking in India: 2000–2001, Mumbai
Reserve Bank of India (2002a) Report of the consultative group of directors of banks/Financial Institutions. (Chairman: A.S. Ganguly), Mumbai
Reserve Bank of India (2002b) Report of the review group on the working of the Local Area Bank Scheme. (Chairman: G. Ramachandran), Mumbai
Reserve Bank of India (2002c) Report of the standing committee on International Financial Standards and Codes. (Chairman: Y.V. Reddy), Mumbai

Reserve Bank of India (2002d) Report on trend and progress of banking in India: 2001–2002, Mumbai

Reserve Bank of India (2003) Report on trend and progress of banking in India: 2002–2003, Mumbai

Reserve Bank of India (2004a) Report of the working group on banking arrangements for implementation of value added tax. (Director: U. Thorat), Mumbai

Reserve Bank of India (2004b) Report on trend and progress of banking in India: 2003–2004, Mumbai

Reserve Bank of India (2005) Report on trend and progress of banking in India: 2004–2005, Mumbai

Reserve Bank of India (2006a) Report of the working group to formulate a scheme for ensuring reasonableness of bank charges. (Chairman: N. Sadasivan), Mumbai

Reserve Bank of India (2006b) Report on trend and progress of banking in India: 2005–2006, Mumbai

Reserve Bank of India (2007) Report on trend and progress of banking in India: 2006–2007, Mumbai

Reserve Bank of India (2008a) Report on trend and progress of banking in India: 2007–2008, Mumbai

Reserve Bank of India (2008b) Evolution of banking in India. Report on currency and finance: 2003–2008, vol 4, pp 74–141

Reserve Bank of India (2008c) Competition and consolidation. Report on currency and finance: 2003–2008, vol 5, pp 349–392

Reserve Bank of India (2008d) Efficiency, productivity and soundness of the banking sector. Report on currency and finance: 2003–2008, vol 5, pp 393–446

Reserve Bank of India (2009a) Handbook of statistics on the Indian economy: 2008–2009, Mumbai

Reserve Bank of India (2009b) Report of the committee on financial sector assessment. (Chairman: R. Mohan), Mumbai

Reserve Bank of India (2009c) Report of the committee to review lead bank scheme. (Chairman: U. Thorat), Mumbai

Reserve Bank of India (2009d) Report on trend and progress of banking in India: 2008–2009, Mumbai

Reserve Bank of India (2009e) Statistical tables relating to banks of India: 2008–2009, Mumbai

Reserve Bank of India (2010) Report on trend and progress of banking in India: 2009–2010, Mumbai

Resti A (1998) Regulation can foster mergers, can mergers foster efficiency? the Italian case. J Econ Bus 50(2):157–169

Rezitis AN (2008) Efficiency and productivity effects of bank mergers: evidence from the Greek banking industry. Econ Model 25(2):236–254

Rezvanian R, Rao N, Mehdian SM (2008) Efficiency change, technological progress and productivity growth of private, public and foreign banks in India: evidence from the post-liberalization era. Appl Financ Econ 18(9):701–713

Rime B, Stiroh KJ (2003) The performance of universal banks: evidence from Switzerland. J Bank Finan 27(11):2121–2150

Rizvi SYA (2001) Post-liberalization efficiency and productivity of the banking sector in Pakistan. Pak Dev Rev 40(4):605–632

Rogers KE (1998) Nontraditional activities and the efficiency of US commercial banks. J Bank Financ 22(4):467–482

Roland C (2008) Banking sector liberalization in India: evaluation of reforms and comparative perspectives on China. Physica-Verlag, Heidelberg

Rutledge RW, Parsons S, Knaebel R (1995) Assessing hospital efficiency over time: an empirical application of data envelopment analysis. J Inf Technol Manage 6(1):13–23

Saha A, Ravisankar TS (2000) Rating of Indian commercial banks: a DEA approach. Eur J Oper Res 124(1):187–203

Sarkar J (2004) The banking industry. In: Gorkan S, Sen A, Vaidya RR (eds) The structure of Indian industry. Oxford University Press, New Delhi

Sarkar J, Sarkar S, Bhaumik SK (1998) Does ownership always matter? Evidence from the Indian banking industry. J Comp Econ 26(2):262–281

Sarma RH (1995) Customer the crown prince of today and monarch of tomorrow. J Indian Inst Bank 66(1):50–52

Sathye M (2001) X-efficiency in Australian banking: an empirical investigation. J Bank Financ 25(3):613–630

Sathye M (2002) Measuring productivity changes in Australian banking: an application of Malmquist indices. Manage Financ 28(9):48–59

Sathye M (2003) Efficiency of banks in a developing economy: the case of India. Eur J Oper Res 148(3):662–671

Schaffnit C, Rosen D, Paradi JC (1997) Best practice analysis of bank branches: an application of DEA in large Canadian bank. Eur J Oper Res 98(2):269–289

Schmid FA (1994) Technical efficiency and returns-to-scale in Austrian commercial banking: 1987–1991. Empirica 21(2):245–253

Schmidt P (1976) On the statistical estimation of parametric frontier production functions. Rev Econ Stat 58(2):238–239

Schmidt P, Sickles R (1984) Production frontiers and panel data. J Bus Econ Stat 2(4):367–374

Schure P, Wagenvoort R, O'Brien D (2004) The efficiency and the conduct of European banks: developments after 1992. Rev Financ Econ 13(4):371–396

Sealey CW Jr, Lindley JT (1977) Inputs, outputs, and a theory of production and cost at depository financial institutions. J Financ 32(4):1251–1266

Seelanatha SL (2007) Efficiency, productivity change and market structure of the banking industry in Srilanka. An unpublished Ph.D. dissertation, School of Accounting, Economics and Finance, Faculty of Business, University of Southern Queensland

Seiford LM (1996) Data envelopment analysis: evolution of the state-of-the-art (1978–1995). J Prod Anal 7(2):99–137

Seiford LM, Thrall RM (1990) Recent developments in DEA: the mathematical programming approach to frontier analysis. J Econom 46(1–2):7–38

Seiford LM, Zhu J (1999) Infeasibility of super efficiency data envelopment analysis models. INFOR 37(2):174–187

Sen K, Vaidya RR (1997) The process of financial liberalization in India. Oxford University Press, New Delhi

Sensarma R (2005) Cost and profit efficiency of Indian banks during 1986–2003: a stochastic frontier analysis. Econ Polit Wkly 40(12):1198–1208

Sensarma R (2006) Are foreign banks always the best? Comparison of state-owned, private and foreign banks in India. Econ Model 23(4):717–735

Sensarma R (2008) Deregulation, ownership, and profitability performance of banks: evidence from India. Appl Financ Econ 18(19):1581–1595

Sexton TR, Silkman RH, Hogan AJ (1986) Data envelopment analysis: critique and extensions. In: Silkman RH (ed) Measuring efficiency: an assessment of data envelopment analysis, vol 32. Jossey-Bass, San Francisco, pp 73–105

Shanmugam KR, Das A (2004) Efficiency of Indian commercial banks during the reform period. Appl Financ Econ 14(9):681–686

Shen Z, Liao H, Weyman-Jones T (2009) Cost efficiency analysis in banking industries of ten Asian countries and regions. J Chin Econ Bus Stud 7(2):199–218

Shephard RW (1970) Theory of cost and production functions. Princeton University Press, Princeton/New Jersey

Sherman HD (1988) Service organization productivity management. The Society of Management Accountants Of Canada, Hamilton

Sherman HD, Gold F (1985) Branch operating efficiency: evaluation with data envelopment analysis. J Bank Financ 9(2):297–315
Shirai S (2002) Road from state to market-assessing the gradual approach to banking sector reforms in India. ADB Institute Research paper series no 32, Asian Development Bank Institute, Tokyo
Shirai S, Rajasekaran P (2002) Is India's banking sector reform successful? KEIO SFC J 1(1):150–163
Siems TF, Clark JA (1997) Rethinking bank efficiency and regulation: how off-balance sheet activities make a difference, Financial industry studies. Federal Reserve Bank of Dallas, Dallas, pp 1–11
Simar L, Wilson PW (1998) Sensitivity analysis of efficiency scores: how to bootstrap in nonparametric frontier models. Manage Sci 44(1):49–61
Singh P (2009) Mergers in Indian banking: impact study using DEA analysis. S Asian J Manage 16(2):7–28
Sowlati T, Paradi JC (2004) Establishing the practical frontier in data envelopment analysis. Omega Int J Manage Sci 32(4):261–272
Staikouras C, Mamatzakis E, Koutsomanoli-Filippaki A (2008) Cost efficiency of the banking industry in the South Eastern European region. Int Financ Mark Inst Money 18(5):483–497
Staub RB, Souza GS, Tabak BM (2010) Evolution of bank efficiency in Brazil: a DEA approach. Eur J Oper Res 202(1):204–213
Stevenson RE (1980) Likelihood functions for generalized stochastic frontier estimation. J Econom 13(1):58–66
Stiroh KJ (2000) How did bank holding companies prosper in the 1990s? J Bank Financ 24(11):1703–1745
Sturm JE, Williams B (2004) Foreign bank entry, deregulation and bank efficiency: lessons from the Australian experience. J Bank Financ 28(7):1775–1799
Sufian F (2004) The efficiency of bank mergers and acquisitions in a developing economy: evidence from Malaysia. Int J Appl Econ Quant Stud 1(4):53–74
Sufian F (2006) The efficiency of non-bank financial institutions: empirical evidence from Malaysia. Int Res J Financ Econ 1(6):49–65
Sufian F (2007) Trends in the efficiency of Singapore's commercial banking groups: a non-stochastic frontier DEA window analysis approach. Int J Prod Perform Manage 56(2):99–136
Sufian F (2009a) Determinants of bank efficiency during unstable macroeconomic environment: empirical evidence from Malaysia. Res Int Bus Financ 23(1):54–77
Sufian F (2009b) The impact of off-balance sheet items on banks' total factor productivity: empirical evidence from the Chinese banking sector. Am J Financ Acc 1(3):213–238
Sufian F (2010) Financial crisis and the efficiency of the Malaysian banking sector: foreign vs. domestic banks. Int J Monetar Econ Financ 3(2):140–158
Sufian F (2011) Banks total factor productivity change in a developing economy: does ownership and origins matter? J Asian Econ 22(1):84–98
Sufian F, Habibullah MS (2009) Nontraditional activities and bank efficiency: empirical evidence from the Chinese banking sector during the post-reform period. Int J Econ Policy Emerg Econ 2(2):107–132
Sufian F, Ibrahim S (2005) An analysis of the relevance of off-balance sheet items in explaining productivity change in post-merger bank performance. Manage Res News 28(4):74–92
Sufian F, Majid MA (2007) Singapore banking efficiency and its relation to stock returns: a DEA window analysis approach. Int J Bus Stud 15(1):83–106
Sufian F, Majid A, Zulkhibri M, Razali H (2008) Efficiency and bank merger in Singapore: a joint estimation of non-parametric, parametric and financial ratios analysis. MPRA paper no 12129. Available via DIALOG. http://mpra.ub.uni-muenchen.de/12129/
Tabak BM, Tecles PL (2010) Estimating a bayesian stochastic frontier for the Indian banking system. Int J Prod Econ 125(1):96–110

Tavares G (2002) A bibliography of data envelopment analysis (1978–2001). Rutcor Research report no 01-02, Rutgers University, New Jersey

Taylor WM, Thompson RG, Thrall RM, Dharmapala PS (1997) DEA/AR efficiency and profitability of Mexican banks: a total income model. Eur J Oper Res 98(2):346–365

Tecles P, Tabak BM (2010) Determinants of bank efficiency: the case of Brazil. Eur J Oper Res 207(3):1587–1598

Thanassoulis E, Boussofiane A, Dyson RG (1995) Exploring output quality targets in the provisions of perinatal care in England using data envelopment analysis. Eur J Oper Res 80(3):588–607

Thanassoulis E (2001) Introduction to the theory and application of data envelopment analysis: a foundation text with integrated software. Kluwer, Dordrecht

Thi NV, Vencappa D (2008) Does the entry mode of foreign banks matter for bank efficiency? Evidence from the Czech Republic, Hungary, and Poland. William Davidson Institute working paper no 925, July. Available via DIALOG. http://wdi.umich.edu/files/publications/workingpapers/wp925.pdf

Thompson RG, Singleton FD, Thrall RM, Smith BA (1986) Comparative site evaluation for locating a high-energy physics lab in Texas. Interfaces 16(6):35–49

Thompson RG, Langemeier LN, Lee C, Thrall RM (1990) The role of multiplier bounds in efficiency analysis with application to Kansas farming. J Econom 46(1–2):93–108

Thrall RM (1996) The lack of invariance of optimal dual solutions under translation. Ann Oper Res 66(2):103–108

Timmer CP (1971) Using a probabilistic frontier production function to measure technical efficiency. J Polit Econ 79(4):776–794

Tochkov K, Nenovsky N (2009) Efficiency of commercial banks in Bulgaria in the wake of EU accession. Bulgarian National Bank, Discussion paper no DP/75/2009, August 2009. Available via DIALOG. http://www.bnb.bg/bnbweb/groups/public/documents/bnb_publication/discussion_2009_75_en. pdf

Tone K (2001) A slacks-based measure of efficiency in data envelopment analysis. Eur J Oper Res 130(3):498–509

Tone K (2002a) A slacks-based measure of super-efficiency in data envelopment analysis. Eur J Oper Res 143(1):32–41

Tone K (2002b) A strange case of the cost and allocative efficiencies in DEA. J Oper Res Soc 53(11):1225–1231

Tortosa-Ausina E (2002a) Bank cost efficiency and output specification. J Prod Anal 18(3):199–222

Tortosa-Ausina E (2002b) Exploring efficiency differences over time in the Spanish banking industry. Eur J Oper Res 139(3):643–664

Tortosa-Ausina E (2003) Nontraditional activities and bank efficiency revisited: a distributional analysis for Spanish financial institutions. J Econ Bus 55(4):371–395

Törnqvist L (1936) The bank of Finland's consumption price index. Bank of Finland Month B 10(1):1–8

Tripe D (2004) Efficiency in integrating banking markets-Australia and New Zealand. A paper presented in Asia-pacific productivity conference, 14–16 July, Brisbane. Available via DIALOG. http://www.rbnz.govt.nz/research/workshops/27apr2004 /27apr04_tripe.pdf

Tsionas EG, Lolos SEG, Christopoulos DK (2003) The performance of the Greek banking system in view of the EMU: results from a non-parametric approach. Econ Model 20(3):571–592

Tulkens H (1993) On FDH efficiency analysis: some methodological issues and applications to retail banking, courts and urban transit. J Prod Anal 4(1–2):183–210

Tulkens H, Malnero A (1994) Nonparametric approach to the assessment of the relative efficiency of bank branches. Center for Operational Research and Econometrics, CORE discussion paper no 1994047, Universite Catholique de Louvain

Tulkens H, van den Eeckaut P (1995) Non-parametric efficiency, progress, and regress measures for panel data: methodological aspects. Eur J Oper Res 80(3):474–499

Turati G (2001) Cost efficiency and profitability in European commercial banking. A Paper prepared for the 7th European workshop on efficiency and productivity analysis, Oviedo, September 2001. Available via DIALOG. http://www.unioviedo.es/7ewepa/pdf/turati.PDF

Valverde SC, Humphrey DB, Fernández FR (2003) Bank deregulation is better than mergers. J Int Financ Mark Inst Money 13(5):429–449

Wagenvoort R, Schure PH (1999) The recursive thick frontier approach to estimating efficiency. Economic and financial report 1999/02, European Investment Bank, Luxembourg. Available via DIALOG. http://www.eib.org/attachments/efs/efr99n02.pdf

Wagenvoort R, Schure PH (2006) A recursive thick frontier approach to estimating production efficiency. Oxf Bull Econ Stat 68(2):183–201

Weill L (2003) Banking efficiency in transition economies: the role of foreign ownership. Econ Transit 11(3):569–592

Weill L (2004) Measuring cost efficiency in European banking: a comparison of frontier techniques. J Prod Anal 21(2):133–152

Weill L (2007) Is there a gap in bank efficiency between CEE and Western European countries? Comp Econ Stud 49(1):101–127

Wezel T (2010) Bank efficiency amid foreign entry: evidence from the Central American region. IMF working paper no WP/10/95

Wheelock DC, Wilson PW (1999) Technical progress, inefficiency, and productivity change in US banking: 1984–1993. J Money Credit Bank 31(2):212–234

Worthington AC (1999) Malmquist indices of productivity change in Australian financial services. J Int Financ Mark Inst Money 9(3):303–320

Wu S (2008) Mergers and acquisitions-an evaluation of the 'four pillars' policy in Australia. Aust Econ Pap 47(2):141–155

Xue M, Harker PT (2002) Note: ranking DMUs with infeasible super-efficiency DEA models. Manage Sci 48(5):705–710

Yildirim C (2002) Evolution of banking efficiency within an unstable macroeconomic environment: the case of Turkish commercial banks. Appl Econ 34(18):2289–2301

Yildirim HS, Philippatos GC (2007) Efficiency of banks: recent evidence from the transition economies of Europe 1993–2000. T Eur J Financ 13(2):123–143

Yoo TH (2005) Indian banking sector reforms: review and prospects. Int Area Rev 8(2):167–189

Zaim O (1995) The effect of financial liberalization on the efficiency of Turkish commercial banks. Appl Financ Econ 5(4):257–264

Zajc P (2006) A comparative study of bank efficiency in Central and Eastern Europe: the role of foreign ownership. Int Financ Rev 6: 117–156

Zhao T, Casu B, Ferrari A (2008) Deregulation and productivity growth: a study of Indian commercial banking. Int J Bus Perform Manage 10(4):318–343

Zhao T, Casu B, Ferrari A (2010) The impact of regulatory reforms on cost structure, ownership and competition in Indian banking. J Bank Financ 34(1):246–254

Zhu J (2003) Quantitative models for performance evaluation and benchmarking: data envelopment analysis with spreadsheets and DEA excel solver. Kluwer Academic, Boston

Index

S. Kumar and R. Gulati, *Deregulation and Efficiency of Indian Banks*, India Studies in Business and Economics, DOI 10.1007/978-81-322-1545-5, © Springer India 2014

The manufacturer's authorised representative in the EU is Springer Nature Customer Service Centre GmbH, Europaplatz 3, 69115 Heidelberg, Germany. If you have any concerns regarding our products, please contact ProductSafety@springernature.com

Printed and bound by CPI Group (UK) Ltd, Croydon, CR0 4YY
22/09/2026
02221058-0017